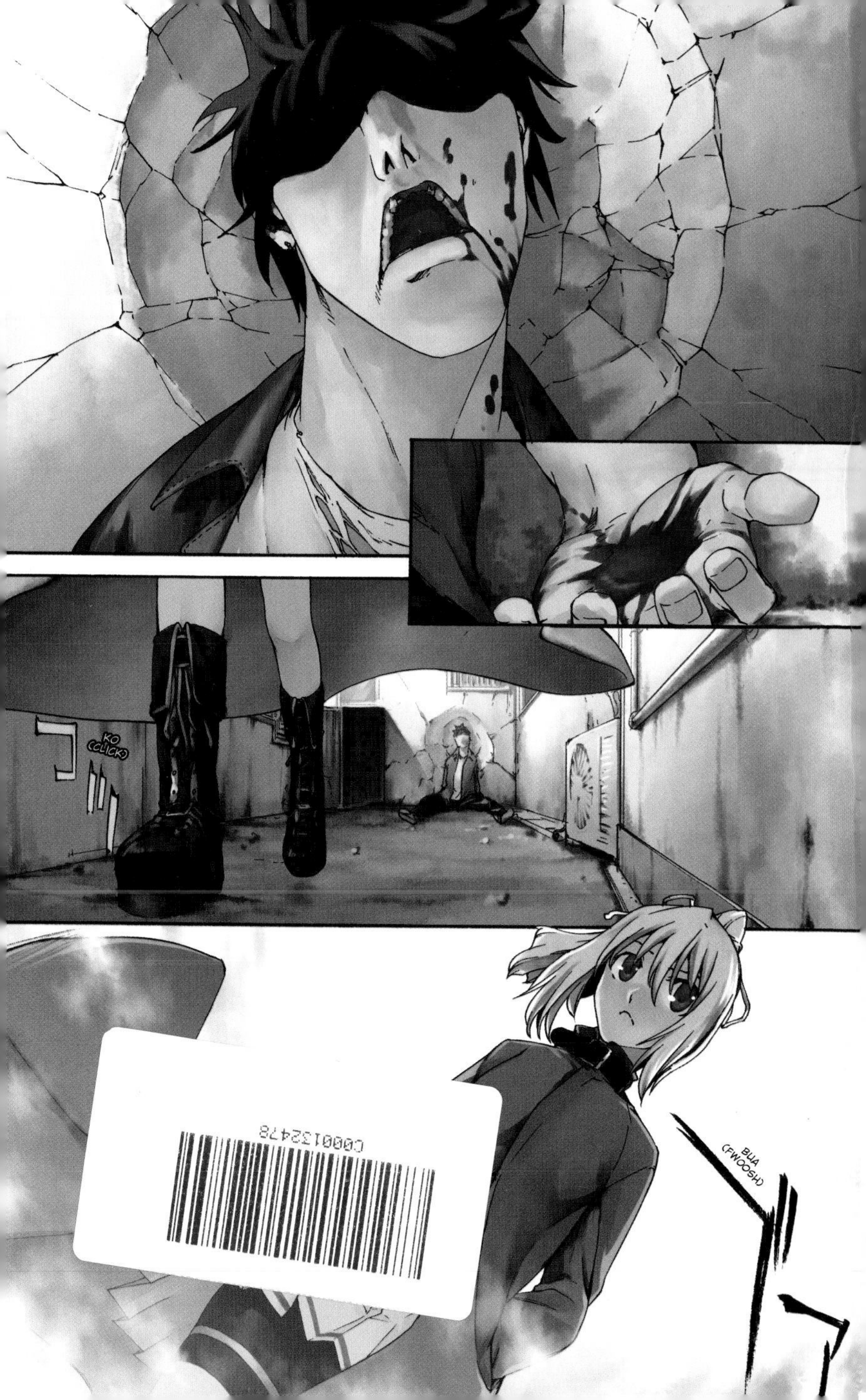
KO
(CLICK)
BUA
(FWOOSH)

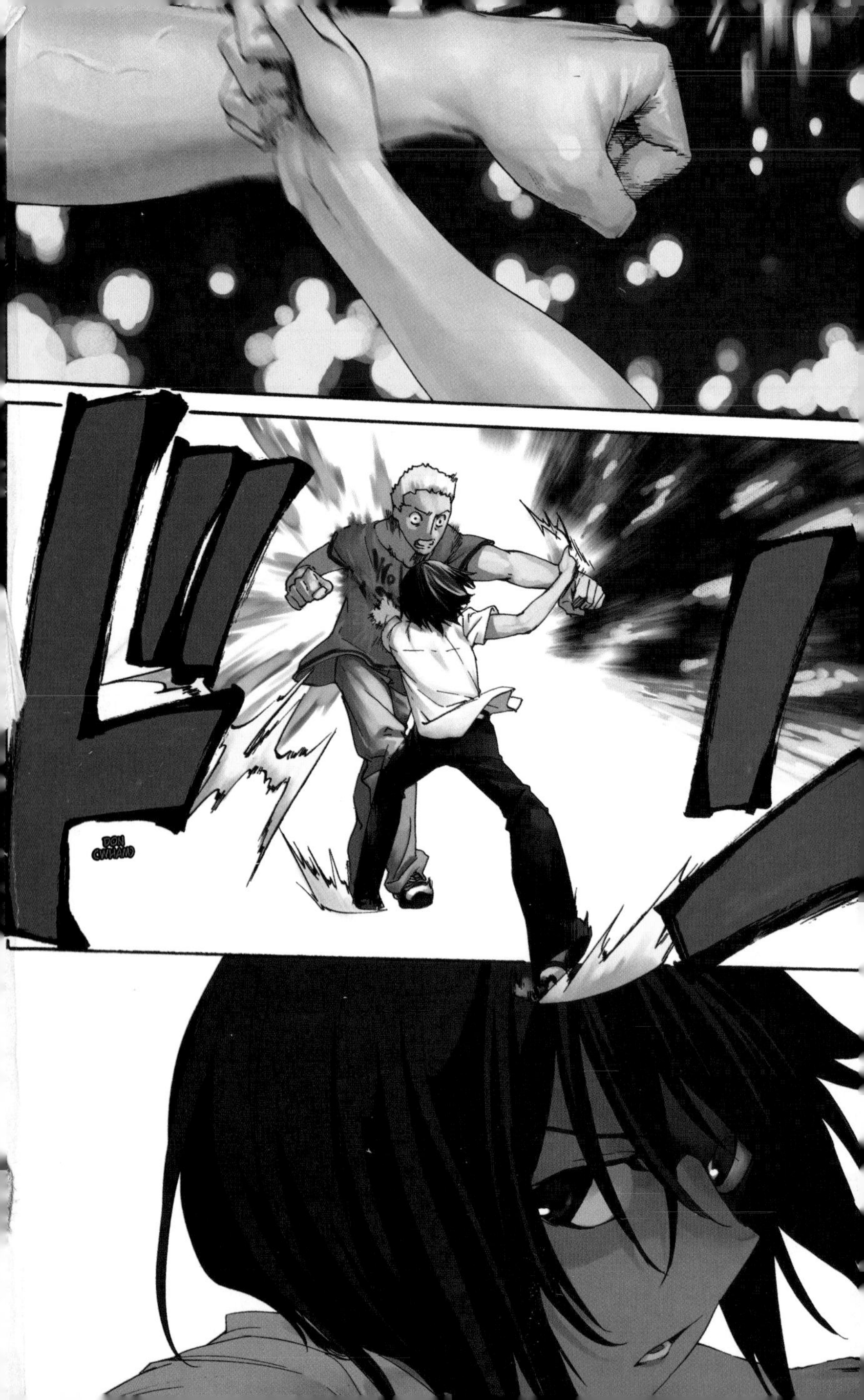
DON (WHAM)

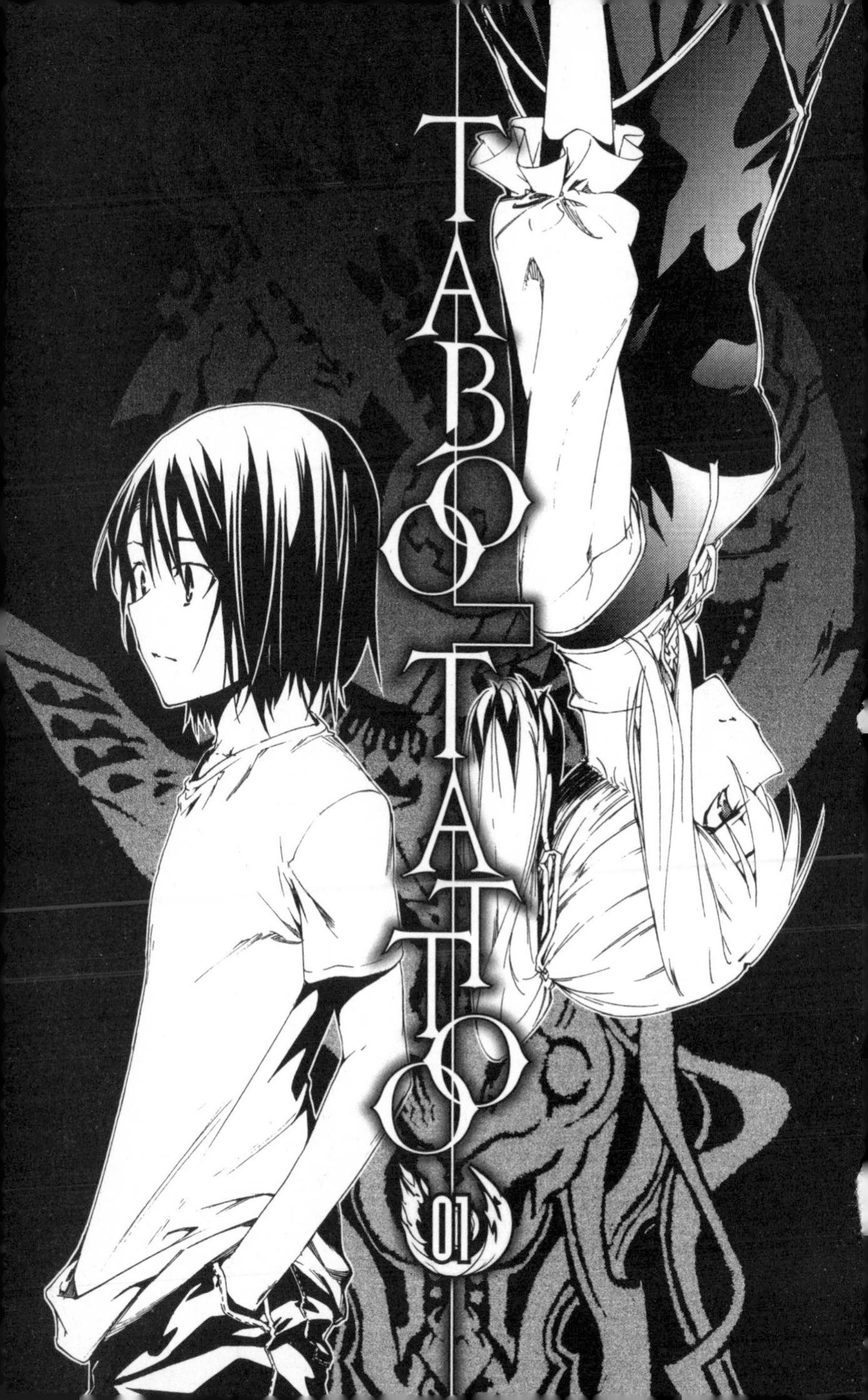
TABOO TATTOO
01

TABOO TATTOO 01

CONTENTS

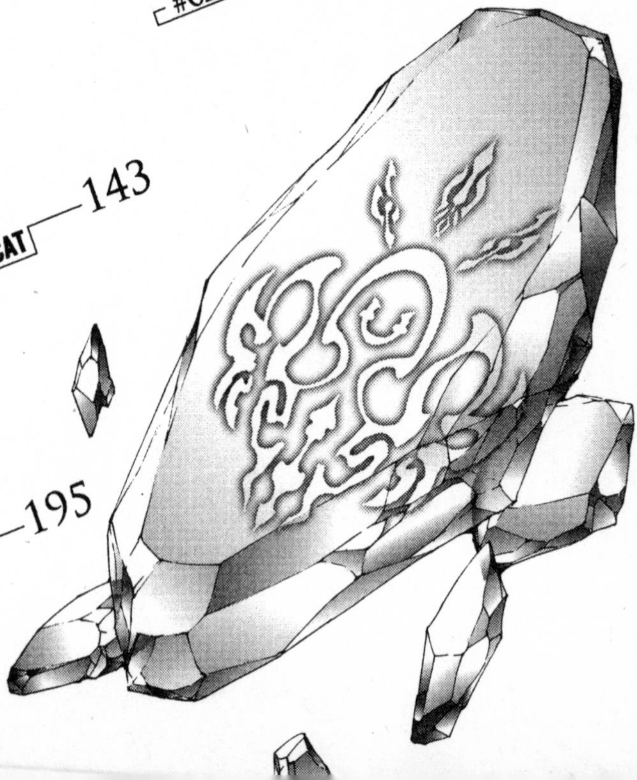

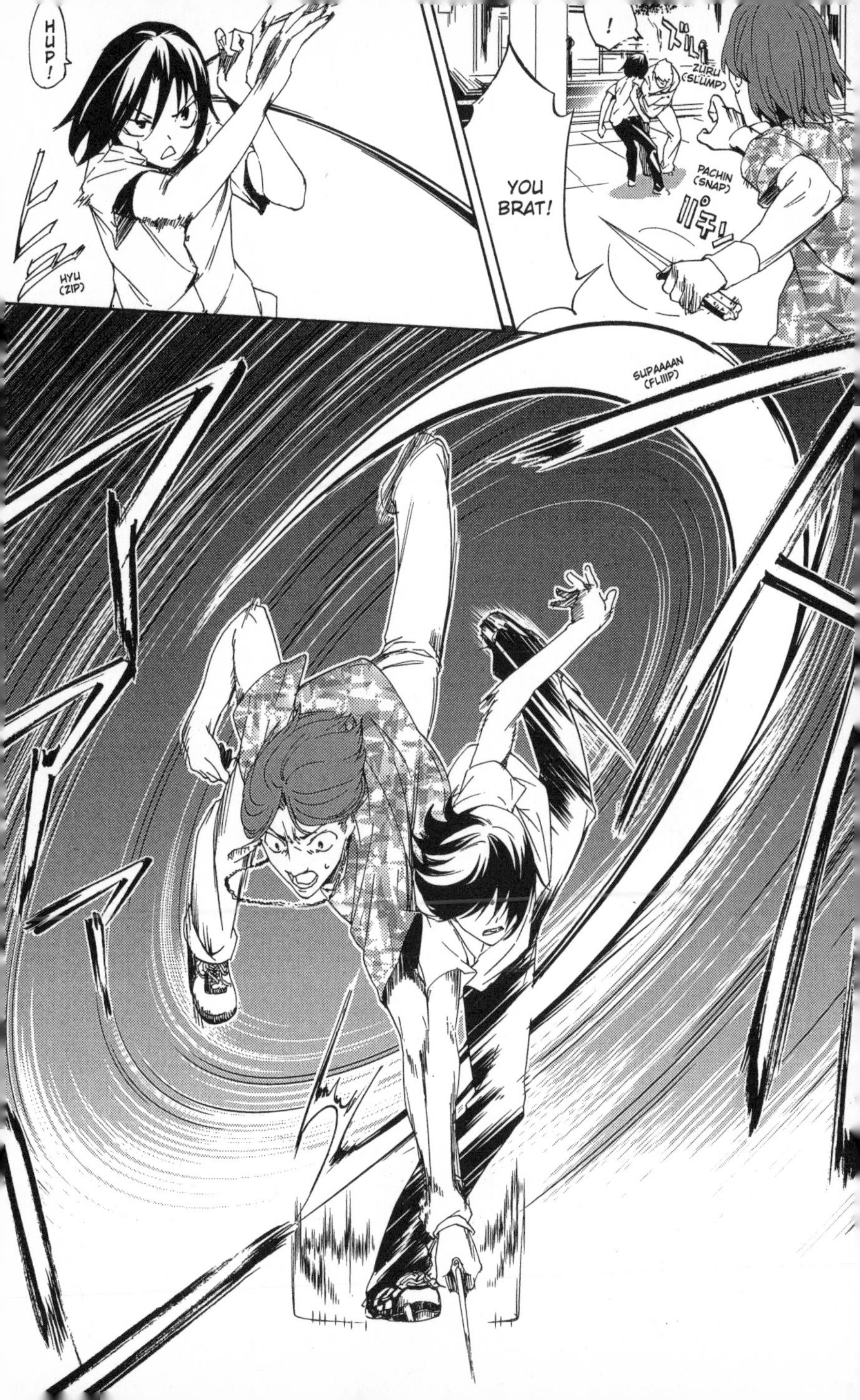

ZURU (SLUMP)
!
YOU BRAT!
PACHIN (SNAP)
HUP!
HYU (ZIP)
SUPAAAAN (FLIIIP)

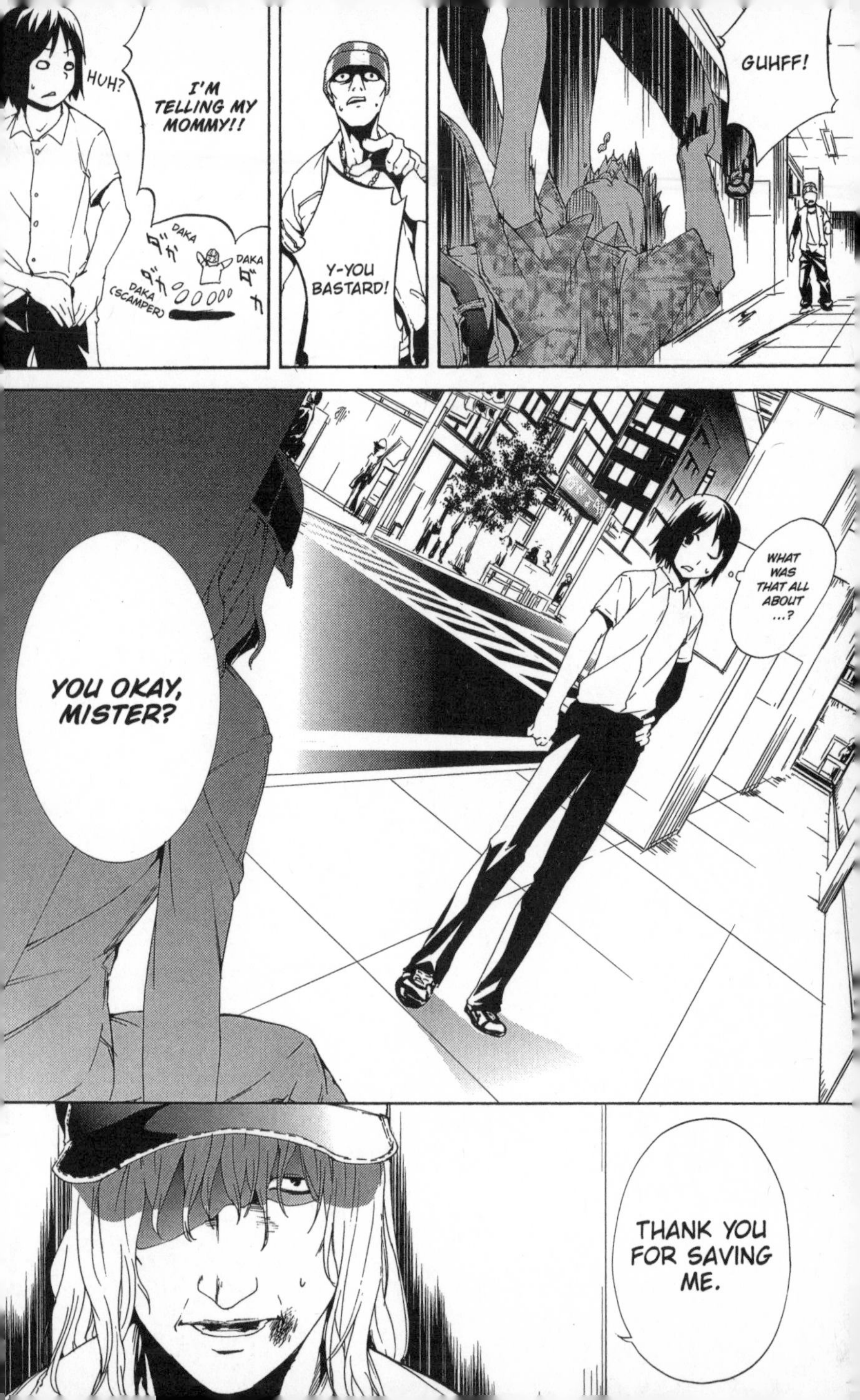
GUHFF!
Y-YOU BASTARD!
I'M TELLING MY MOMMY!!
HUH?
DAKA DAKA DAKA (SCAMPER)
WHAT WAS THAT ALL ABOUT ...?
YOU OKAY, MISTER?
THANK YOU FOR SAVING ME.

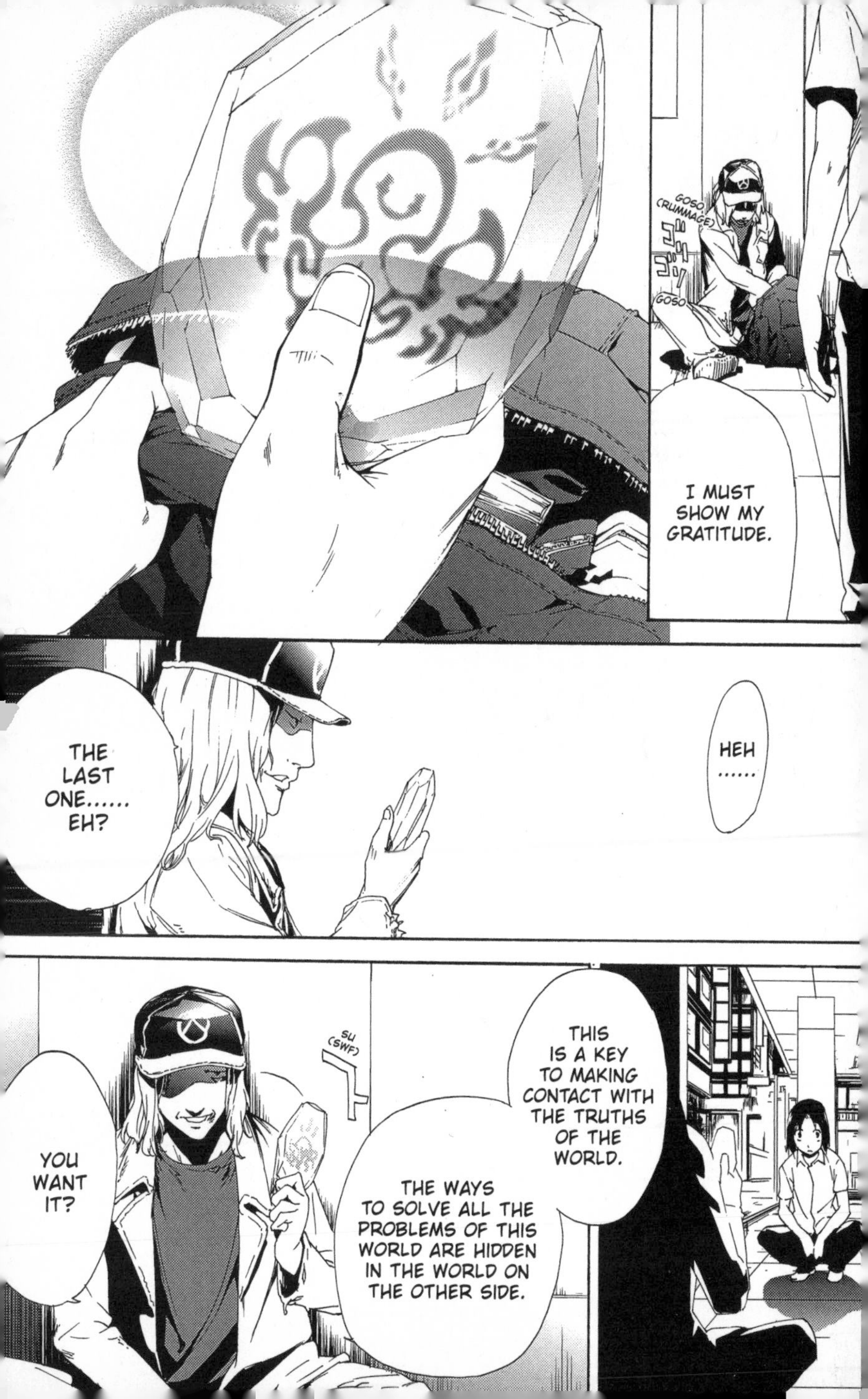
GOSO (RUMMAGE)
GOSO
I MUST SHOW MY GRATITUDE.
HEH ......
THE LAST ONE...... EH?
THIS IS A KEY TO MAKING CONTACT WITH THE TRUTHS OF THE WORLD.
THE WAYS TO SOLVE ALL THE PROBLEMS OF THIS WORLD ARE HIDDEN IN THE WORLD ON THE OTHER SIDE.
SU (SWF)
YOU WANT IT?

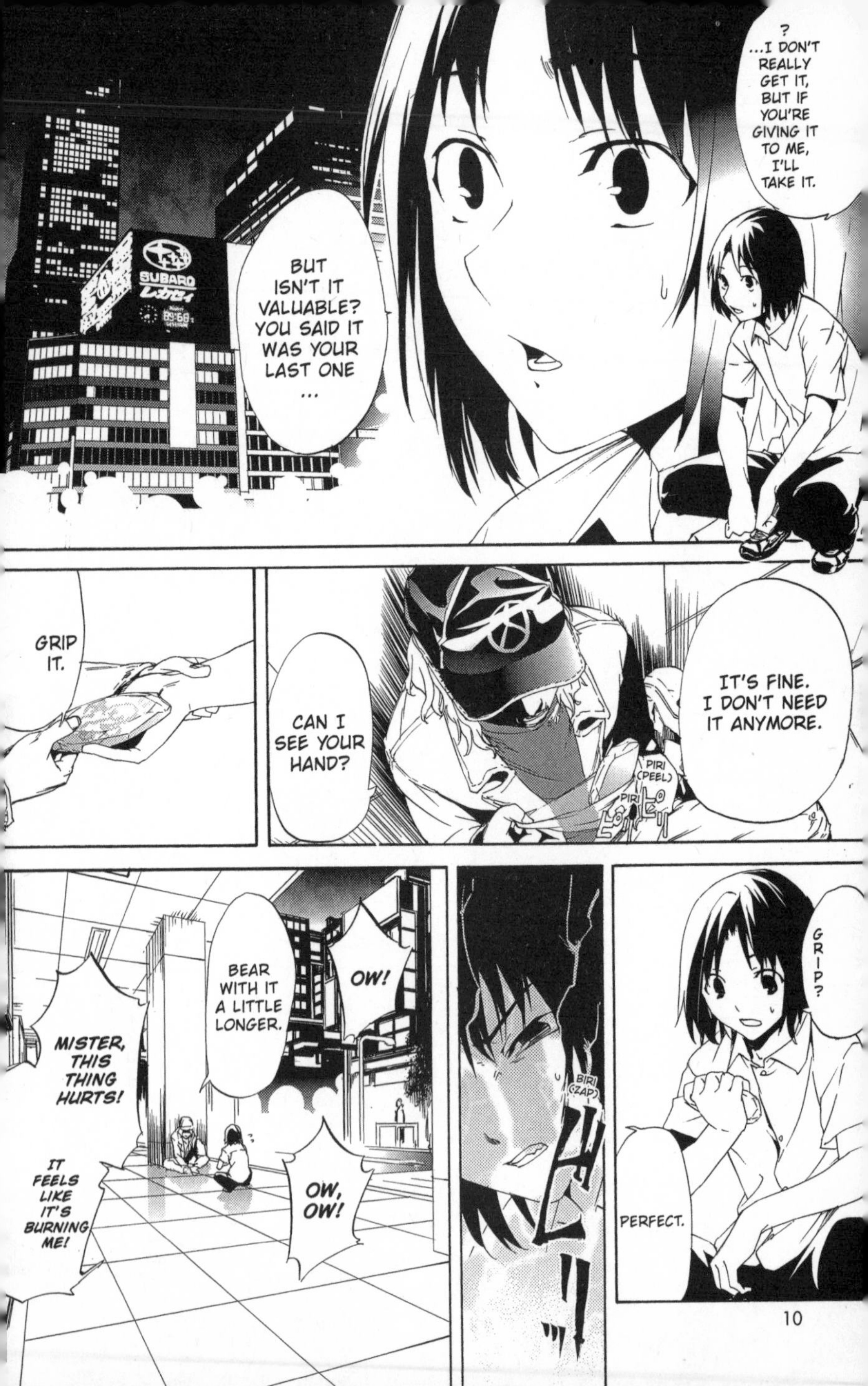
? ...I DON'T REALLY GET IT, BUT IF YOU'RE GIVING IT TO ME, I'LL TAKE IT.
BUT ISN'T IT VALUABLE? YOU SAID IT WAS YOUR LAST ONE ...
IT'S FINE. I DON'T NEED IT ANYMORE.
PIRI (PEEL)
PIRI
CAN I SEE YOUR HAND?
GRIP IT.
GRIP?
PERFECT.
BIRI (ZAP)
OW!
BEAR WITH IT A LITTLE LONGER.
OW, OW!
MISTER, THIS THING HURTS!
IT FEELS LIKE IT'S BURNING ME!

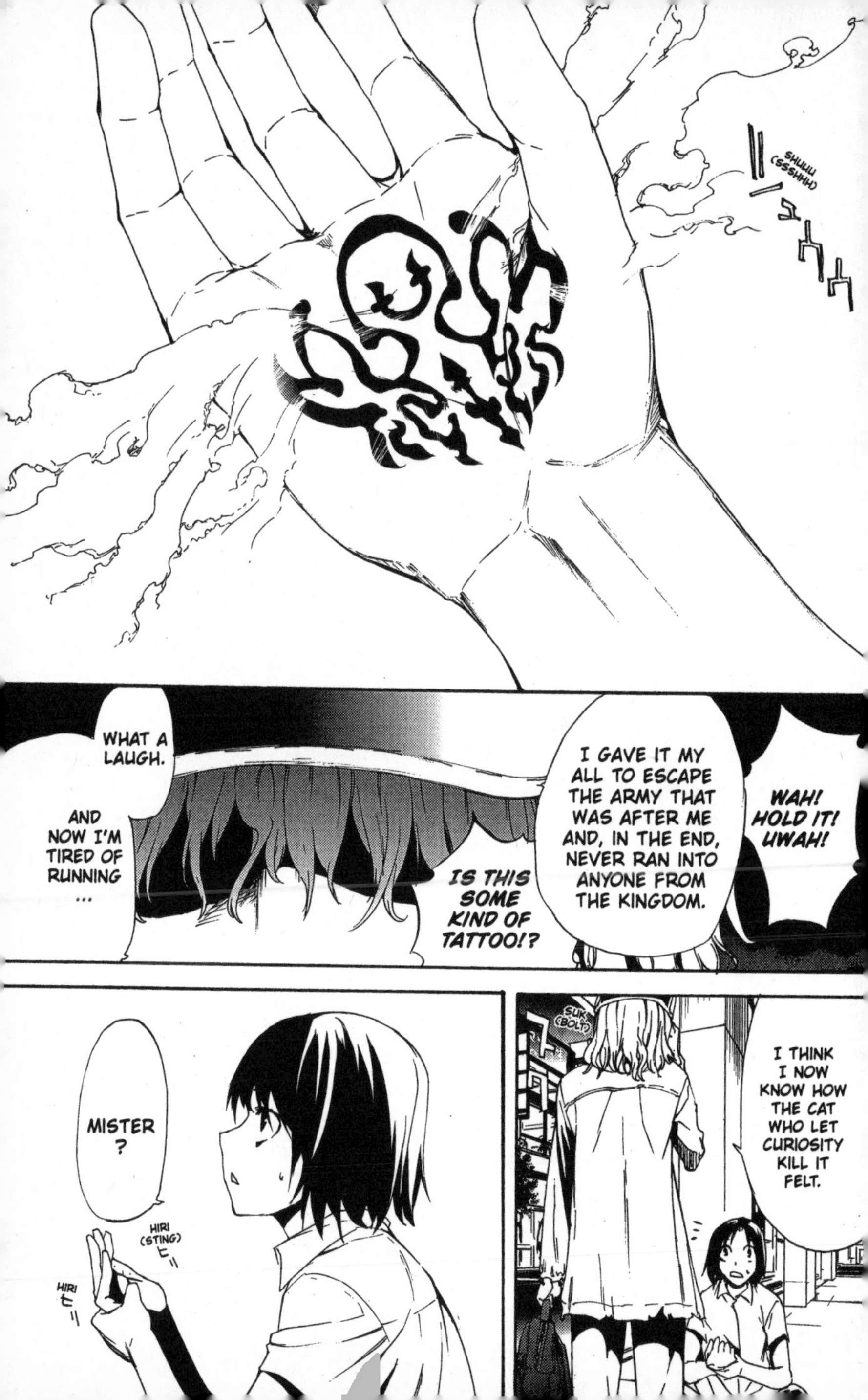
SHUUU (SSSHHH)
WAH! HOLD IT! UWAH!
I GAVE IT MY ALL TO ESCAPE THE ARMY THAT WAS AFTER ME AND, IN THE END, NEVER RAN INTO ANYONE FROM THE KINGDOM.
IS THIS SOME KIND OF TATTOO!?
WHAT A LAUGH.
AND NOW I'M TIRED OF RUNNING...
SUK (BOLT)
I THINK I NOW KNOW HOW THE CAT WHO LET CURIOSITY KILL IT FELT.
MISTER?
HIRI (STING)
HIRI

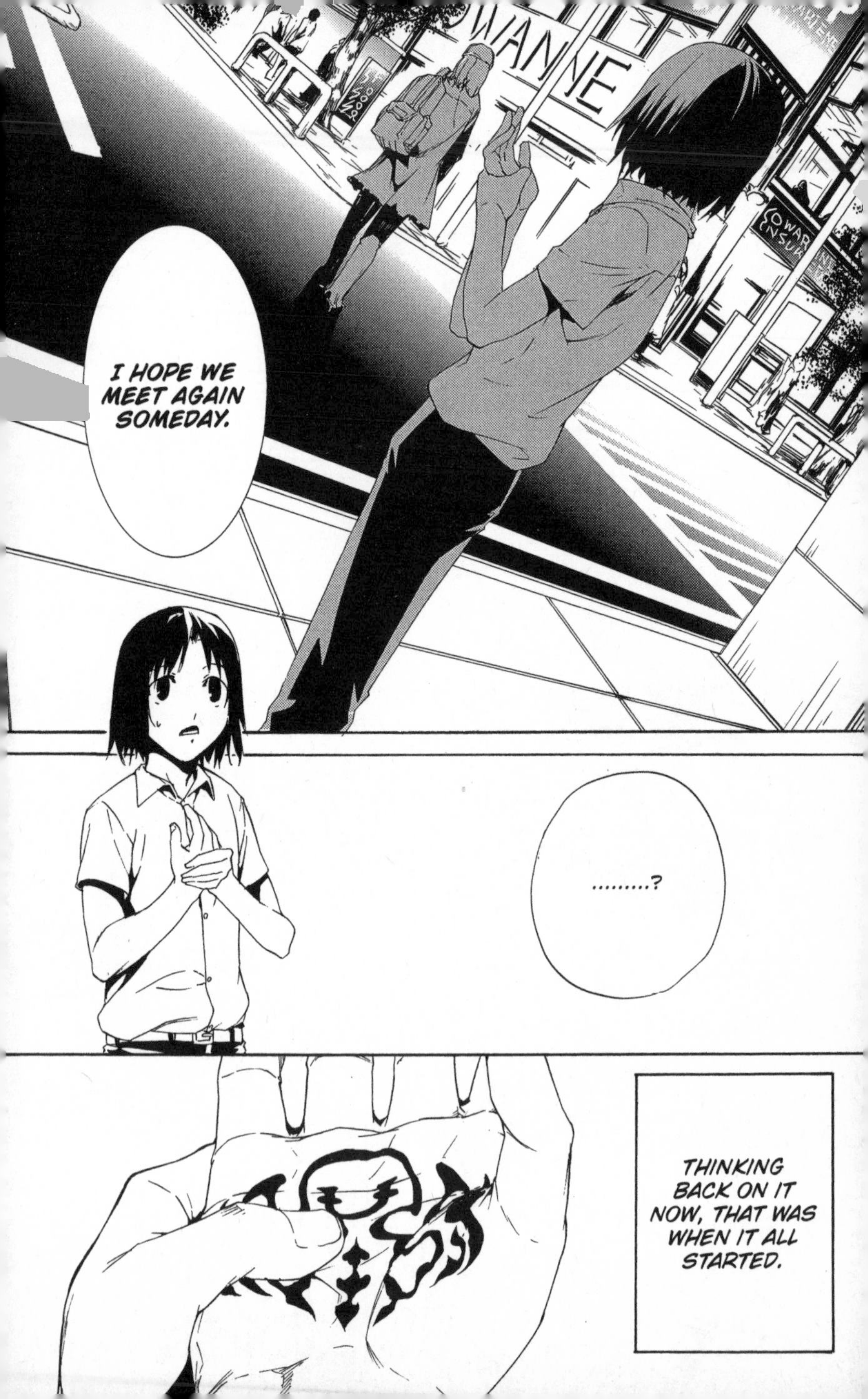
I HOPE WE MEET AGAIN SOMEDAY.
..........?
THINKING BACK ON IT NOW, THAT WAS WHEN IT ALL STARTED.

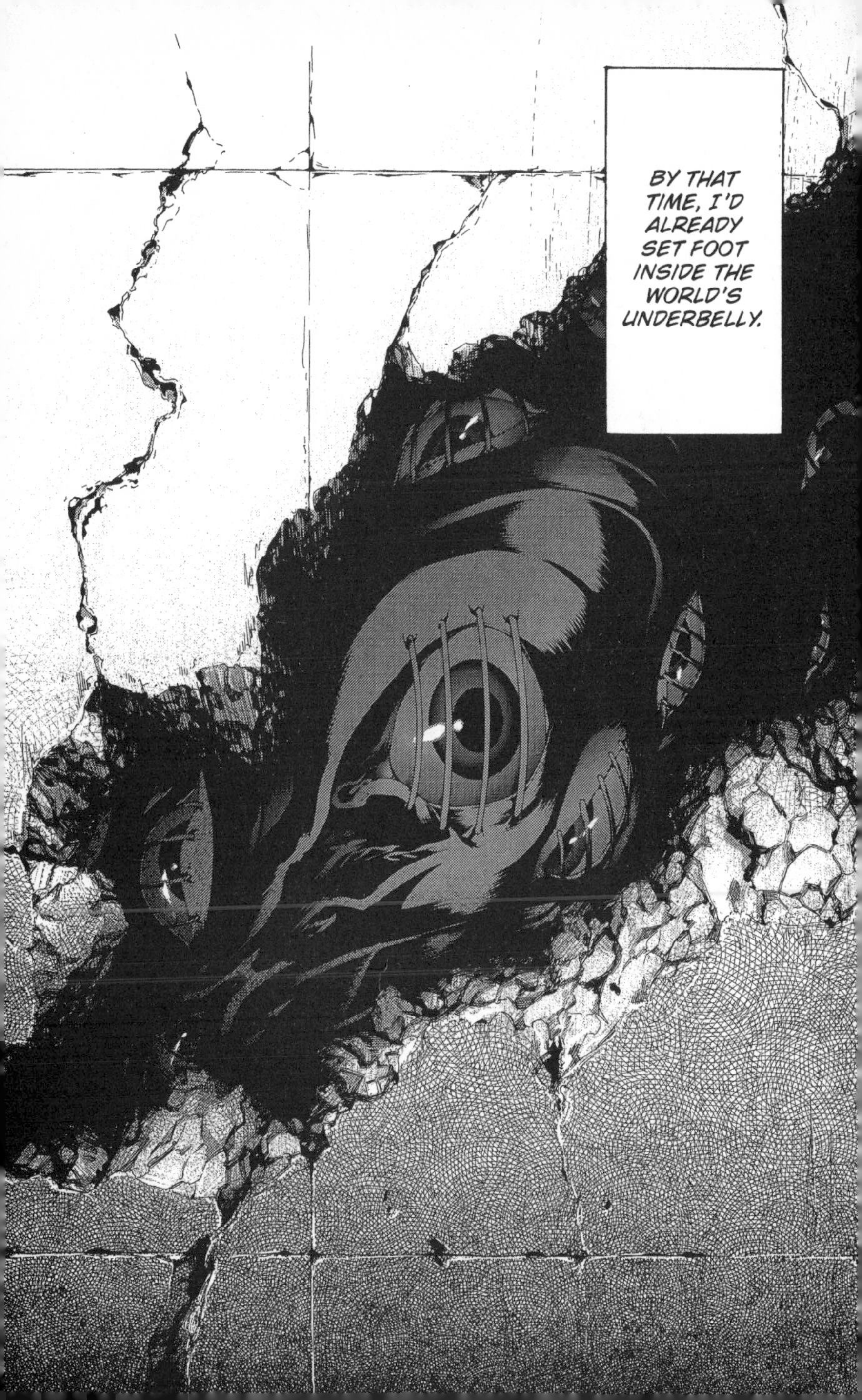
BY THAT TIME, I'D ALREADY SET FOOT INSIDE THE WORLD'S UNDERBELLY.

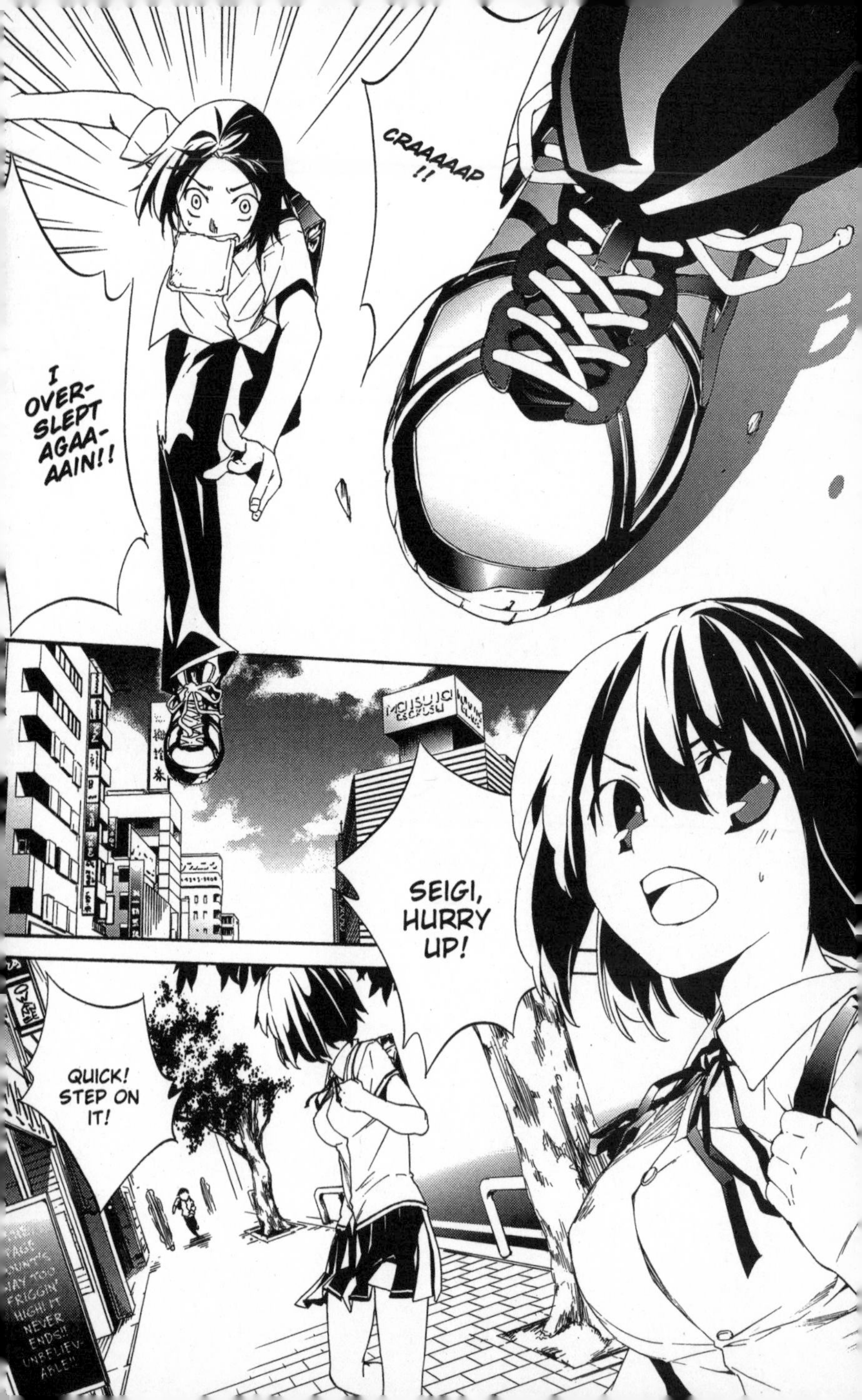
CRAAAAAP!!
I OVER-SLEPT AGAA-AAIN!!
SEIGI, HURRY UP!
QUICK! STEP ON IT!
FRIGGIN' HIGH! IT NEVER ENDS!! UNBELIEV-ABLE!!

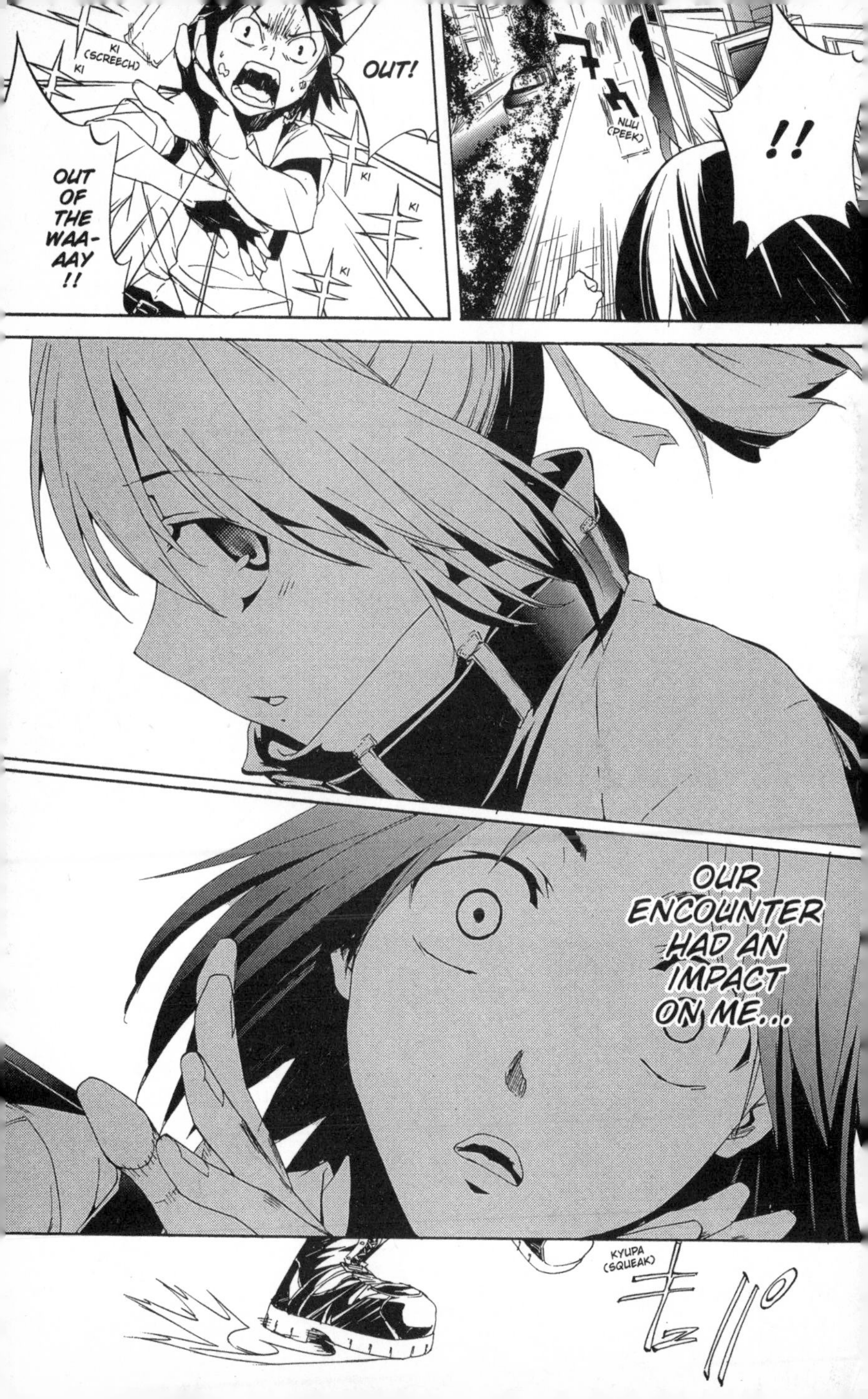
!!
NUU (PEEK)
KI (SCREECH) KI
OUT!
OUT OF THE WAA-AAY!!
KI
KI
KI
OUR ENCOUNTER HAD AN IMPACT ON ME...
KYUPA (SQUEAK)

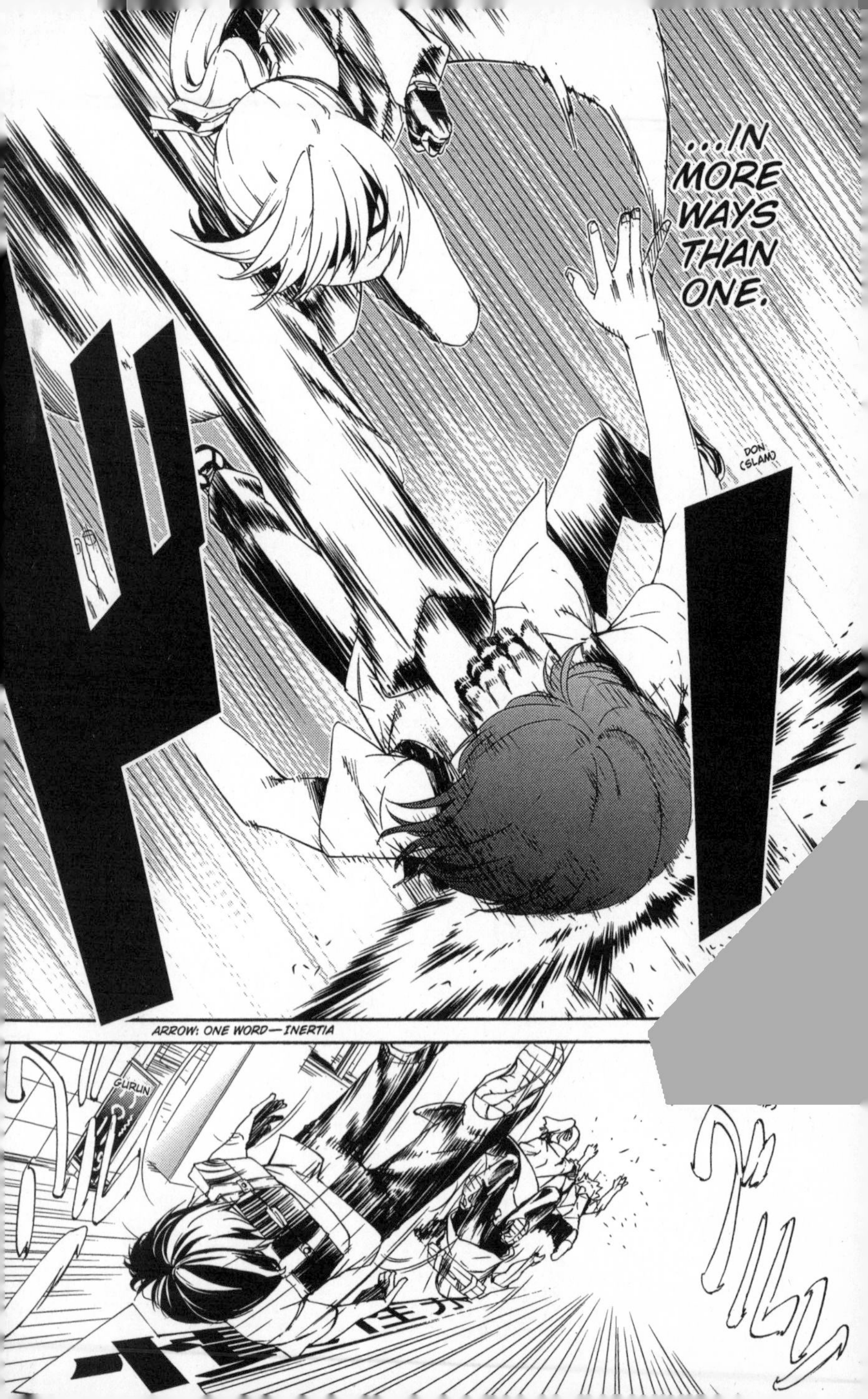
...IN MORE WAYS THAN ONE.
DON (SLAM)
ARROW: ONE WORD—INERTIA
GURUN

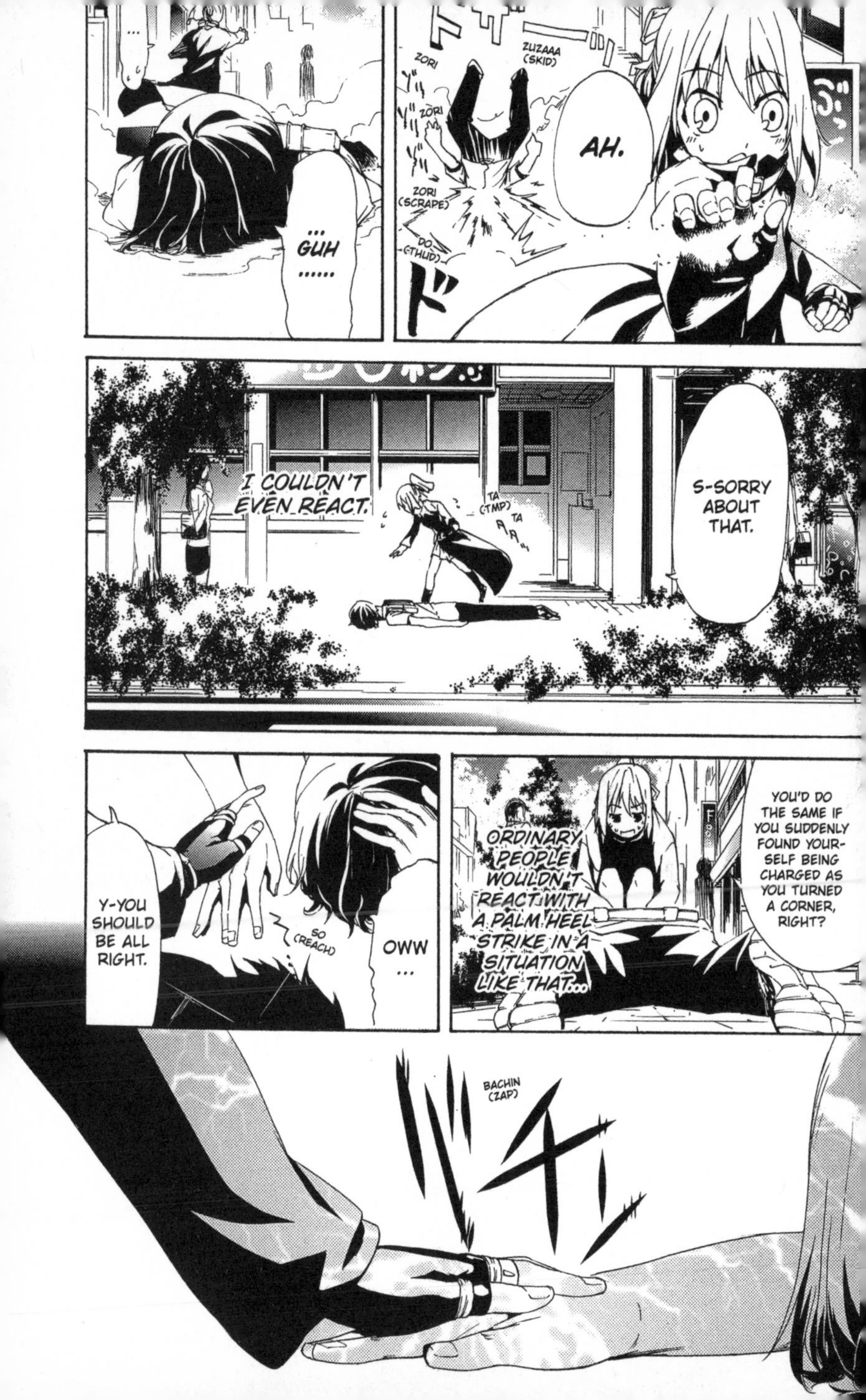
ZUZAAA (SKID)
AH.
ZORI
ZORI
ZORI (SCRAPE)
DO (THUD)
...
...GUH ......
S-SORRY ABOUT THAT.
TA (TMP) TA
I COULDN'T EVEN REACT.
YOU'D DO THE SAME IF YOU SUDDENLY FOUND YOUR-SELF BEING CHARGED AS YOU TURNED A CORNER, RIGHT?
ORDINARY PEOPLE WOULDN'T REACT WITH A PALM HEEL STRIKE IN A SITUATION LIKE THAT...
OWW ...
SO (REACH)
Y-YOU SHOULD BE ALL RIGHT.
BACHIN (ZAP)

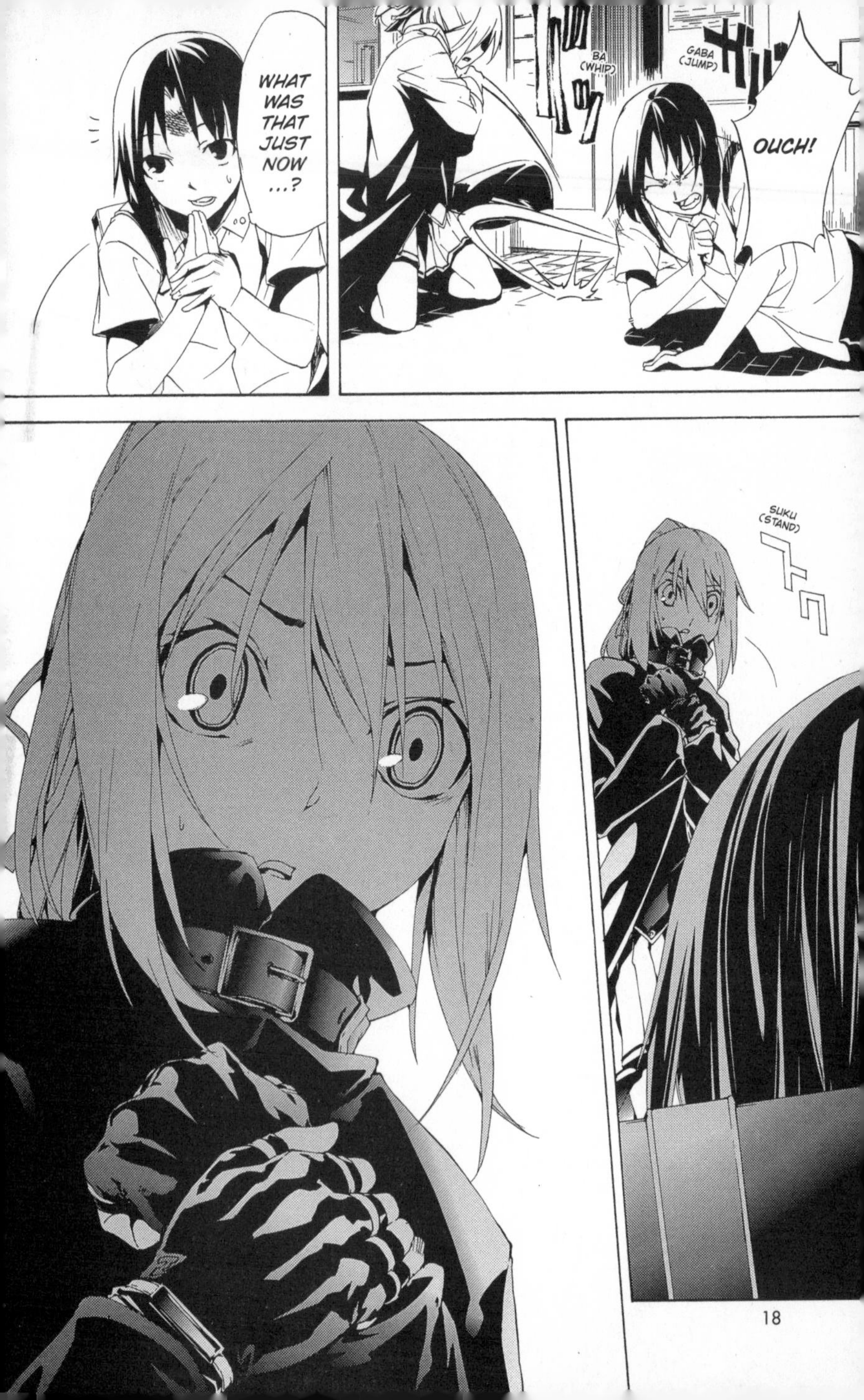
GABA (JUMP)
BA (WHIP)
OUCH!
WHAT WAS THAT JUST NOW ...?
SUKU (STAND)

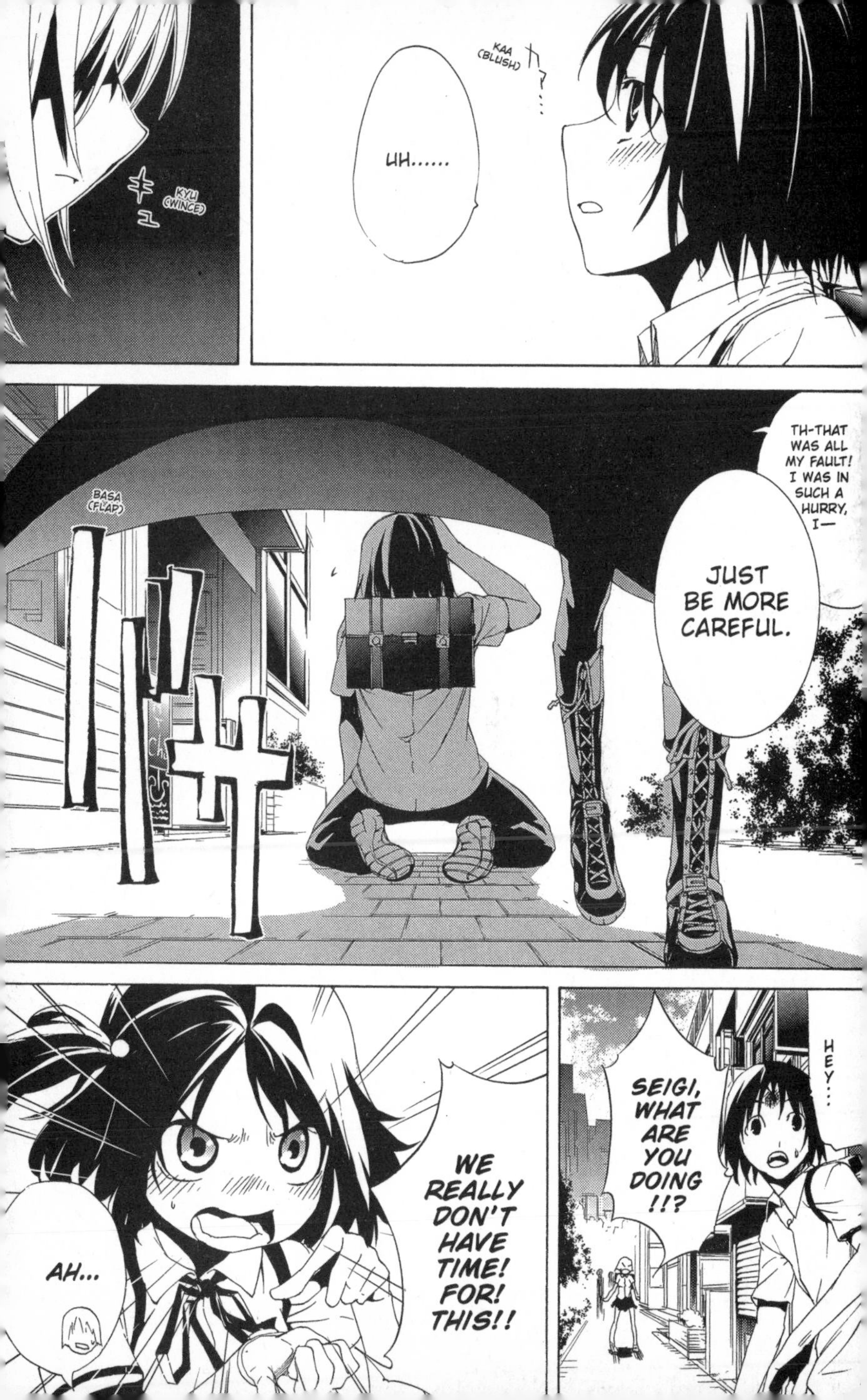
KAA (BLUSH)
UH......
KYU (WINCE)
TH-THAT WAS ALL MY FAULT! I WAS IN SUCH A HURRY, I—
JUST BE MORE CAREFUL.
BASA (FLAP)
HEY...
SEIGI, WHAT ARE YOU DOING!!?
WE REALLY DON'T HAVE TIME! FOR! THIS!!
AH...

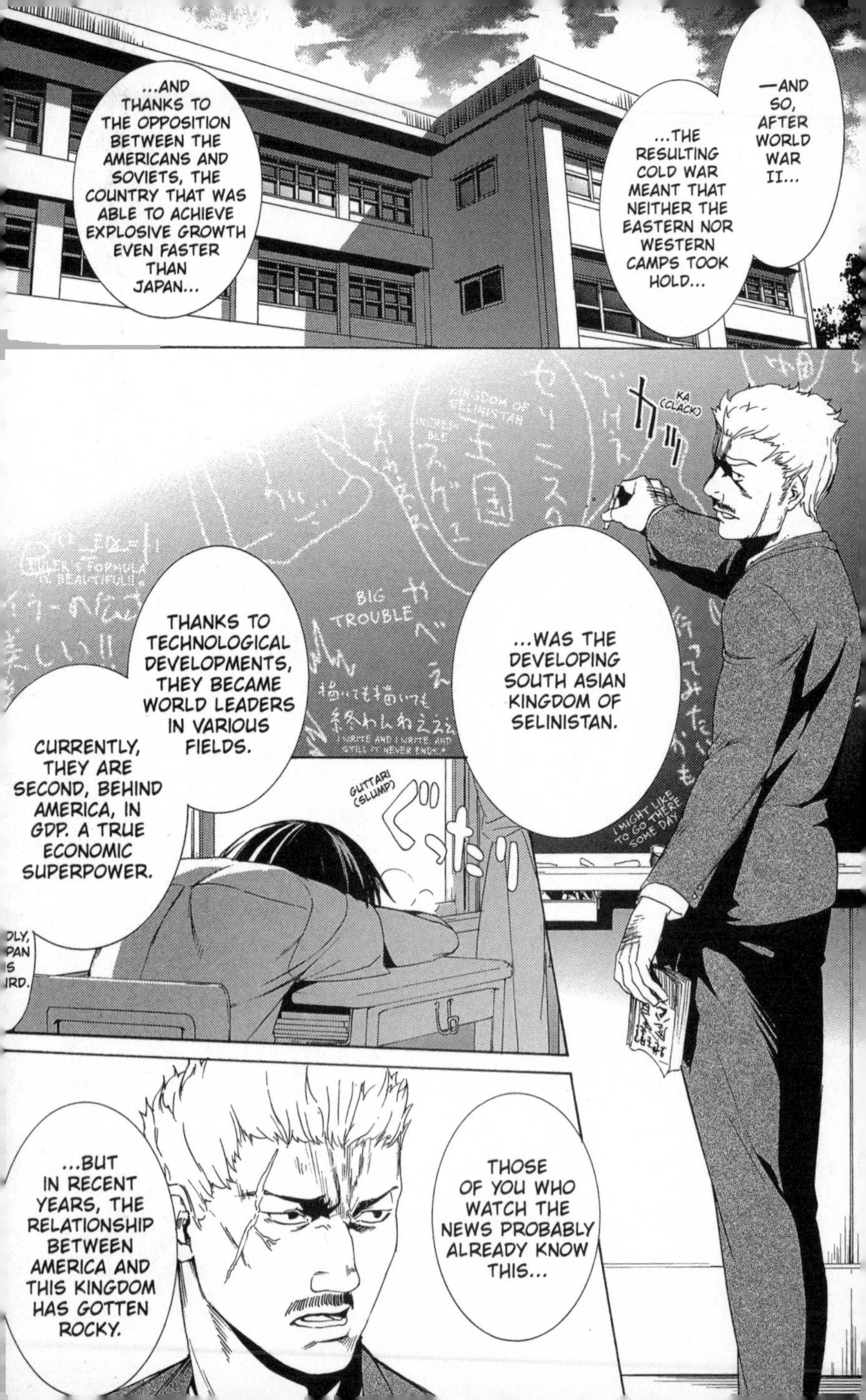
—AND SO, AFTER WORLD WAR II...
...THE RESULTING COLD WAR MEANT THAT NEITHER THE EASTERN NOR WESTERN CAMPS TOOK HOLD...
...AND THANKS TO THE OPPOSITION BETWEEN THE AMERICANS AND SOVIETS, THE COUNTRY THAT WAS ABLE TO ACHIEVE EXPLOSIVE GROWTH EVEN FASTER THAN JAPAN...
KA (CLACK)
KINGDOM OF SELINISTAN
BIG TROUBLE
I WRITE AND I WRITE AND STILL IT NEVER ENDS
I MIGHT LIKE TO GO THERE SOME DAY
...WAS THE DEVELOPING SOUTH ASIAN KINGDOM OF SELINISTAN.
THANKS TO TECHNOLOGICAL DEVELOPMENTS, THEY BECAME WORLD LEADERS IN VARIOUS FIELDS.
CURRENTLY, THEY ARE SECOND, BEHIND AMERICA, IN GDP. A TRUE ECONOMIC SUPERPOWER.
GUTTARI (SLUMP)
THOSE OF YOU WHO WATCH THE NEWS PROBABLY ALREADY KNOW THIS...
...BUT IN RECENT YEARS, THE RELATIONSHIP BETWEEN AMERICA AND THIS KINGDOM HAS GOTTEN ROCKY.

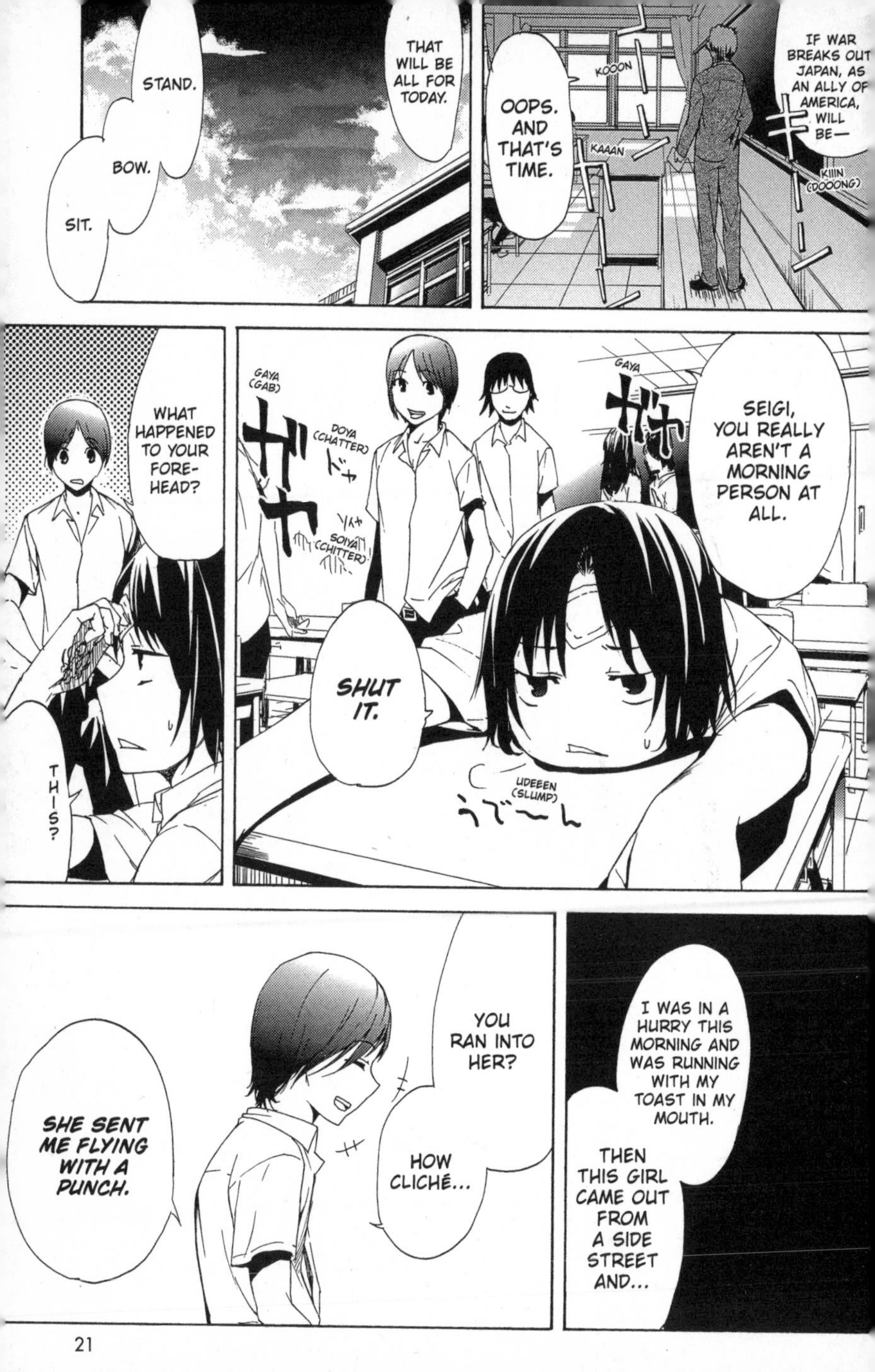
IF WAR BREAKS OUT JAPAN, AS AN ALLY OF AMERICA, WILL BE—
KIIN (DOOONG)
KOOON
KAAAN
OOPS. AND THAT'S TIME.
THAT WILL BE ALL FOR TODAY.
STAND.
BOW.
SIT.
GAYA
SEIGI, YOU REALLY AREN'T A MORNING PERSON AT ALL.
GAYA (GAB)
DOYA (CHATTER)
SOIYA (CHITTER)
SHUT IT.
UDEEEN (SLUMP)
うで～ん
WHAT HAPPENED TO YOUR FOREHEAD?
THIS?
I WAS IN A HURRY THIS MORNING AND WAS RUNNING WITH MY TOAST IN MY MOUTH.
THEN THIS GIRL CAME OUT FROM A SIDE STREET AND...
YOU RAN INTO HER?
HOW CLICHÉ...
SHE SENT ME FLYING WITH A PUNCH.

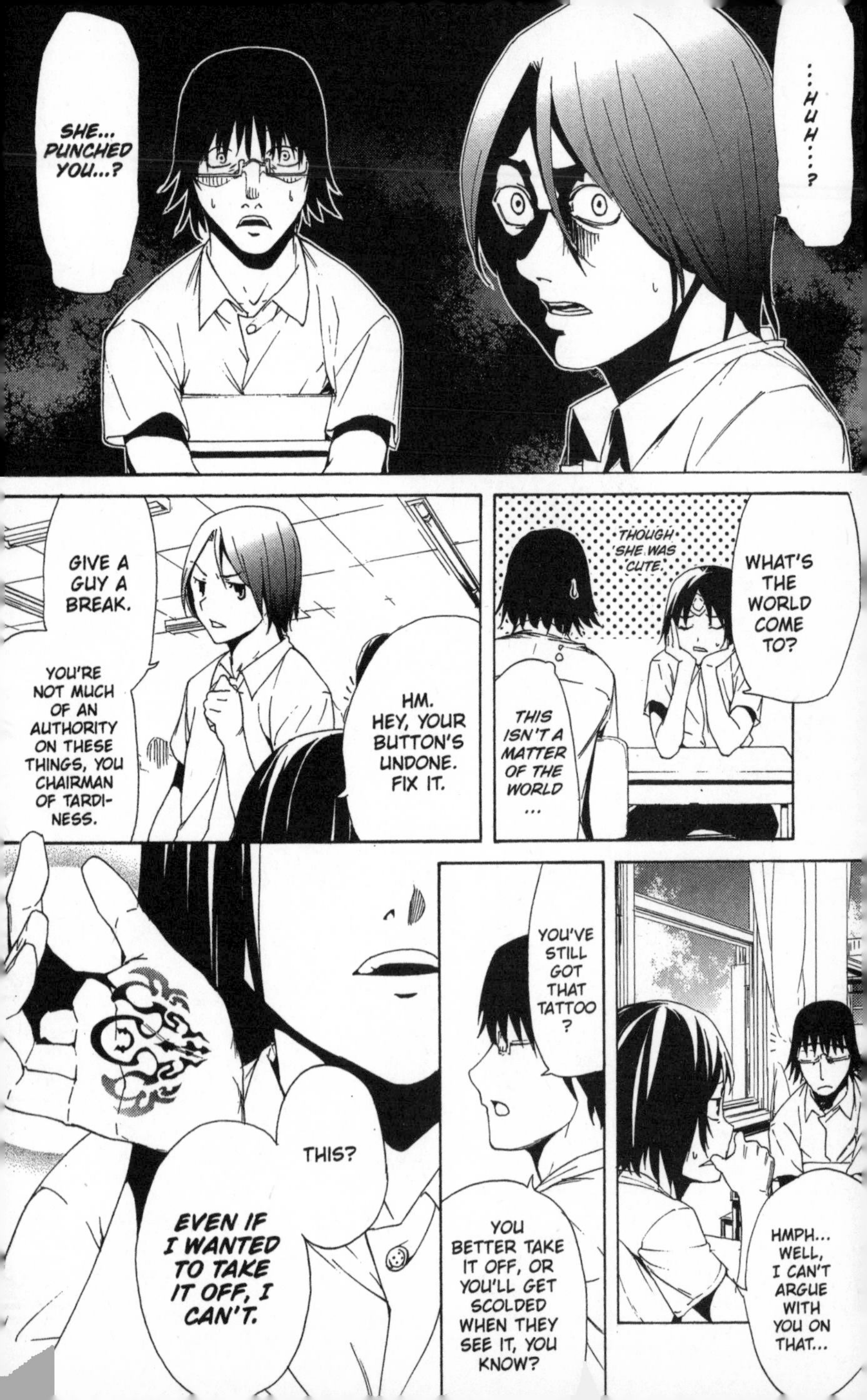
...HUH...?
SHE... PUNCHED YOU...?
WHAT'S THE WORLD COME TO?
THOUGH SHE WAS CUTE.
THIS ISN'T A MATTER OF THE WORLD ...
HM. HEY, YOUR BUTTON'S UNDONE. FIX IT.
GIVE A GUY A BREAK.
YOU'RE NOT MUCH OF AN AUTHORITY ON THESE THINGS, YOU CHAIRMAN OF TARDINESS.
HMPH... WELL, I CAN'T ARGUE WITH YOU ON THAT...
YOU'VE STILL GOT THAT TATTOO?
THIS?
YOU BETTER TAKE IT OFF, OR YOU'LL GET SCOLDED WHEN THEY SEE IT, YOU KNOW?
EVEN IF I WANTED TO TAKE IT OFF, I CAN'T.

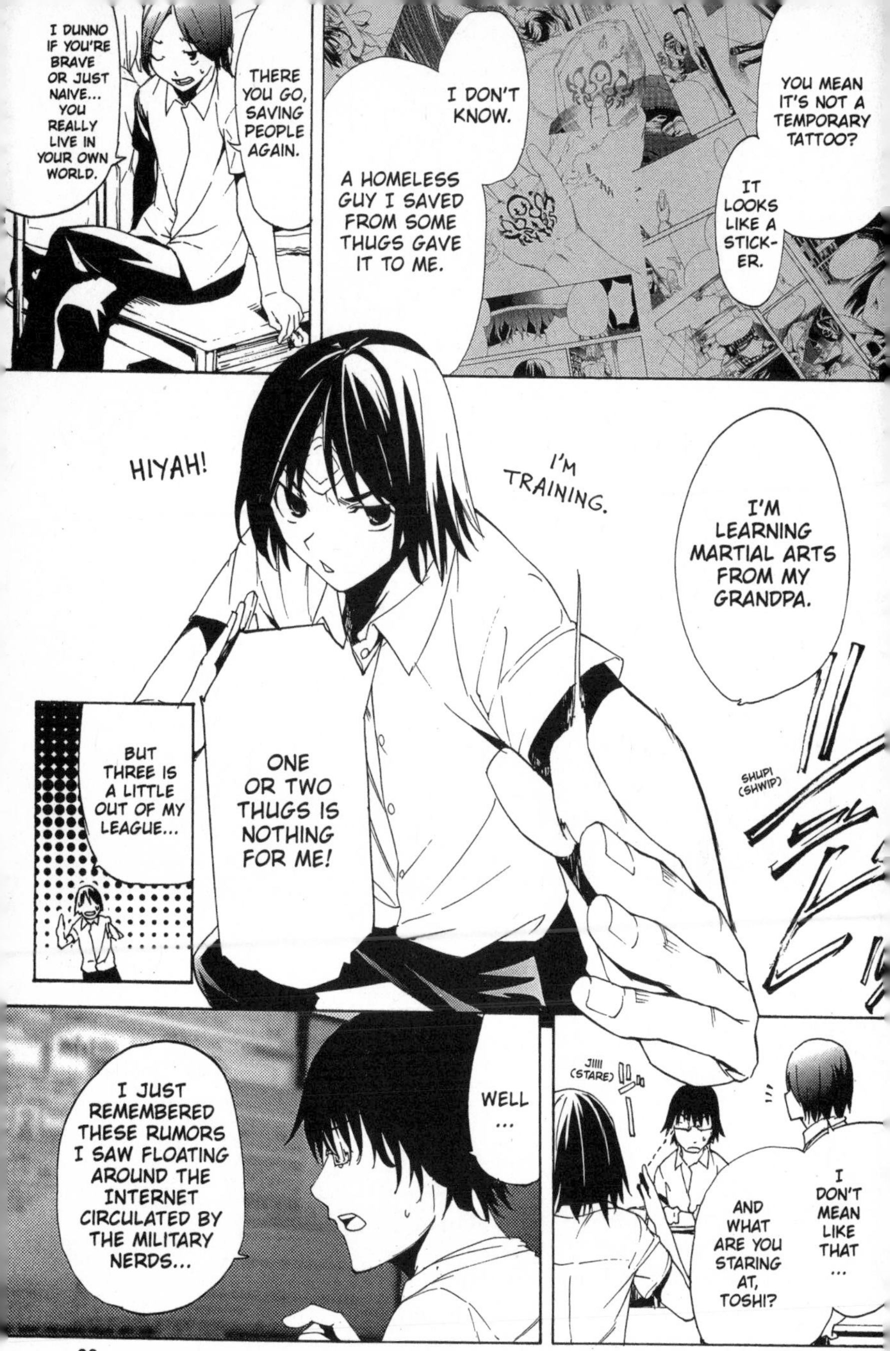
YOU MEAN IT'S NOT A TEMPORARY TATTOO?
IT LOOKS LIKE A STICK-ER.
I DON'T KNOW.
A HOMELESS GUY I SAVED FROM SOME THUGS GAVE IT TO ME.
THERE YOU GO, SAVING PEOPLE AGAIN.
I DUNNO IF YOU'RE BRAVE OR JUST NAIVE... YOU REALLY LIVE IN YOUR OWN WORLD.
I'M LEARNING MARTIAL ARTS FROM MY GRANDPA.
I'M TRAINING.
HIYAH!
SHUPI (SHWIP)
ONE OR TWO THUGS IS NOTHING FOR ME!
BUT THREE IS A LITTLE OUT OF MY LEAGUE...
JIIII (STARE)
I DON'T MEAN LIKE THAT...
AND WHAT ARE YOU STARING AT, TOSHI?
WELL...
I JUST REMEMBERED THESE RUMORS I SAW FLOATING AROUND THE INTERNET CIRCULATED BY THE MILITARY NERDS...

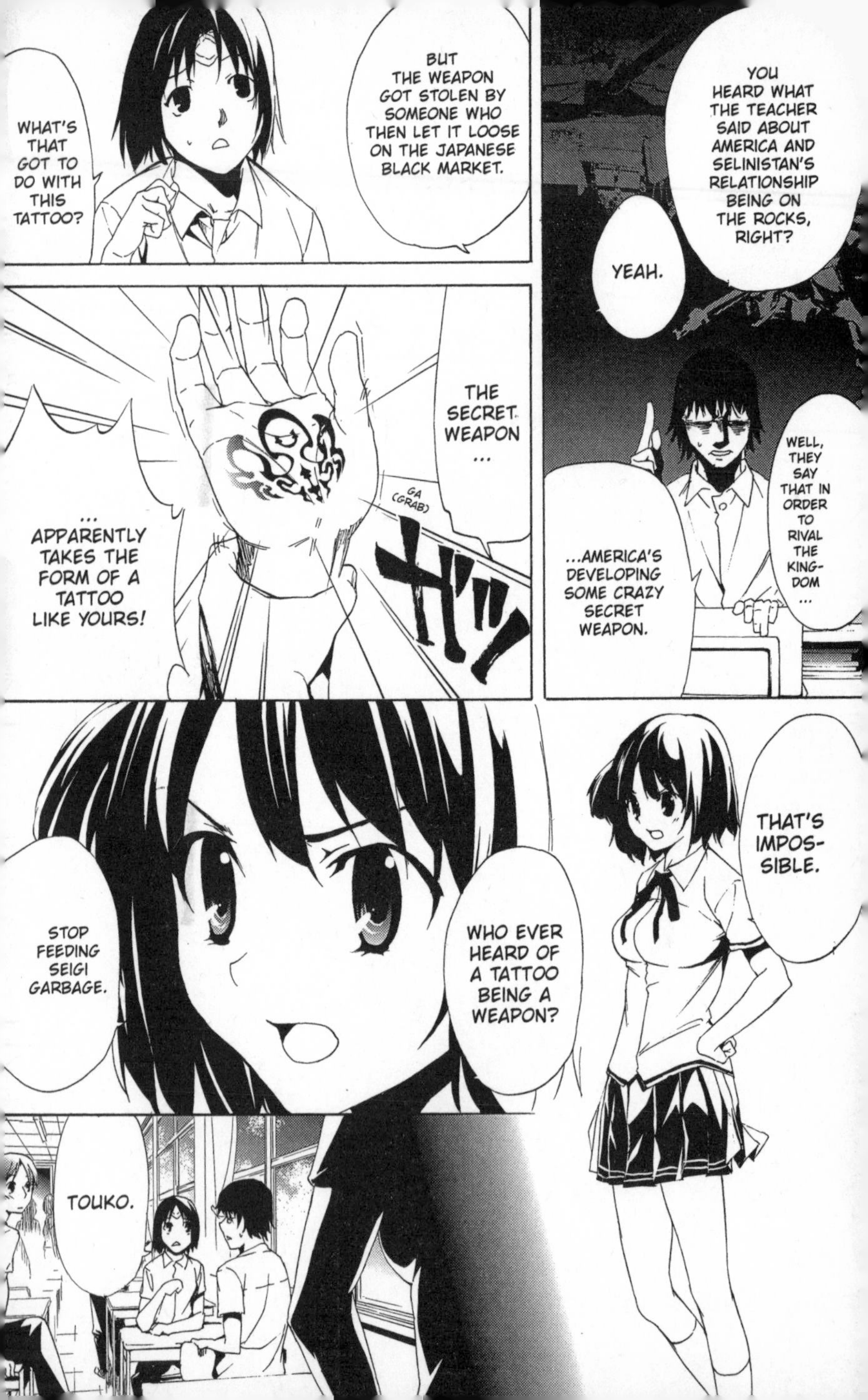
YOU HEARD WHAT THE TEACHER SAID ABOUT AMERICA AND SELINISTAN'S RELATIONSHIP BEING ON THE ROCKS, RIGHT?
YEAH.
WELL, THEY SAY THAT IN ORDER TO RIVAL THE KING-DOM ...
...AMERICA'S DEVELOPING SOME CRAZY SECRET WEAPON.
BUT THE WEAPON GOT STOLEN BY SOMEONE WHO THEN LET IT LOOSE ON THE JAPANESE BLACK MARKET.
WHAT'S THAT GOT TO DO WITH THIS TATTOO?
THE SECRET WEAPON ...
GA (GRAB)
... APPARENTLY TAKES THE FORM OF A TATTOO LIKE YOURS!
THAT'S IMPOS-SIBLE.
WHO EVER HEARD OF A TATTOO BEING A WEAPON?
STOP FEEDING SEIGI GARBAGE.
TOUKO.

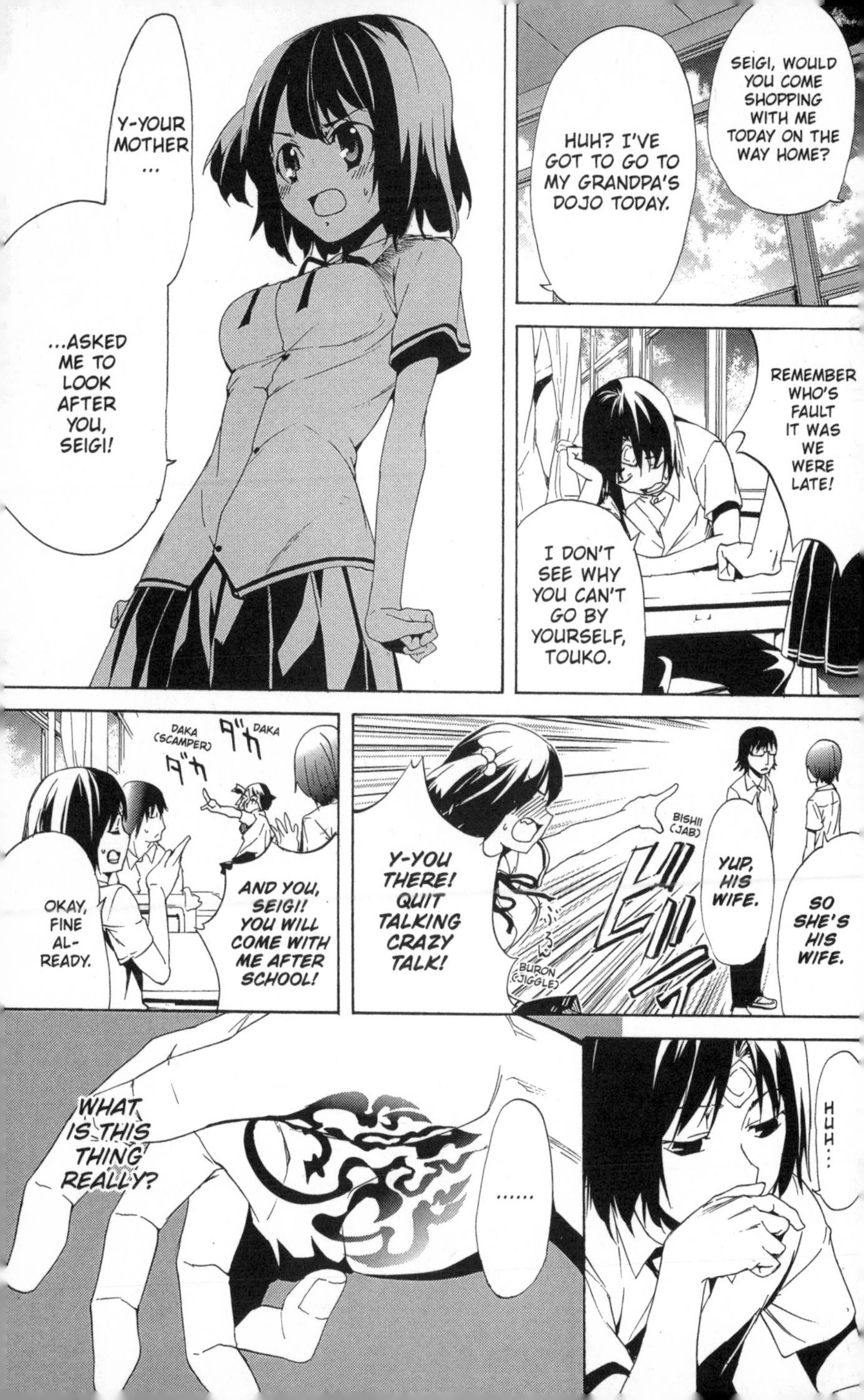
SEIGI, WOULD YOU COME SHOPPING WITH ME TODAY ON THE WAY HOME?
HUH? I'VE GOT TO GO TO MY GRANDPA'S DOJO TODAY.
REMEMBER WHO'S FAULT IT WAS WE WERE LATE!
I DON'T SEE WHY YOU CAN'T GO BY YOURSELF, TOUKO.
Y-YOUR MOTHER ...
...ASKED ME TO LOOK AFTER YOU, SEIGI!
SO SHE'S HIS WIFE.
YUP, HIS WIFE.
BISHI! (JAB)
Y-YOU THERE! QUIT TALKING CRAZY TALK!
BURON (JIGGLE)
DAKA DAKA (SCAMPER)
AND YOU, SEIGI! YOU WILL COME WITH ME AFTER SCHOOL!
OKAY, FINE AL-READY.
HUH...
......
WHAT IS THIS THING REALLY?

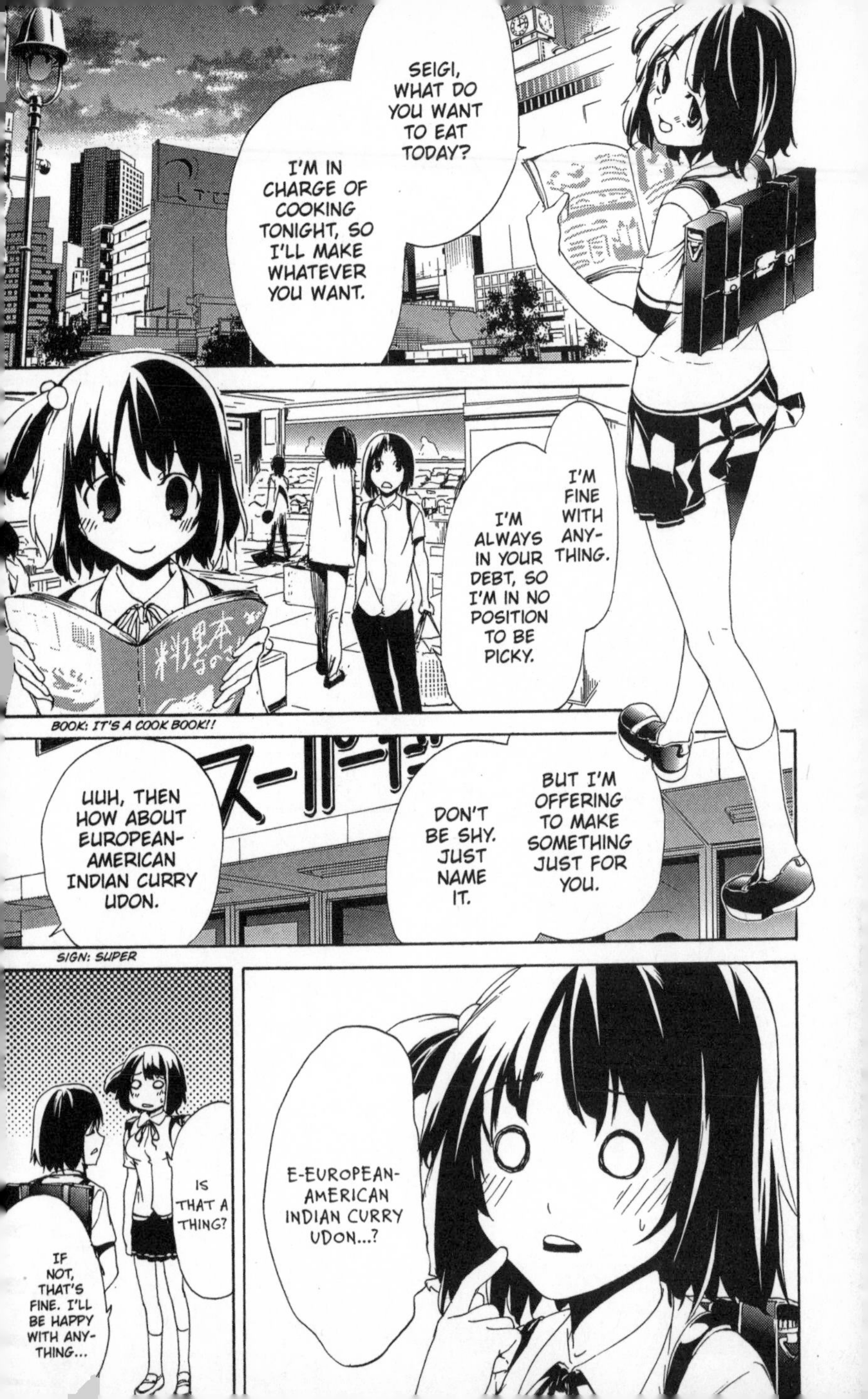
SEIGI, WHAT DO YOU WANT TO EAT TODAY?
I'M IN CHARGE OF COOKING TONIGHT, SO I'LL MAKE WHATEVER YOU WANT.
I'M FINE WITH ANY-THING.
I'M ALWAYS IN YOUR DEBT, SO I'M IN NO POSITION TO BE PICKY.
BOOK: IT'S A COOK BOOK!!
BUT I'M OFFERING TO MAKE SOMETHING JUST FOR YOU.
DON'T BE SHY. JUST NAME IT.
UUH, THEN HOW ABOUT EUROPEAN-AMERICAN INDIAN CURRY UDON.
SIGN: SUPER
E-EUROPEAN-AMERICAN INDIAN CURRY UDON...?
IS THAT A THING?
IF NOT, THAT'S FINE. I'LL BE HAPPY WITH ANY-THING...

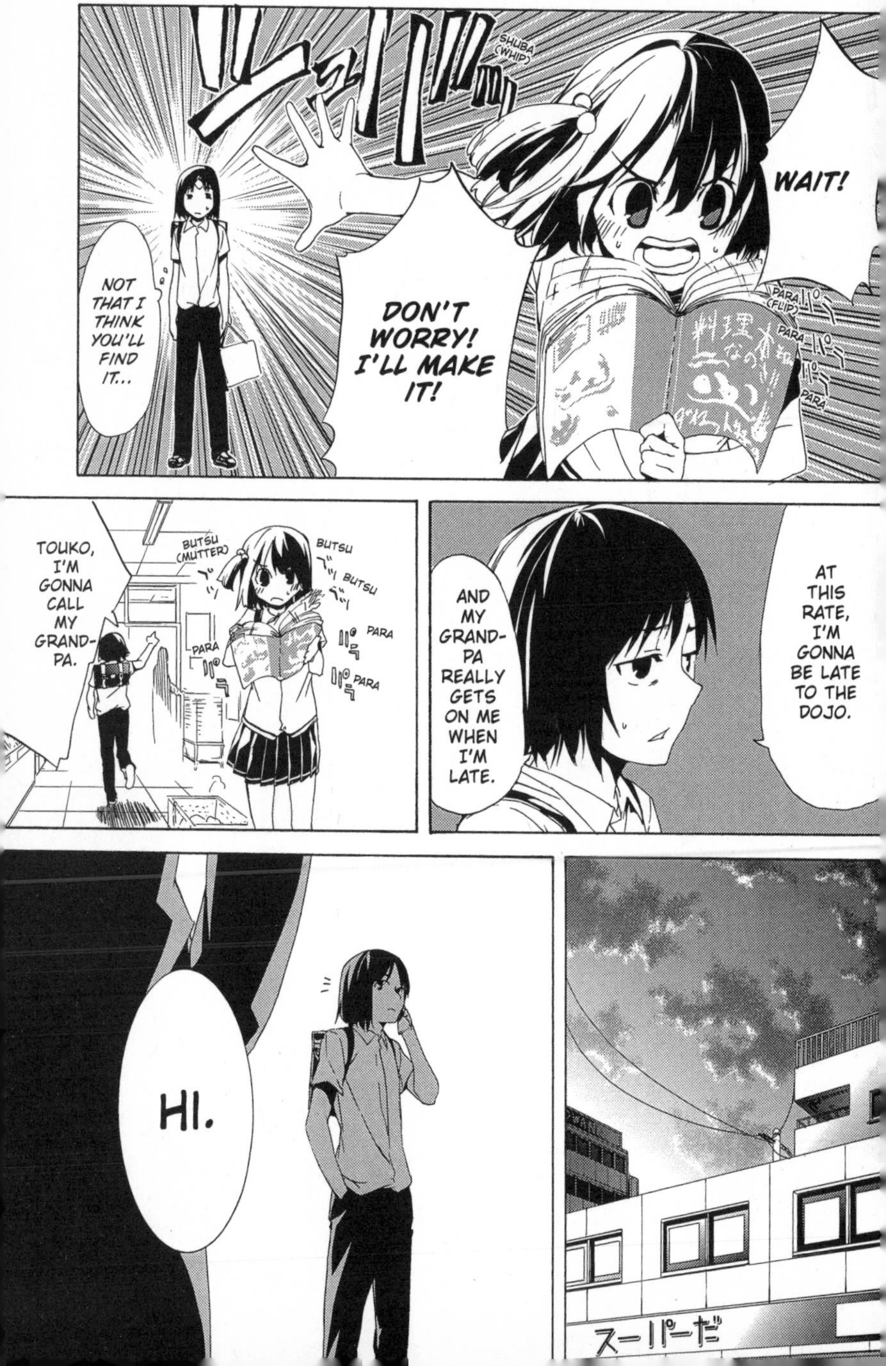
WAIT!
SHUBA (WHIP)
PARA (FLIP)
PARA
PARA
DON'T WORRY! I'LL MAKE IT!
NOT THAT I THINK YOU'LL FIND IT...
AT THIS RATE, I'M GONNA BE LATE TO THE DOJO.
AND MY GRANDPA REALLY GETS ON ME WHEN I'M LATE.
BUTSU
BUTSU
BUTSU (MUTTER)
PARA
PARA
PARA
TOUKO, I'M GONNA CALL MY GRAND-PA.
スーパーだ
HI.

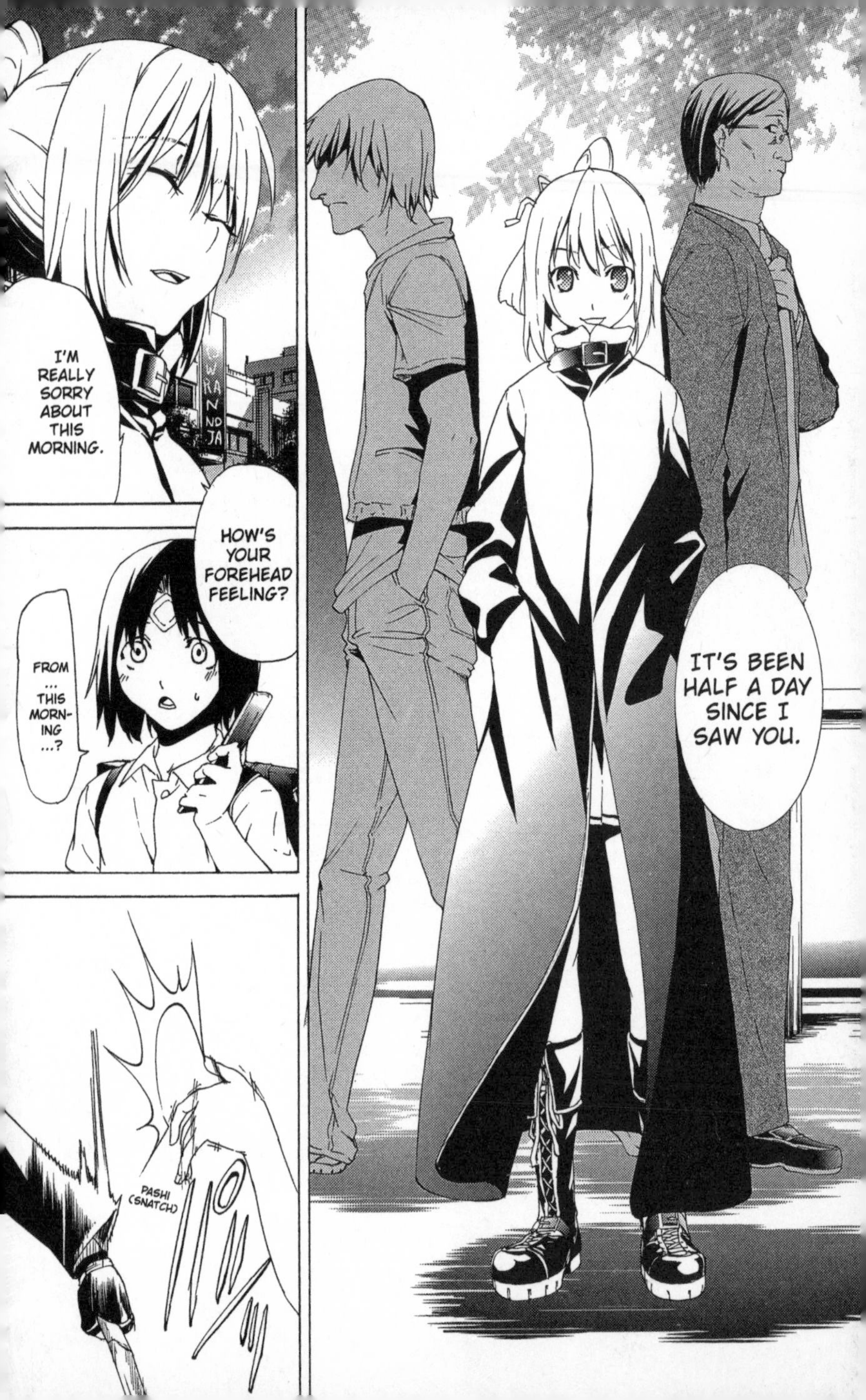
IT'S BEEN HALF A DAY SINCE I SAW YOU.
I'M REALLY SORRY ABOUT THIS MORNING.
HOW'S YOUR FOREHEAD FEELING?
FROM ... THIS MORNING ...?
PASHI (SNATCH)

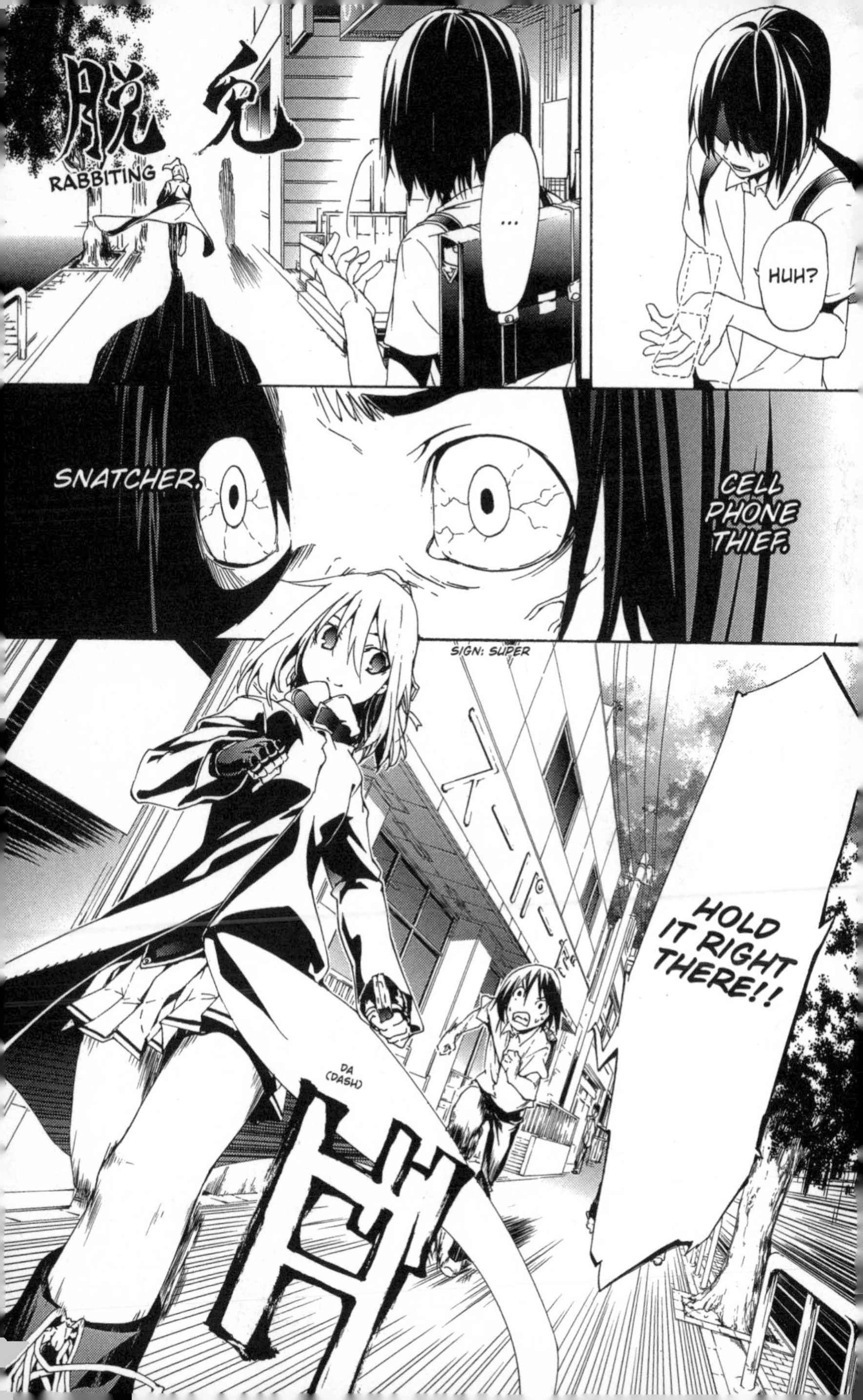

HUH?
...
脱兎
RABBITING
CELL PHONE THIEF.
SNATCHER.
HOLD IT RIGHT THERE!!
SIGN: SUPER
DA (DASH)

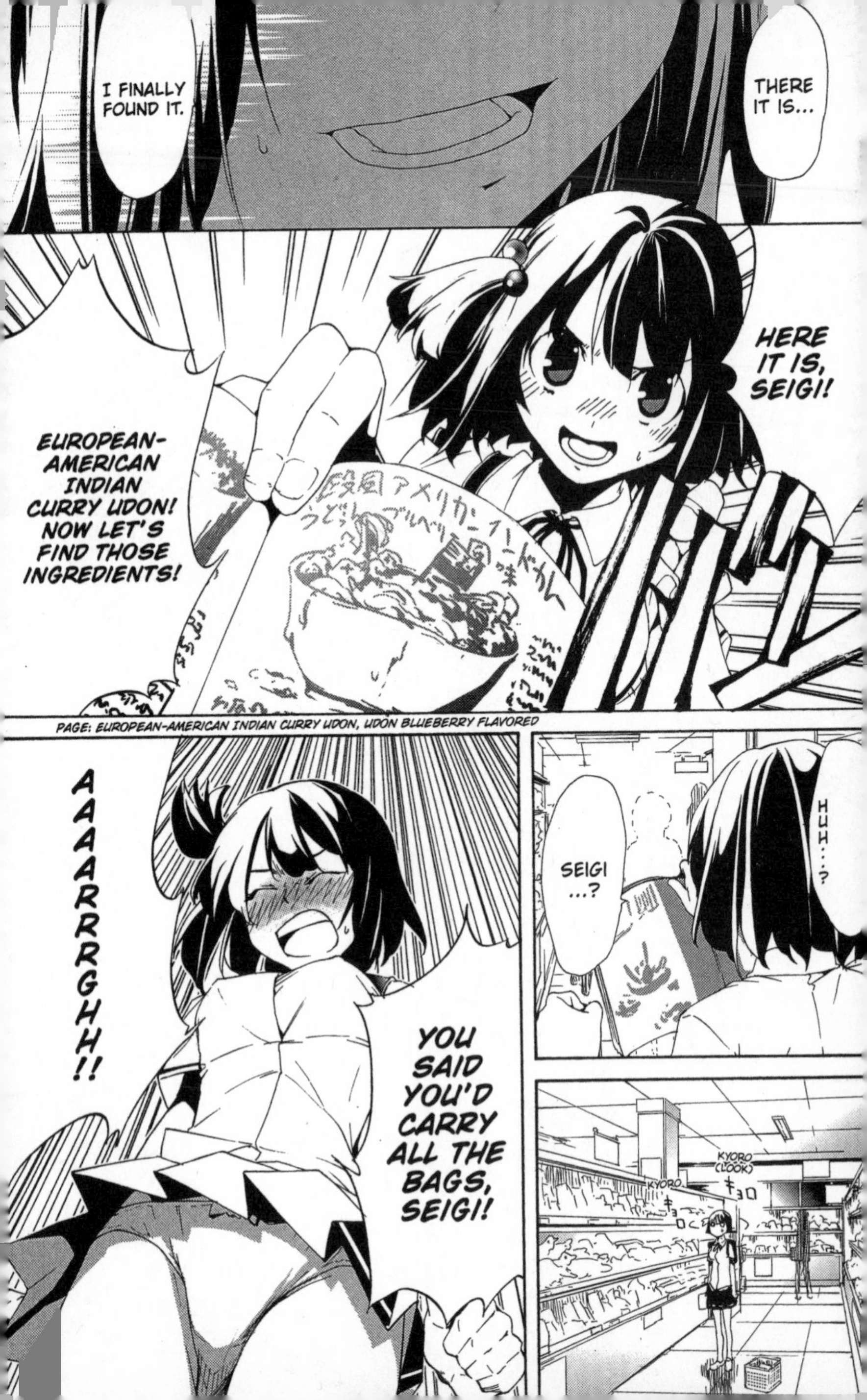
THERE IT IS...
I FINALLY FOUND IT.
HERE IT IS, SEIGI!
EUROPEAN-AMERICAN INDIAN CURRY UDON! NOW LET'S FIND THOSE INGREDIENTS!
PAGE: EUROPEAN-AMERICAN INDIAN CURRY UDON, UDON BLUEBERRY FLAVORED
HUH...?
SEIGI...?
KYORO (LOOK)
KYORO
YOU SAID YOU'D CARRY ALL THE BAGS, SEIGI!
AAAAARRRRGHH!!

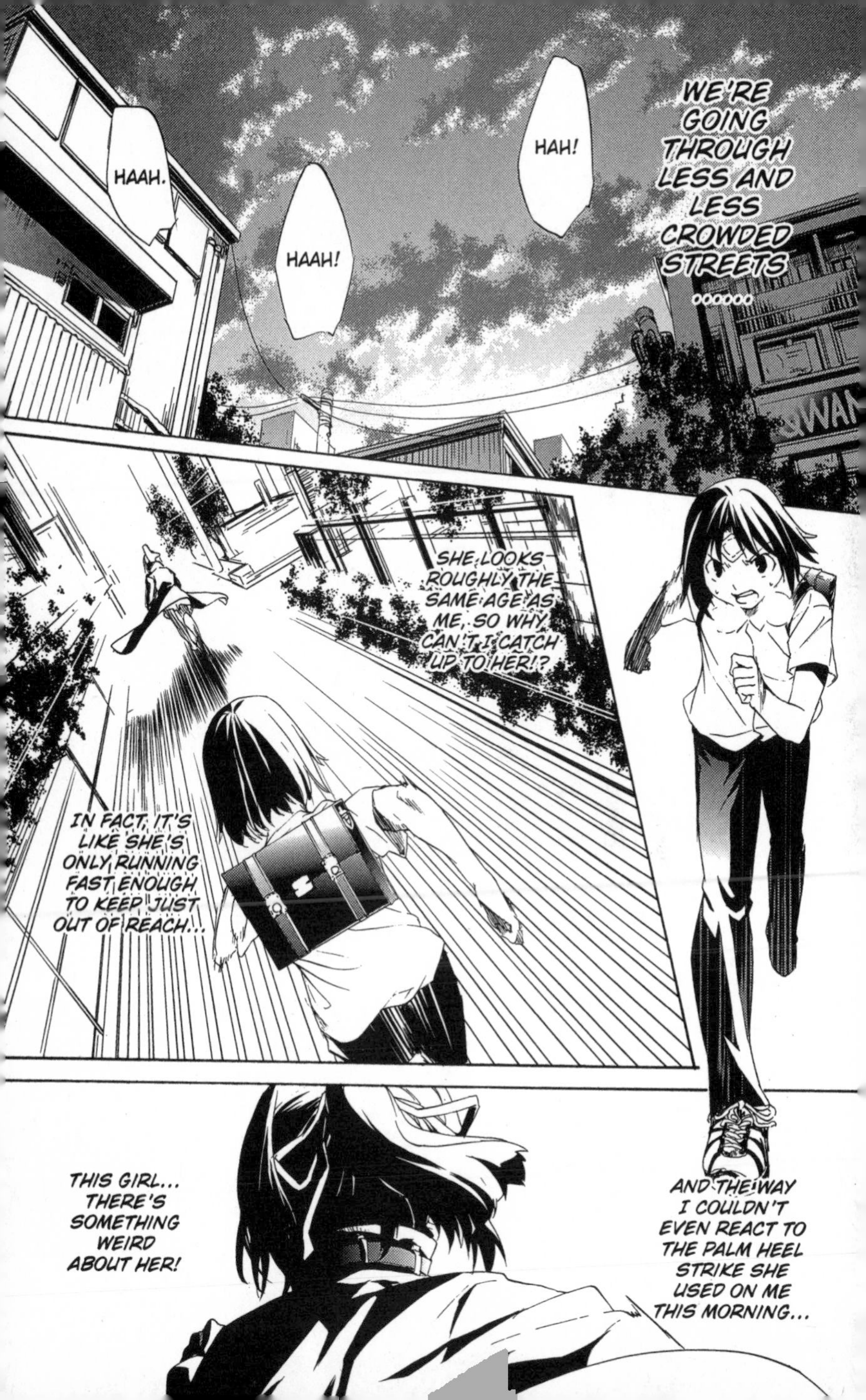
WE'RE GOING THROUGH LESS AND LESS CROWDED STREETS......
HAH!
HAAH!
HAAH.
SHE LOOKS ROUGHLY THE SAME AGE AS ME, SO WHY CAN'T I CATCH UP TO HER!?
IN FACT, IT'S LIKE SHE'S ONLY RUNNING FAST ENOUGH TO KEEP JUST OUT OF REACH...
AND THE WAY I COULDN'T EVEN REACT TO THE PALM HEEL STRIKE SHE USED ON ME THIS MORNING...
THIS GIRL... THERE'S SOMETHING WEIRD ABOUT HER!

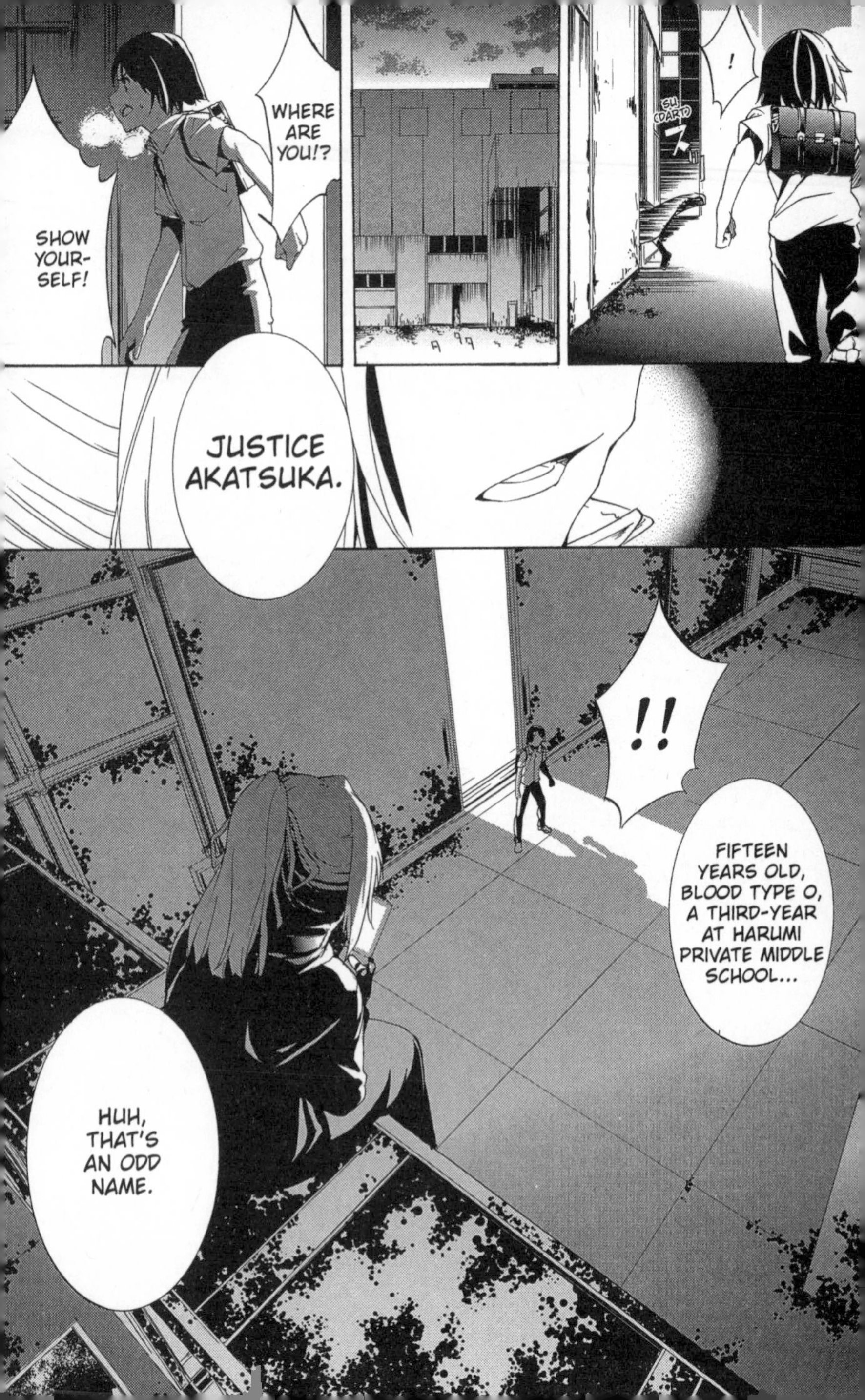
!
SU (DART)
WHERE ARE YOU!?
SHOW YOUR-SELF!
JUSTICE AKATSUKA.
!!
FIFTEEN YEARS OLD, BLOOD TYPE O, A THIRD-YEAR AT HARUMI PRIVATE MIDDLE SCHOOL...
HUH, THAT'S AN ODD NAME.

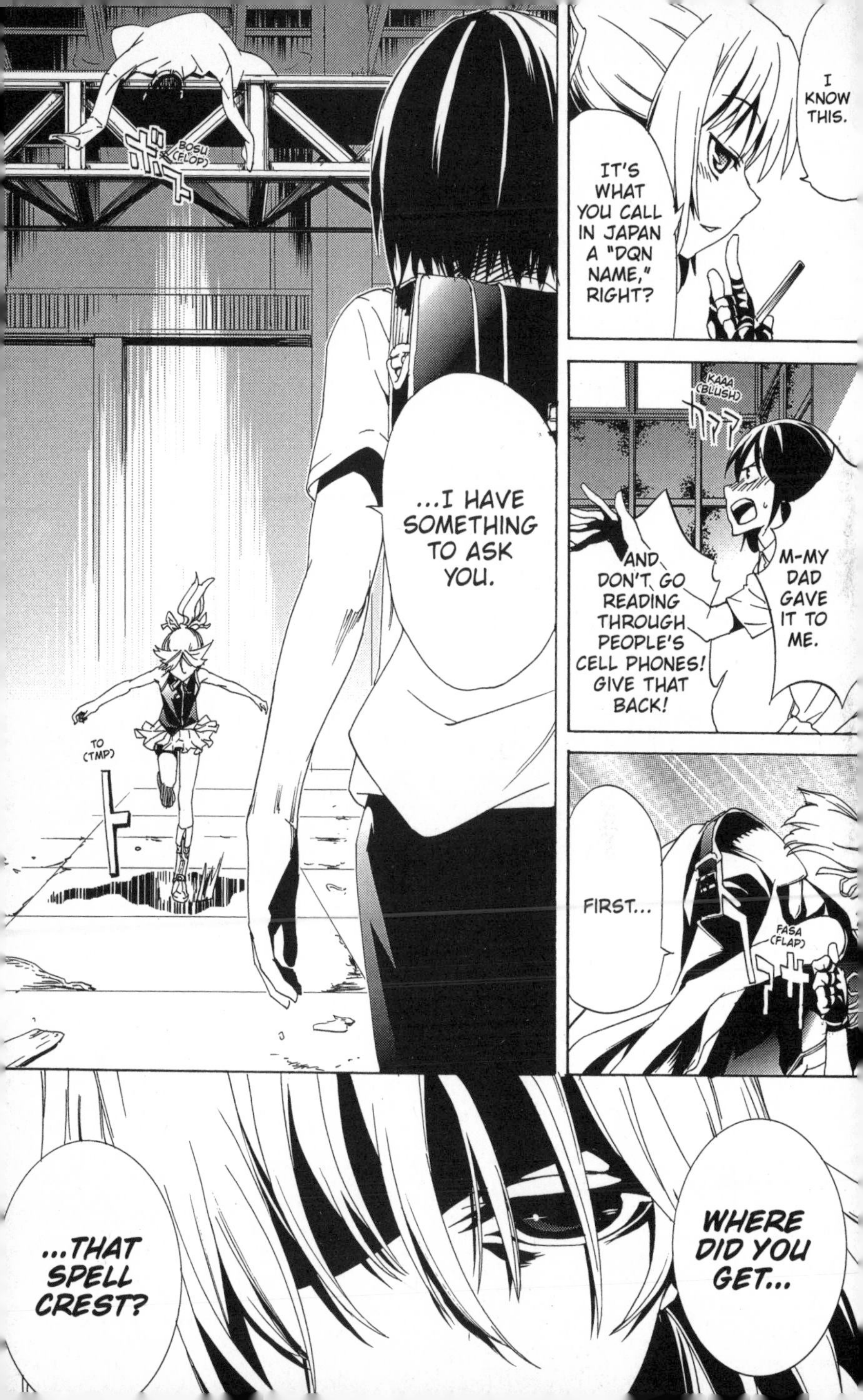
I KNOW THIS.
IT'S WHAT YOU CALL IN JAPAN A "DQN NAME," RIGHT?
KAAA (BLUSH)
M-MY DAD GAVE IT TO ME.
AND DON'T GO READING THROUGH PEOPLE'S CELL PHONES! GIVE THAT BACK!
FIRST...
FASA (FLAP)
BOSU (FLOP)
...I HAVE SOMETHING TO ASK YOU.
TO (TMP)
WHERE DID YOU GET...
...THAT SPELL CREST?

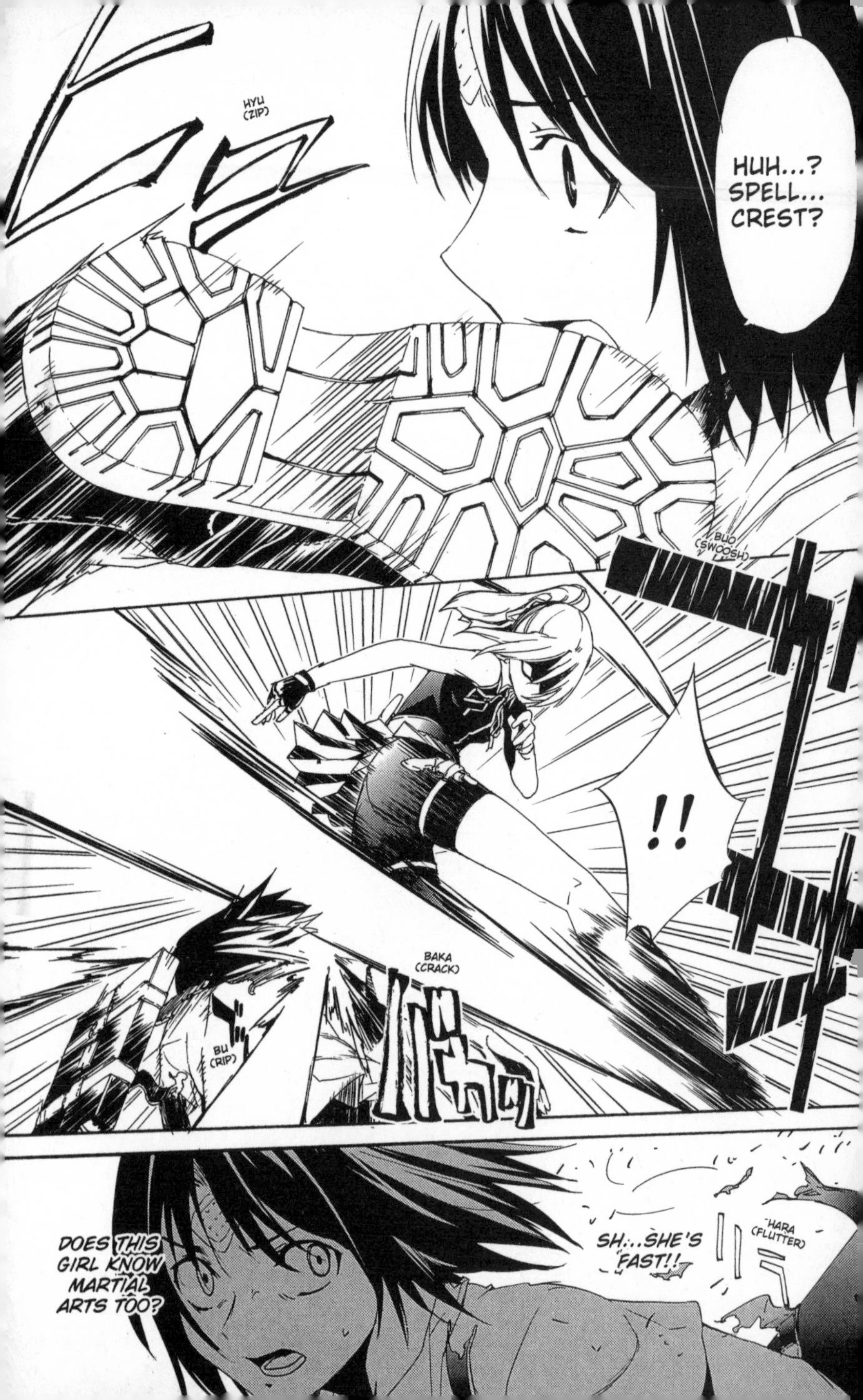
HUH...? SPELL... CREST?
HYU (ZIP)
BUO (SWOOSH)
!!
BAKA (CRACK)
BU (RIP)
HARA (FLUTTER)
SH...SHE'S FAST!!
DOES THIS GIRL KNOW MARTIAL ARTS TOO?

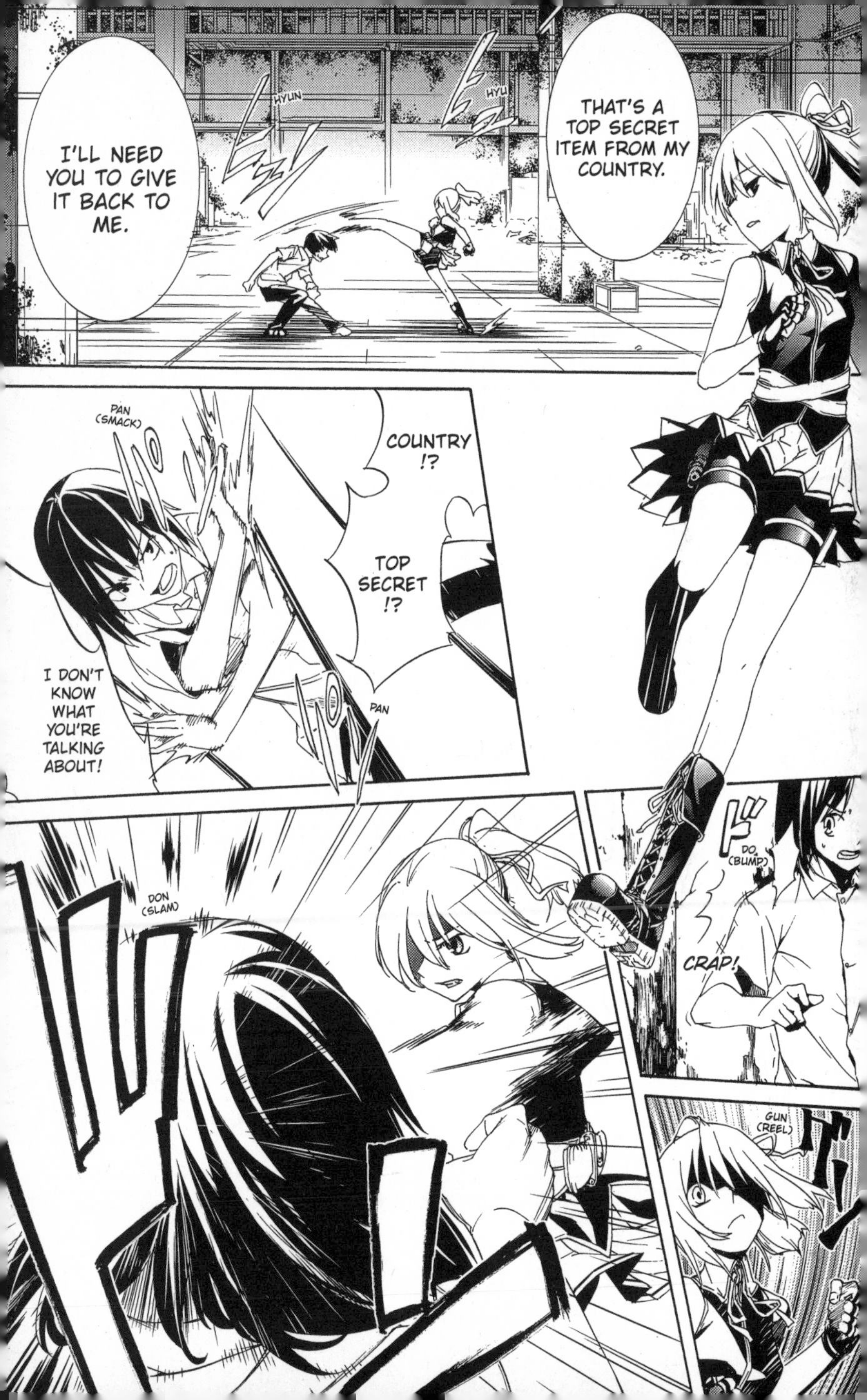
THAT'S A TOP SECRET ITEM FROM MY COUNTRY.
HYU
HYUN
I'LL NEED YOU TO GIVE IT BACK TO ME.
COUNTRY !?
TOP SECRET !?
PAN (SMACK)
PAN
I DON'T KNOW WHAT YOU'RE TALKING ABOUT!
DO (BUMP)
CRAP!
GUN (REEL)
DON (SLAM)

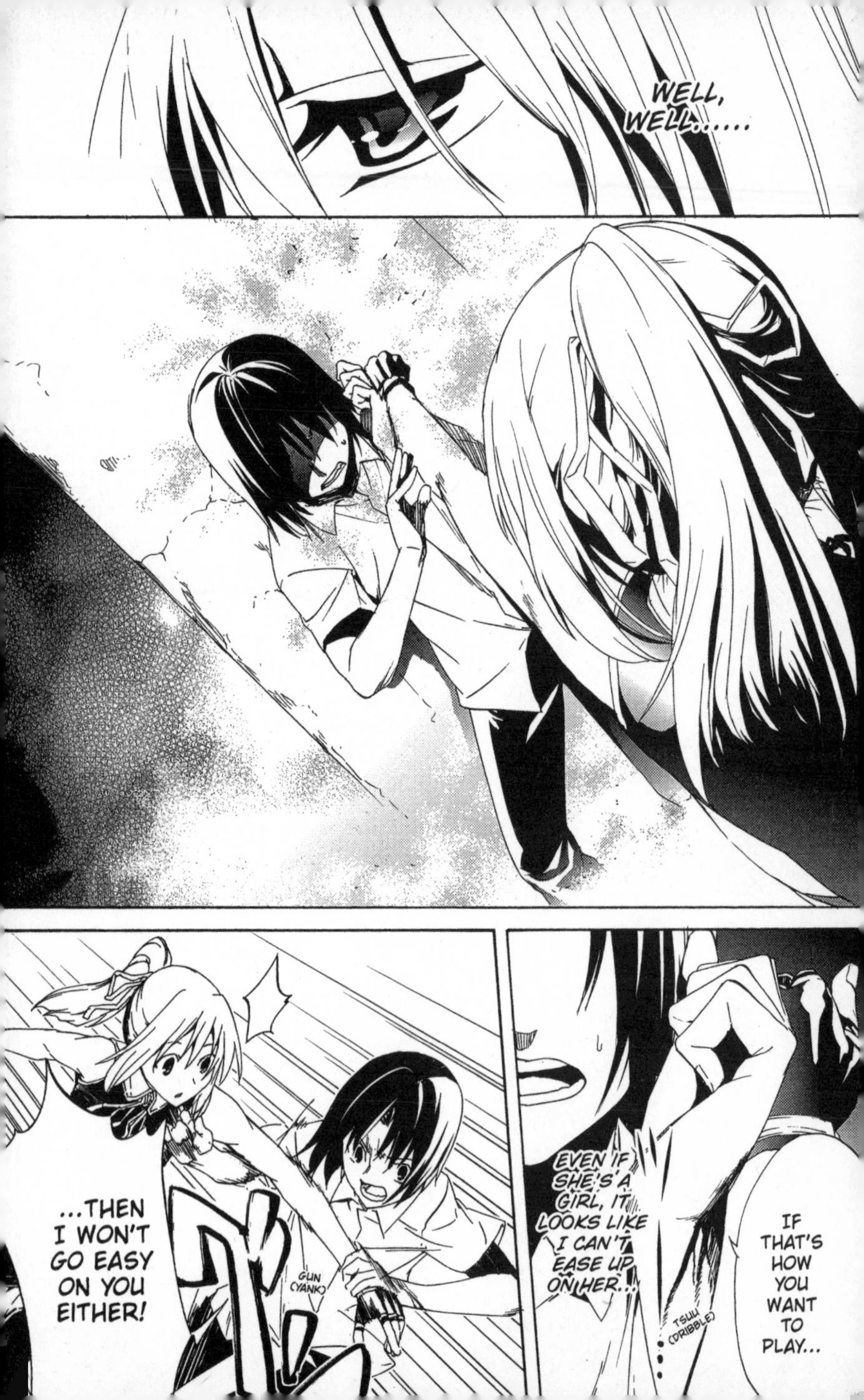
WELL, WELL......
IF THAT'S HOW YOU WANT TO PLAY...
TSUU (DRIBBLE)
EVEN IF SHE'S A GIRL, IT LOOKS LIKE I CAN'T EASE UP ON HER...
GUN (YANK)
...THEN I WON'T GO EASY ON YOU EITHER!

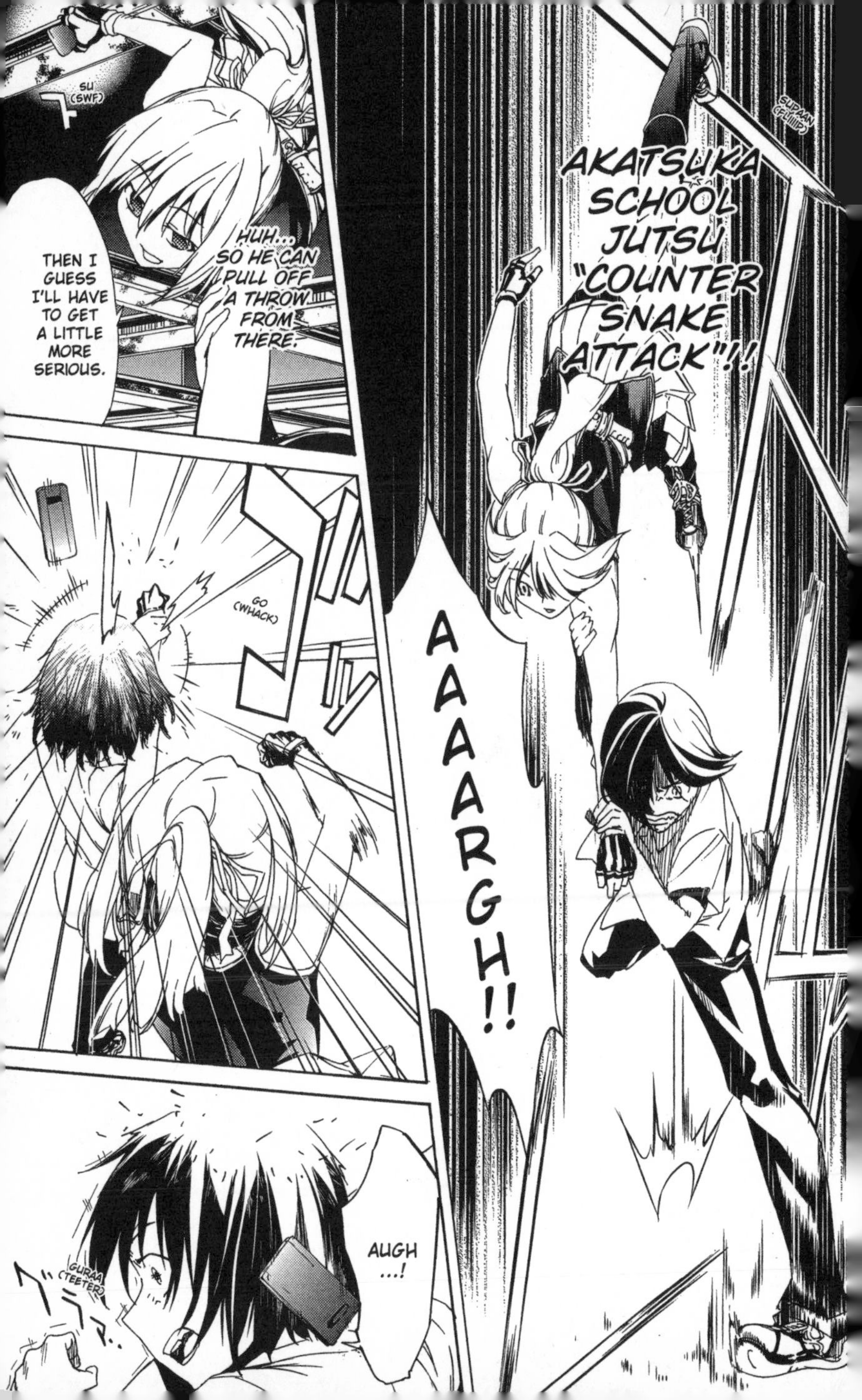
SUPAAN
(FLIIIIP)
AKATSUKA SCHOOL JUTSU "COUNTER SNAKE ATTACK"!!
AAAAARGH!!
SU
(SWF)
HUH... SO HE CAN PULL OFF A THROW FROM THERE.
THEN I GUESS I'LL HAVE TO GET A LITTLE MORE SERIOUS.
GO
(WHACK)
AUGH ...!
GURAA
(TEETER)

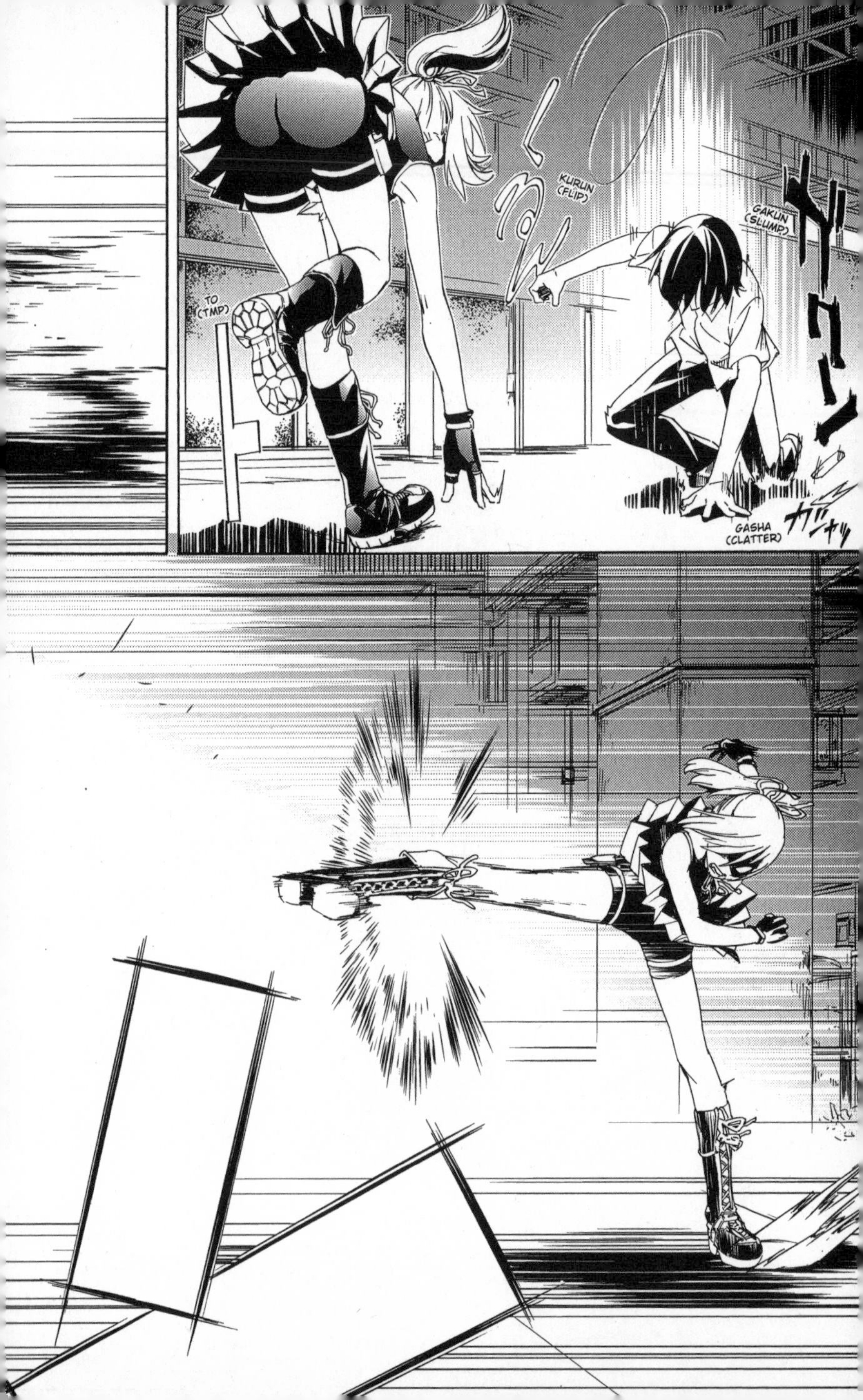
GAKUN
(SLUMP)
KURUN
(FLIP)
GASHA
(CLATTER)
TO
(TMP)

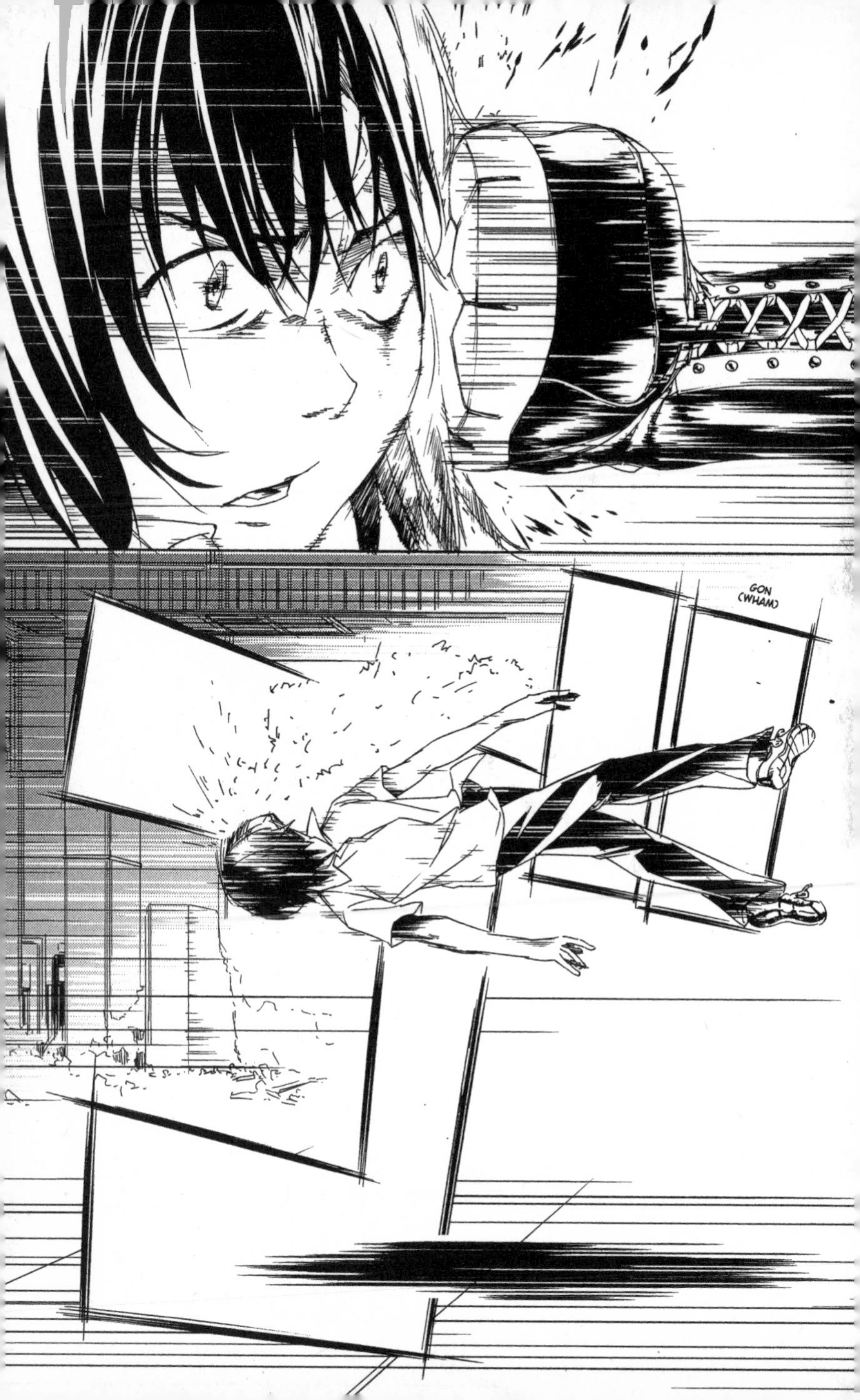
GON
(WHAM)

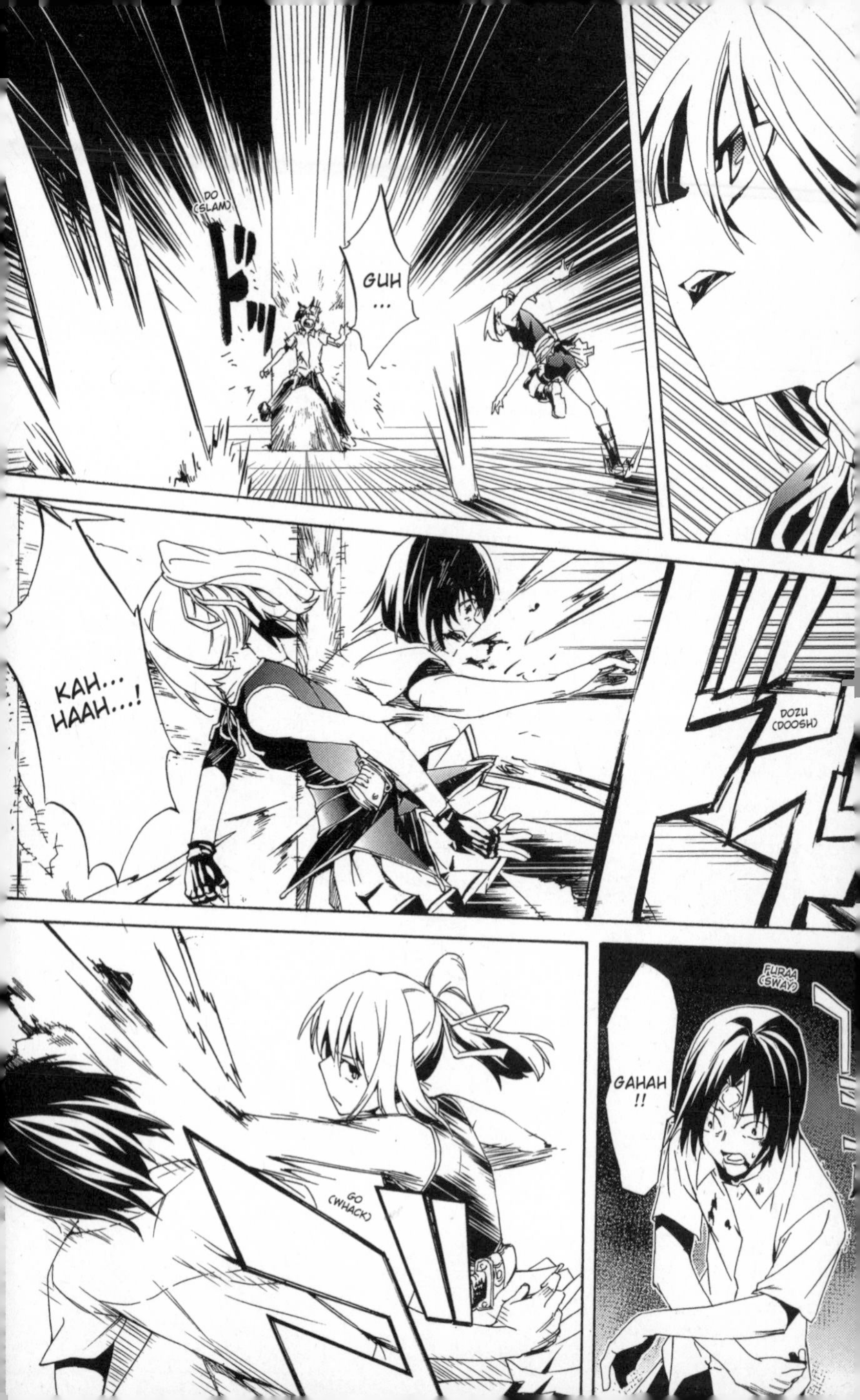
DO (SLAM)
ドッ
GUH ...
DOZU (DOOSH)
KAH... HAAH...!
FURAA (SWAY)
GAHAH !!
GO (WHACK)

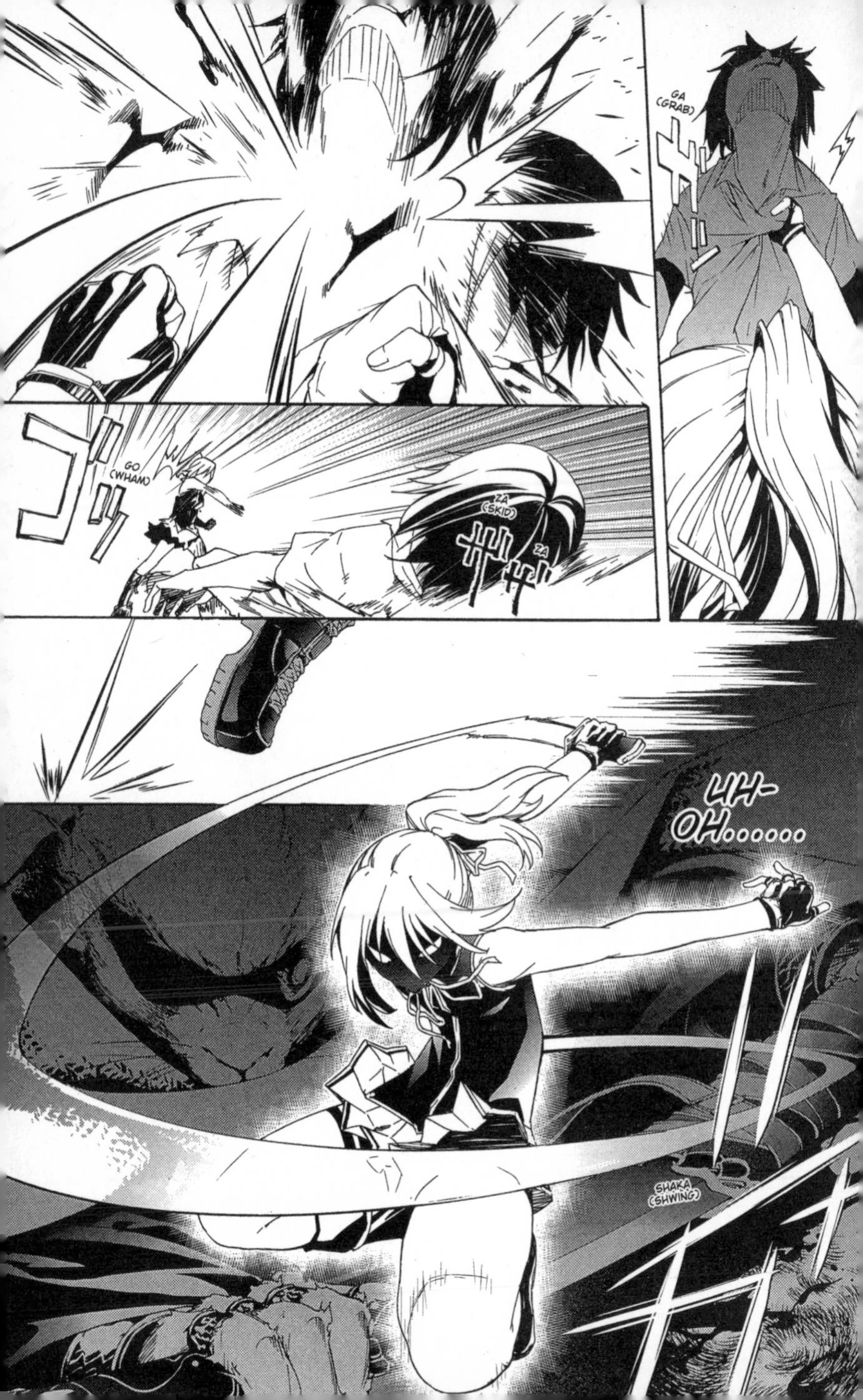
GA (GRAB)
GO (WHAM)
ZA (SKID)
ZA
UH-OH.oooooo
SHAKA (SHWING)

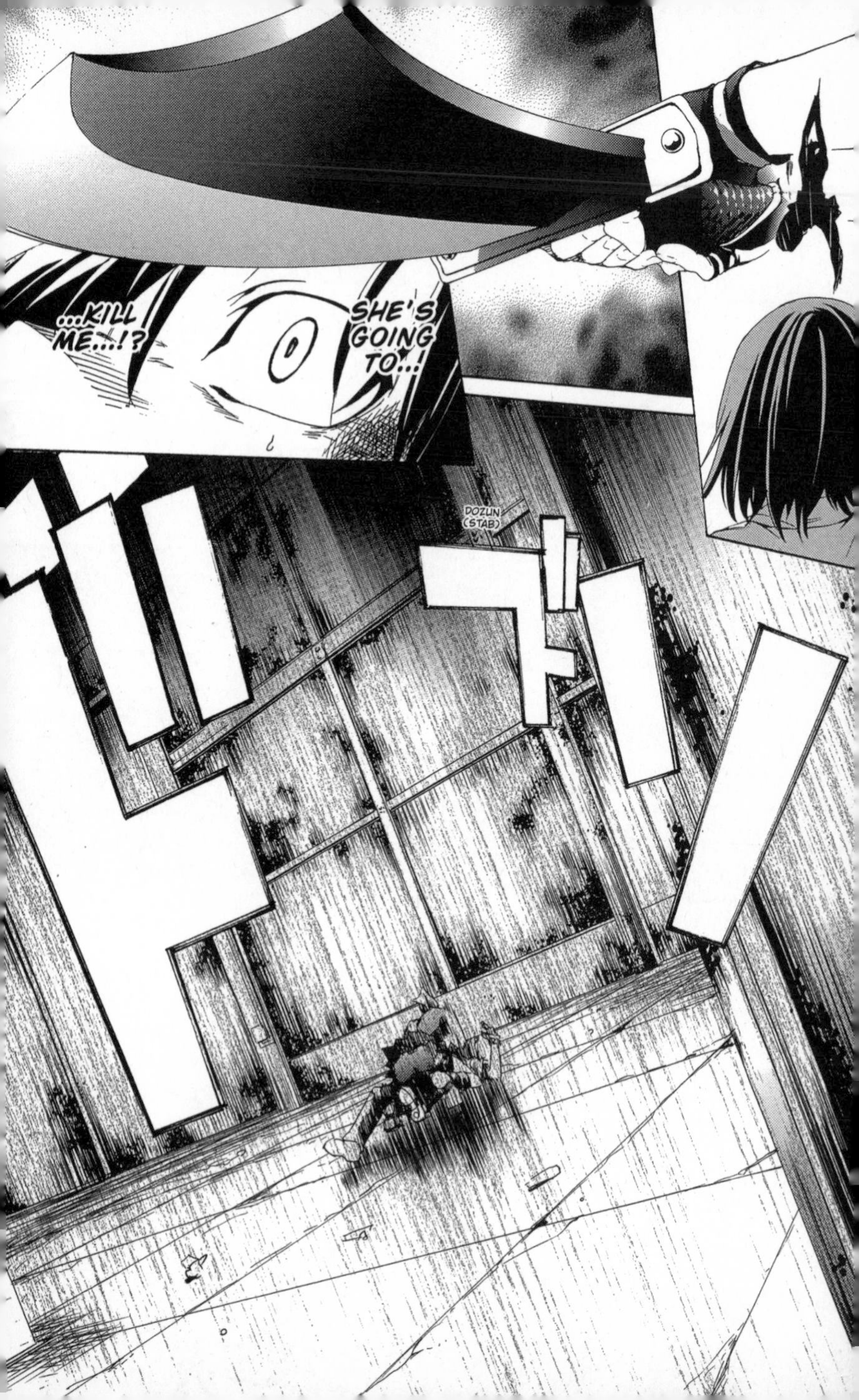
SHE'S GOING TO...!
...KILL ME...!?
DOZUN (STAB)

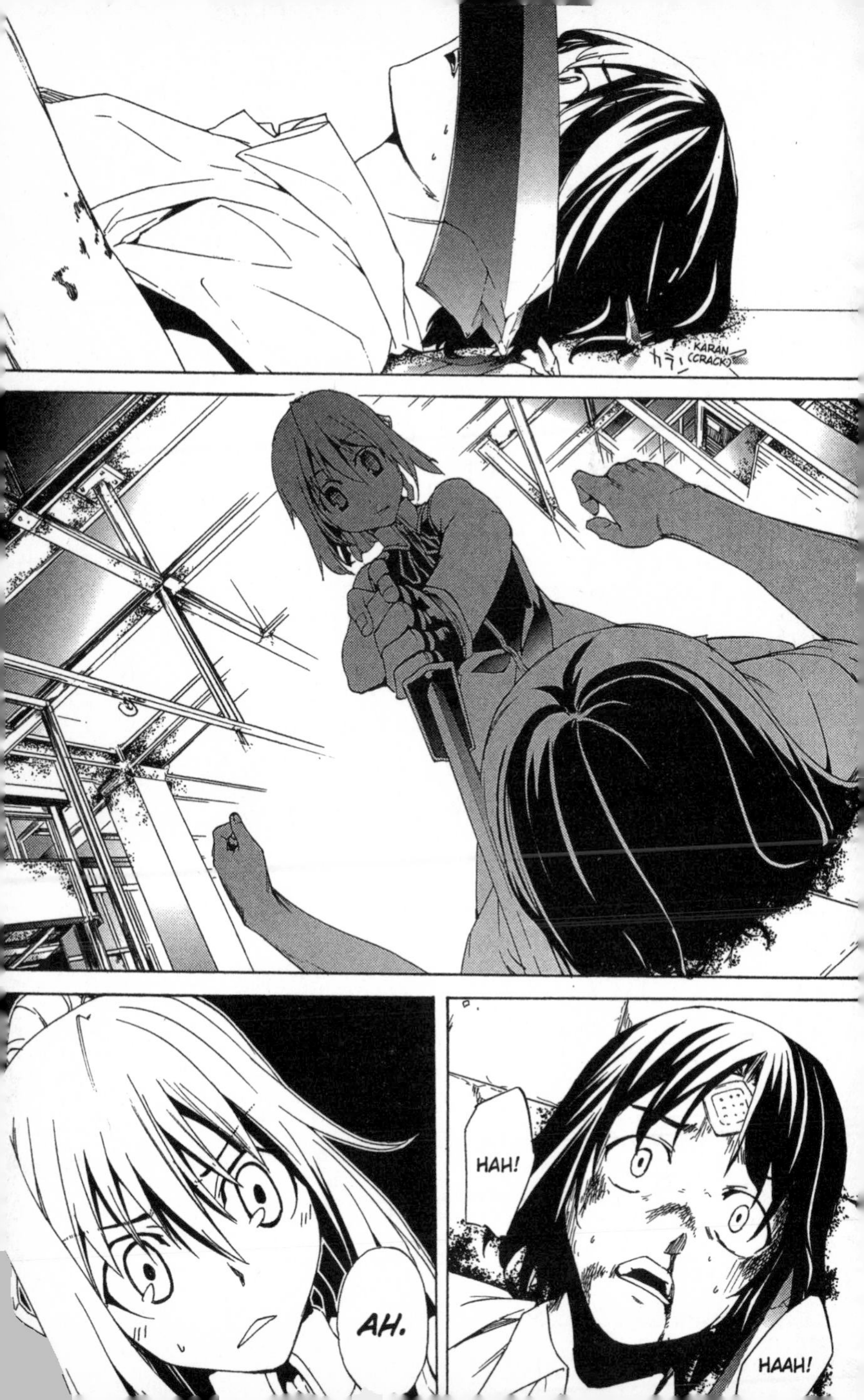
カラン
KARAN
(CRACK)
HAH!
HAAH!
AH.

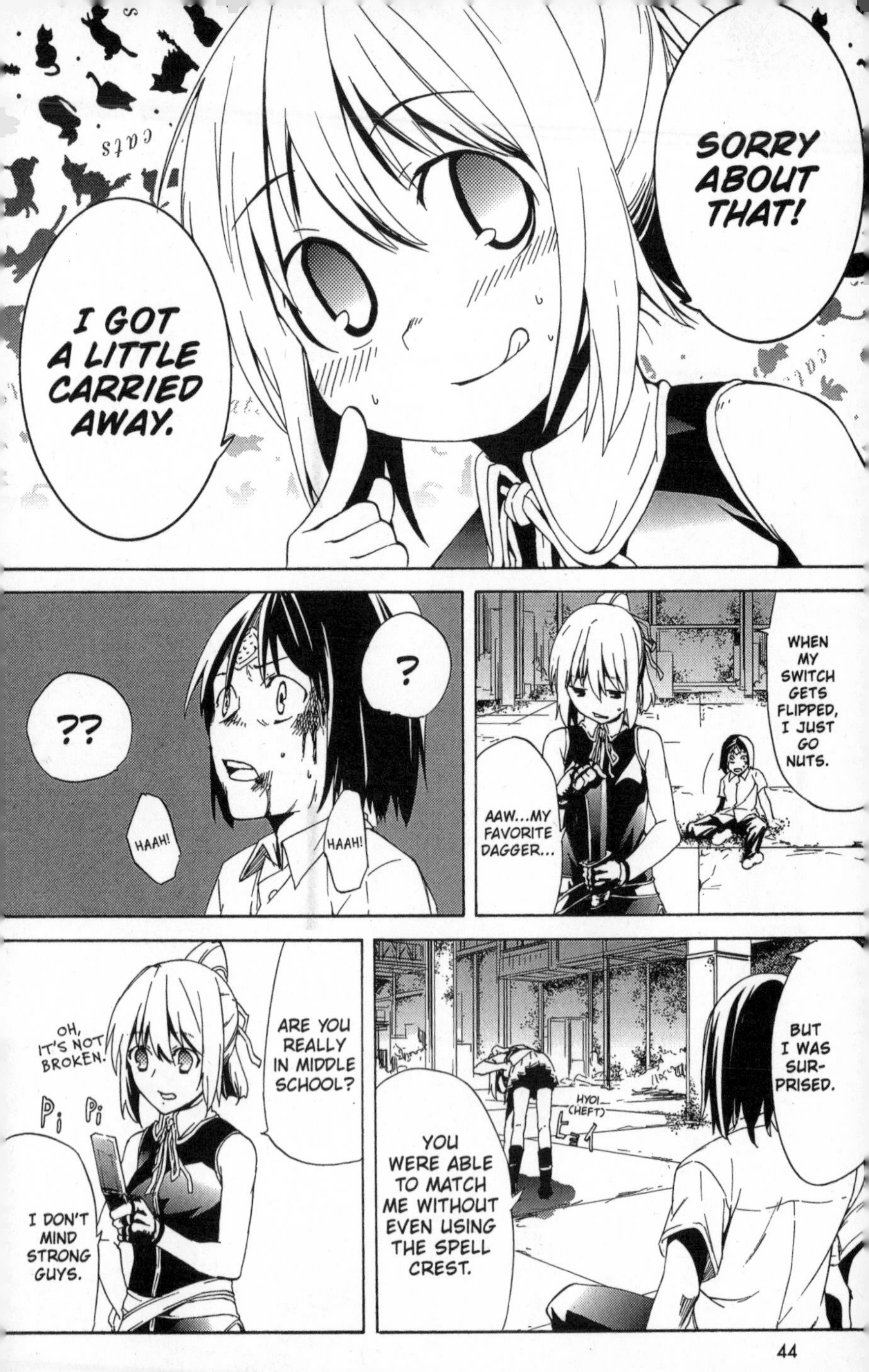
SORRY ABOUT THAT!
I GOT A LITTLE CARRIED AWAY.
WHEN MY SWITCH GETS FLIPPED, I JUST GO NUTS.
AAW...MY FAVORITE DAGGER...
?
??
HAAH!
HAAH!
BUT I WAS SUR-PRISED.
YOU WERE ABLE TO MATCH ME WITHOUT EVEN USING THE SPELL CREST.
HYOI (HEFT)
ARE YOU REALLY IN MIDDLE SCHOOL?
OH, IT'S NOT BROKEN.
Pi Pi
I DON'T MIND STRONG GUYS.

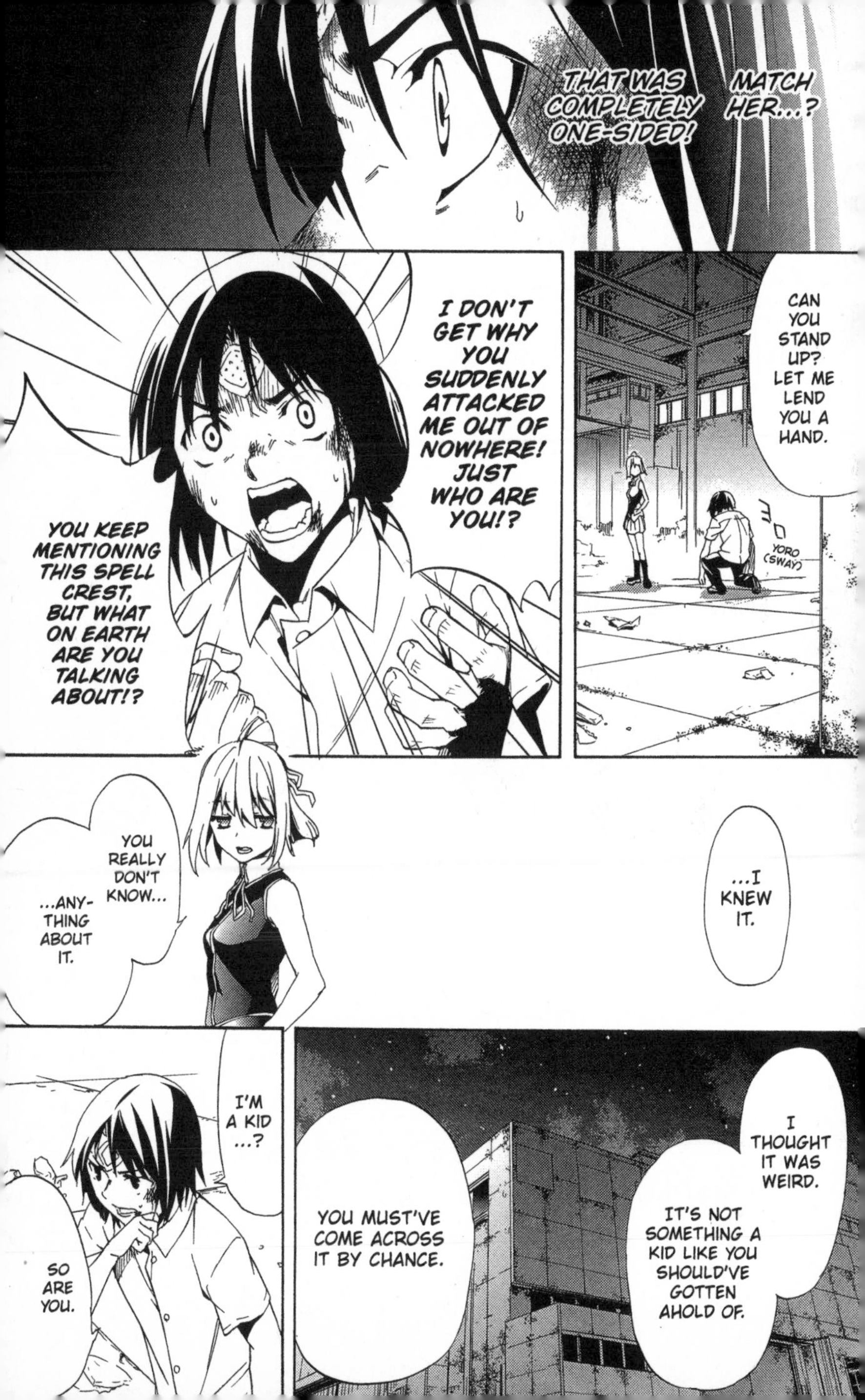
MATCH HER...?
THAT WAS COMPLETELY ONE-SIDED!
CAN YOU STAND UP? LET ME LEND YOU A HAND.
YORO (SWAY)
I DON'T GET WHY YOU SUDDENLY ATTACKED ME OUT OF NOWHERE! JUST WHO ARE YOU!?
YOU KEEP MENTIONING THIS SPELL CREST, BUT WHAT ON EARTH ARE YOU TALKING ABOUT!?
...I KNEW IT.
YOU REALLY DON'T KNOW...
...ANY-THING ABOUT IT.
I THOUGHT IT WAS WEIRD.
IT'S NOT SOMETHING A KID LIKE YOU SHOULD'VE GOTTEN AHOLD OF.
YOU MUST'VE COME ACROSS IT BY CHANCE.
I'M A KID...?
SO ARE YOU.

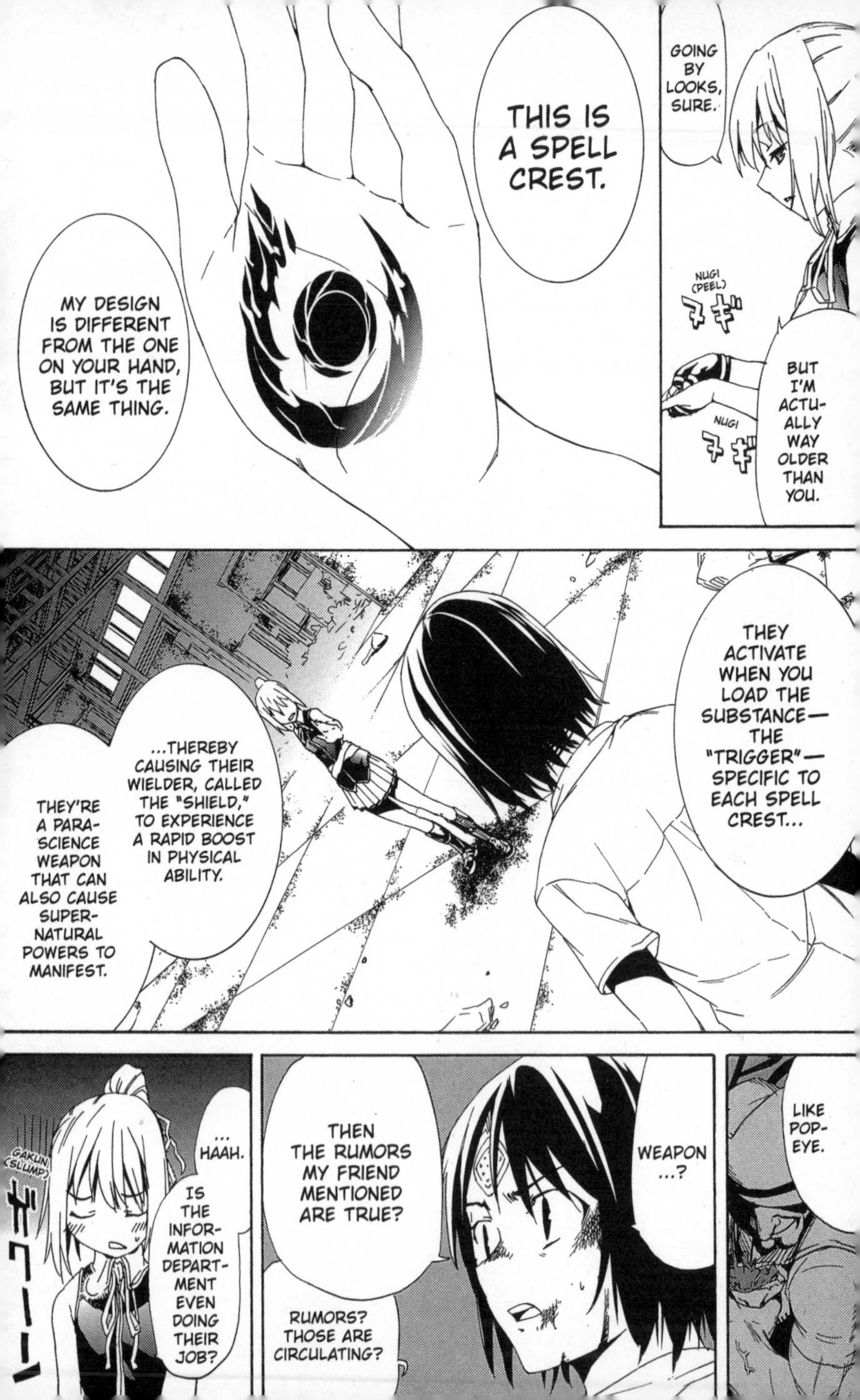
GOING BY LOOKS, SURE.
NUGI (PEEL)
ヌギ
BUT I'M ACTUALLY WAY OLDER THAN YOU.
NUGI
ヌギ
THIS IS A SPELL CREST.
MY DESIGN IS DIFFERENT FROM THE ONE ON YOUR HAND, BUT IT'S THE SAME THING.
THEY ACTIVATE WHEN YOU LOAD THE SUBSTANCE—THE "TRIGGER"—SPECIFIC TO EACH SPELL CREST...
...THEREBY CAUSING THEIR WIELDER, CALLED THE "SHIELD," TO EXPERIENCE A RAPID BOOST IN PHYSICAL ABILITY.
THEY'RE A PARA-SCIENCE WEAPON THAT CAN ALSO CAUSE SUPER-NATURAL POWERS TO MANIFEST.
LIKE POP-EYE.
WEAPON ...?
THEN THE RUMORS MY FRIEND MENTIONED ARE TRUE?
RUMORS? THOSE ARE CIRCULATING?
... HAAH.
IS THE INFORMATION DEPARTMENT EVEN DOING THEIR JOB?
GAKUN (SLUMP)

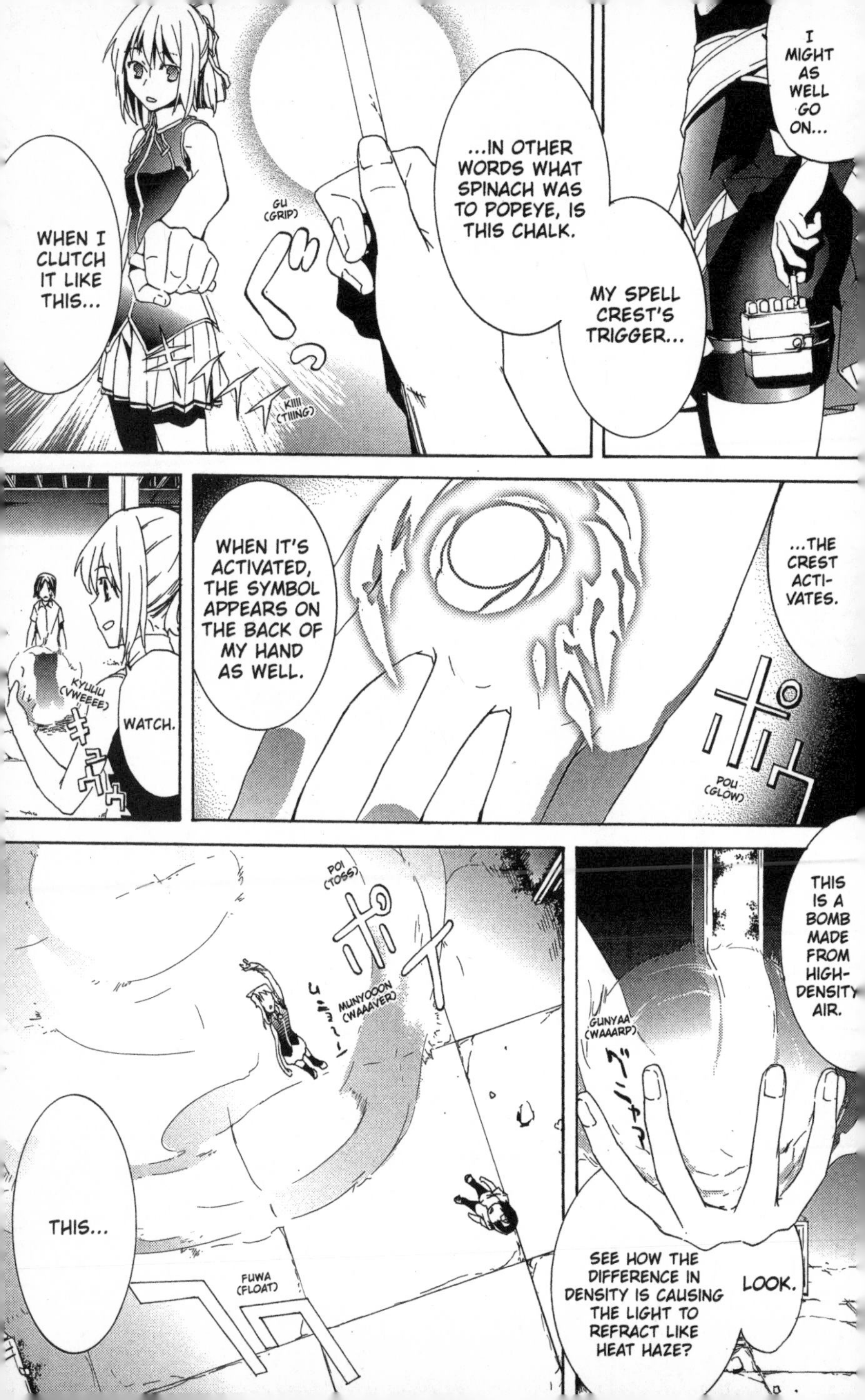
I MIGHT AS WELL GO ON...
...IN OTHER WORDS WHAT SPINACH WAS TO POPEYE, IS THIS CHALK.
MY SPELL CREST'S TRIGGER...
GU (GRIP)
WHEN I CLUTCH IT LIKE THIS...
KIIII (TIIING)
...THE CREST ACTIVATES.
POU (GLOW)
WHEN IT'S ACTIVATED, THE SYMBOL APPEARS ON THE BACK OF MY HAND AS WELL.
WATCH.
KYULUU (VWEEEE)
THIS IS A BOMB MADE FROM HIGH-DENSITY AIR.
LOOK.
SEE HOW THE DIFFERENCE IN DENSITY IS CAUSING THE LIGHT TO REFRACT LIKE HEAT HAZE?
GUNYAA (WAAARP)
POI (TOSS)
MUNYOOON (WAAAVER)
THIS...
FUWA (FLOAT)

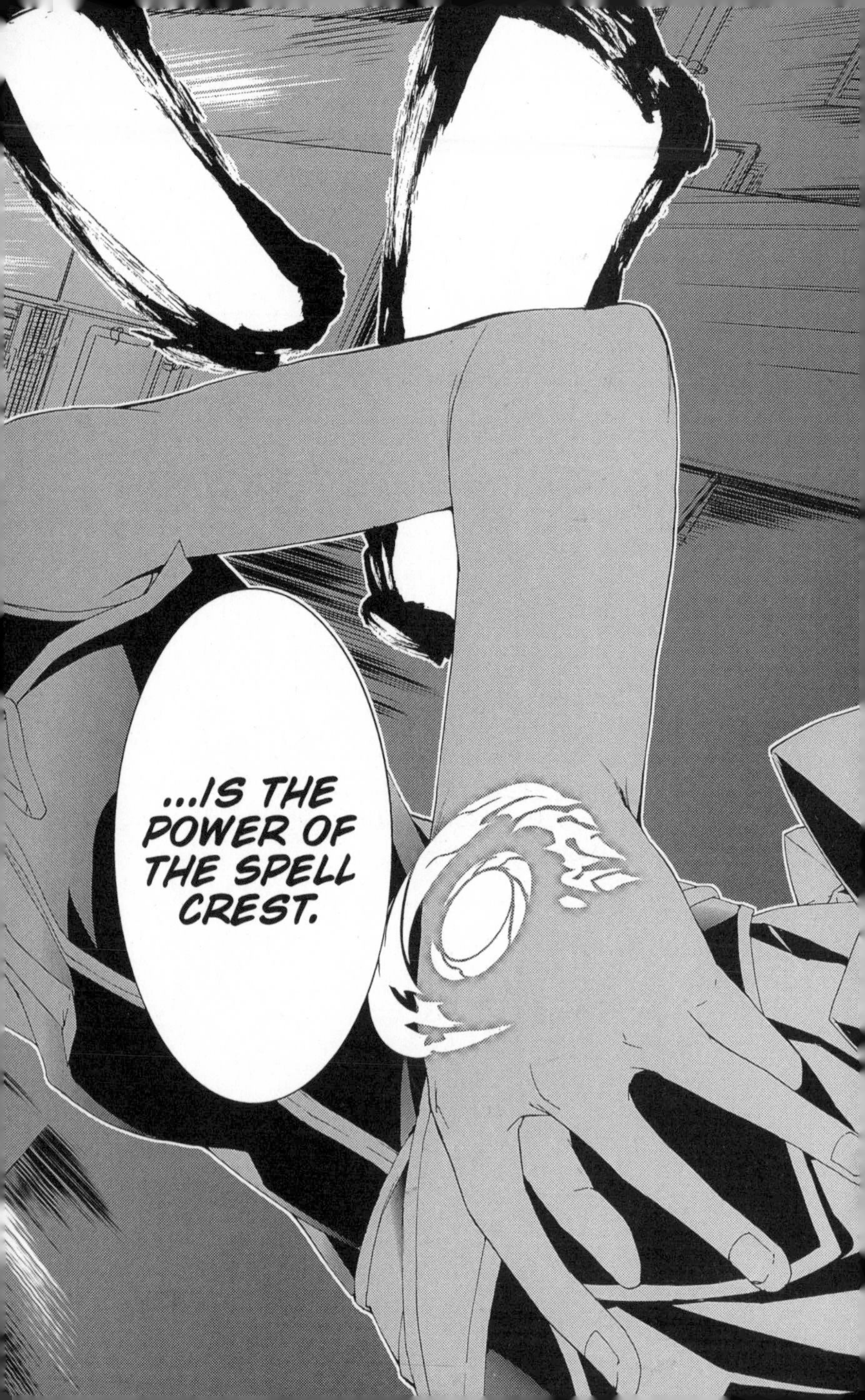
...IS THE POWER OF THE SPELL CREST.

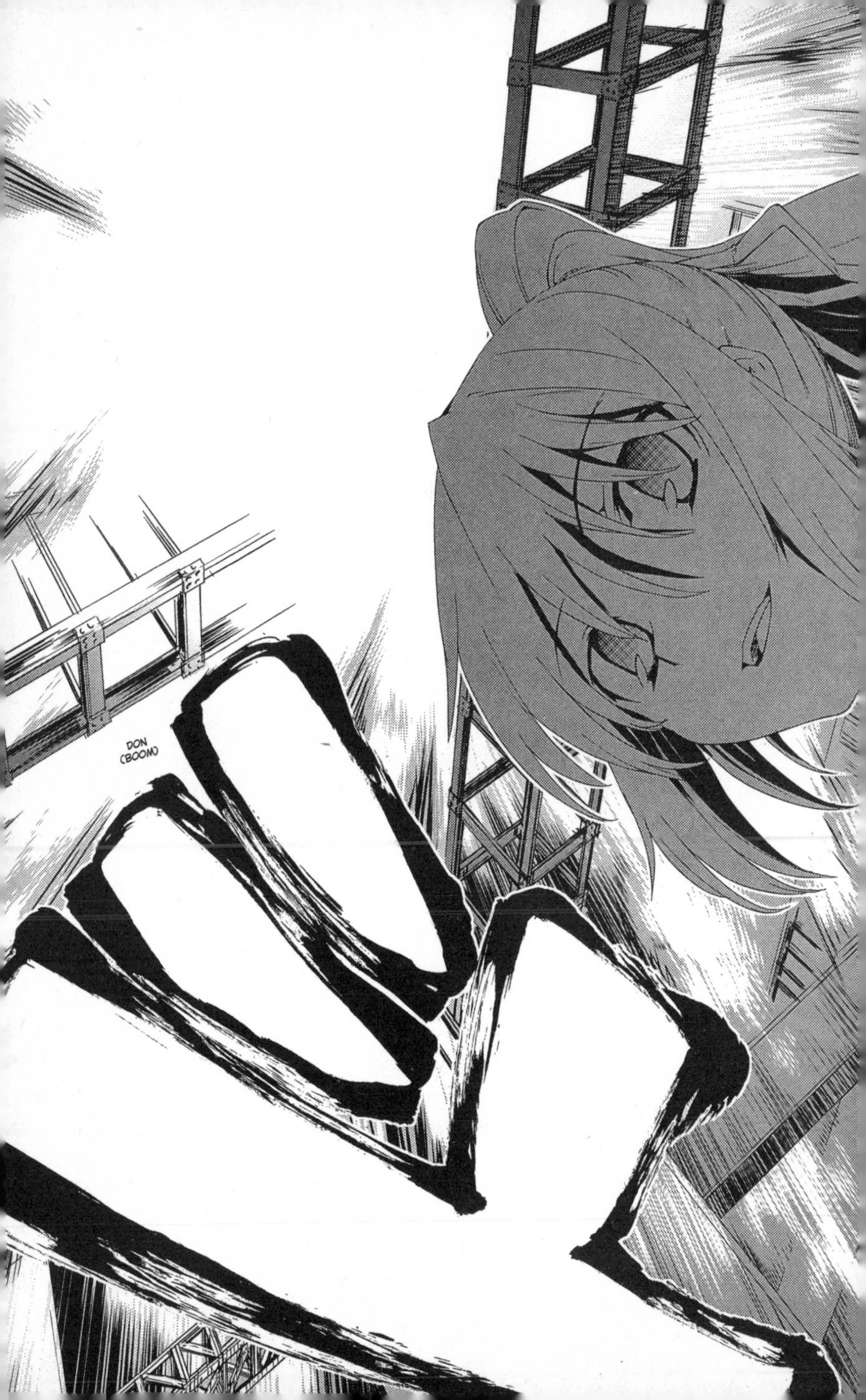
DON
(BOOM)

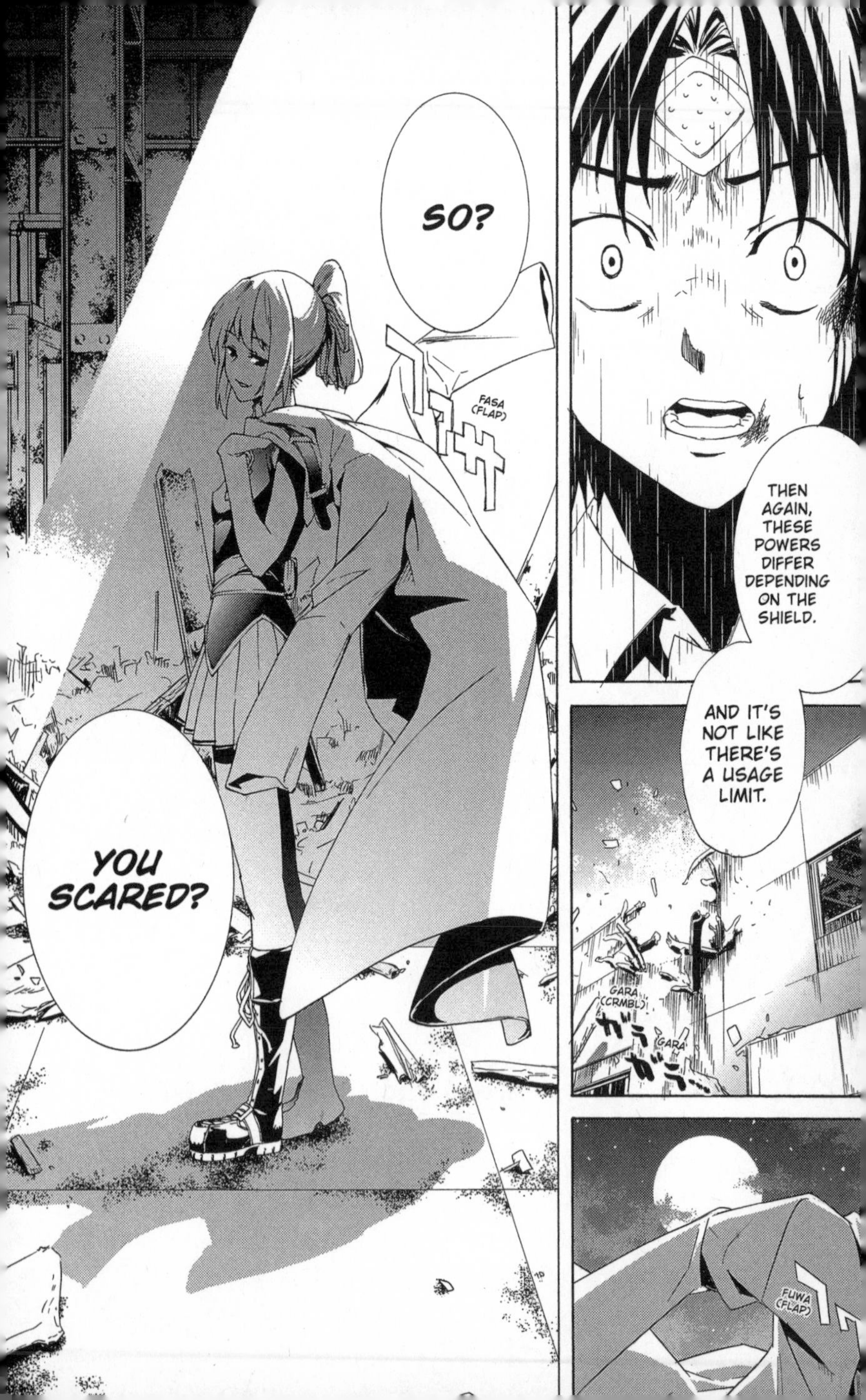

THEN AGAIN, THESE POWERS DIFFER DEPENDING ON THE SHIELD.
AND IT'S NOT LIKE THERE'S A USAGE LIMIT.
GARA (CRMBL)
GARA
FUWA (FLAP)
SO?
FASA (FLAP)
YOU SCARED?

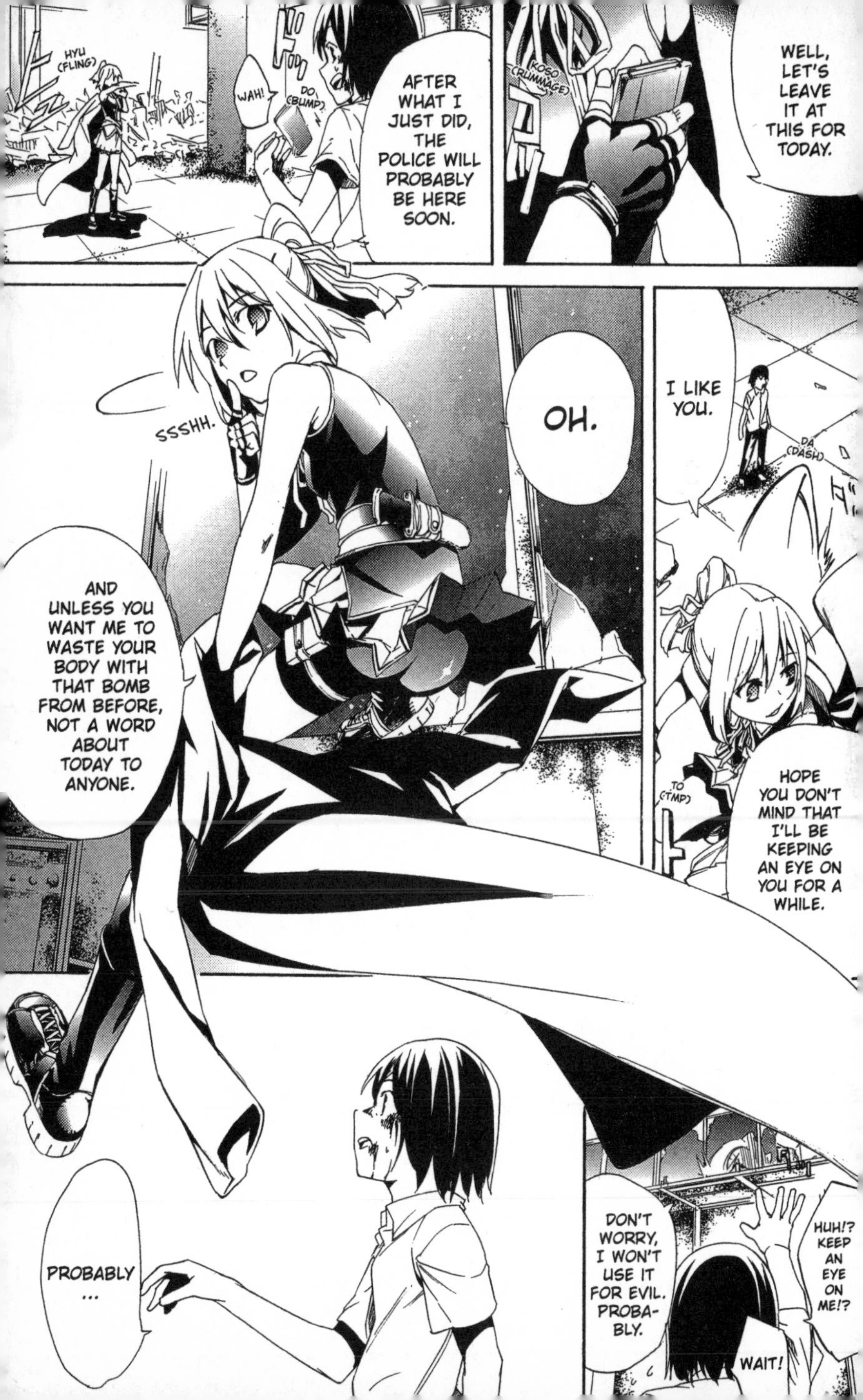
WELL, LET'S LEAVE IT AT THIS FOR TODAY.
KOSO (RUMMAGE)
AFTER WHAT I JUST DID, THE POLICE WILL PROBABLY BE HERE SOON.
DO (BUMP)
WAH!
HYU (FLING)
I LIKE YOU.
DA (DASH)
HOPE YOU DON'T MIND THAT I'LL BE KEEPING AN EYE ON YOU FOR A WHILE.
TO (TMP)
OH.
SSSHH.
AND UNLESS YOU WANT ME TO WASTE YOUR BODY WITH THAT BOMB FROM BEFORE, NOT A WORD ABOUT TODAY TO ANYONE.
HUH!? KEEP AN EYE ON ME!?
WAIT!
DON'T WORRY, I WON'T USE IT FOR EVIL. PROBA-BLY.
PROBABLY ...

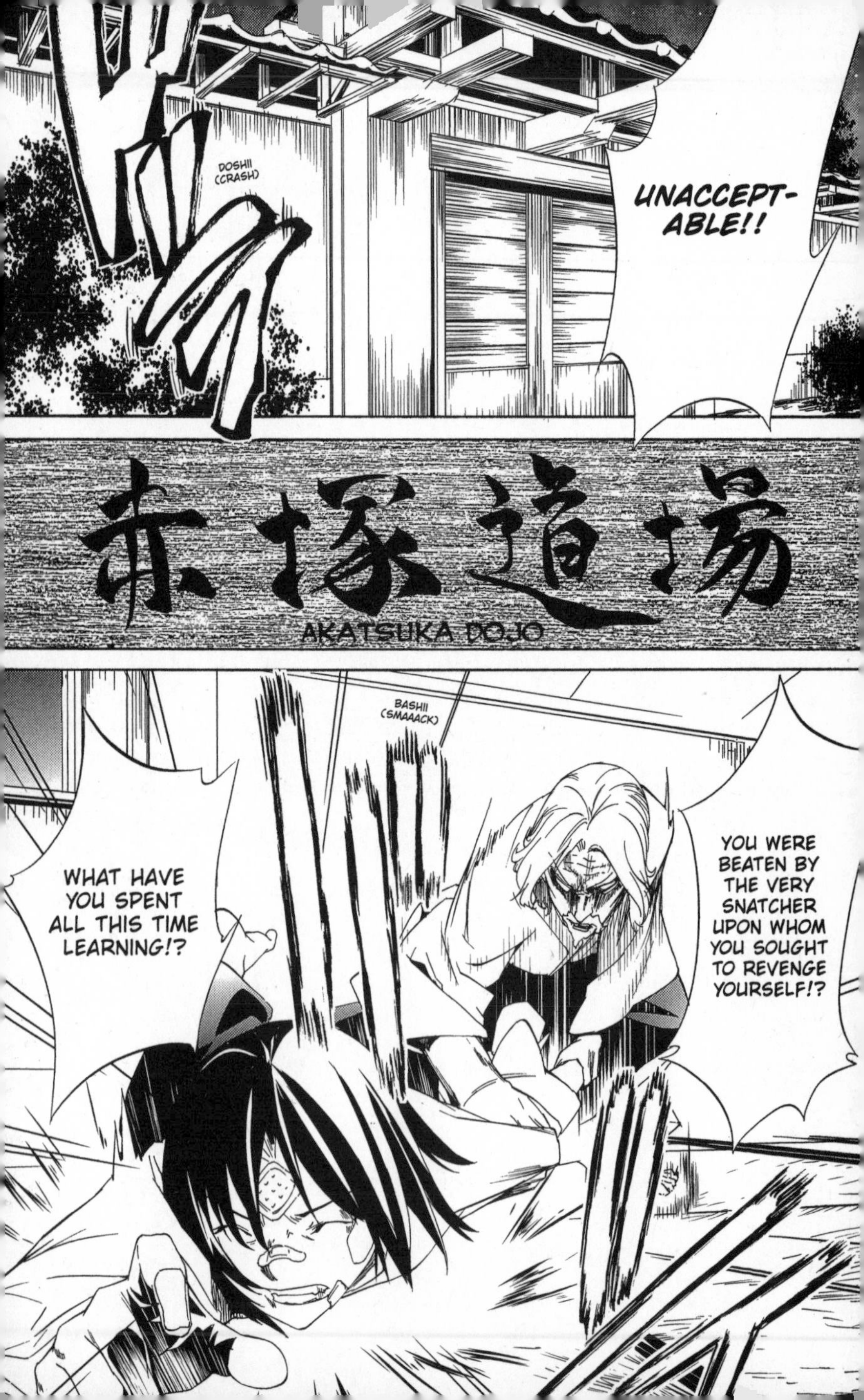
UNACCEPT-ABLE!!
DOSHII (CRASH)
赤塚道場
AKATSUKA DOJO
YOU WERE BEATEN BY THE VERY SNATCHER UPON WHOM YOU SOUGHT TO REVENGE YOURSELF!?
BASHII (SMAAACK)
WHAT HAVE YOU SPENT ALL THIS TIME LEARNING!?

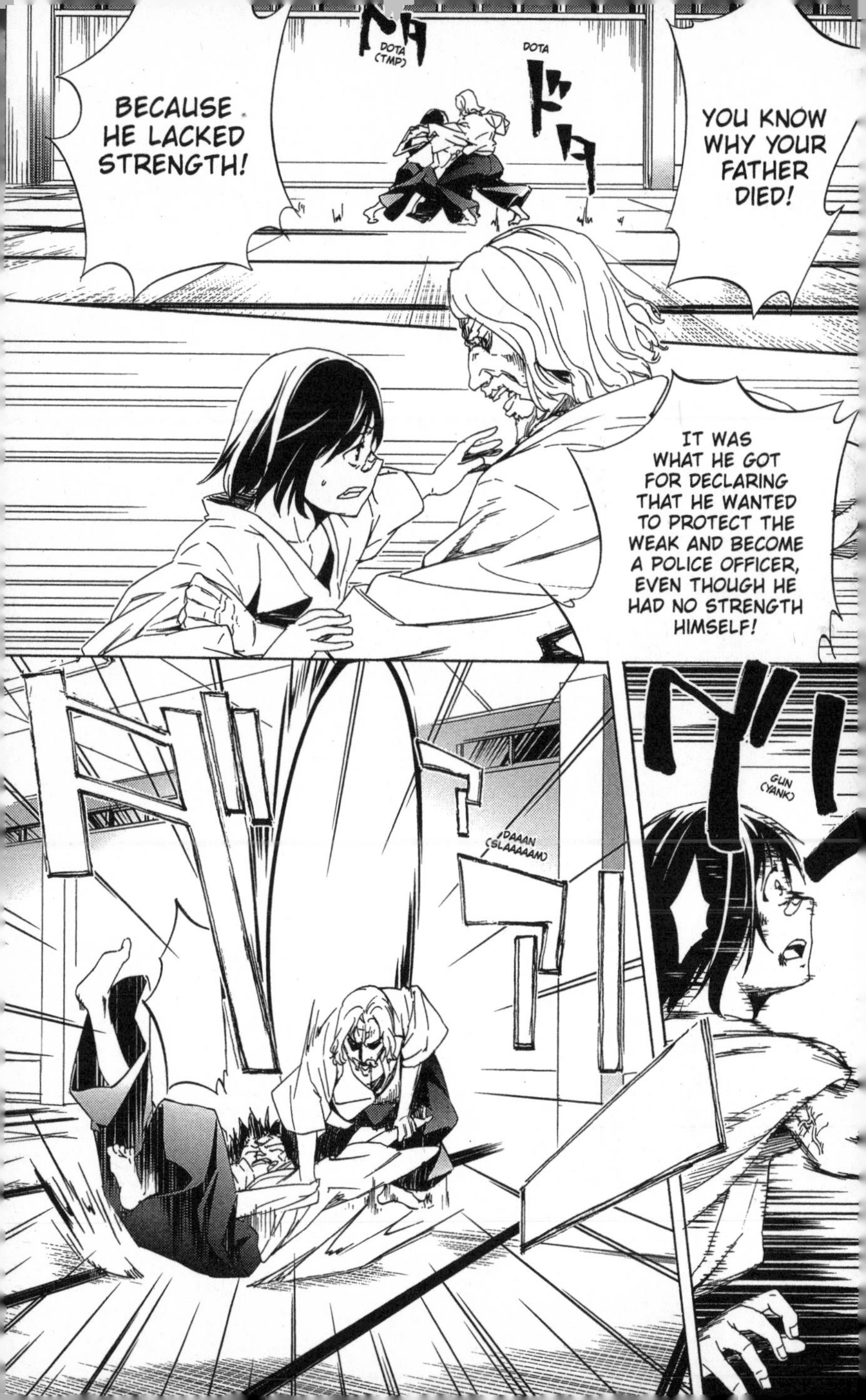
YOU KNOW WHY YOUR FATHER DIED!
DOTA
DOTA (TMP)
BECAUSE HE LACKED STRENGTH!
IT WAS WHAT HE GOT FOR DECLARING THAT HE WANTED TO PROTECT THE WEAK AND BECOME A POLICE OFFICER, EVEN THOUGH HE HAD NO STRENGTH HIMSELF!
GUN (YANK)
DAAAN (SLAAAAAM)

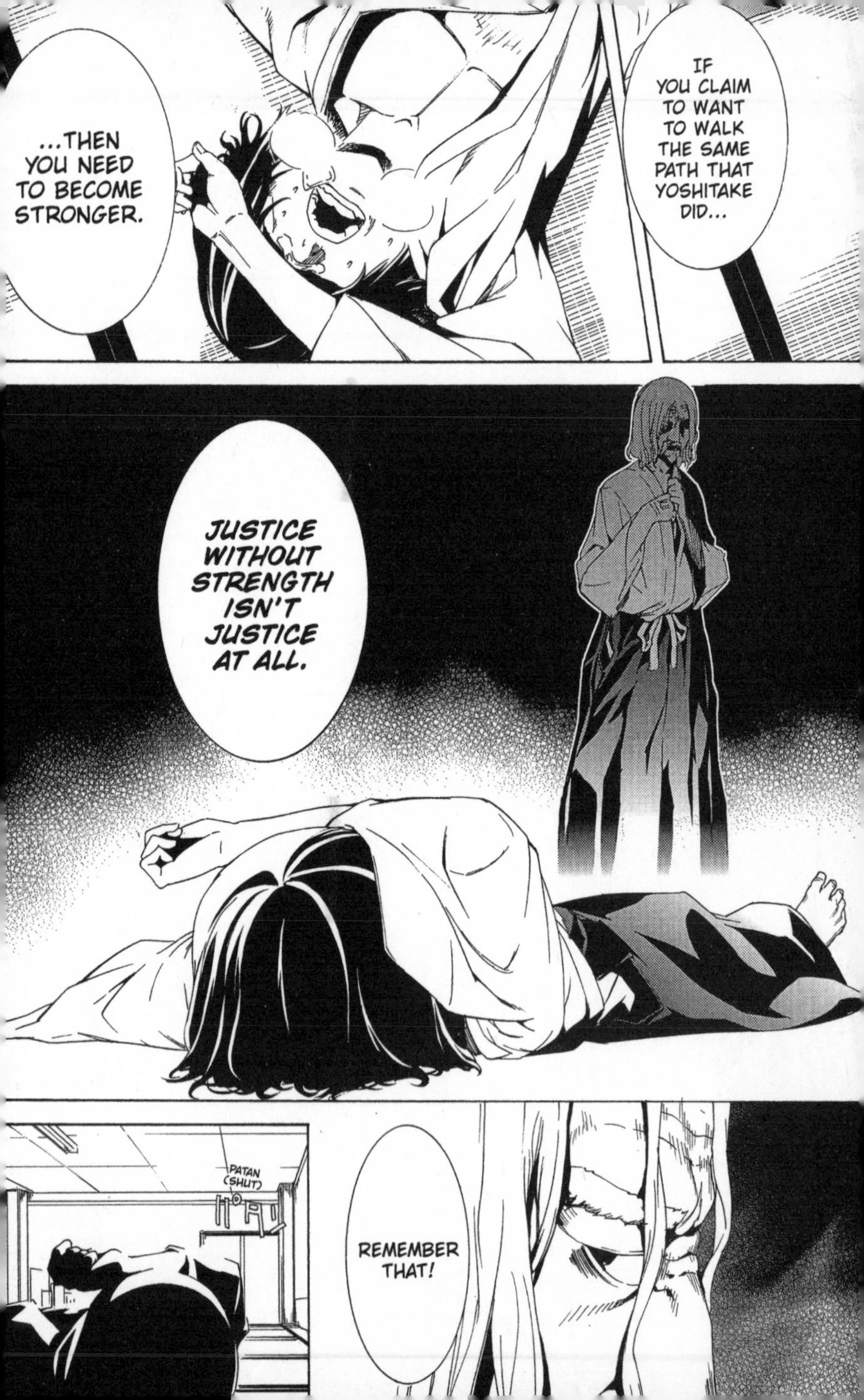
IF YOU CLAIM TO WANT TO WALK THE SAME PATH THAT YOSHITAKE DID...
...THEN YOU NEED TO BECOME STRONGER.
JUSTICE WITHOUT STRENGTH ISN'T JUSTICE AT ALL.
REMEMBER THAT!
PATAN (SHUT)

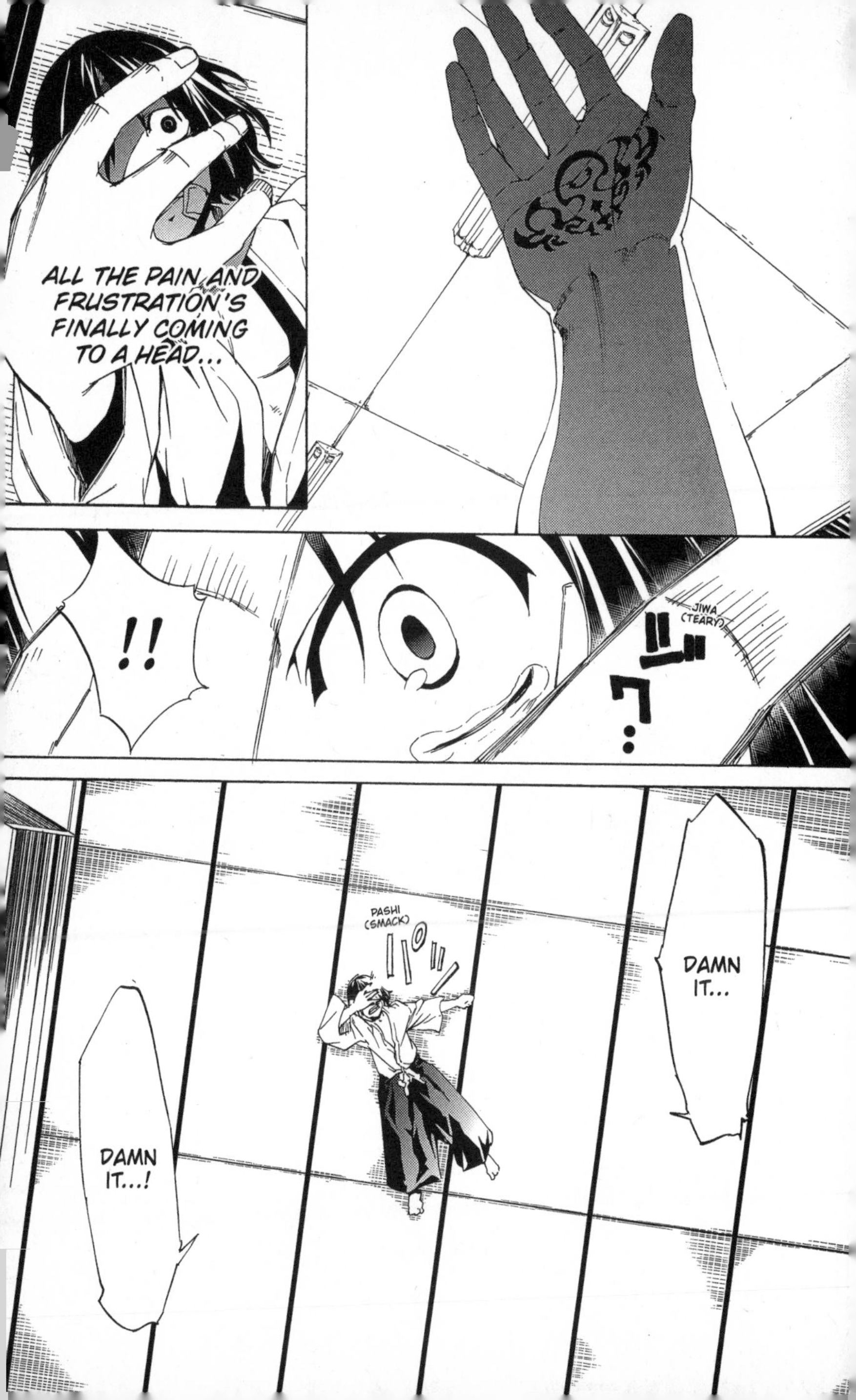
ALL THE PAIN AND FRUSTRATION'S FINALLY COMING TO A HEAD...
JIWA (TEARY)
!!
PASHI (SMACK)
DAMN IT...
DAMN IT...!

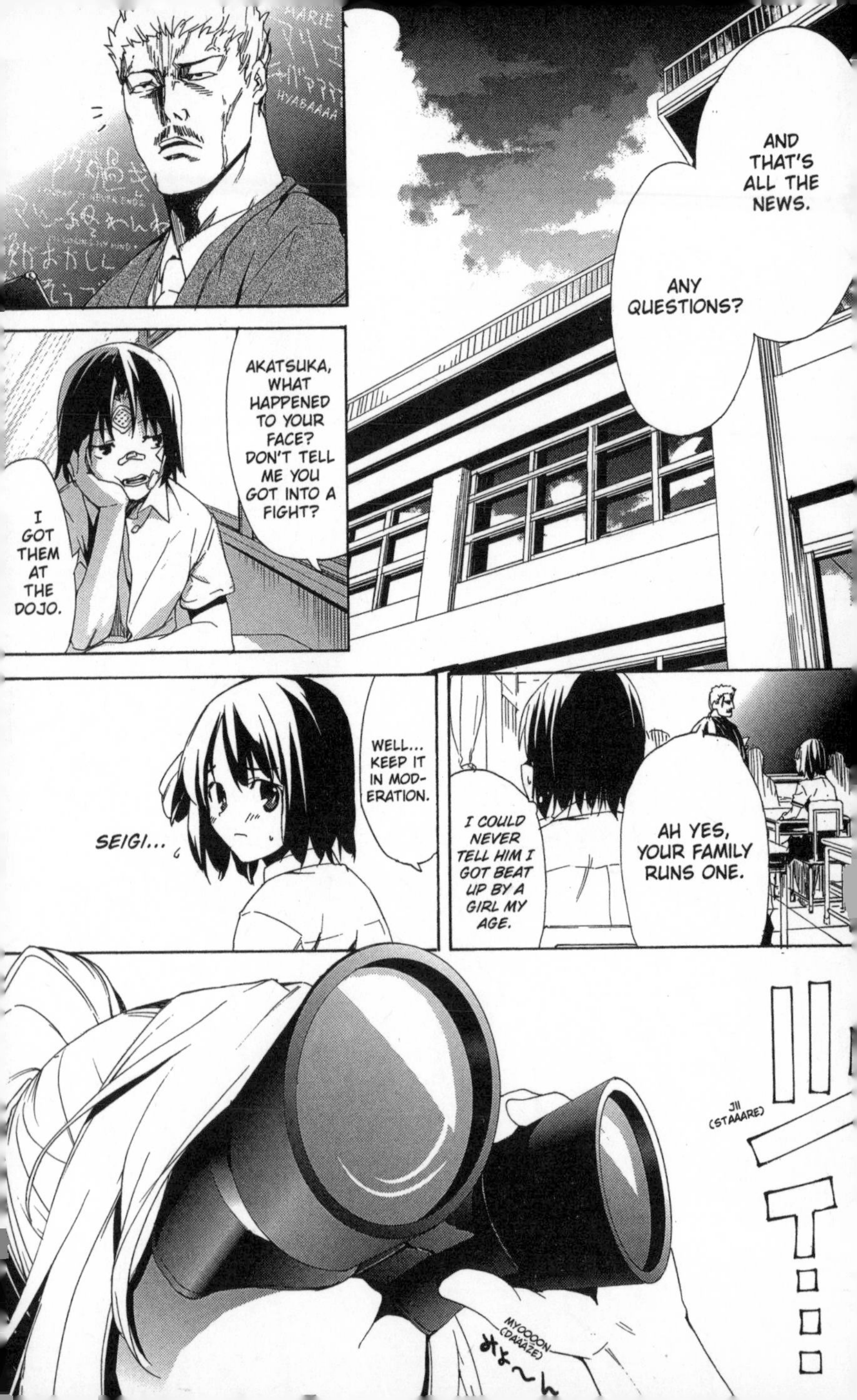

AND THAT'S ALL THE NEWS.
ANY QUESTIONS?
HYABAAAA
AKATSUKA, WHAT HAPPENED TO YOUR FACE? DON'T TELL ME YOU GOT INTO A FIGHT?
I GOT THEM AT THE DOJO.
AH YES, YOUR FAMILY RUNS ONE.
I COULD NEVER TELL HIM I GOT BEAT UP BY A GIRL MY AGE.
WELL... KEEP IT IN MODERATION.
SEIGI...
JII (STAAARE)
MYOOOON (DAAAZE)
みょ〜ん

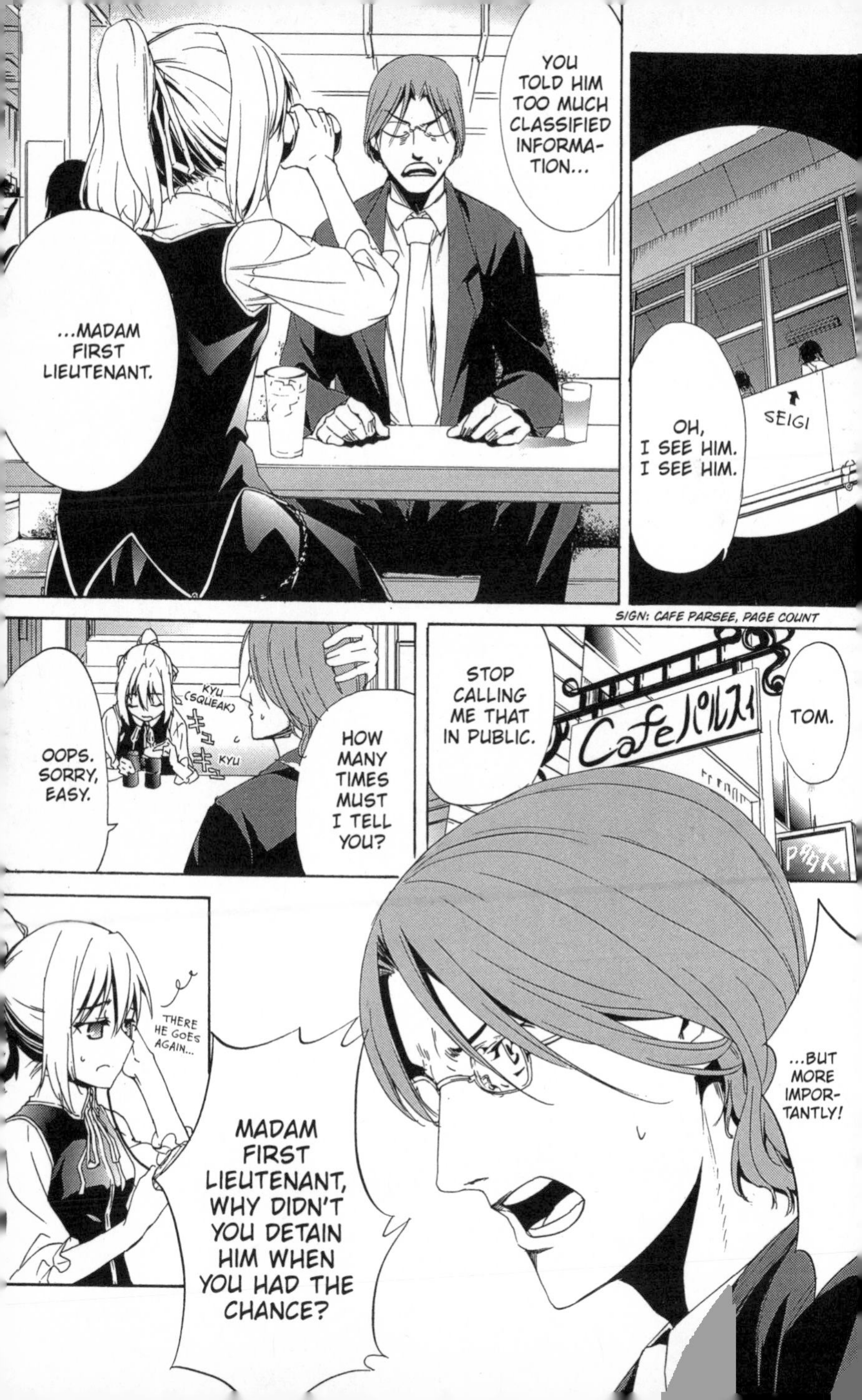
SEIGI
OH, I SEE HIM. I SEE HIM.
YOU TOLD HIM TOO MUCH CLASSIFIED INFORMATION...
...MADAM FIRST LIEUTENANT.
SIGN: CAFE PARSEE, PAGE COUNT
TOM.
Cafeパルスィ
STOP CALLING ME THAT IN PUBLIC.
HOW MANY TIMES MUST I TELL YOU?
KYU (SQUEAK)
KYU
OOPS. SORRY, EASY.
...BUT MORE IMPORTANTLY!
MADAM FIRST LIEUTENANT, WHY DIDN'T YOU DETAIN HIM WHEN YOU HAD THE CHANCE?
THERE HE GOES AGAIN...

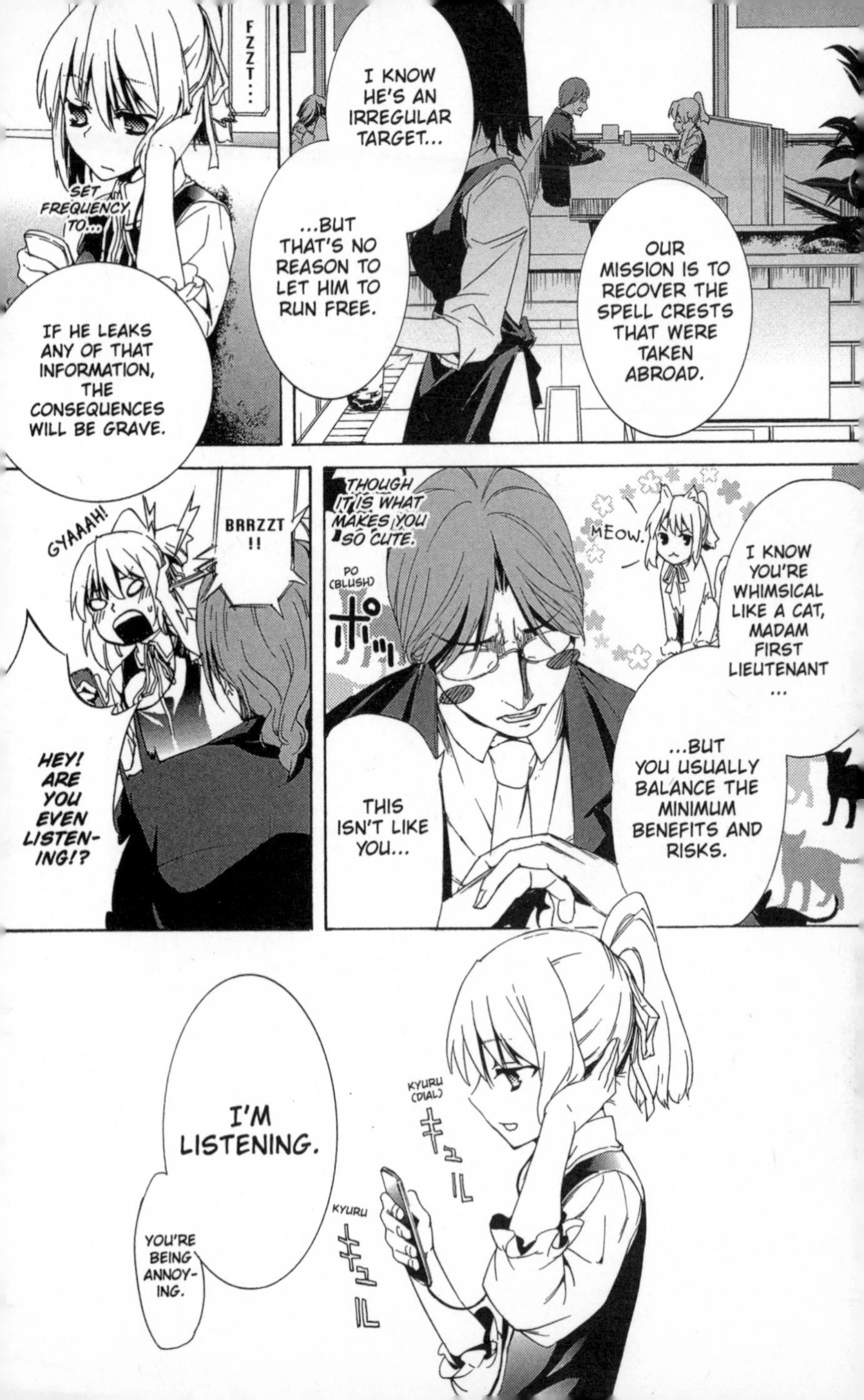
OUR MISSION IS TO RECOVER THE SPELL CRESTS THAT WERE TAKEN ABROAD.
I KNOW HE'S AN IRREGULAR TARGET...
...BUT THAT'S NO REASON TO LET HIM TO RUN FREE.
FZZZT...
SET FREQUENCY TO...
IF HE LEAKS ANY OF THAT INFORMATION, THE CONSEQUENCES WILL BE GRAVE.
I KNOW YOU'RE WHIMSICAL LIKE A CAT, MADAM FIRST LIEUTENANT...
MEOW.
THOUGH IT IS WHAT MAKES YOU SO CUTE.
PO (BLUSH)
...BUT YOU USUALLY BALANCE THE MINIMUM BENEFITS AND RISKS.
THIS ISN'T LIKE YOU...
BRRZZT !!
GYAAAH!
HEY! ARE YOU EVEN LISTEN-ING!?
KYURU (DIAL)
I'M LISTENING.
KYURU
YOU'RE BEING ANNOY-ING.

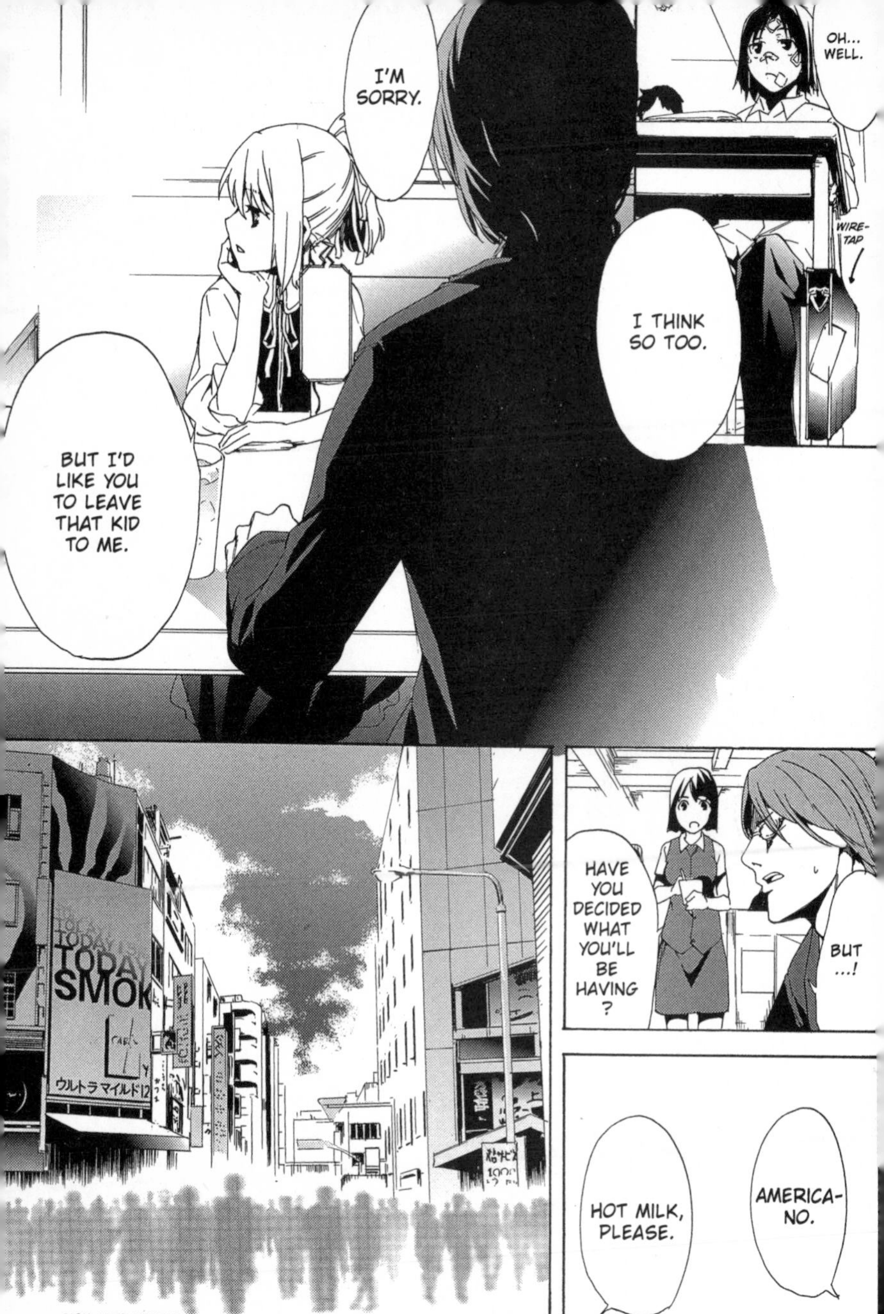
OH... WELL.
WIRE-TAP
I'M SORRY.
I THINK SO TOO.
BUT I'D LIKE YOU TO LEAVE THAT KID TO ME.
BUT ...!
HAVE YOU DECIDED WHAT YOU'LL BE HAVING?
AMERICA-NO.
HOT MILK, PLEASE.
TODAY SMOK
ウルトラマイルド12
SIGN: ULTRA MILD 12

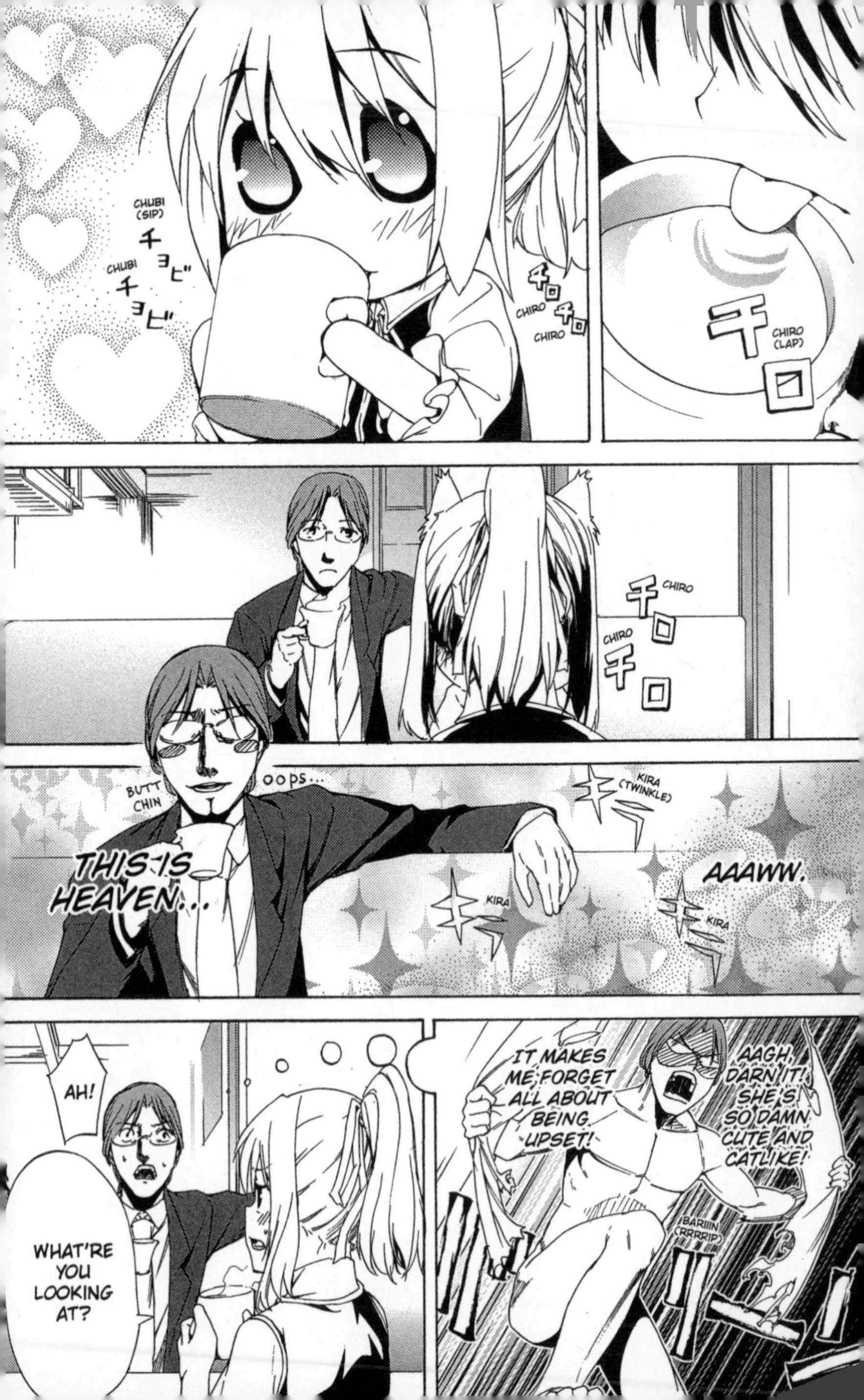
チロ
CHIRO (LAP)
チロ
CHIRO
チロ
CHIRO
チョビ
CHUBI (SIP)
チョビ
CHUBI
チロ
CHIRO
チロ
CHIRO
キラ
KIRA (TWINKLE)
AAAWW.
キラ
KIRA
キラ
KIRA
oops...
BUTT CHIN
THIS IS HEAVEN...
AAGH, DARN IT! SHE'S SO DAMN CUTE AND CATLIKE!
IT MAKES ME FORGET ALL ABOUT BEING UPSET!
BARIIIN (RRRRIP)
AH!
WHAT'RE YOU LOOKING AT?

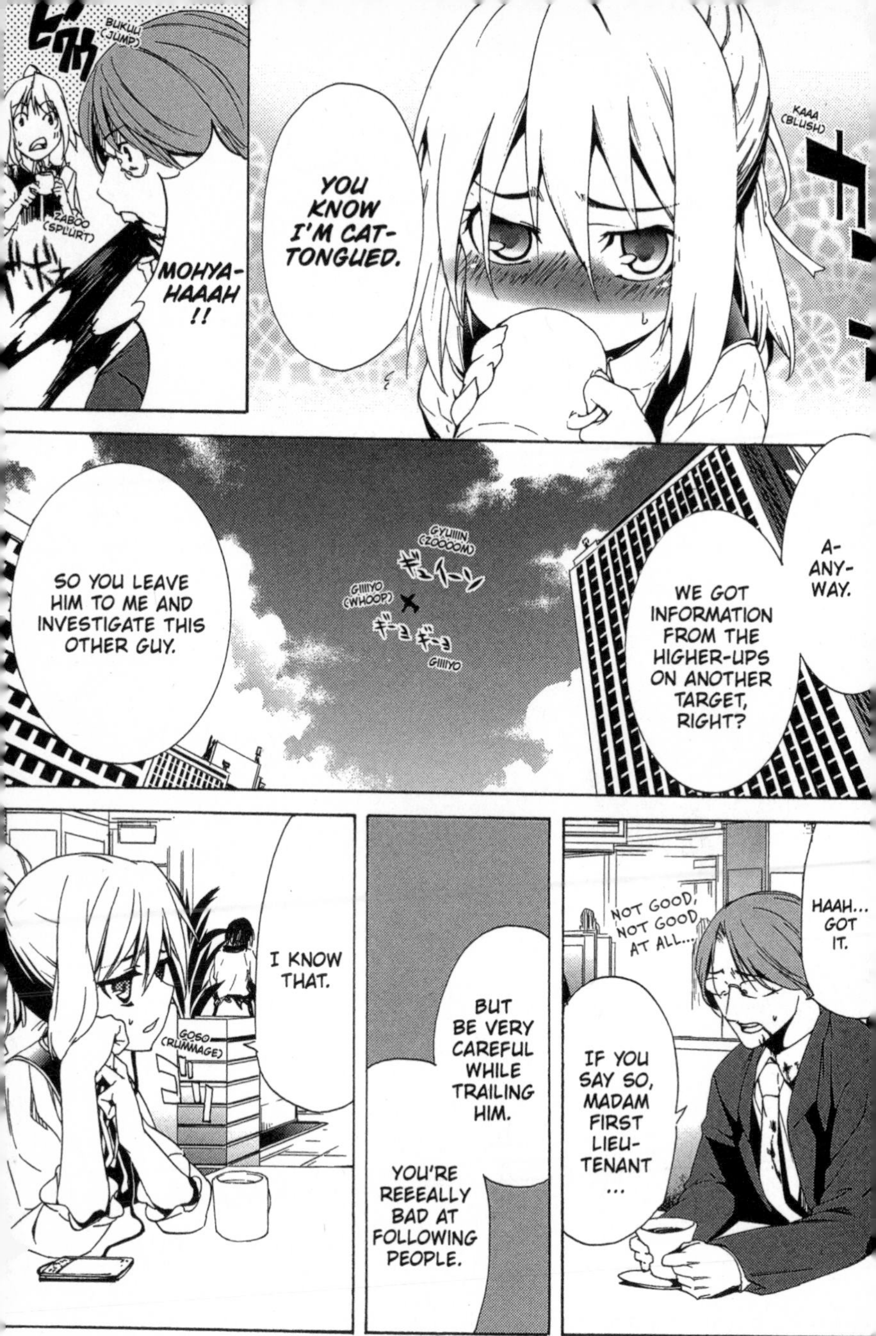
KAAA (BLUSH)
YOU KNOW I'M CAT-TONGUED.
BUKUU (JUMP)
ZABOO (SPLURT)
MOHYA-HAAAH!!
A-ANYWAY.
WE GOT INFORMATION FROM THE HIGHER-UPS ON ANOTHER TARGET, RIGHT?
GYUIIIN (ZOOOOOM)
ギュイーン
GIIIIYO (WHOOP)
ギョ ギョ
GIIIIYO
SO YOU LEAVE HIM TO ME AND INVESTIGATE THIS OTHER GUY.
HAAH... GOT IT.
NOT GOOD, NOT GOOD AT ALL...
IF YOU SAY SO, MADAM FIRST LIEU-TENANT...
BUT BE VERY CAREFUL WHILE TRAILING HIM.
YOU'RE REEEALLY BAD AT FOLLOWING PEOPLE.
I KNOW THAT.
GOSO (RUMMAGE)

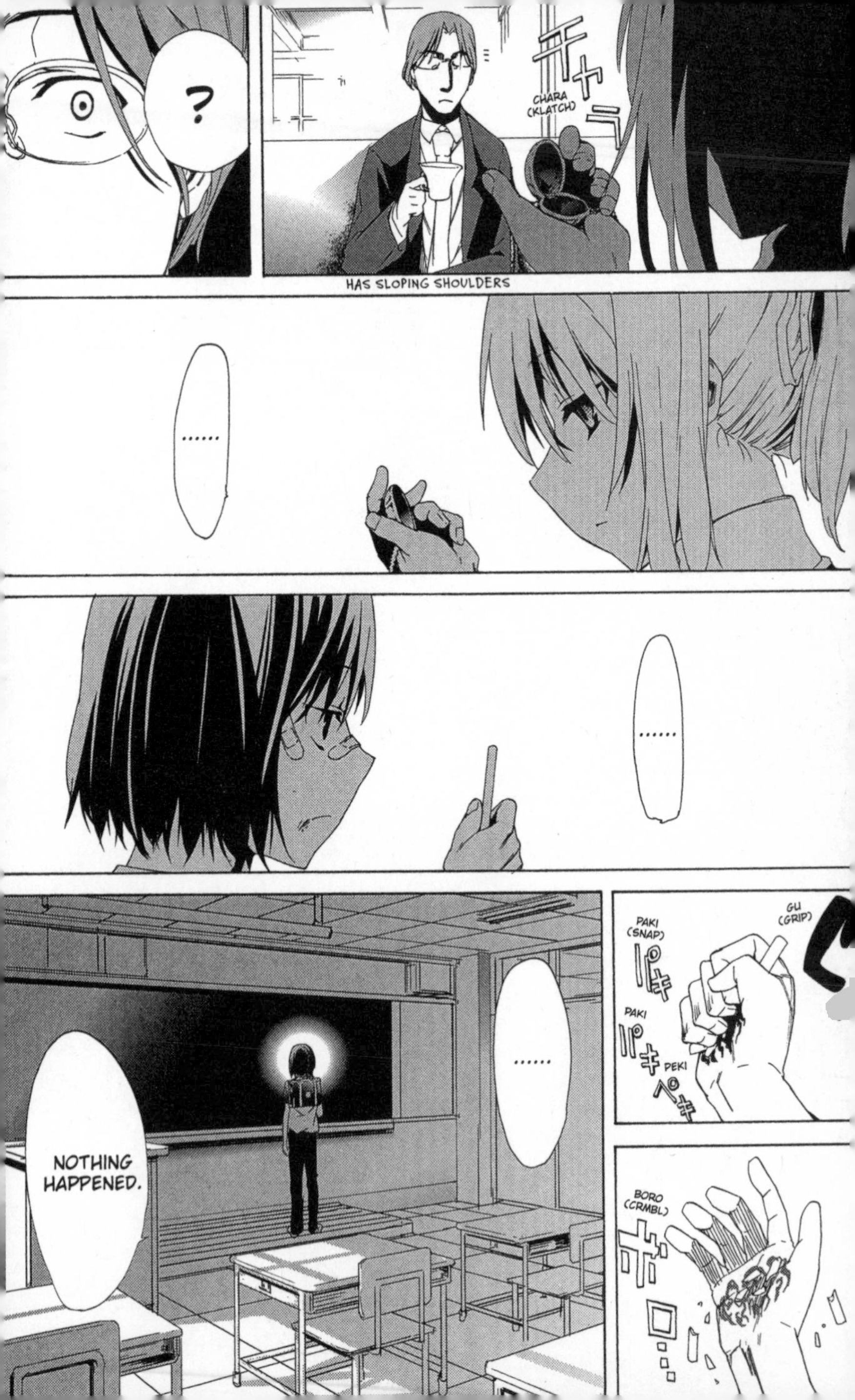
CHARA (KLATCH)
HAS SLOPING SHOULDERS
?
......
......
GU (GRIP)
PAKI (SNAP)
PAKI
PEKI
BORO (CRMBL)
......
NOTHING HAPPENED.

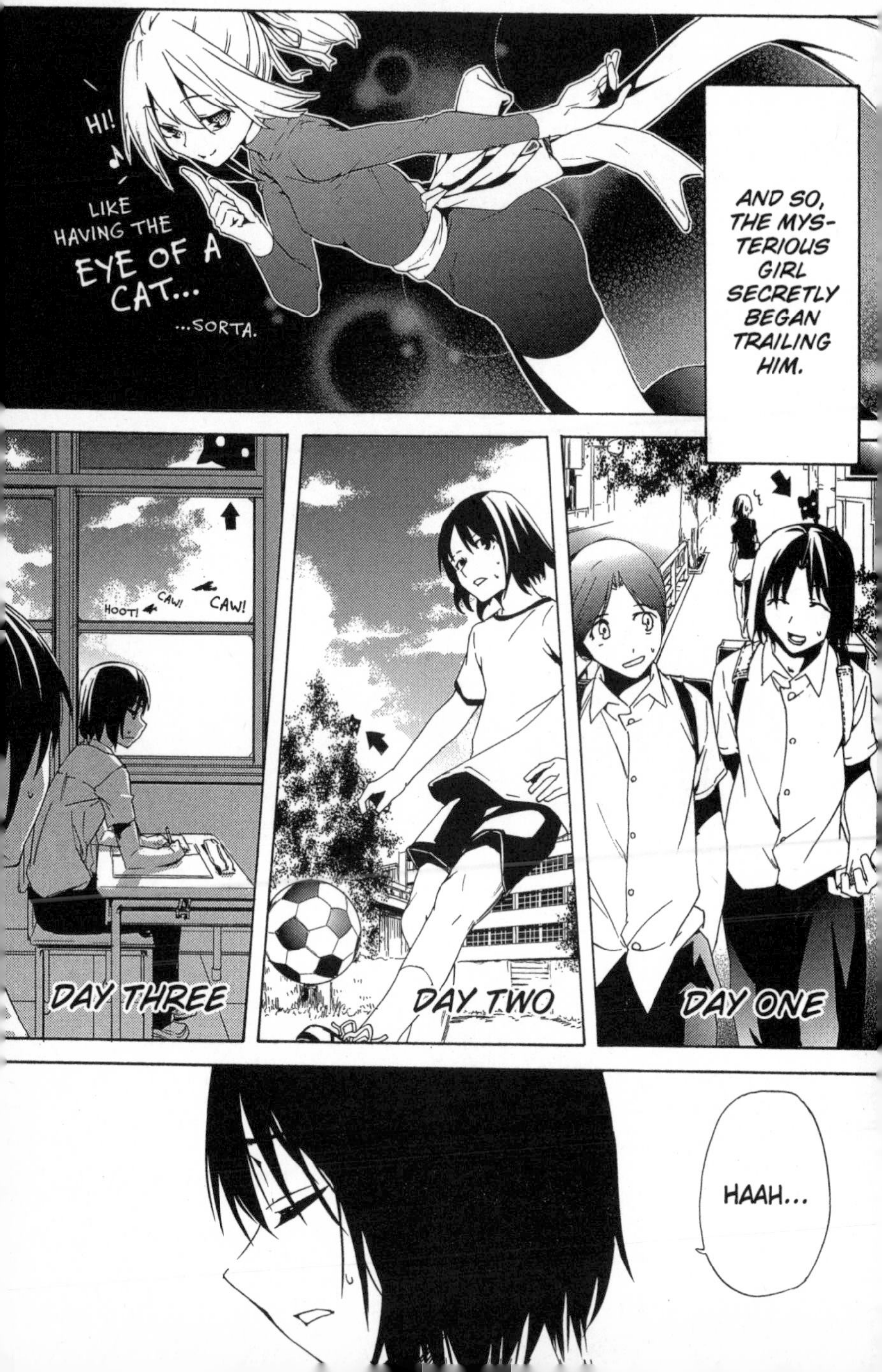
AND SO, THE MYS-TERIOUS GIRL SECRETLY BEGAN TRAILING HIM.
HI! ♪
LIKE HAVING THE EYE OF A CAT...
...SORTA.
DAY ONE
DAY TWO
CAW!
CAW!
HOOT!
DAY THREE
HAAH...

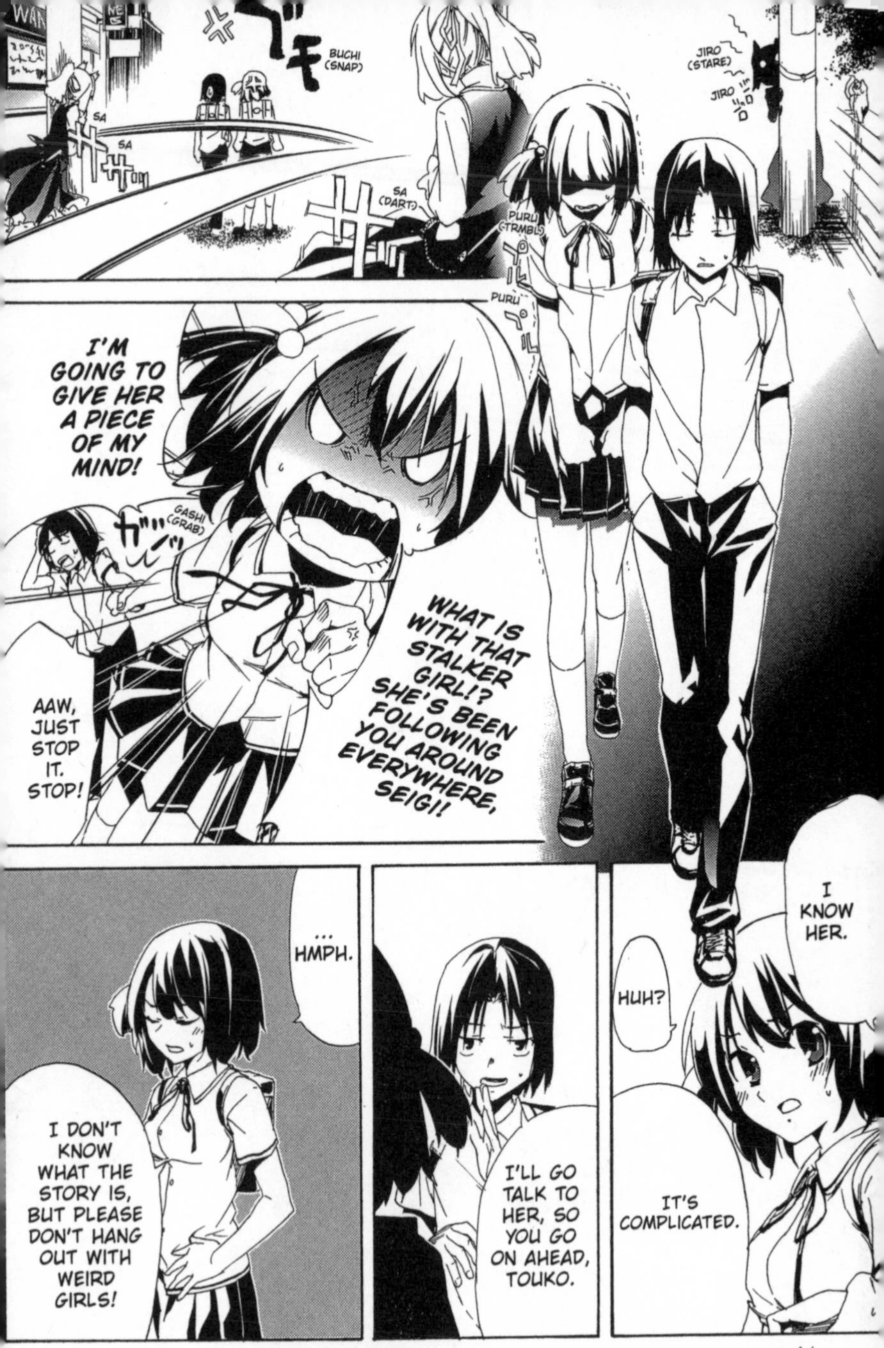
JIRO (STARE)
JIRO
PURU (TRMBL)
PURU
BUCHI (SNAP)
SA
SA
SA (DART)
WHAT IS WITH THAT STALKER GIRL!? SHE'S BEEN FOLLOWING YOU AROUND EVERYWHERE, SEIG!!
I'M GOING TO GIVE HER A PIECE OF MY MIND!
GASHI (GRAB)
AAW, JUST STOP IT. STOP!
I KNOW HER.
HUH?
IT'S COMPLICATED.
I'LL GO TALK TO HER, SO YOU GO ON AHEAD, TOUKO.
... HMPH.
I DON'T KNOW WHAT THE STORY IS, BUT PLEASE DON'T HANG OUT WITH WEIRD GIRLS!

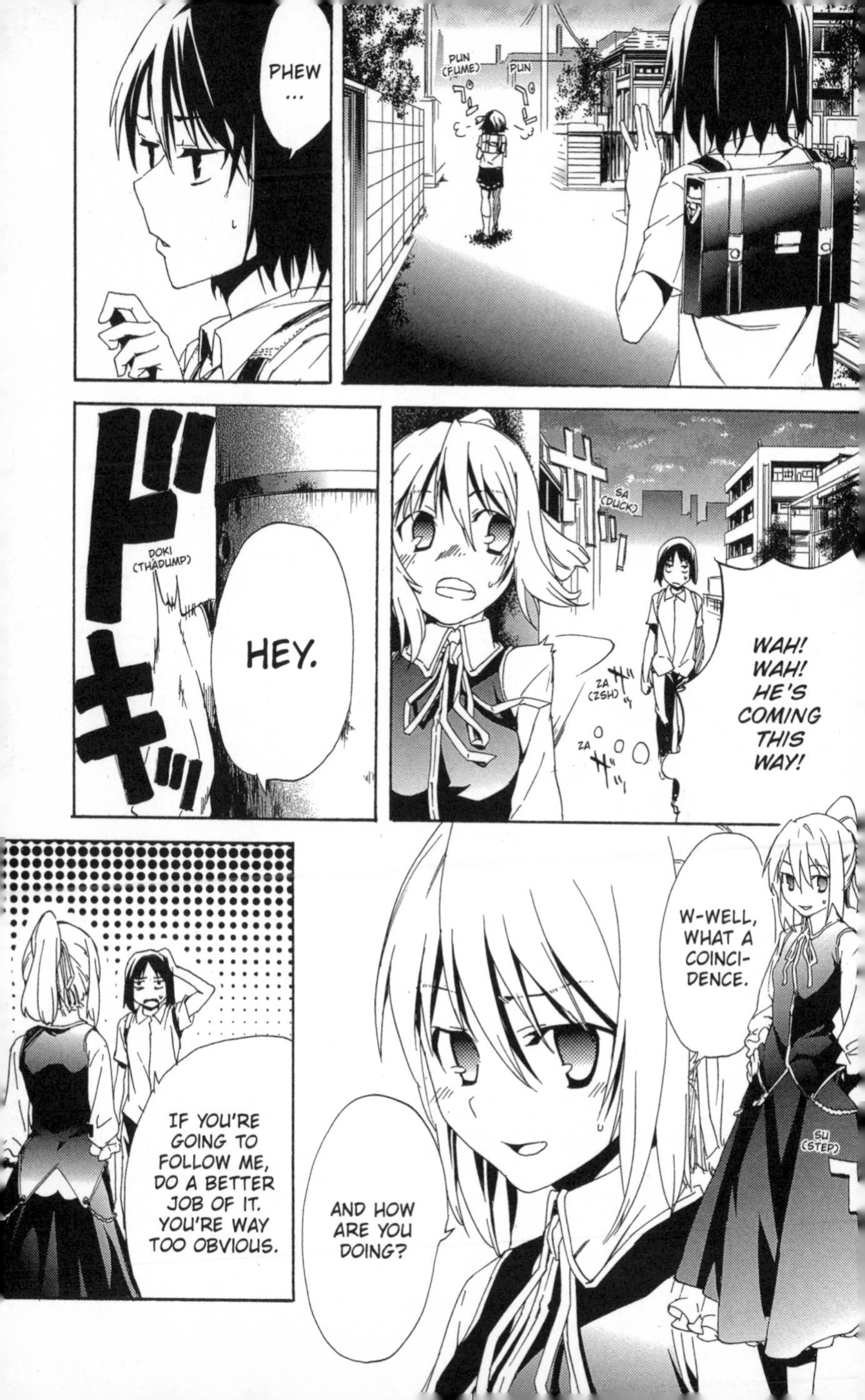
PUN
PUN (FUME)
PHEW ...
SA (DUCK)
WAH! WAH! HE'S COMING THIS WAY!
ZA (ZSH)
ZA
HEY.
DOKI (THADUMP)
ドキッ
W-WELL, WHAT A COINCI-DENCE.
SU (STEP)
AND HOW ARE YOU DOING?
IF YOU'RE GOING TO FOLLOW ME, DO A BETTER JOB OF IT. YOU'RE WAY TOO OBVIOUS.

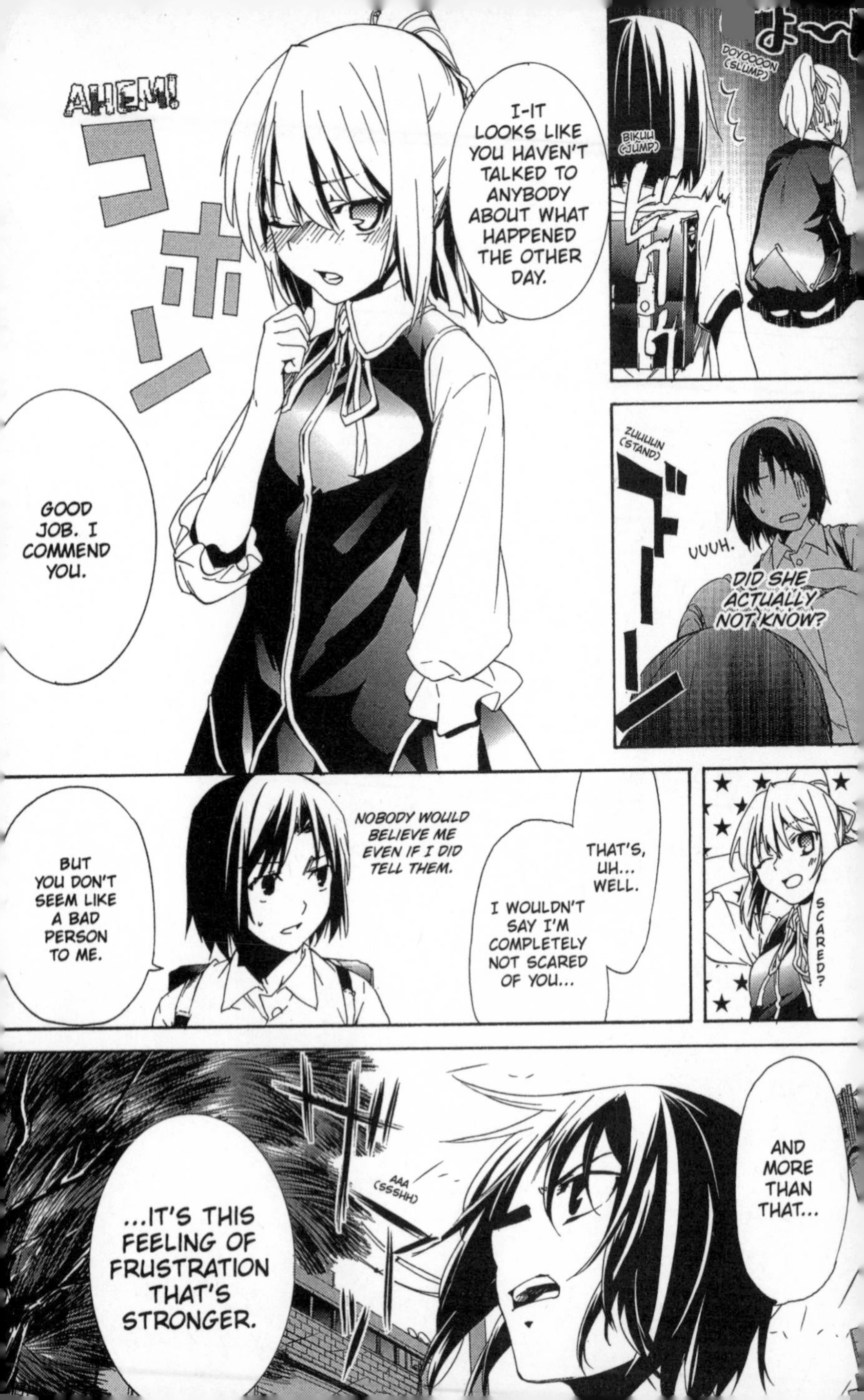
DOYOOOON (SLUMP)
BIKUU (JUMP)
ZUUUUN (STAND)
UUUH.
DID SHE ACTUALLY NOT KNOW?
AHEM!
コホン
I-IT LOOKS LIKE YOU HAVEN'T TALKED TO ANYBODY ABOUT WHAT HAPPENED THE OTHER DAY.
GOOD JOB. I COMMEND YOU.
SCARED?
THAT'S, UH... WELL.
I WOULDN'T SAY I'M COMPLETELY NOT SCARED OF YOU...
NOBODY WOULD BELIEVE ME EVEN IF I DID TELL THEM.
BUT YOU DON'T SEEM LIKE A BAD PERSON TO ME.
AND MORE THAN THAT...
AAA (SSSHH)
...IT'S THIS FEELING OF FRUSTRATION THAT'S STRONGER.

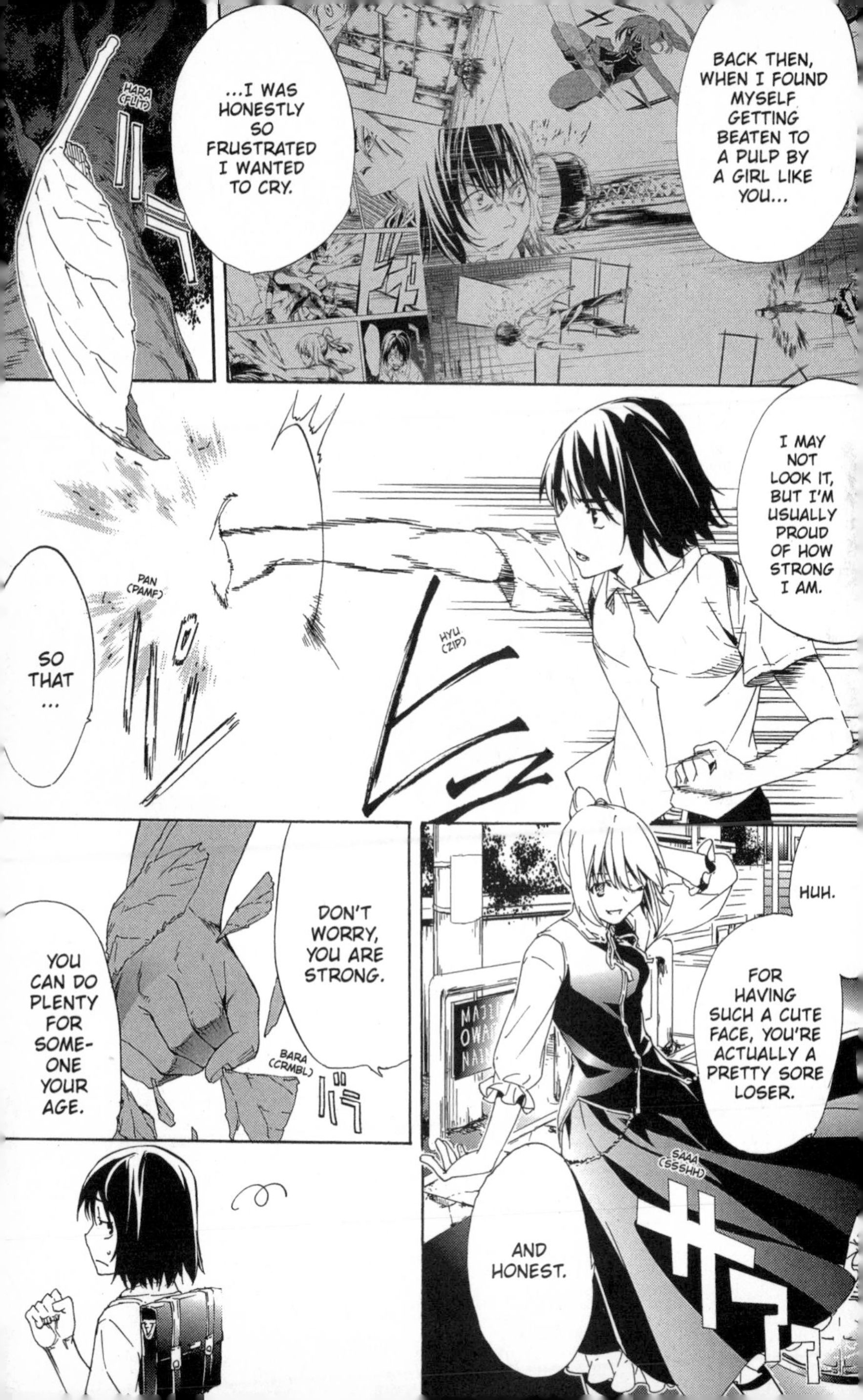
BACK THEN, WHEN I FOUND MYSELF GETTING BEATEN TO A PULP BY A GIRL LIKE YOU...
...I WAS HONESTLY SO FRUSTRATED I WANTED TO CRY.
HARA (FLIP)
I MAY NOT LOOK IT, BUT I'M USUALLY PROUD OF HOW STRONG I AM.
HYU (ZIP)
PAN (PAMF)
SO THAT ...
HUH.
FOR HAVING SUCH A CUTE FACE, YOU'RE ACTUALLY A PRETTY SORE LOSER.
DON'T WORRY, YOU ARE STRONG.
YOU CAN DO PLENTY FOR SOME-ONE YOUR AGE.
BARA (CRMBL)
SAAA (SSSHH)
AND HONEST.

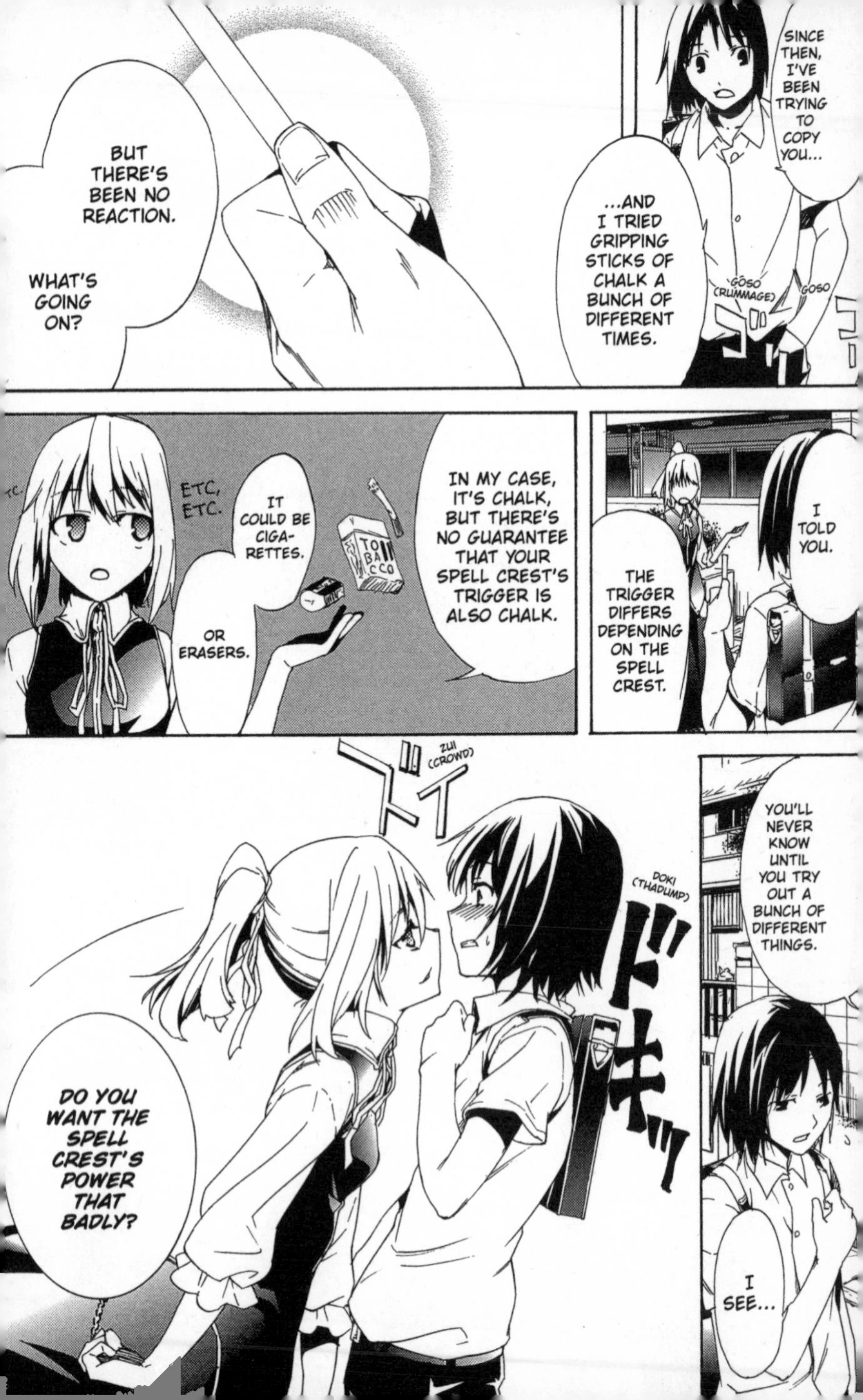
SINCE THEN, I'VE BEEN TRYING TO COPY YOU...
...AND I TRIED GRIPPING STICKS OF CHALK A BUNCH OF DIFFERENT TIMES.
GOSO (RUMMAGE) GOSO
BUT THERE'S BEEN NO REACTION.
WHAT'S GOING ON?
I TOLD YOU.
THE TRIGGER DIFFERS DEPENDING ON THE SPELL CREST.
IN MY CASE, IT'S CHALK, BUT THERE'S NO GUARANTEE THAT YOUR SPELL CREST'S TRIGGER IS ALSO CHALK.
IT COULD BE CIGARETTES.
TOBACCO
ETC, ETC.
OR ERASERS.
YOU'LL NEVER KNOW UNTIL YOU TRY OUT A BUNCH OF DIFFERENT THINGS.
I SEE...
ZUI (CROWD)
DOKI (THADUMP)
DO YOU WANT THE SPELL CREST'S POWER THAT BADLY?

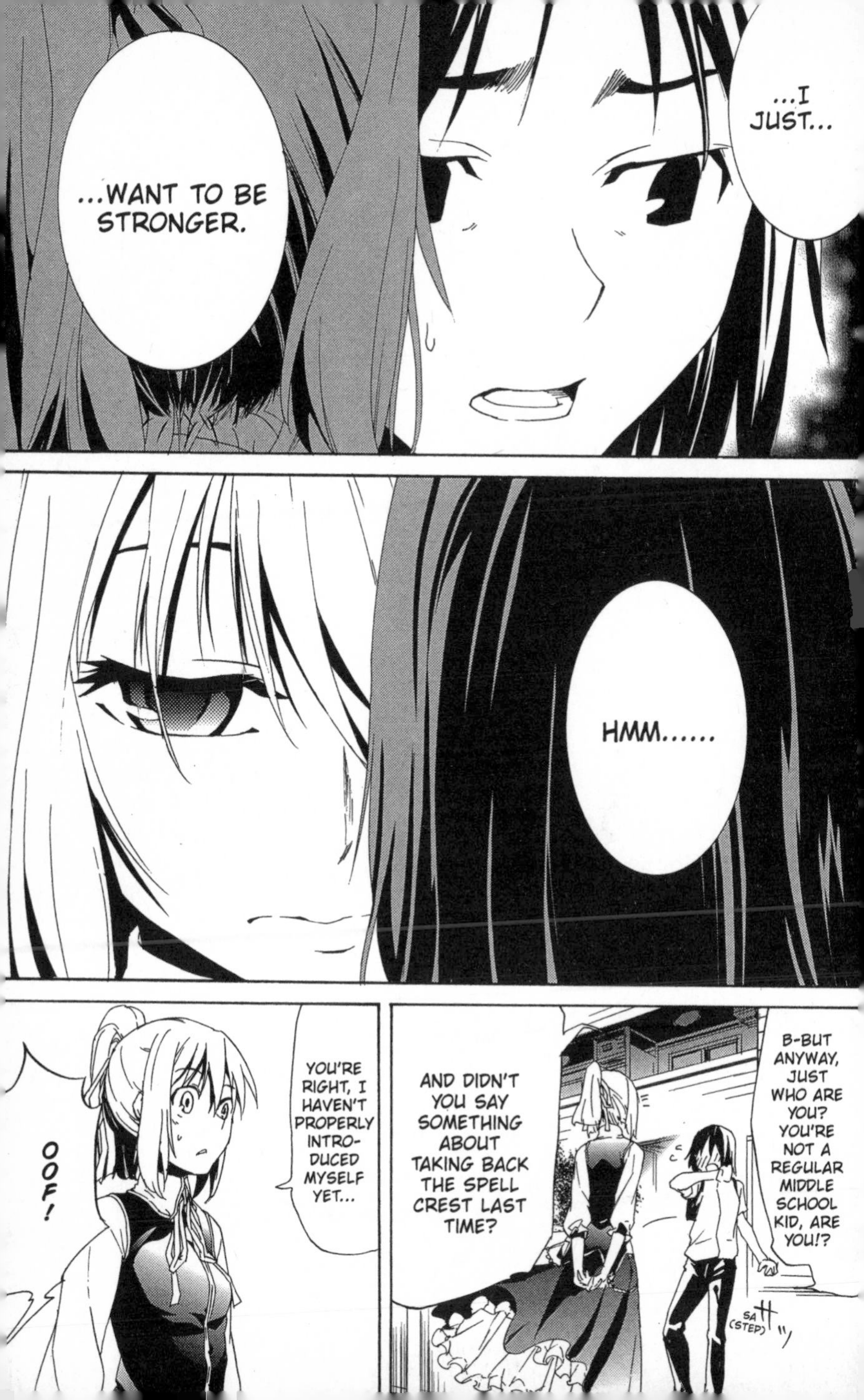
...I JUST...
...WANT TO BE STRONGER.
HMM......
B-BUT ANYWAY, JUST WHO ARE YOU? YOU'RE NOT A REGULAR MIDDLE SCHOOL KID, ARE YOU!?
AND DIDN'T YOU SAY SOMETHING ABOUT TAKING BACK THE SPELL CREST LAST TIME?
SA (STEP)
YOU'RE RIGHT, I HAVEN'T PROPERLY INTRO-DUCED MYSELF YET...
OOF!

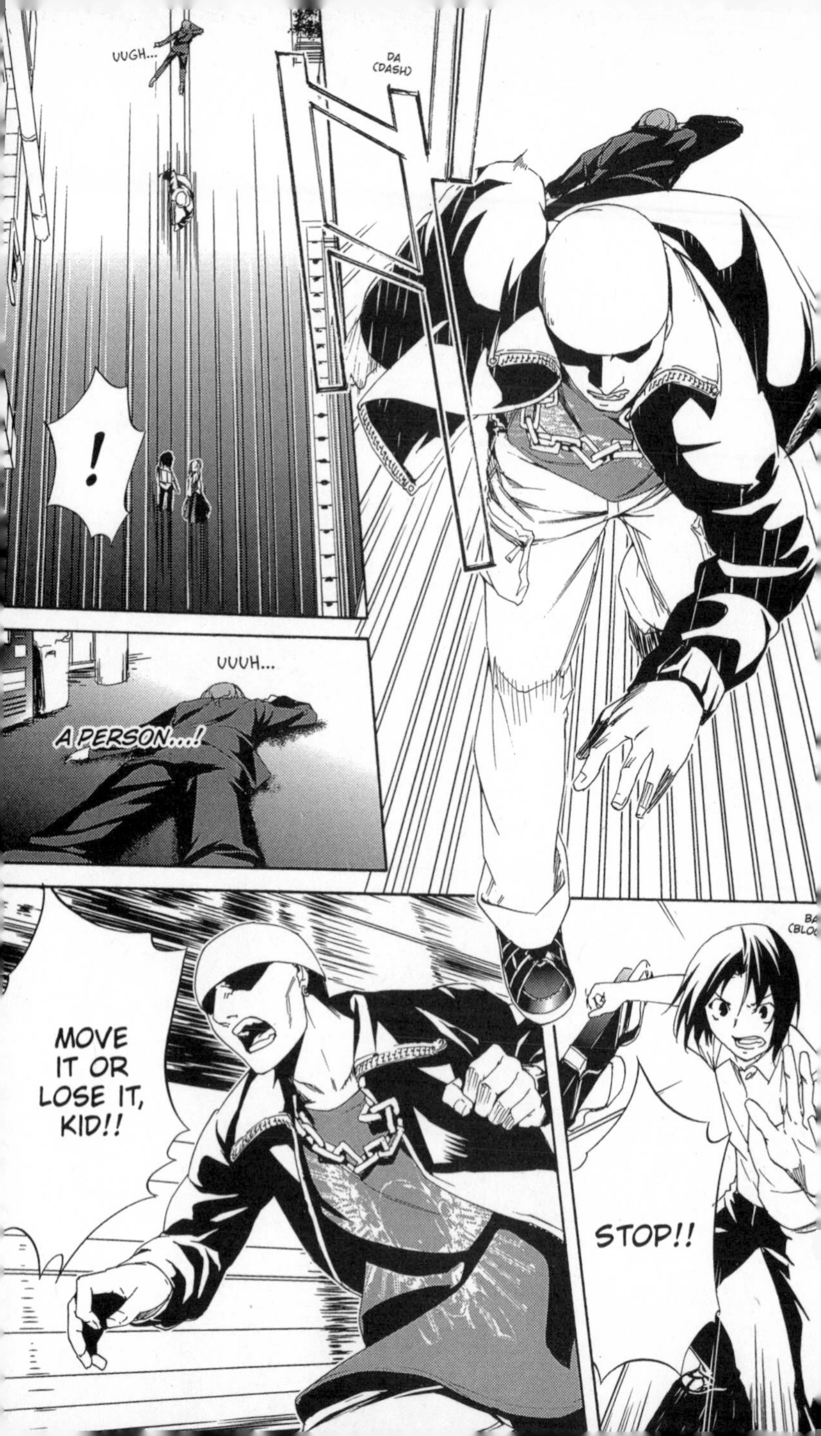
DA
(DASH)
UUGH...
!
UUUH...
A PERSON...!
BA
(BLOC
MOVE IT OR LOSE IT, KID!!
STOP!!

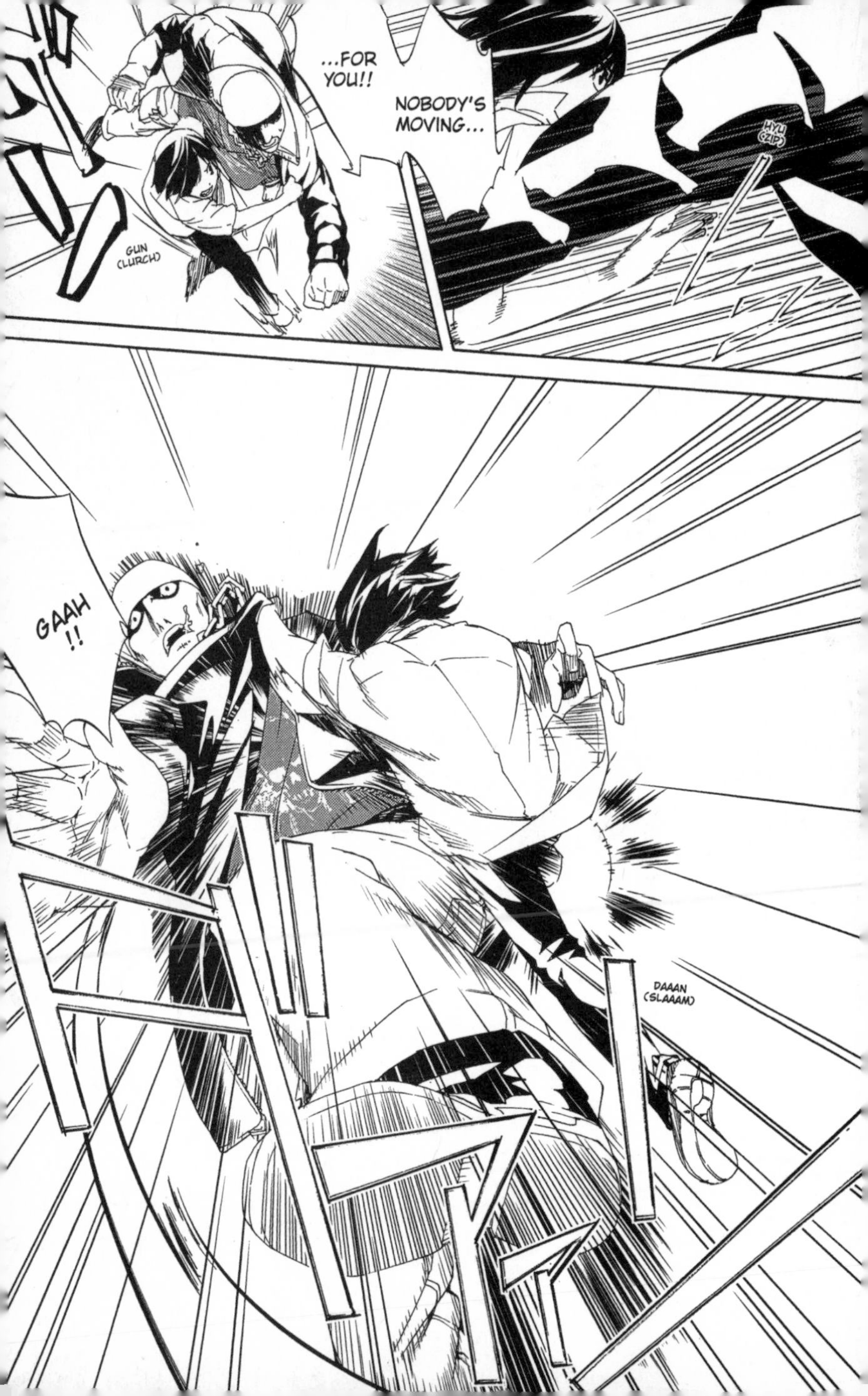

HYU (ZIP)
NOBODY'S MOVING...
...FOR YOU!!
GUN (LURCH)
GAAH !!
DAAAN (SLAAAM)

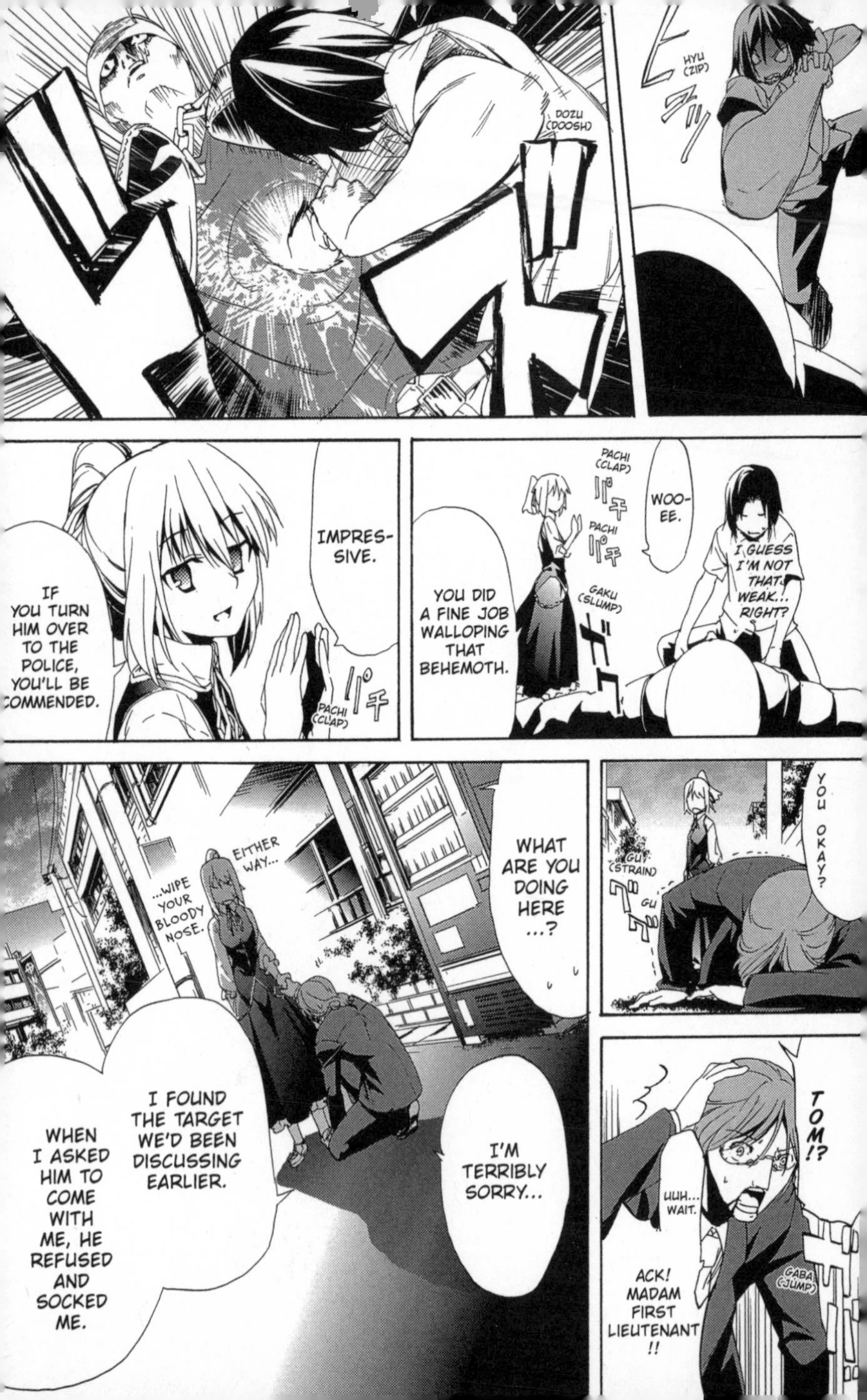
HYU (ZIP)
DOZU (DOOSH)
PACHI (CLAP)
PACHI
WOO-EE.
I GUESS I'M NOT THAT WEAK... RIGHT?
GAKU (SLUMP)
YOU DID A FINE JOB WALLOPING THAT BEHEMOTH.
IMPRES-SIVE.
PACHI (CLAP)
IF YOU TURN HIM OVER TO THE POLICE, YOU'LL BE COMMENDED.
YOU OKAY?
GU (STRAIN)
GU
TOM!?
UUH... WAIT.
GABA (JUMP)
ACK! MADAM FIRST LIEUTENANT!!
WHAT ARE YOU DOING HERE ...?
EITHER WAY...
...WIPE YOUR BLOODY NOSE.
I'M TERRIBLY SORRY...
I FOUND THE TARGET WE'D BEEN DISCUSSING EARLIER.
WHEN I ASKED HIM TO COME WITH ME, HE REFUSED AND SOCKED ME.

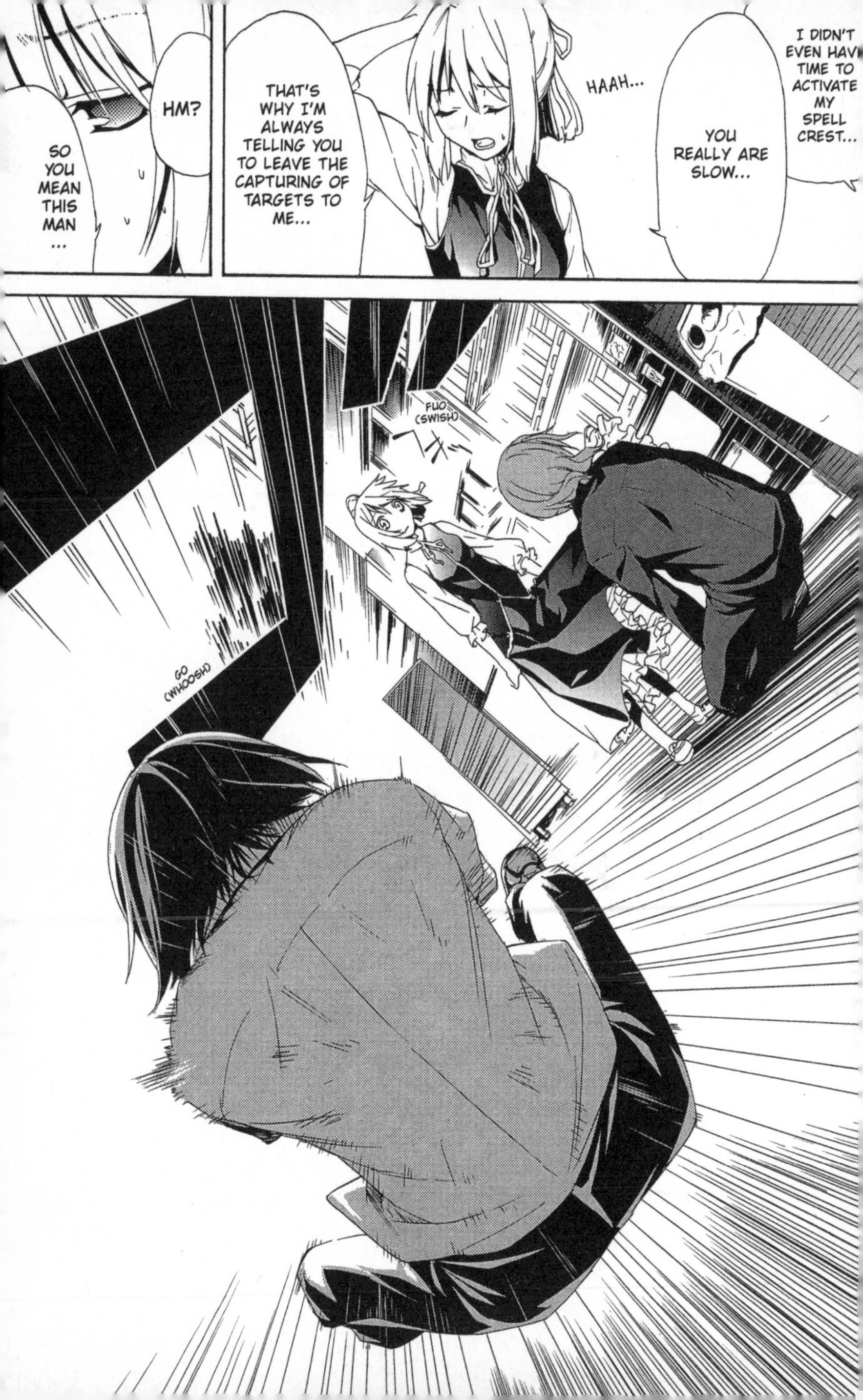
I DIDN'T EVEN HAV TIME TO ACTIVATE MY SPELL CREST...
YOU REALLY ARE SLOW...
HAAH...
THAT'S WHY I'M ALWAYS TELLING YOU TO LEAVE THE CAPTURING OF TARGETS TO ME...
HM?
SO YOU MEAN THIS MAN ...
FUO (SWISH)
GO (WHOOSH)

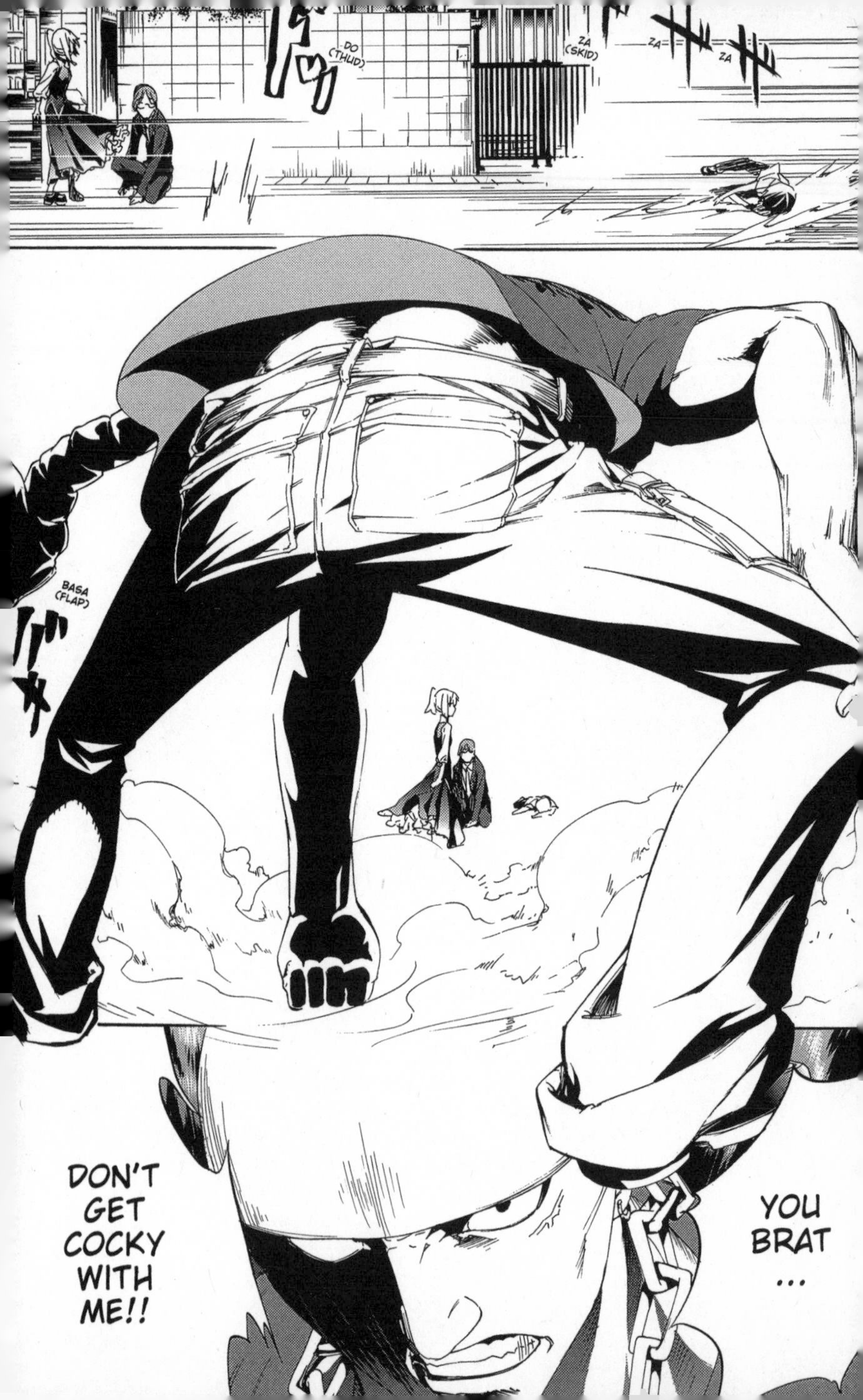
ZA
ZA
ZA
(SKID)
DO
(THUD)
BASA
(FLAP)
YOU BRAT...
DON'T GET COCKY WITH ME!!

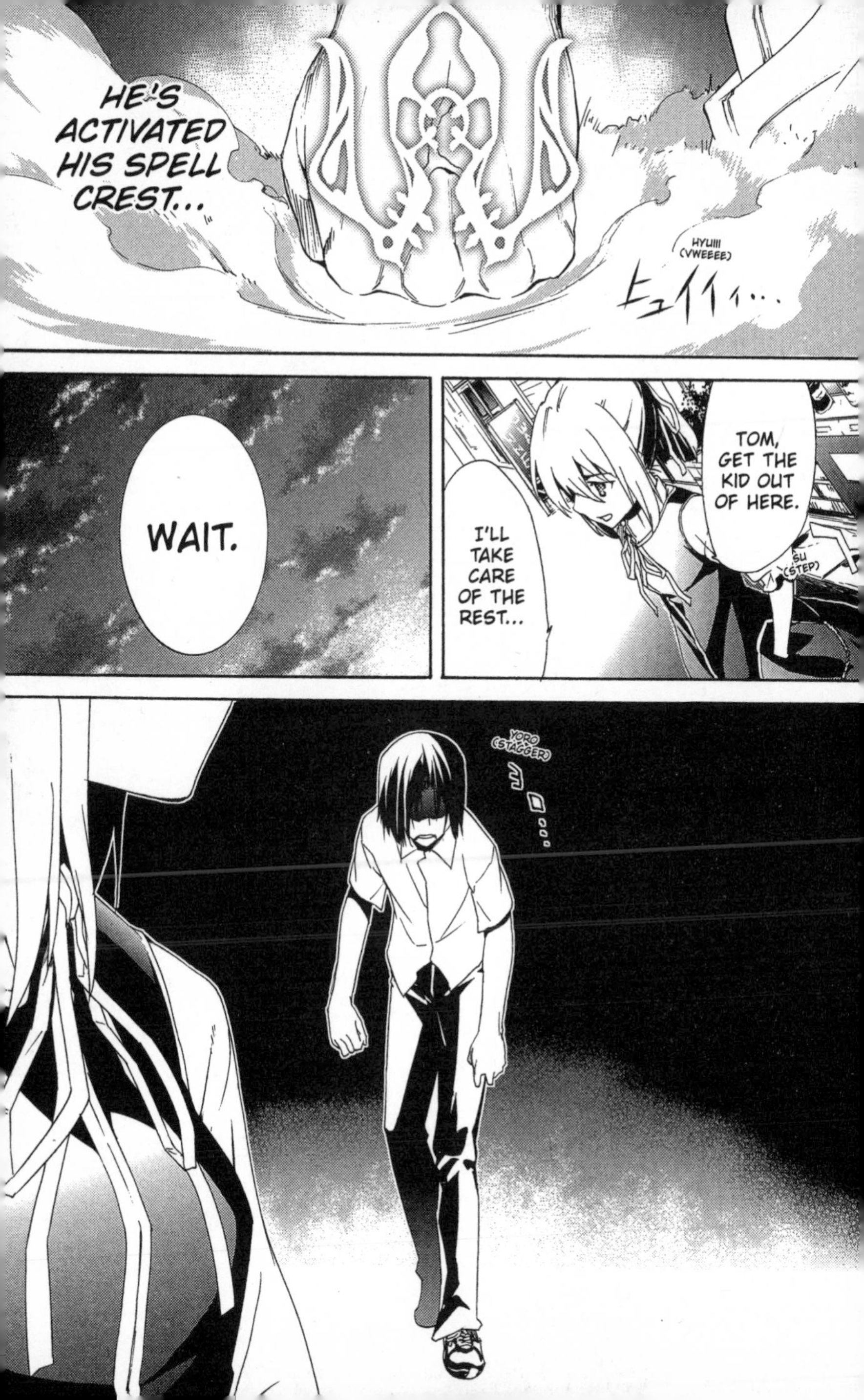
HE'S ACTIVATED HIS SPELL CREST...
HYUIII (VWEEEE)
ヒュイイィ...
TOM, GET THE KID OUT OF HERE.
I'LL TAKE CARE OF THE REST...
SU (STEP)
WAIT.
YORO (STAGGER)
ヨロ...

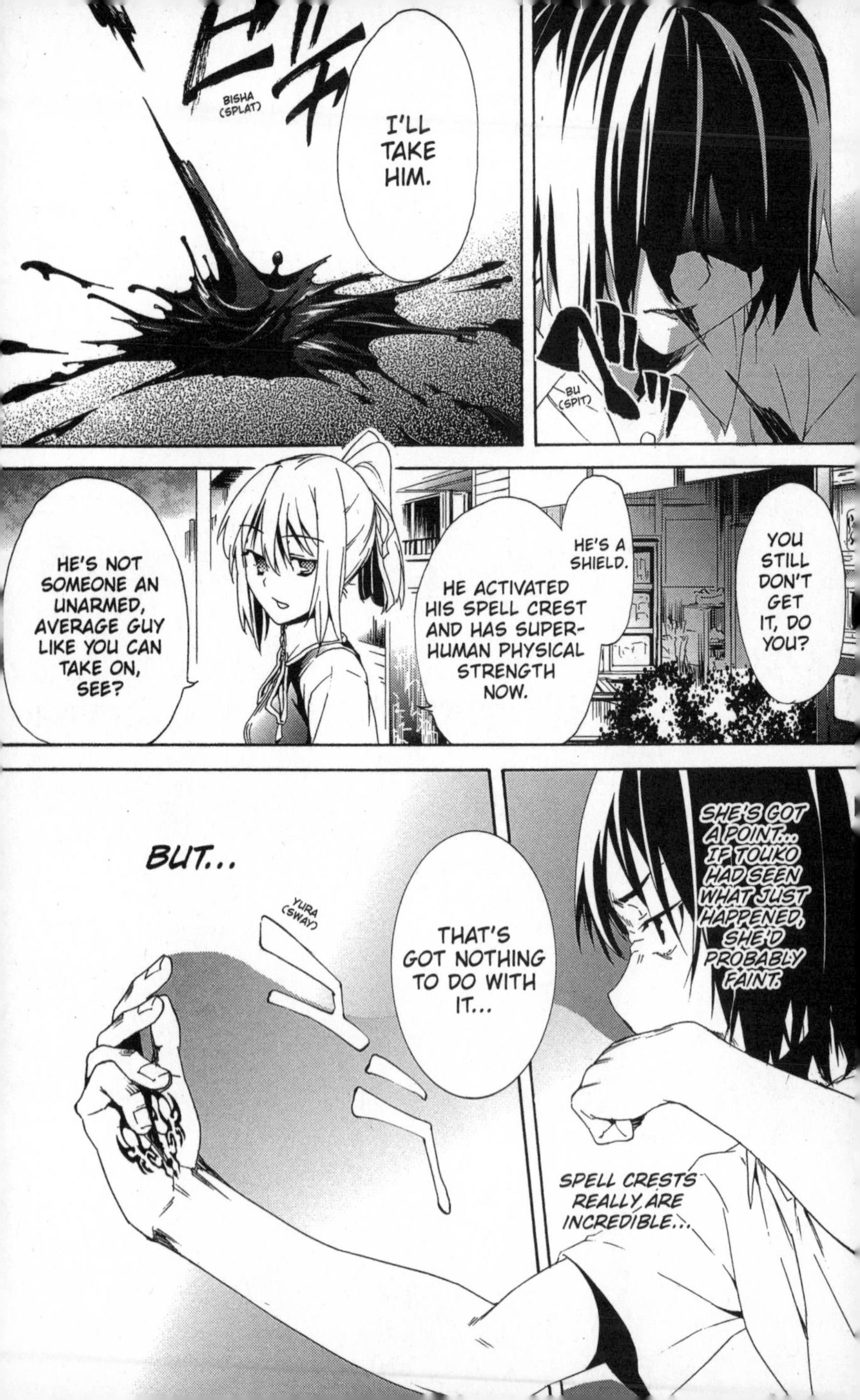
BU (SPIT)
I'LL TAKE HIM.
BISHA (SPLAT)
YOU STILL DON'T GET IT, DO YOU?
HE'S A SHIELD.
HE ACTIVATED HIS SPELL CREST AND HAS SUPER-HUMAN PHYSICAL STRENGTH NOW.
HE'S NOT SOMEONE AN UNARMED, AVERAGE GUY LIKE YOU CAN TAKE ON, SEE?
SHE'S GOT A POINT... IF TOUKO HAD SEEN WHAT JUST HAPPENED, SHE'D PROBABLY FAINT.
SPELL CRESTS REALLY ARE INCREDIBLE...
THAT'S GOT NOTHING TO DO WITH IT...
YURA (SWAY)
BUT...

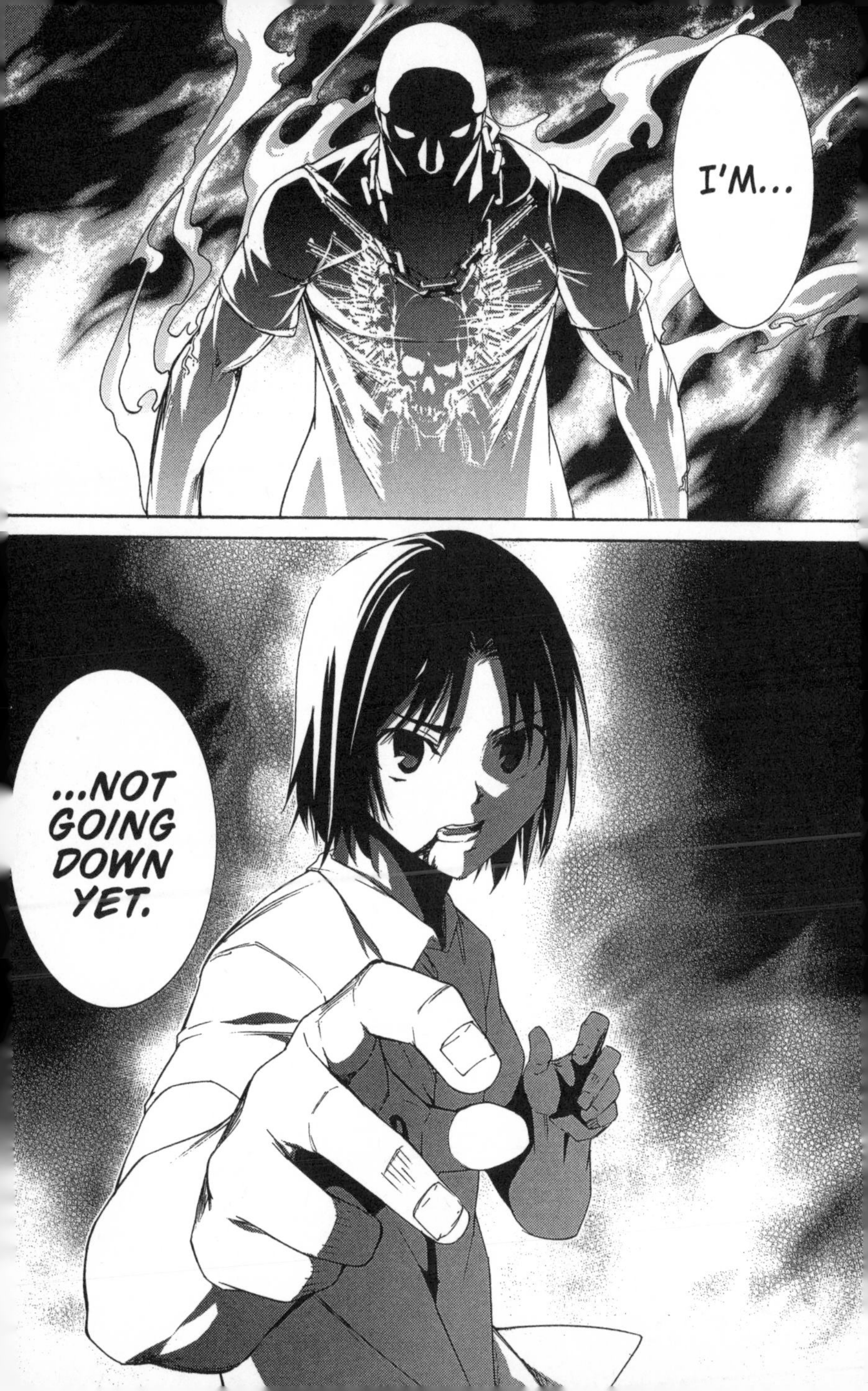
I'M...
...NOT GOING DOWN YET.

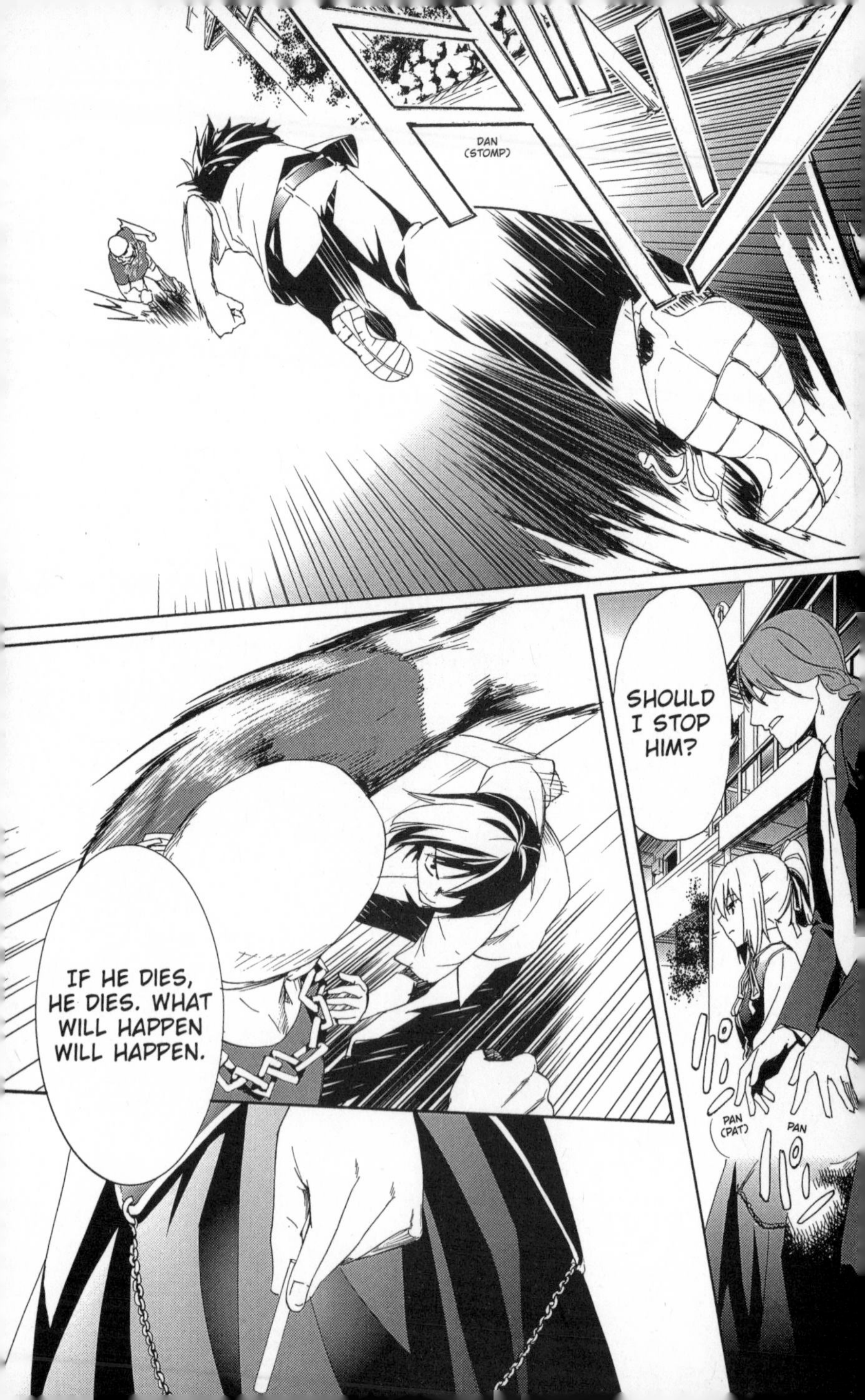
DAN
(STOMP)
SHOULD I STOP HIM?
PAN
(PAT)
PAN
IF HE DIES, HE DIES. WHAT WILL HAPPEN WILL HAPPEN.

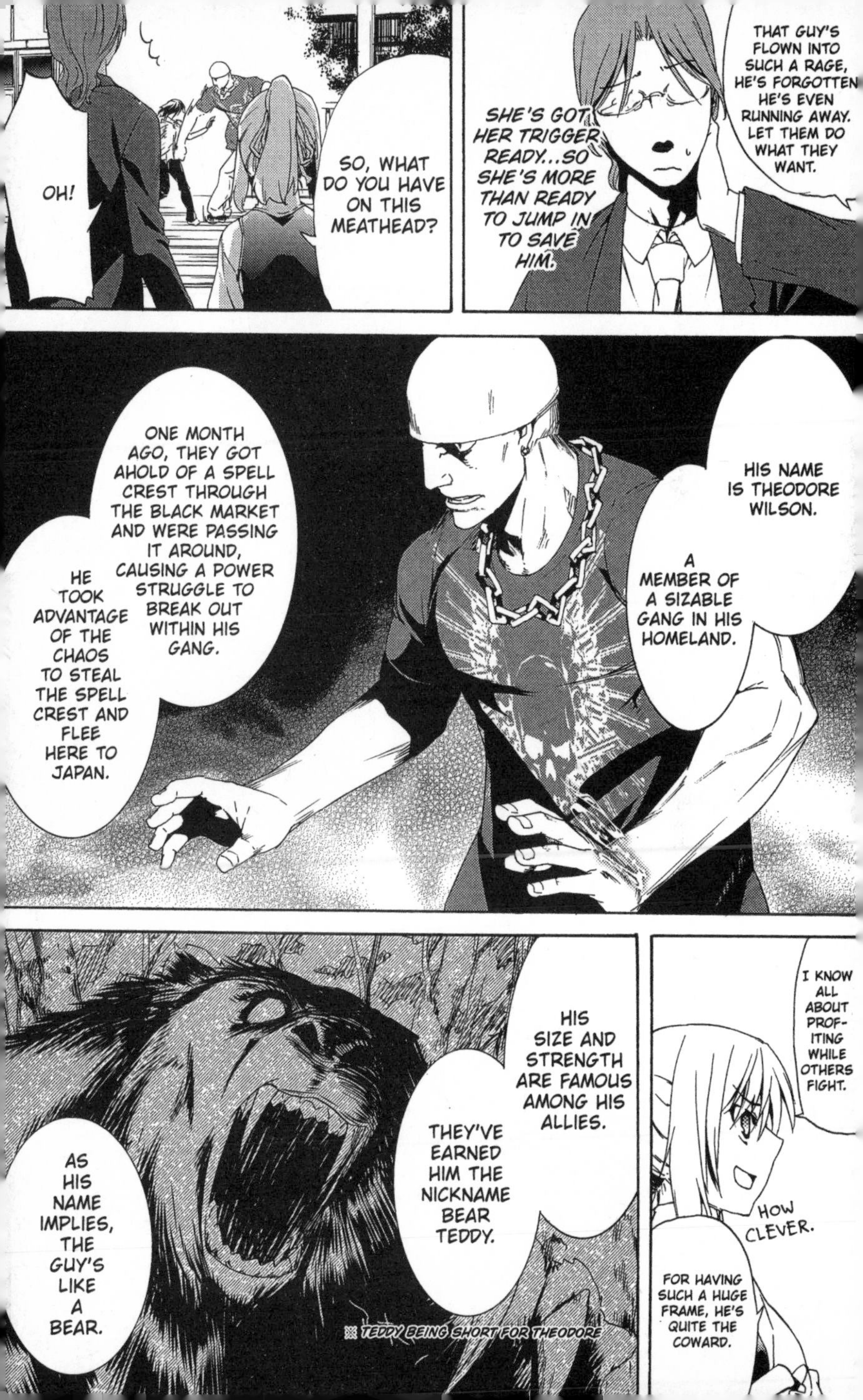
THAT GUY'S FLOWN INTO SUCH A RAGE, HE'S FORGOTTEN HE'S EVEN RUNNING AWAY. LET THEM DO WHAT THEY WANT.
SHE'S GOT HER TRIGGER READY...SO SHE'S MORE THAN READY TO JUMP IN TO SAVE HIM.
SO, WHAT DO YOU HAVE ON THIS MEATHEAD?
OH!
HIS NAME IS THEODORE WILSON.
A MEMBER OF A SIZABLE GANG IN HIS HOMELAND.
ONE MONTH AGO, THEY GOT AHOLD OF A SPELL CREST THROUGH THE BLACK MARKET AND WERE PASSING IT AROUND, CAUSING A POWER STRUGGLE TO BREAK OUT WITHIN HIS GANG.
HE TOOK ADVANTAGE OF THE CHAOS TO STEAL THE SPELL CREST AND FLEE HERE TO JAPAN.
I KNOW ALL ABOUT PROF-ITING WHILE OTHERS FIGHT.
HOW CLEVER.
FOR HAVING SUCH A HUGE FRAME, HE'S QUITE THE COWARD.
HIS SIZE AND STRENGTH ARE FAMOUS AMONG HIS ALLIES.
THEY'VE EARNED HIM THE NICKNAME BEAR TEDDY.
AS HIS NAME IMPLIES, THE GUY'S LIKE A BEAR.
※ TEDDY BEING SHORT FOR THEODORE

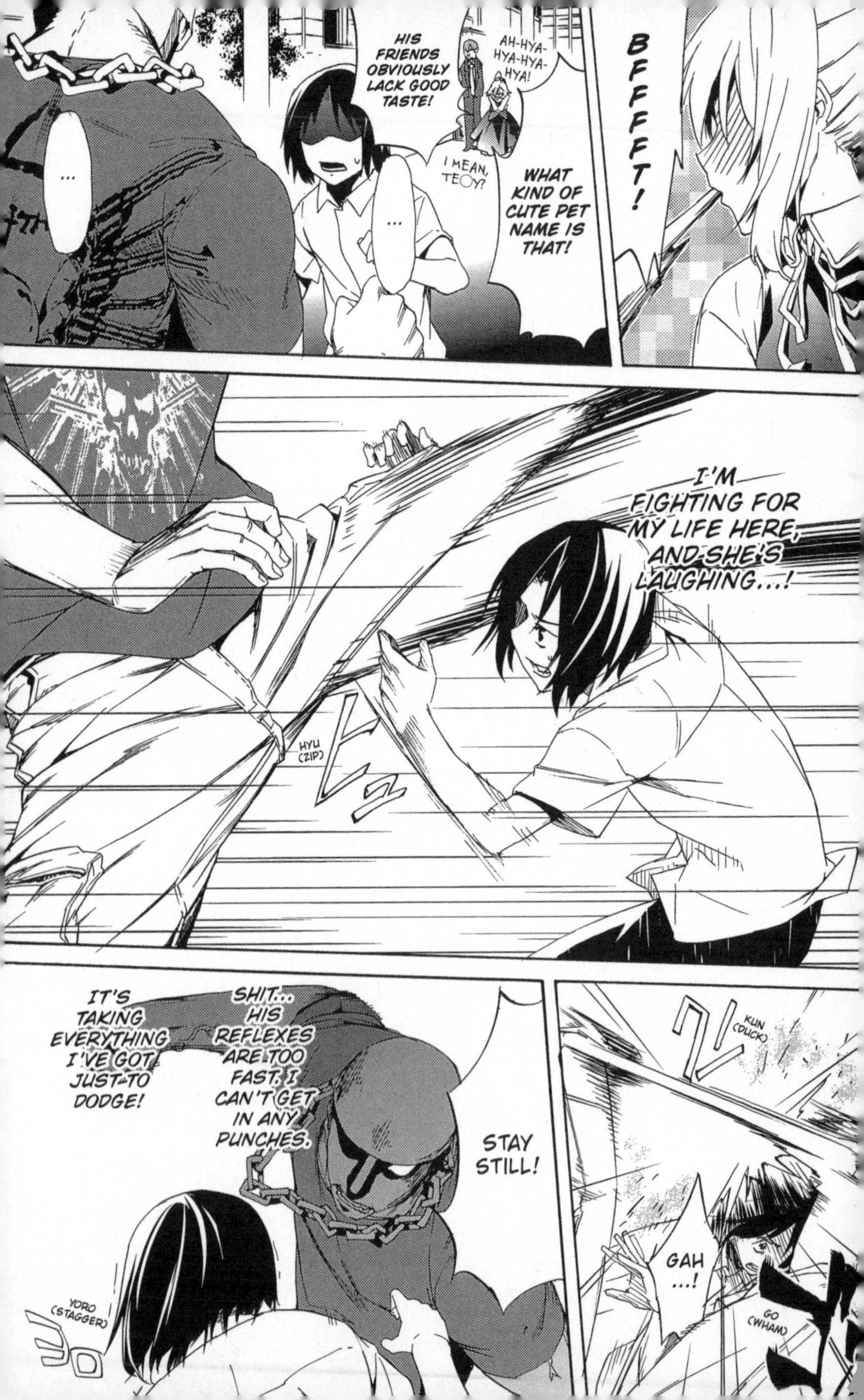
BFFFFFT!
AH-HYA-HYA-HYA-HYA!
HIS FRIENDS OBVIOUSLY LACK GOOD TASTE!
WHAT KIND OF CUTE PET NAME IS THAT!
I MEAN, TE◯Y?
...
...
I'M FIGHTING FOR MY LIFE HERE, AND SHE'S LAUGHING...!
HYU (ZIP)
KUN (DUCK)
GAH ...!
GO (WHAM)
STAY STILL!
SHIT... HIS REFLEXES ARE TOO FAST. I CAN'T GET IN ANY PUNCHES.
IT'S TAKING EVERYTHING I'VE GOT JUST TO DODGE!
YORO (STAGGER)

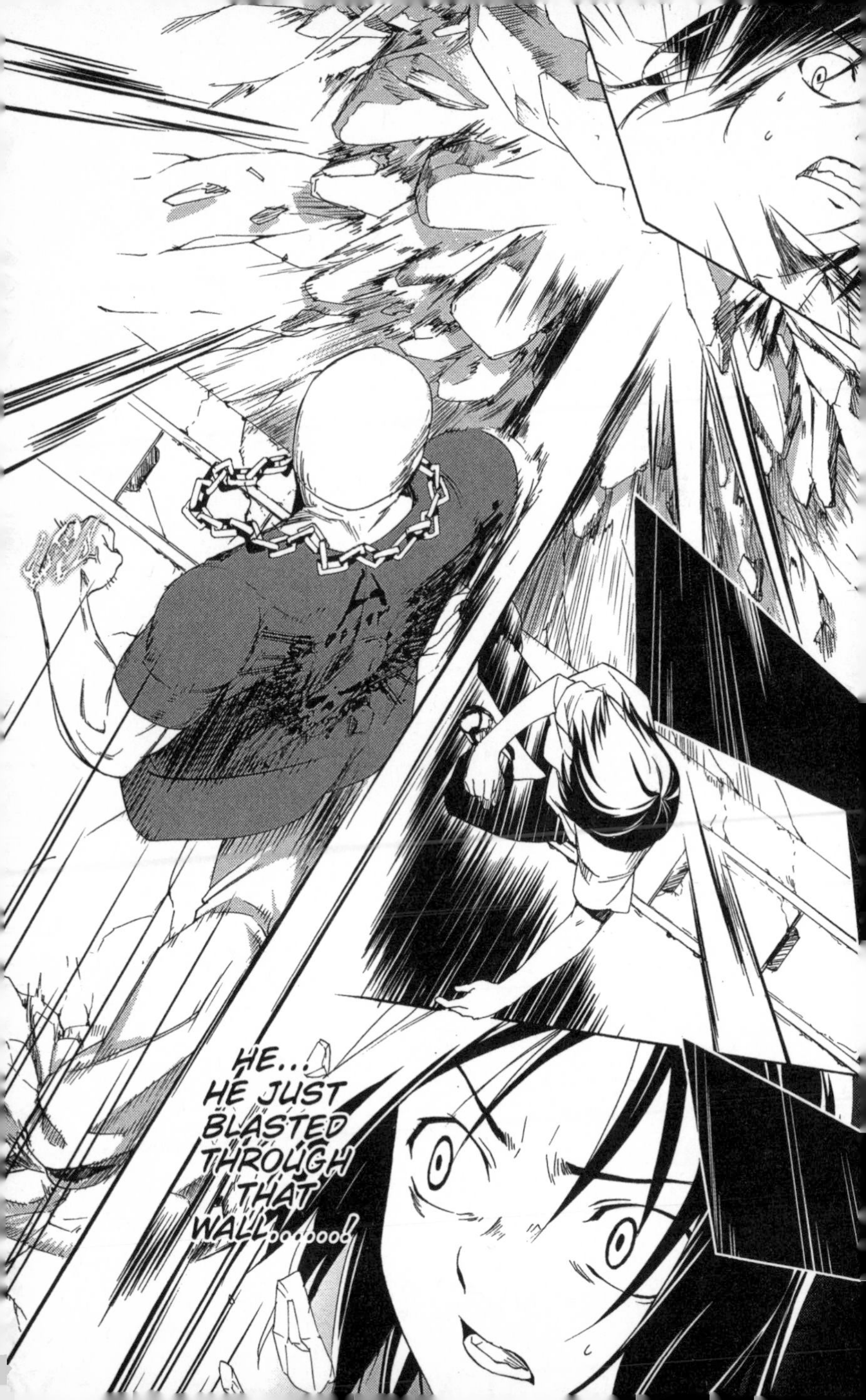
HE... HE JUST BLASTED THROUGH THAT WALL...!

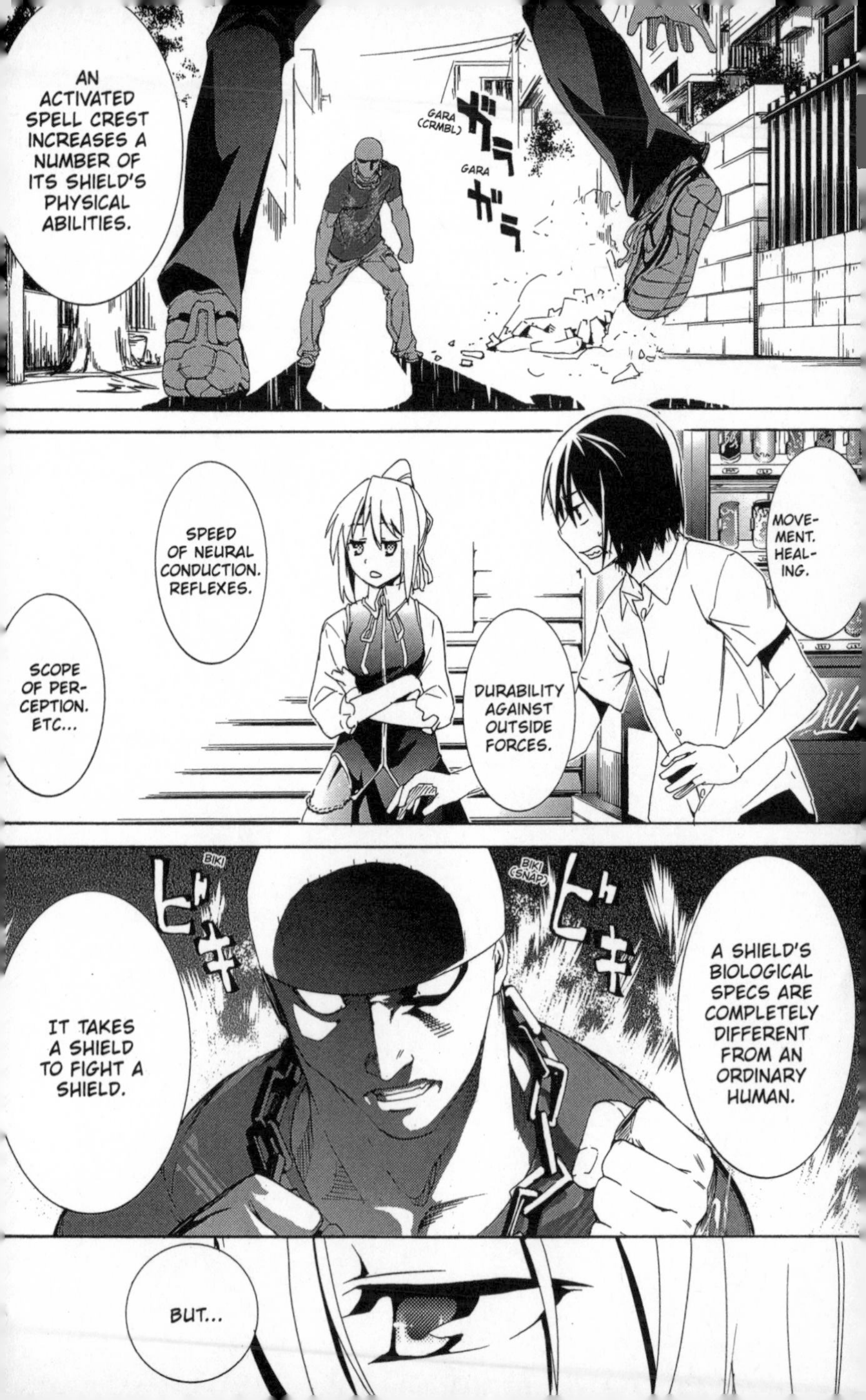
GARA (CRMBL)
GARA
AN ACTIVATED SPELL CREST INCREASES A NUMBER OF ITS SHIELD'S PHYSICAL ABILITIES.
MOVEMENT. HEALING.
SPEED OF NEURAL CONDUCTION. REFLEXES.
DURABILITY AGAINST OUTSIDE FORCES.
SCOPE OF PERCEPTION. ETC...
BIKI (SNAP)
A SHIELD'S BIOLOGICAL SPECS ARE COMPLETELY DIFFERENT FROM AN ORDINARY HUMAN.
BIKI
IT TAKES A SHIELD TO FIGHT A SHIELD.
BUT...

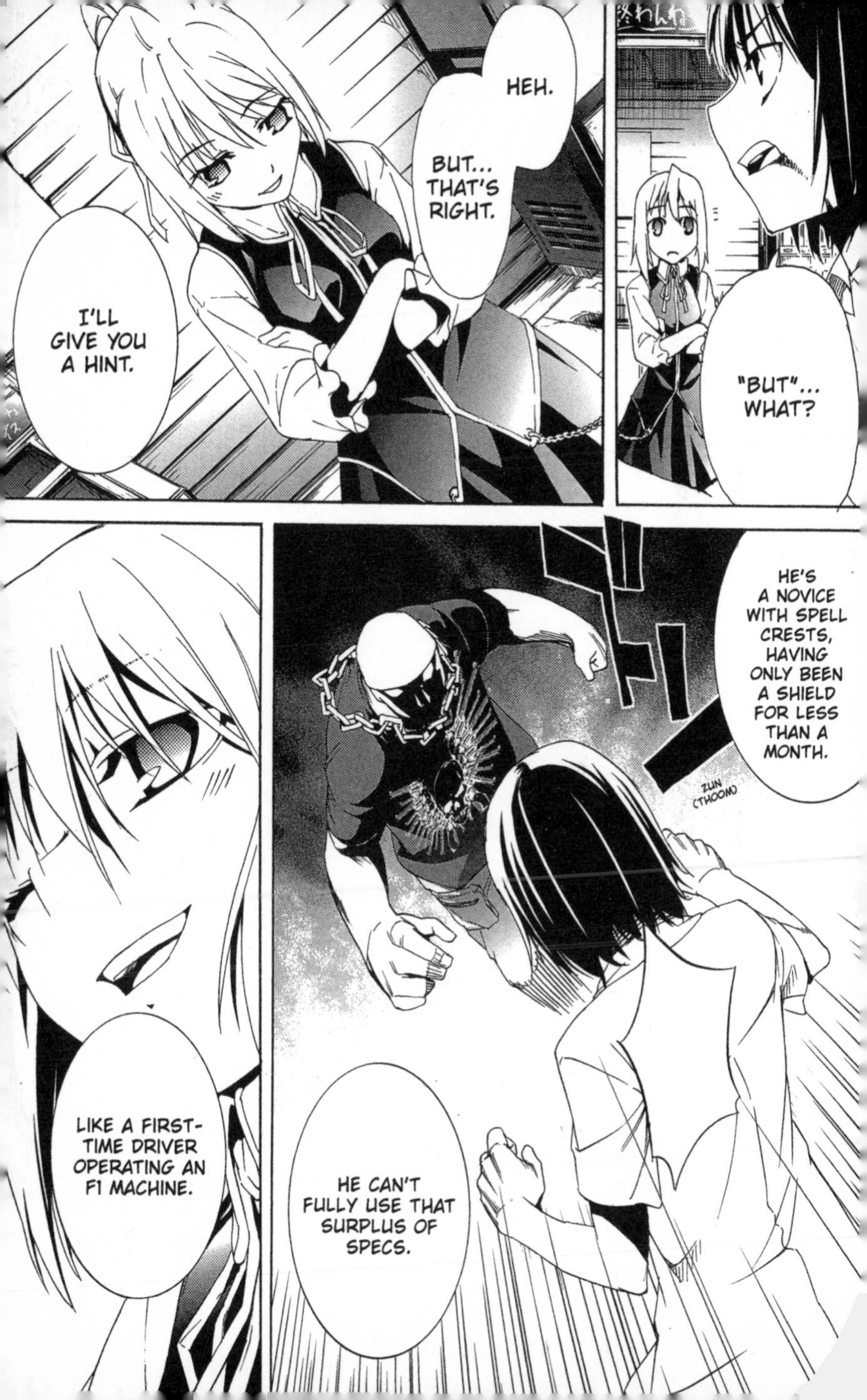
"BUT"... WHAT?
HEH.
BUT... THAT'S RIGHT.
I'LL GIVE YOU A HINT.
HE'S A NOVICE WITH SPELL CRESTS, HAVING ONLY BEEN A SHIELD FOR LESS THAN A MONTH.
ZUN (THOOM)
HE CAN'T FULLY USE THAT SURPLUS OF SPECS.
LIKE A FIRST-TIME DRIVER OPERATING AN F1 MACHINE.

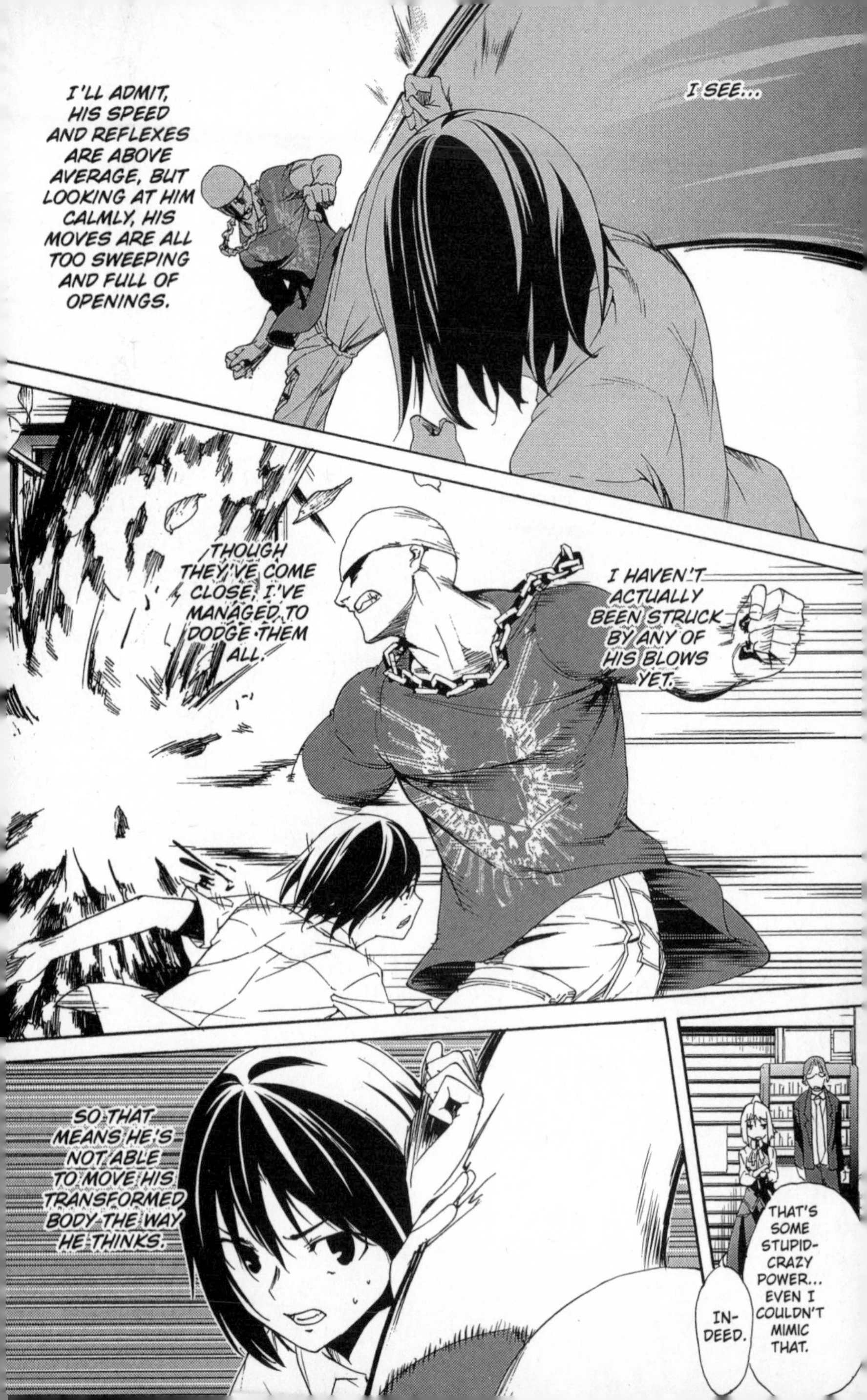
I SEE...
I'LL ADMIT, HIS SPEED AND REFLEXES ARE ABOVE AVERAGE, BUT LOOKING AT HIM CALMLY, HIS MOVES ARE ALL TOO SWEEPING AND FULL OF OPENINGS.
I HAVEN'T ACTUALLY BEEN STRUCK BY ANY OF HIS BLOWS YET.
THOUGH THEY'VE COME CLOSE, I'VE MANAGED TO DODGE THEM ALL.
THAT'S SOME STUPID-CRAZY POWER... EVEN I COULDN'T MIMIC THAT.
IN-DEED.
SO THAT MEANS HE'S NOT ABLE TO MOVE HIS TRANSFORMED BODY THE WAY HE THINKS.

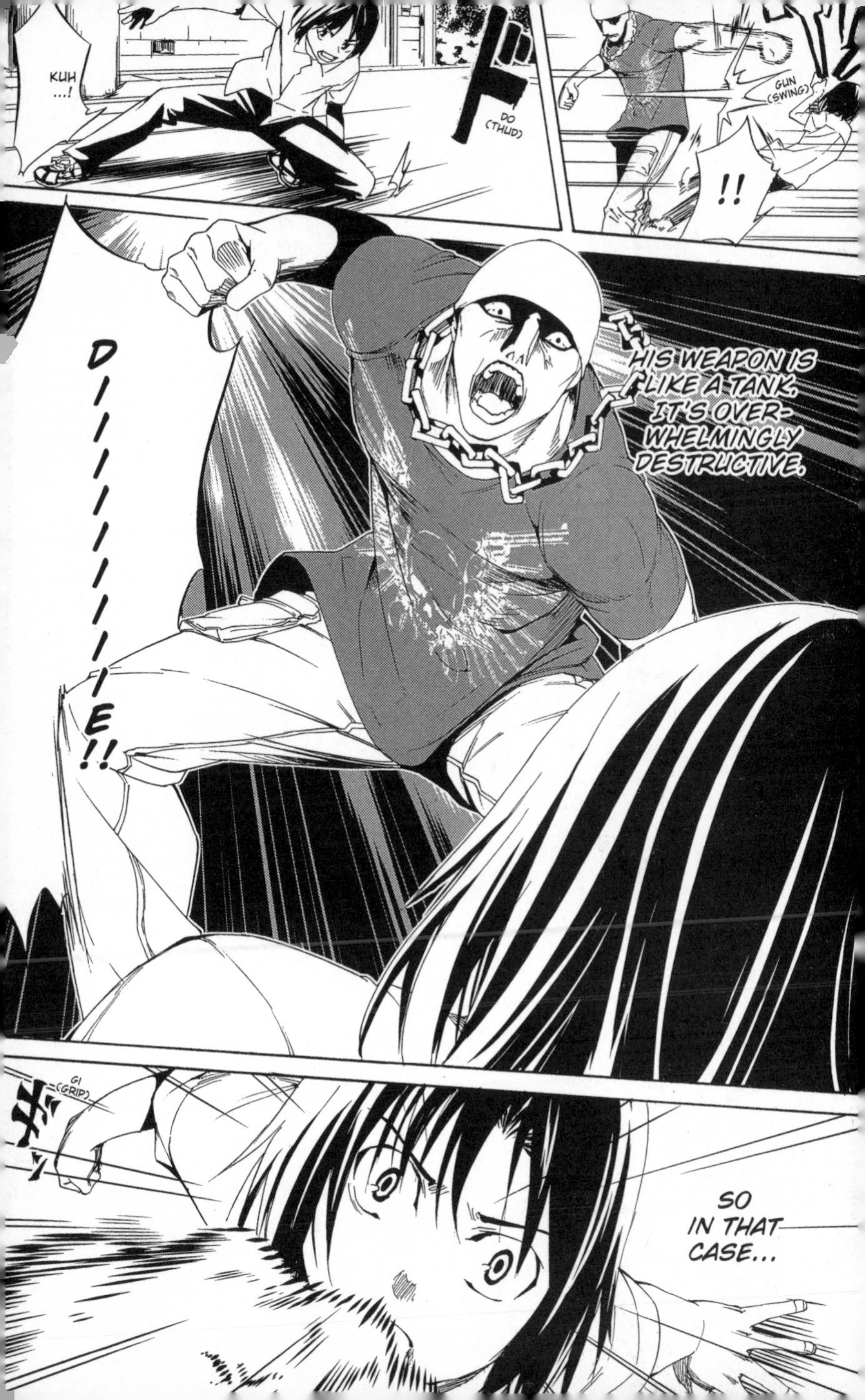
GUN (SWING)
!!
DO (THUD)
KUH ...!
HIS WEAPON IS LIKE A TANK. IT'S OVER-WHELMINGLY DESTRUCTIVE.
DIIIIIIIIIIIIE!!
SO IN THAT CASE...
GI (GRIP)
ギッ

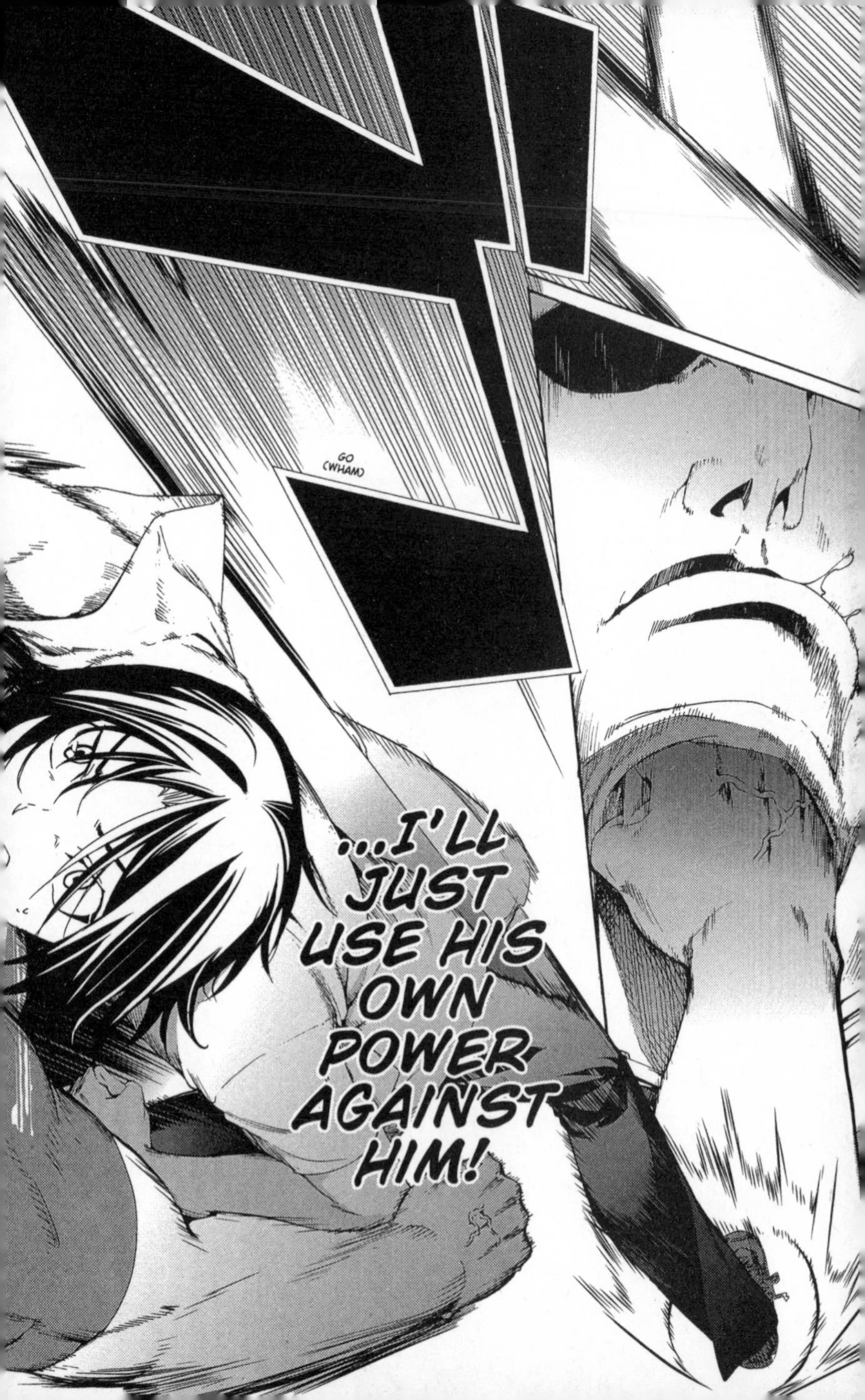
GO
(WHAM)
...I'LL JUST USE HIS OWN POWER AGAINST HIM!

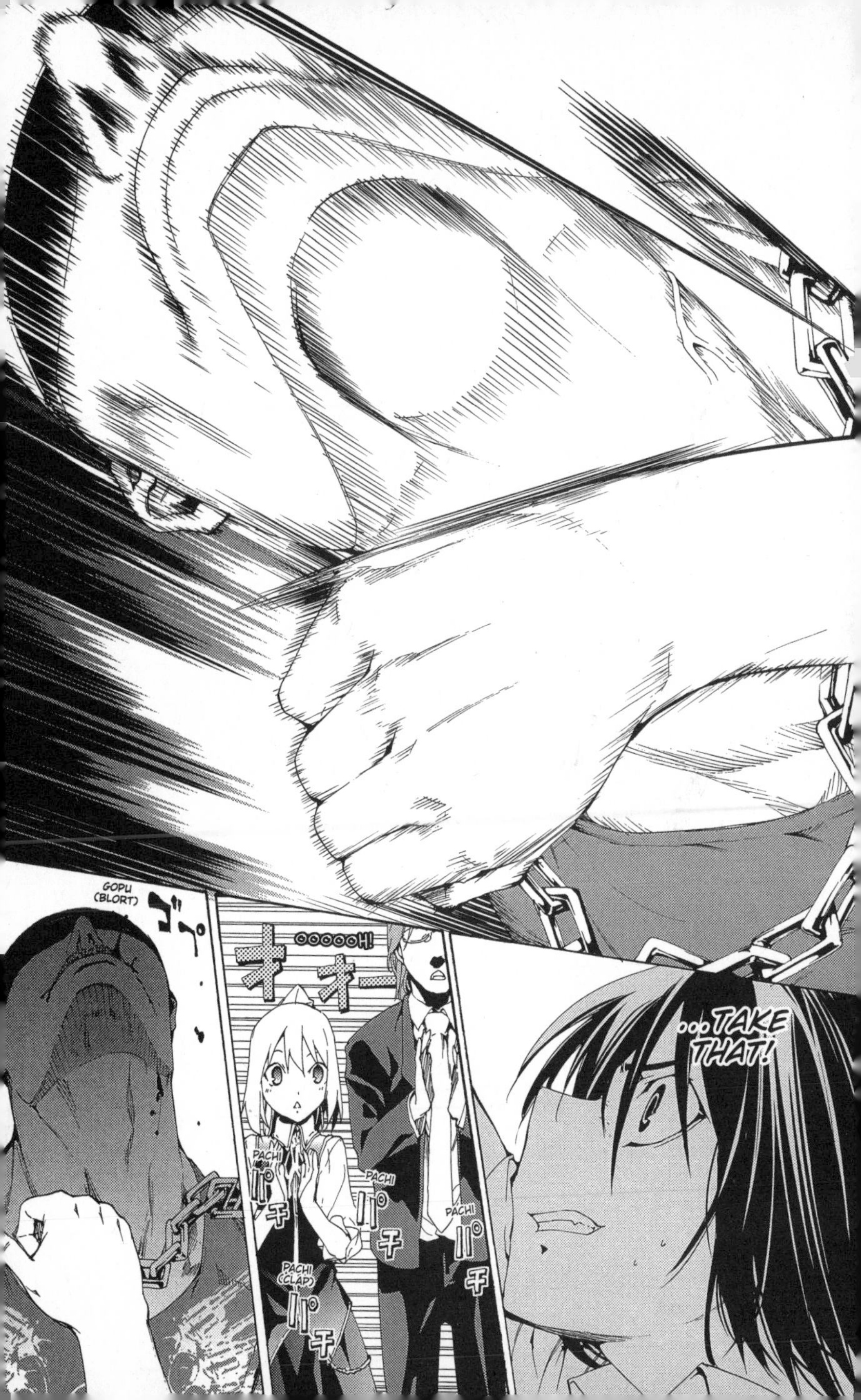
...TAKE THAT!
OOOOOH!
オオー
PACHI
パチ
PACHI
パチ
PACHI
パチ
PACHI (CLAP)
パチ
GOPU (BLORT)
ゴプ

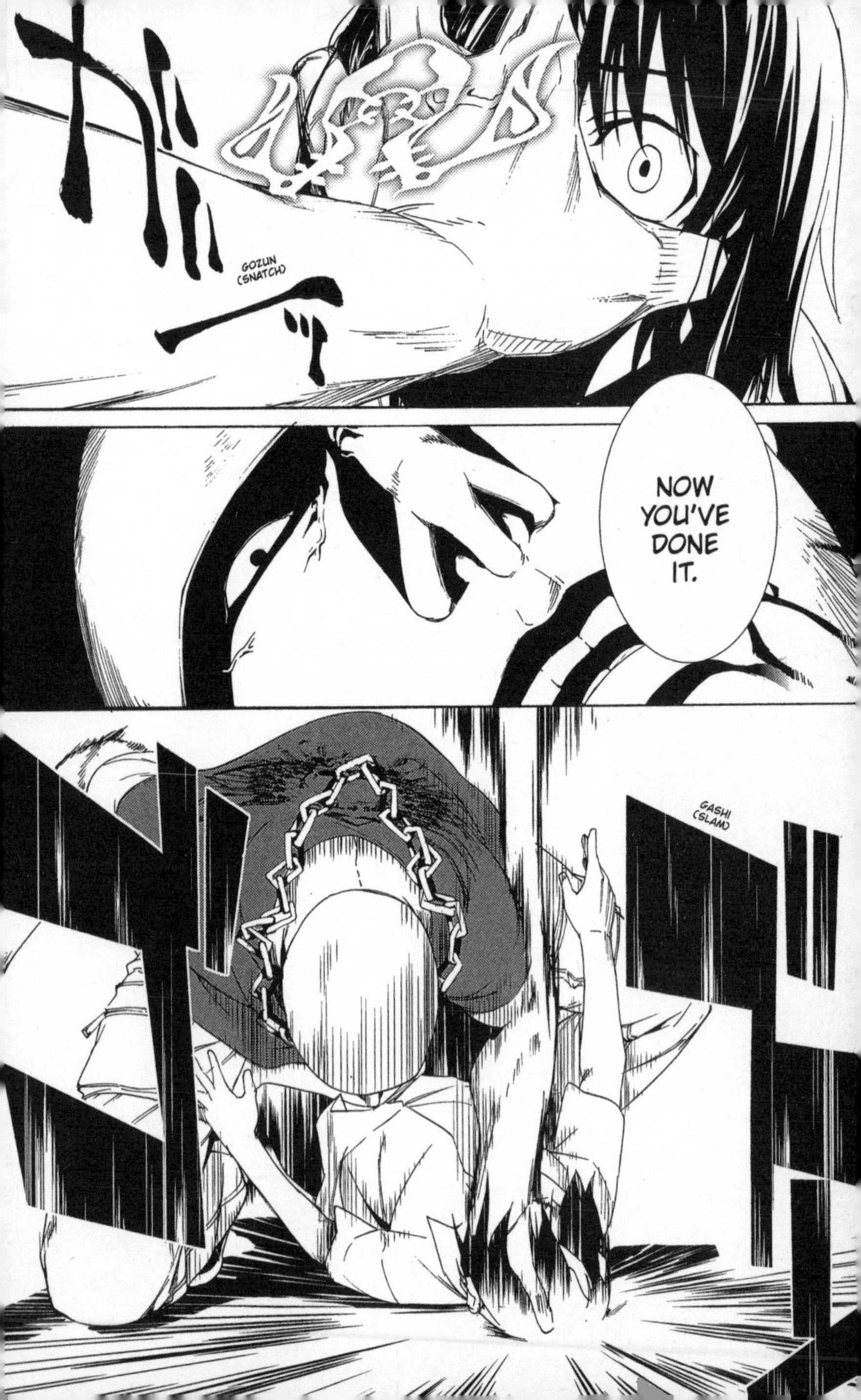
GOZUN (SNATCH)
NOW YOU'VE DONE IT.
GASHI (SLAM)

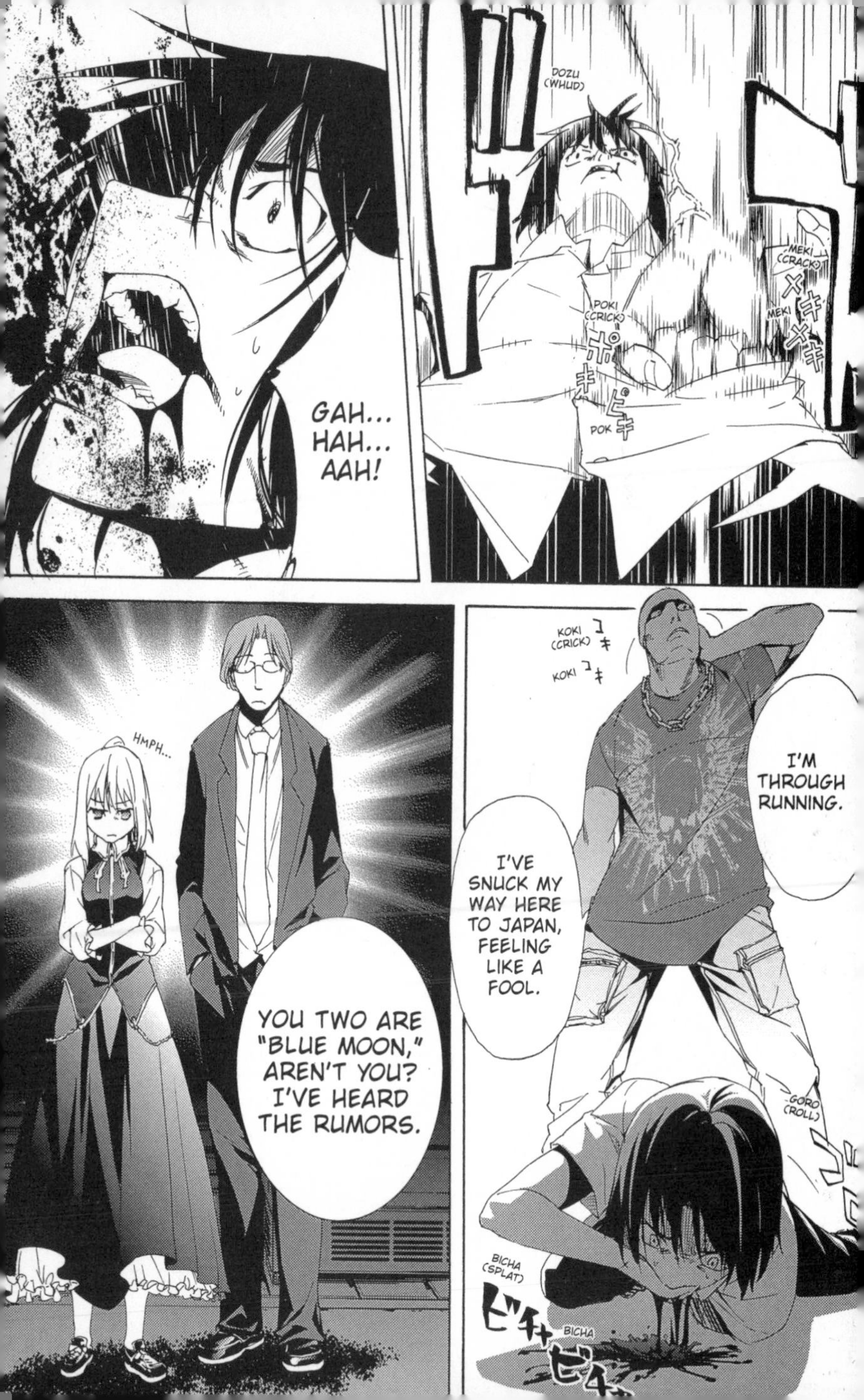
DOZU (WHUD)
MEKI (CRACK)
MEKI
POKI (CRICK)
POK
GAH... HAH... AAH!
KOKI (CRICK)
KOKI
I'M THROUGH RUNNING.
I'VE SNUCK MY WAY HERE TO JAPAN, FEELING LIKE A FOOL.
GORO (ROLL)
BICHA (SPLAT)
BICHA
HMPH...
YOU TWO ARE "BLUE MOON," AREN'T YOU? I'VE HEARD THE RUMORS.

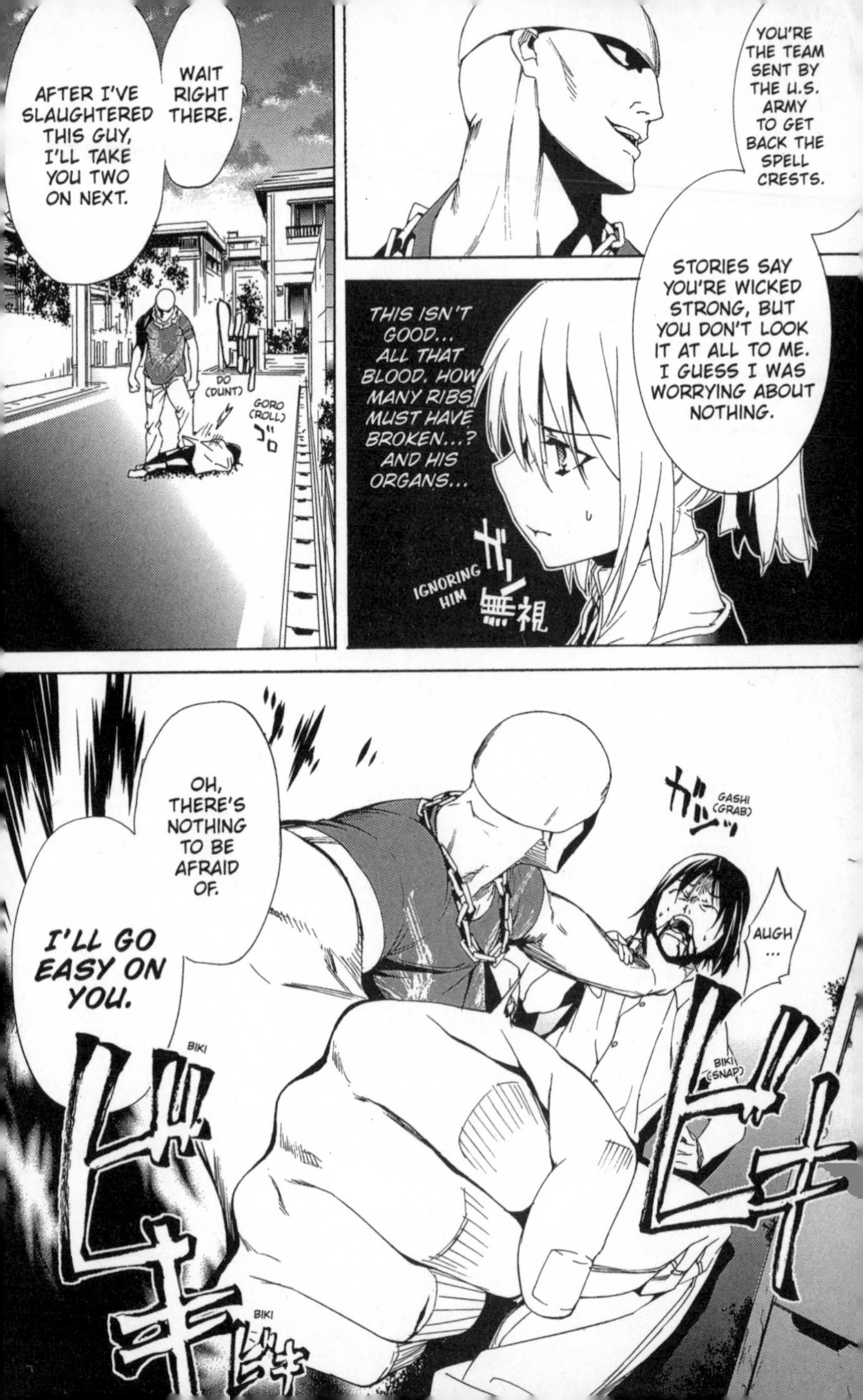

YOU'RE THE TEAM SENT BY THE U.S. ARMY TO GET BACK THE SPELL CRESTS.
STORIES SAY YOU'RE WICKED STRONG, BUT YOU DON'T LOOK IT AT ALL TO ME. I GUESS I WAS WORRYING ABOUT NOTHING.
THIS ISN'T GOOD... ALL THAT BLOOD. HOW MANY RIBS MUST HAVE BROKEN...? AND HIS ORGANS...
IGNORING HIM 無視
WAIT RIGHT THERE.
AFTER I'VE SLAUGHTERED THIS GUY, I'LL TAKE YOU TWO ON NEXT.
DO (DUNT)
GORO (ROLL) ゴロ
GASHI (GRAB)
AUGH...
BIKI (SNAP)
OH, THERE'S NOTHING TO BE AFRAID OF.
I'LL GO EASY ON YOU.
BIKI
BIKI

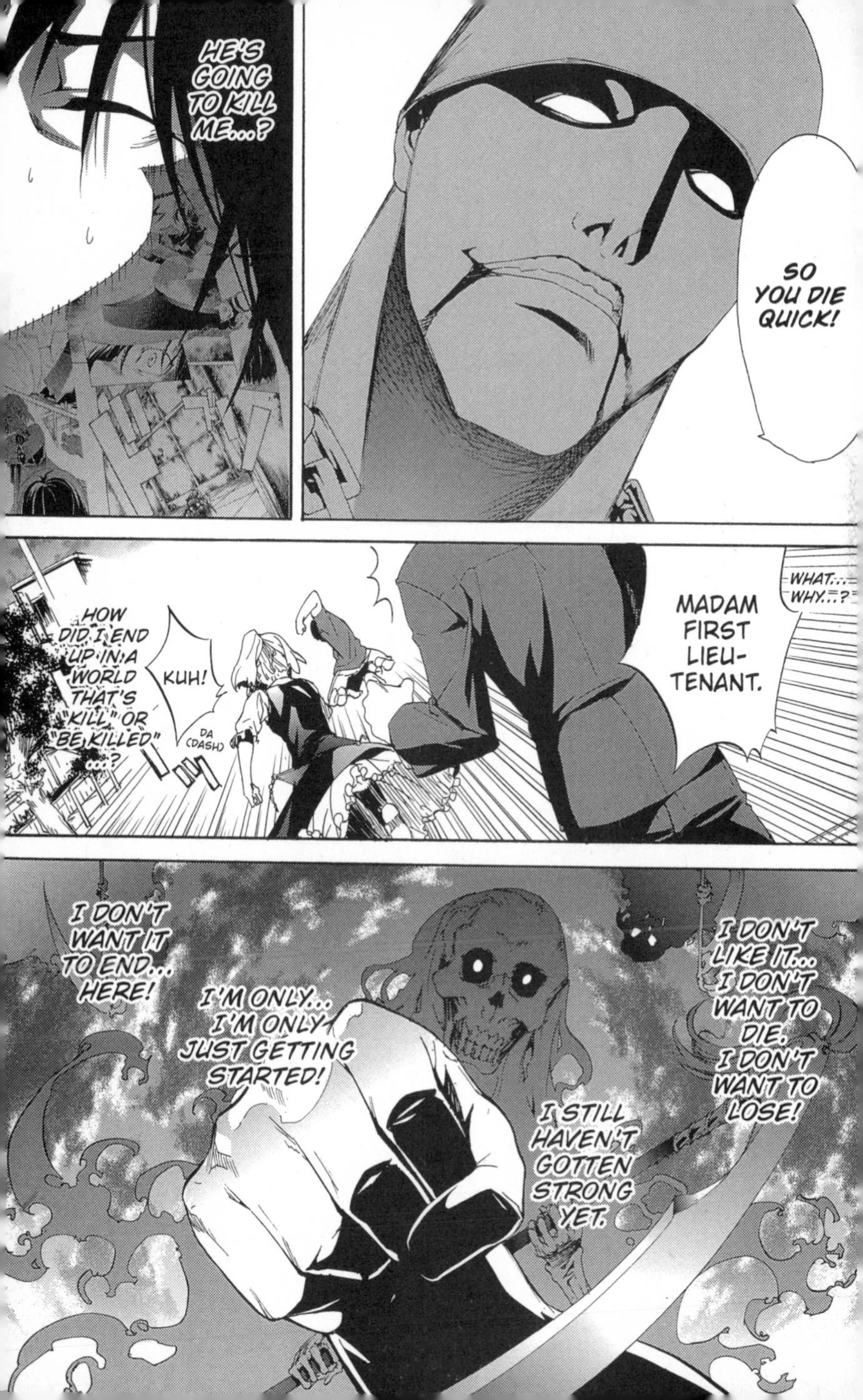
SO YOU DIE QUICK!
HE'S GOING TO KILL ME...?
WHAT... WHY...?
MADAM FIRST LIEU-TENANT.
KUH!
DA (DASH)
HOW DID I END UP IN A WORLD THAT'S "KILL" OR "BE KILLED"...?
I DON'T LIKE IT... I DON'T WANT TO DIE. I DON'T WANT TO LOSE!
I STILL HAVEN'T GOTTEN STRONG YET.
I'M ONLY... I'M ONLY JUST GETTING STARTED!
I DON'T WANT IT TO END... HERE!

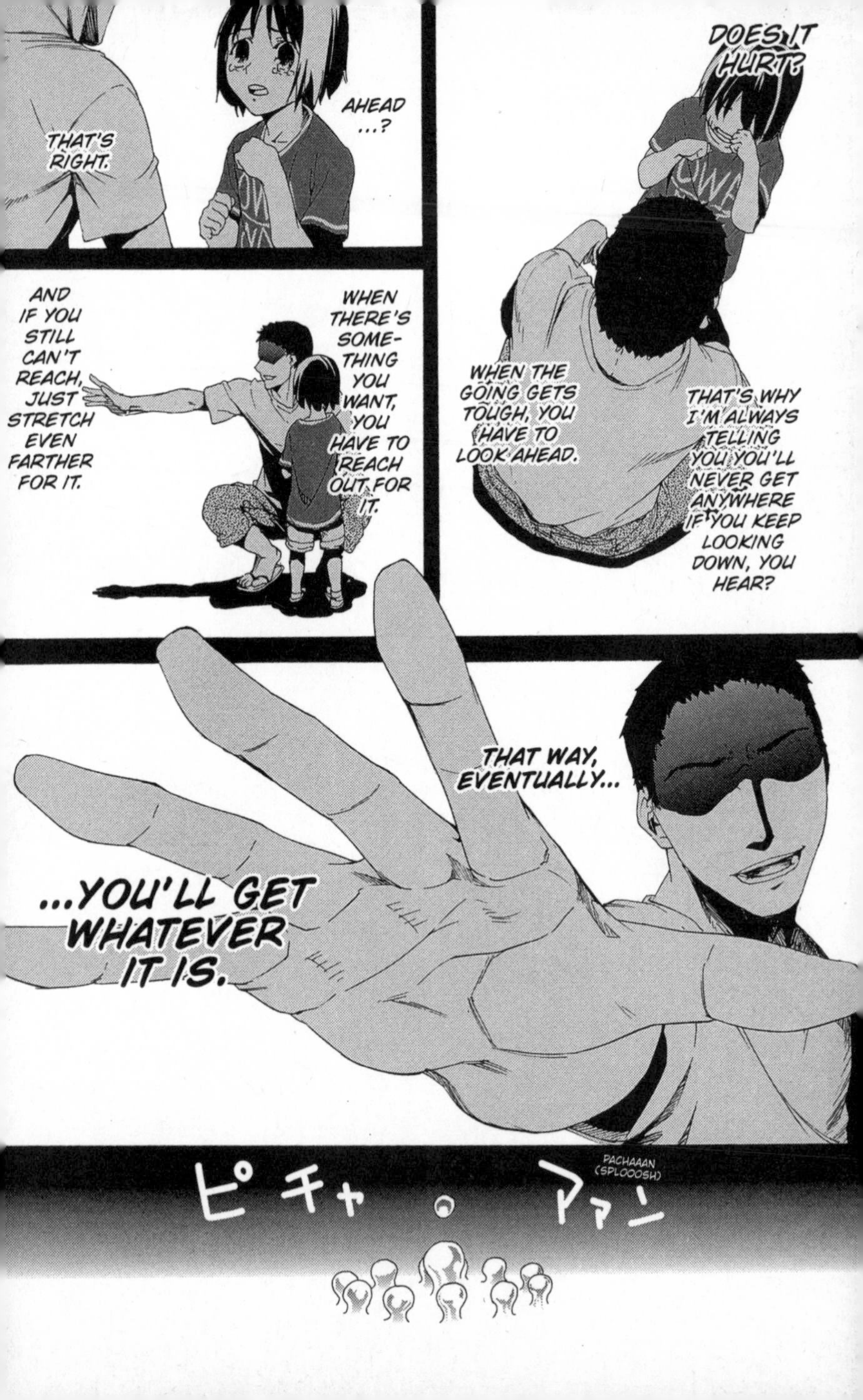
DOES IT HURT?
THAT'S WHY I'M ALWAYS TELLING YOU YOU'LL NEVER GET ANYWHERE IF YOU KEEP LOOKING DOWN, YOU HEAR?
WHEN THE GOING GETS TOUGH, YOU HAVE TO LOOK AHEAD.
AHEAD ...?
THAT'S RIGHT.
WHEN THERE'S SOME-THING YOU WANT, YOU HAVE TO REACH OUT FOR IT.
AND IF YOU STILL CAN'T REACH, JUST STRETCH EVEN FARTHER FOR IT.
THAT WAY, EVENTUALLY...
...YOU'LL GET WHATEVER IT IS.
PACHAAAN (SPLOOOSH)
ピチャ。アァン

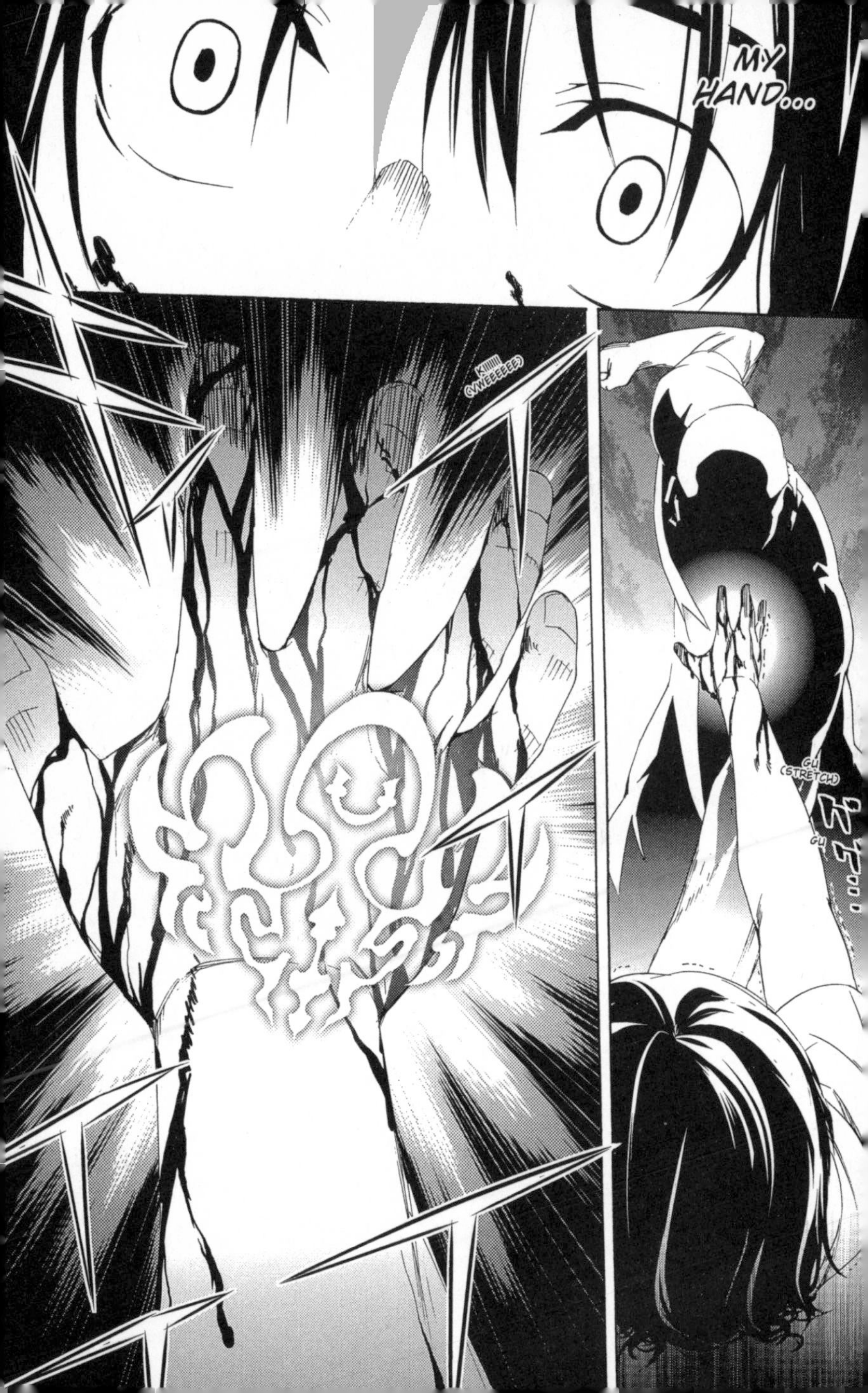
MY HAND...
GU (STRETCH)
GU
KIIIIII (VWEEEEEE)

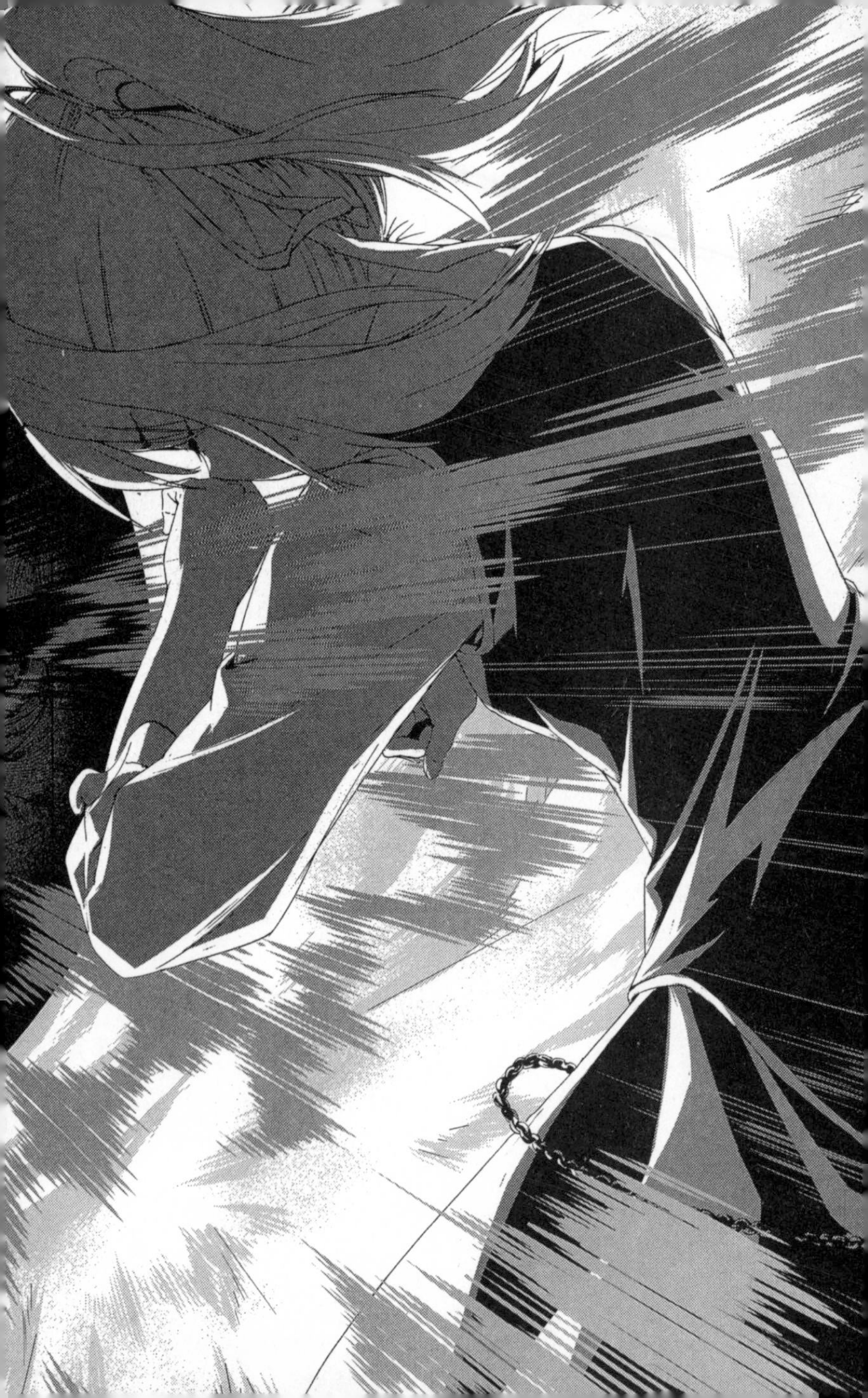

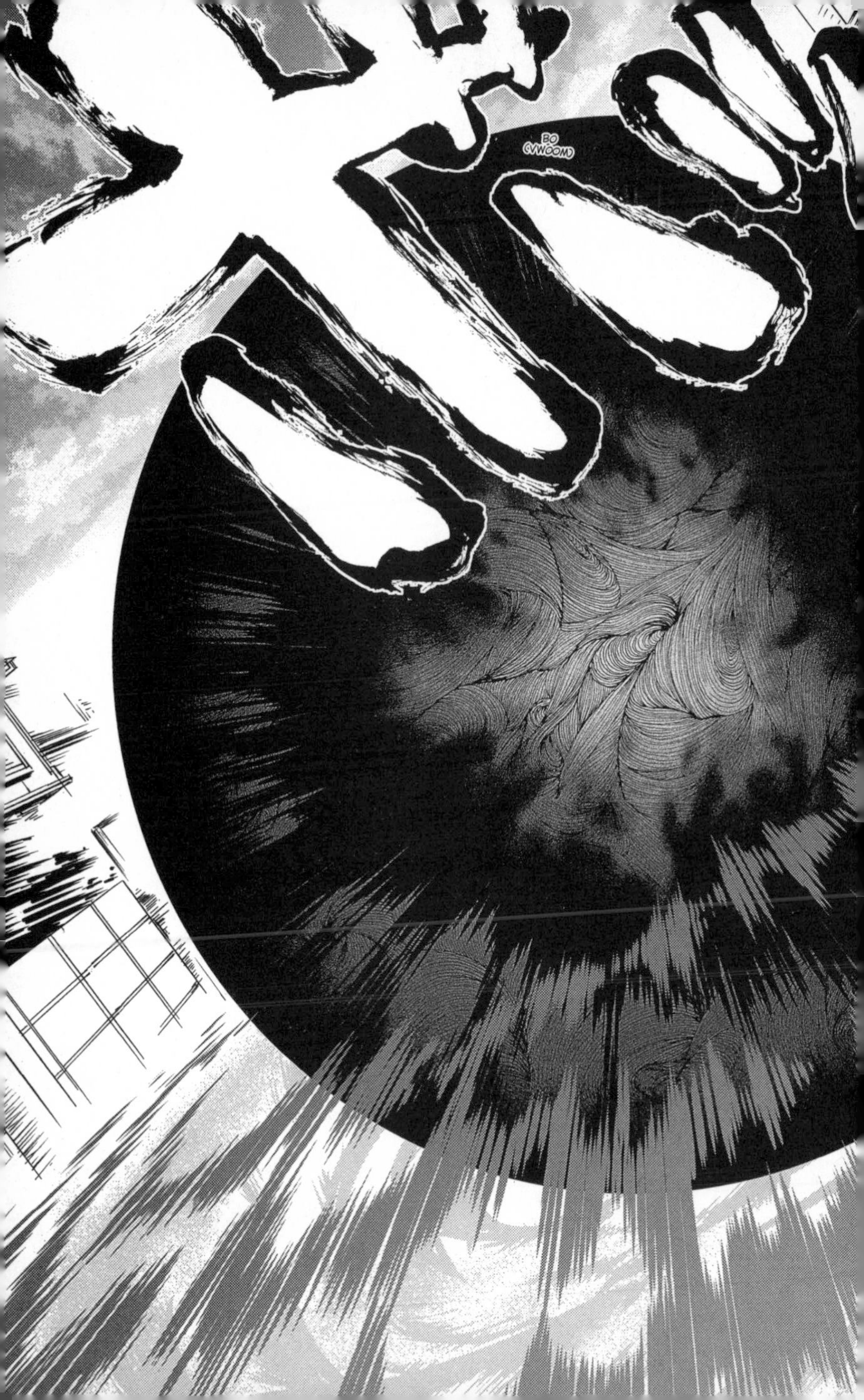
BO
(VWOOM)

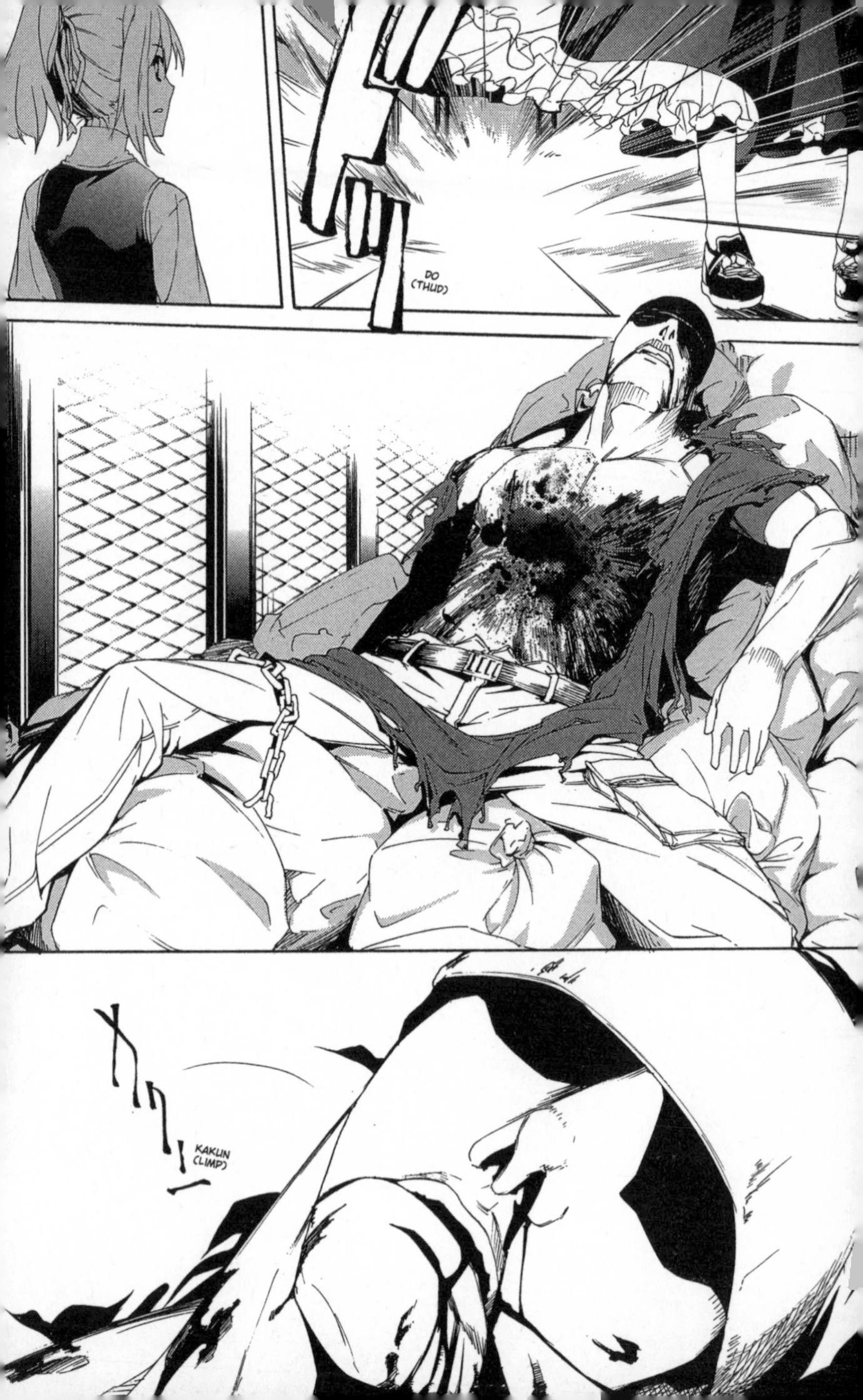
DO
(THUD)
KAKUN
(LIMP)

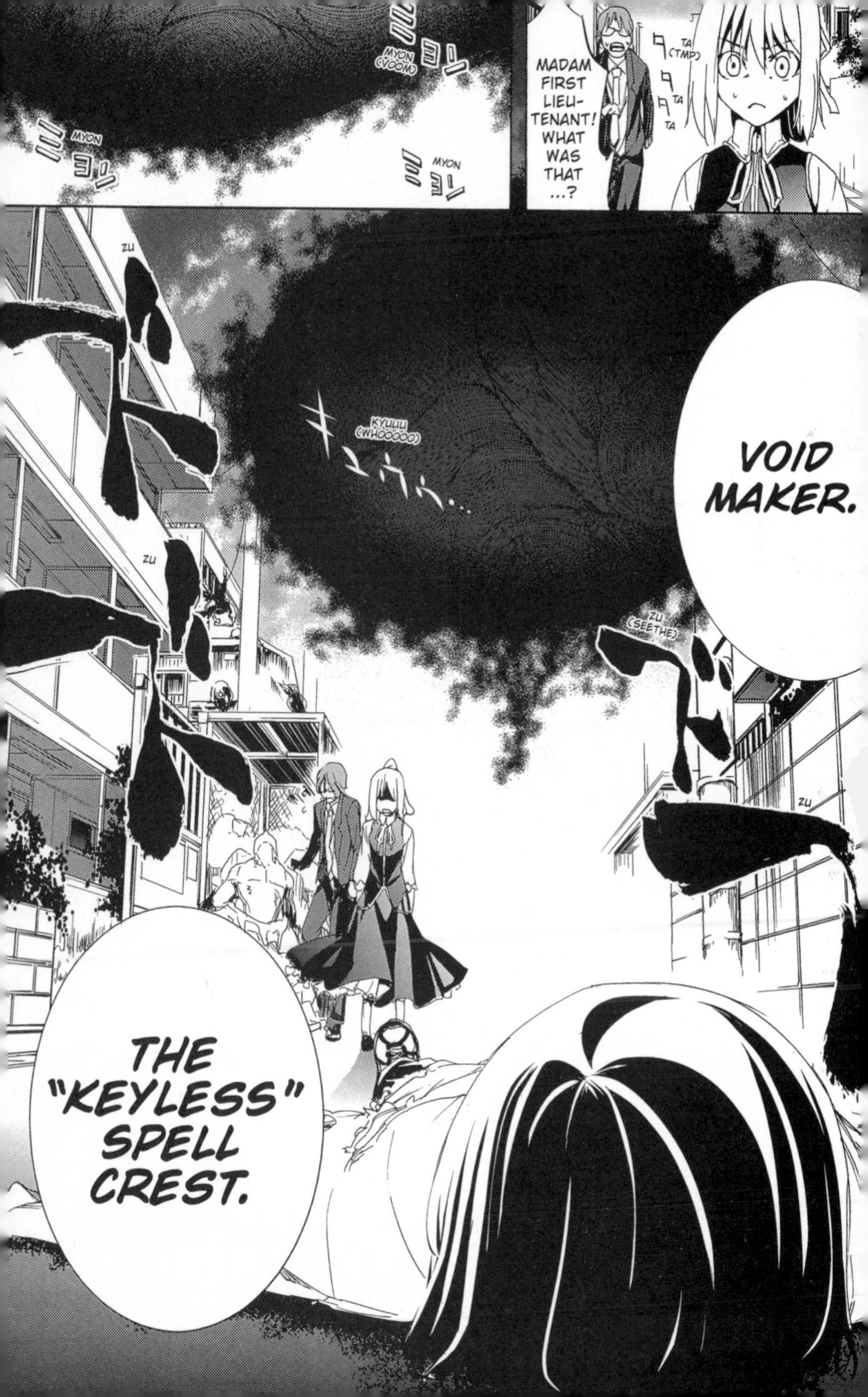
TA (TMP)
TA
TA
MADAM FIRST LIEU- TENANT! WHAT WAS THAT ...?
MYON (VOOM)
MYON
MYON
VOID MAKER.
ZU (SEETHE)
ZU
KYUUU (WHOOOOO)
ZU
ZU
THE "KEYLESS" SPELL CREST.

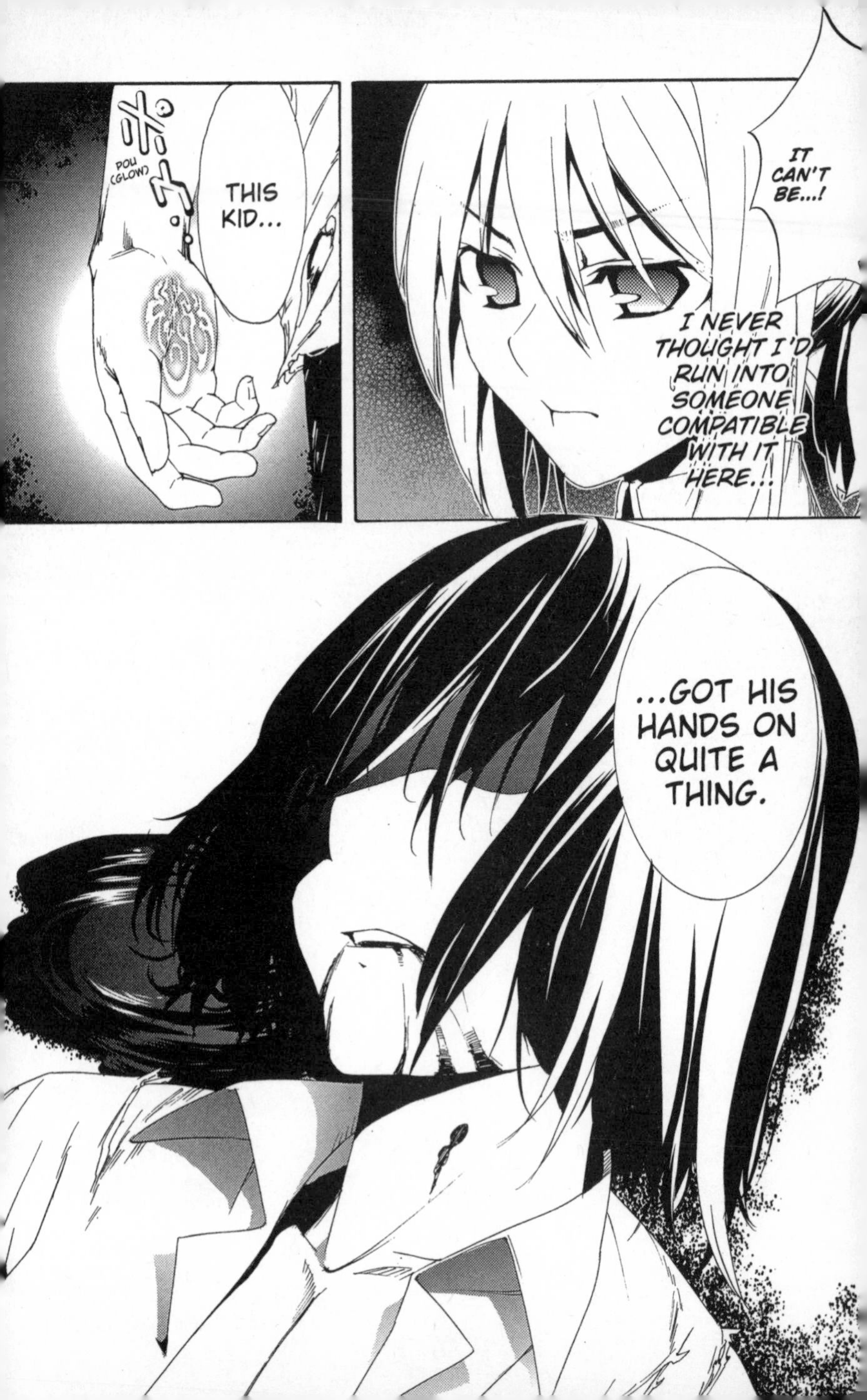
IT CAN'T BE...!
I NEVER THOUGHT I'D RUN INTO SOMEONE COMPATIBLE WITH IT HERE...
POU (GLOW)
THIS KID...
...GOT HIS HANDS ON QUITE A THING.

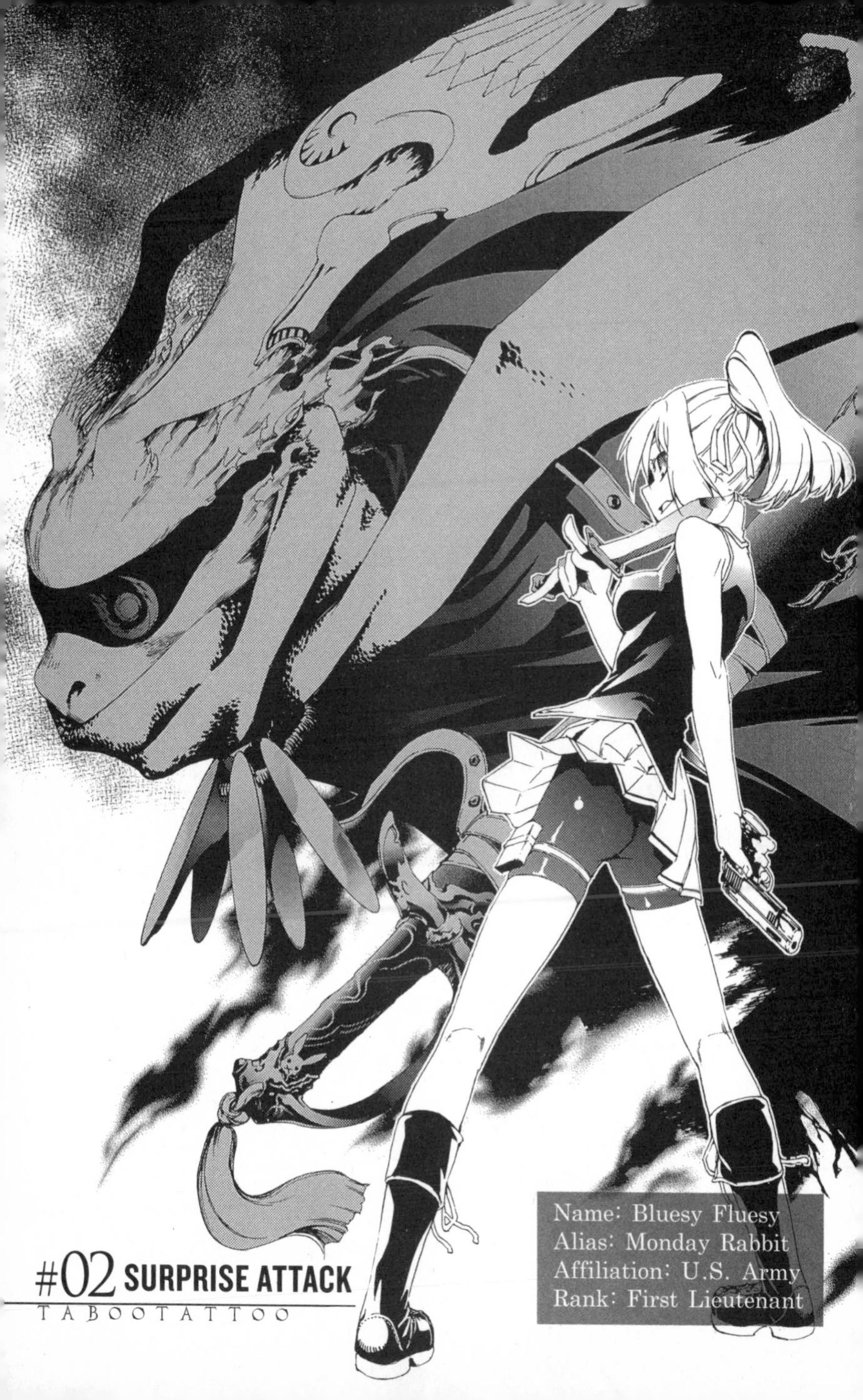
Name: Bluesy Fluesy
Alias: Monday Rabbit
Affiliation: U.S. Army
Rank: First Lieutenant
#02 SURPRISE ATTACK
TABOOTATTOO

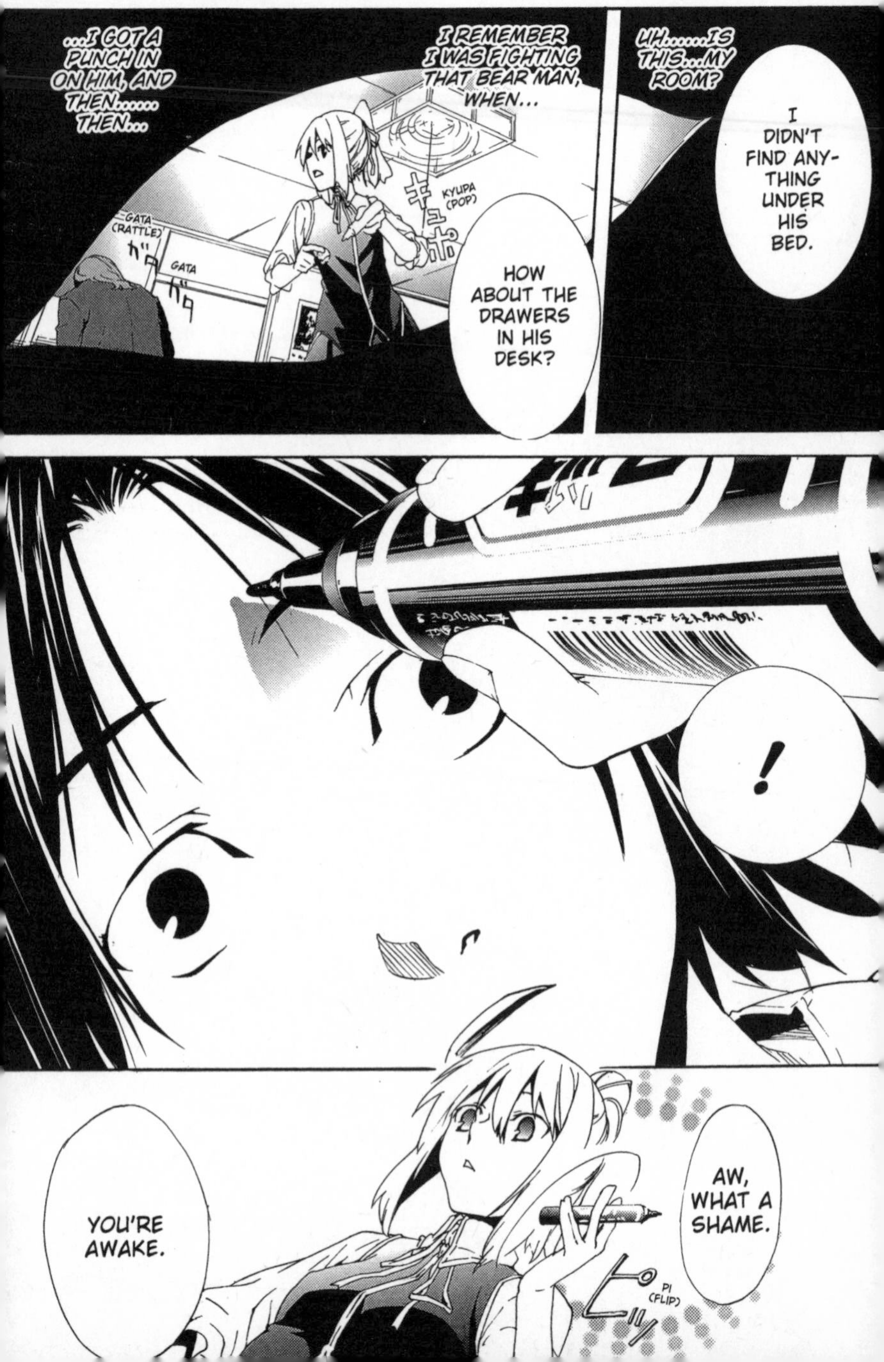
UH......IS THIS...MY ROOM?
I DIDN'T FIND ANY-THING UNDER HIS BED.
I REMEMBER I WAS FIGHTING THAT BEAR MAN, WHEN...
...I GOT A PUNCH IN ON HIM, AND THEN...... THEN...
KYUPA (POP)
HOW ABOUT THE DRAWERS IN HIS DESK?
GATA (RATTLE)
GATA
!
AW, WHAT A SHAME.
PI (FLIP)
YOU'RE AWAKE.

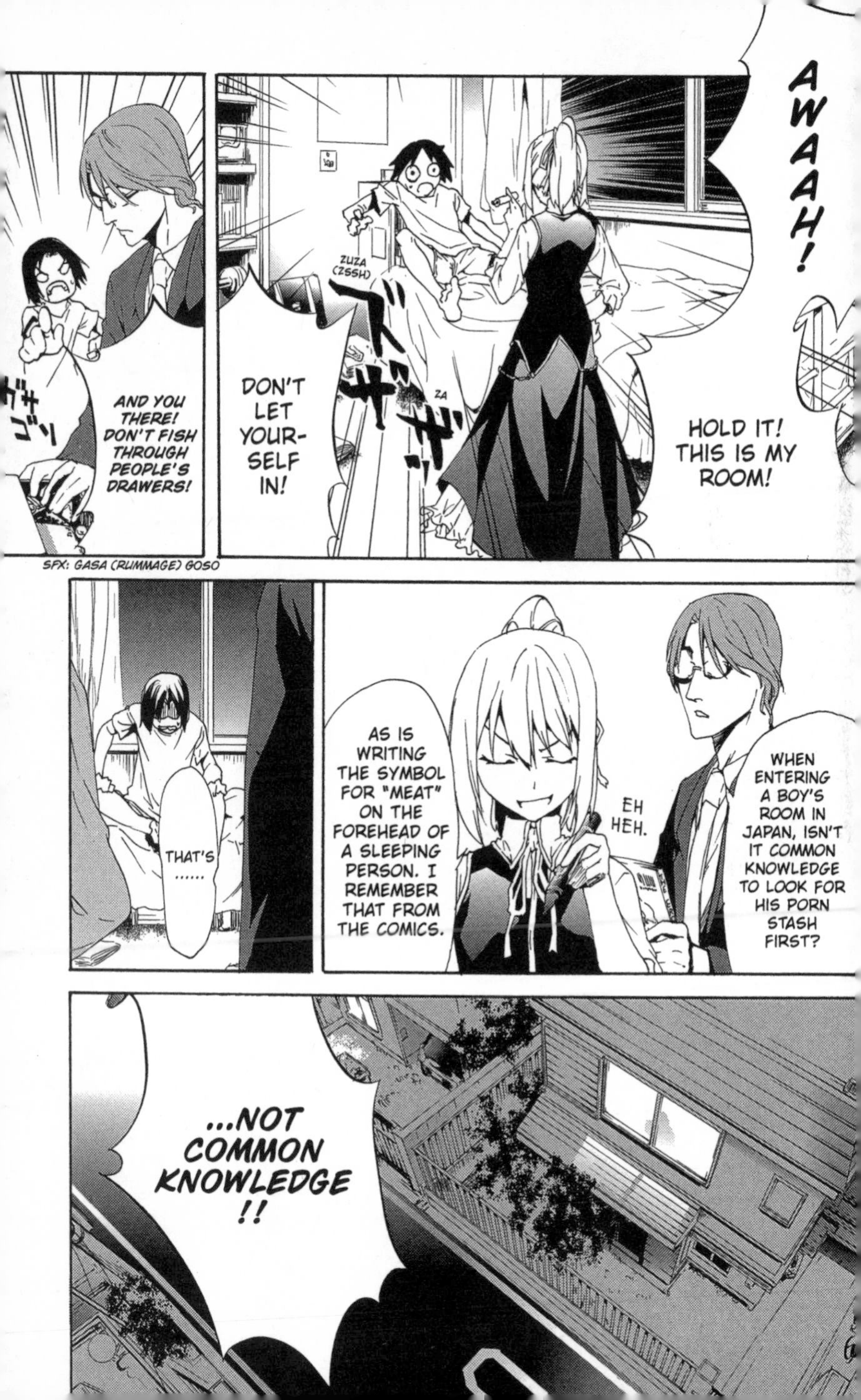
AWAAAH!
HOLD IT! THIS IS MY ROOM!
ZUZA (ZSSH)
ZA
DON'T LET YOURSELF IN!
AND YOU THERE! DON'T FISH THROUGH PEOPLE'S DRAWERS!
SFX: GASA (RUMMAGE) GOSO
WHEN ENTERING A BOY'S ROOM IN JAPAN, ISN'T IT COMMON KNOWLEDGE TO LOOK FOR HIS PORN STASH FIRST?
EH HEH.
AS IS WRITING THE SYMBOL FOR "MEAT" ON THE FOREHEAD OF A SLEEPING PERSON. I REMEMBER THAT FROM THE COMICS.
THAT'S ......
...NOT COMMON KNOWLEDGE!!

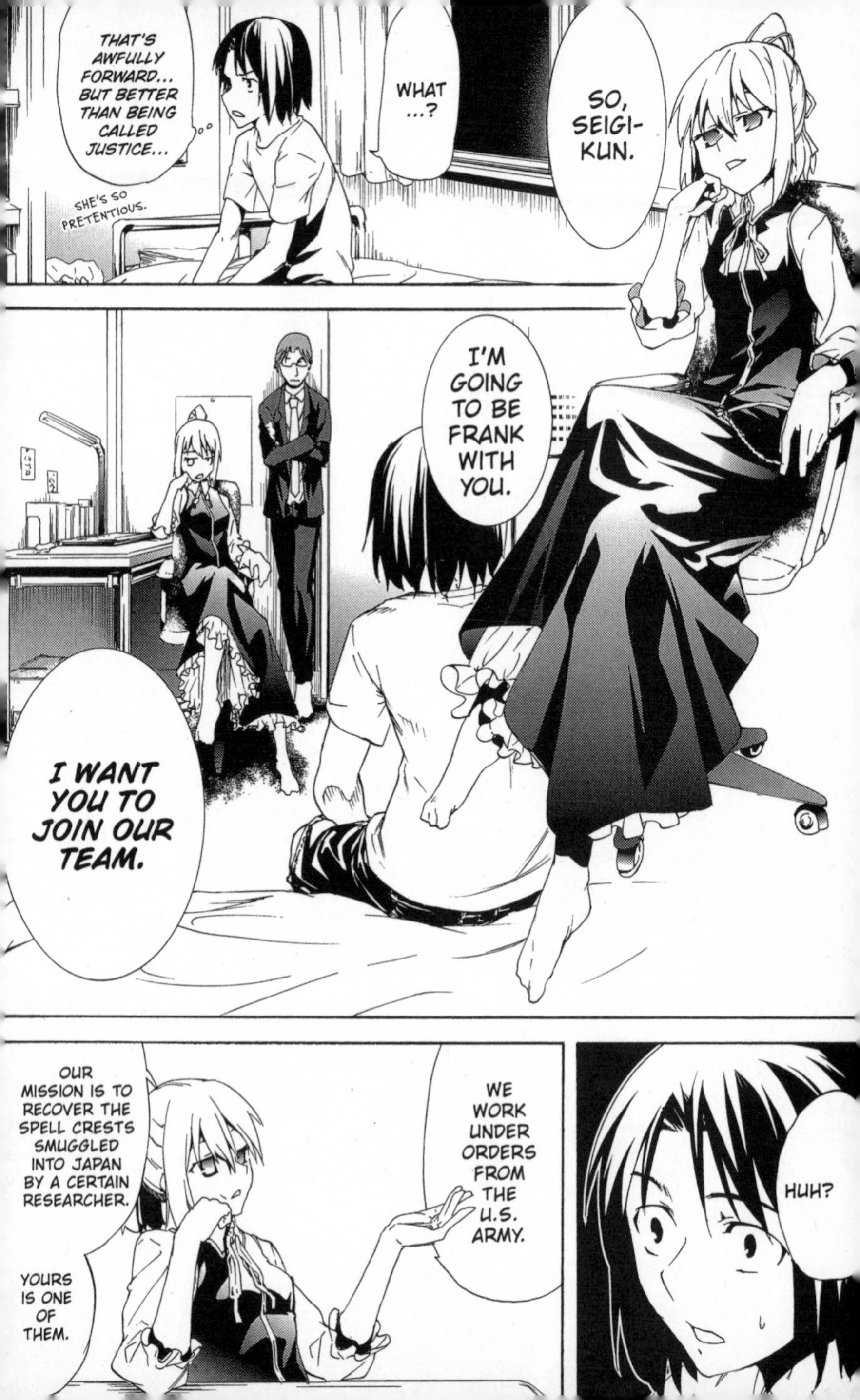
SO, SEIGI-KUN.
WHAT ...?
THAT'S AWFULLY FORWARD... BUT BETTER THAN BEING CALLED JUSTICE...
SHE'S SO PRETENTIOUS.
I'M GOING TO BE FRANK WITH YOU.
I WANT YOU TO JOIN OUR TEAM.
HUH?
WE WORK UNDER ORDERS FROM THE U.S. ARMY.
OUR MISSION IS TO RECOVER THE SPELL CRESTS SMUGGLED INTO JAPAN BY A CERTAIN RESEARCHER.
YOURS IS ONE OF THEM.

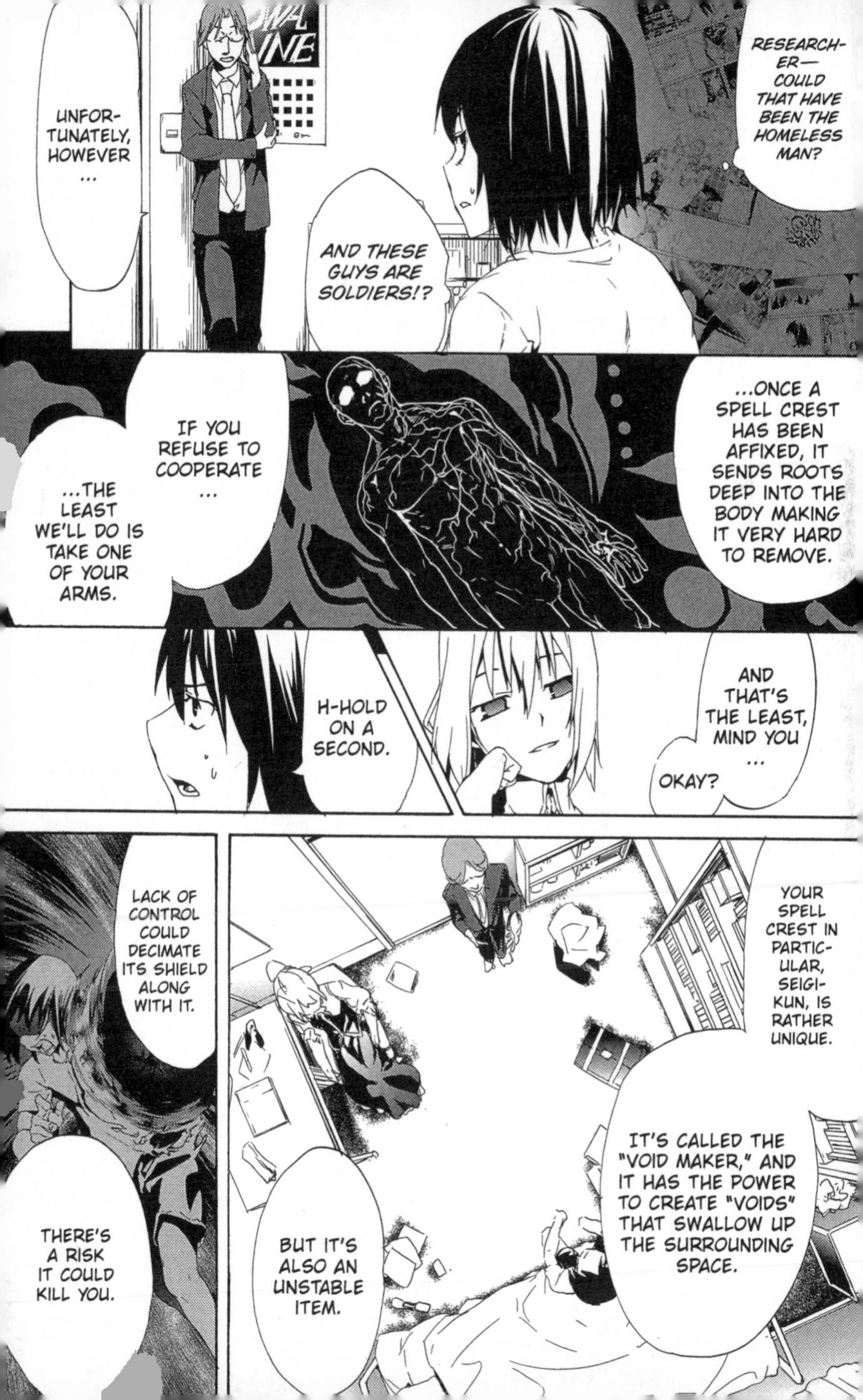
RESEARCHER—COULD THAT HAVE BEEN THE HOMELESS MAN?
AND THESE GUYS ARE SOLDIERS!?
UNFORTUNATELY, HOWEVER ...
...ONCE A SPELL CREST HAS BEEN AFFIXED, IT SENDS ROOTS DEEP INTO THE BODY MAKING IT VERY HARD TO REMOVE.
IF YOU REFUSE TO COOPERATE ...
...THE LEAST WE'LL DO IS TAKE ONE OF YOUR ARMS.
AND THAT'S THE LEAST, MIND YOU ...
OKAY?
H-HOLD ON A SECOND.
YOUR SPELL CREST IN PARTICULAR, SEIGI-KUN, IS RATHER UNIQUE.
IT'S CALLED THE "VOID MAKER," AND IT HAS THE POWER TO CREATE "VOIDS" THAT SWALLOW UP THE SURROUNDING SPACE.
BUT IT'S ALSO AN UNSTABLE ITEM.
LACK OF CONTROL COULD DECIMATE ITS SHIELD ALONG WITH IT.
THERE'S A RISK IT COULD KILL YOU.

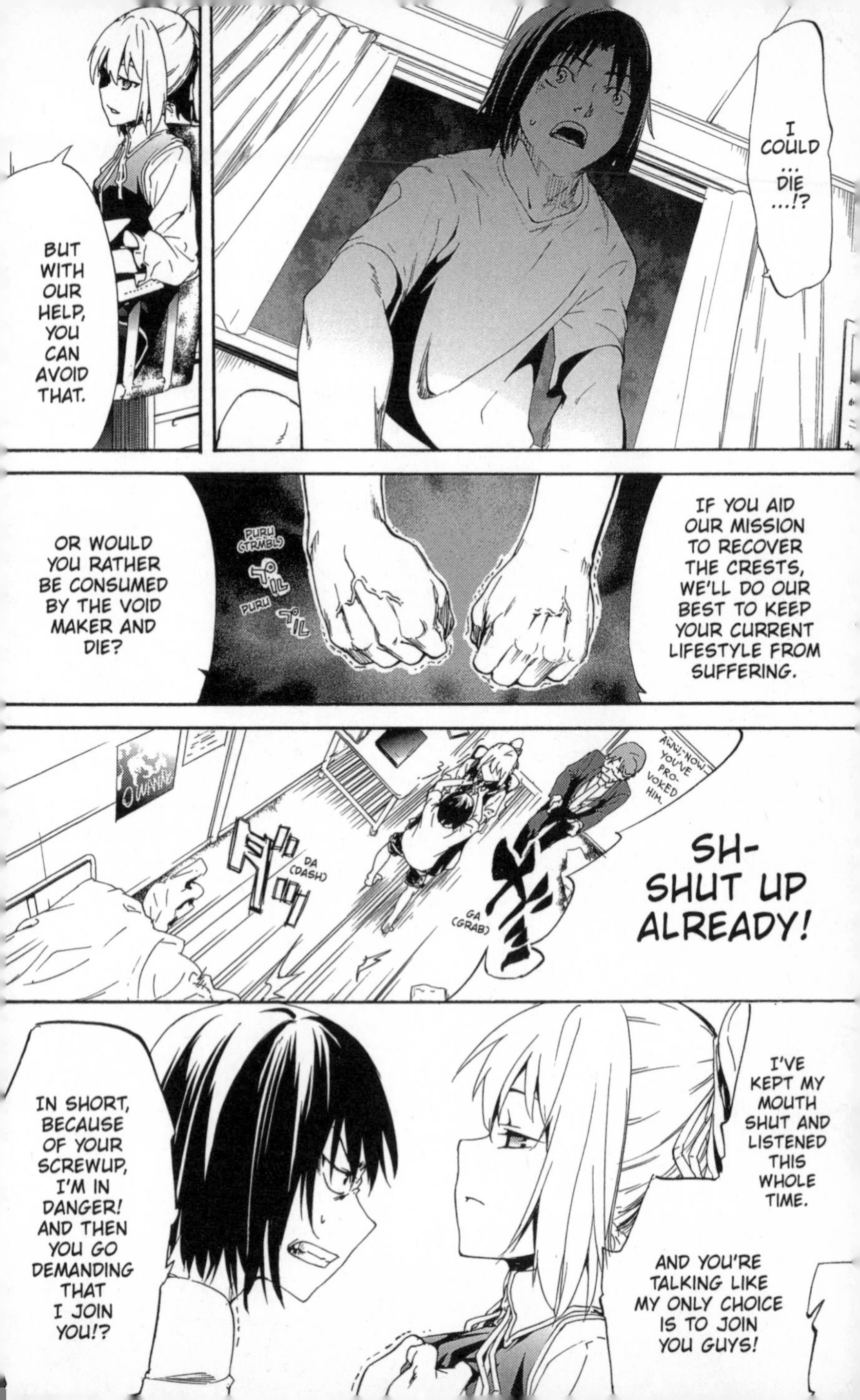
I COULD ... DIE ...!?
BUT WITH OUR HELP, YOU CAN AVOID THAT.
IF YOU AID OUR MISSION TO RECOVER THE CRESTS, WE'LL DO OUR BEST TO KEEP YOUR CURRENT LIFESTYLE FROM SUFFERING.
PURU (TRMBL)
PURU
OR WOULD YOU RATHER BE CONSUMED BY THE VOID MAKER AND DIE?
AWW, NOW YOU'VE PROVOKED HIM.
SH- SHUT UP ALREADY!
GA (GRAB)
DA (DASH)
I'VE KEPT MY MOUTH SHUT AND LISTENED THIS WHOLE TIME.
AND YOU'RE TALKING LIKE MY ONLY CHOICE IS TO JOIN YOU GUYS!
IN SHORT, BECAUSE OF YOUR SCREWUP, I'M IN DANGER! AND THEN YOU GO DEMANDING THAT I JOIN YOU!?

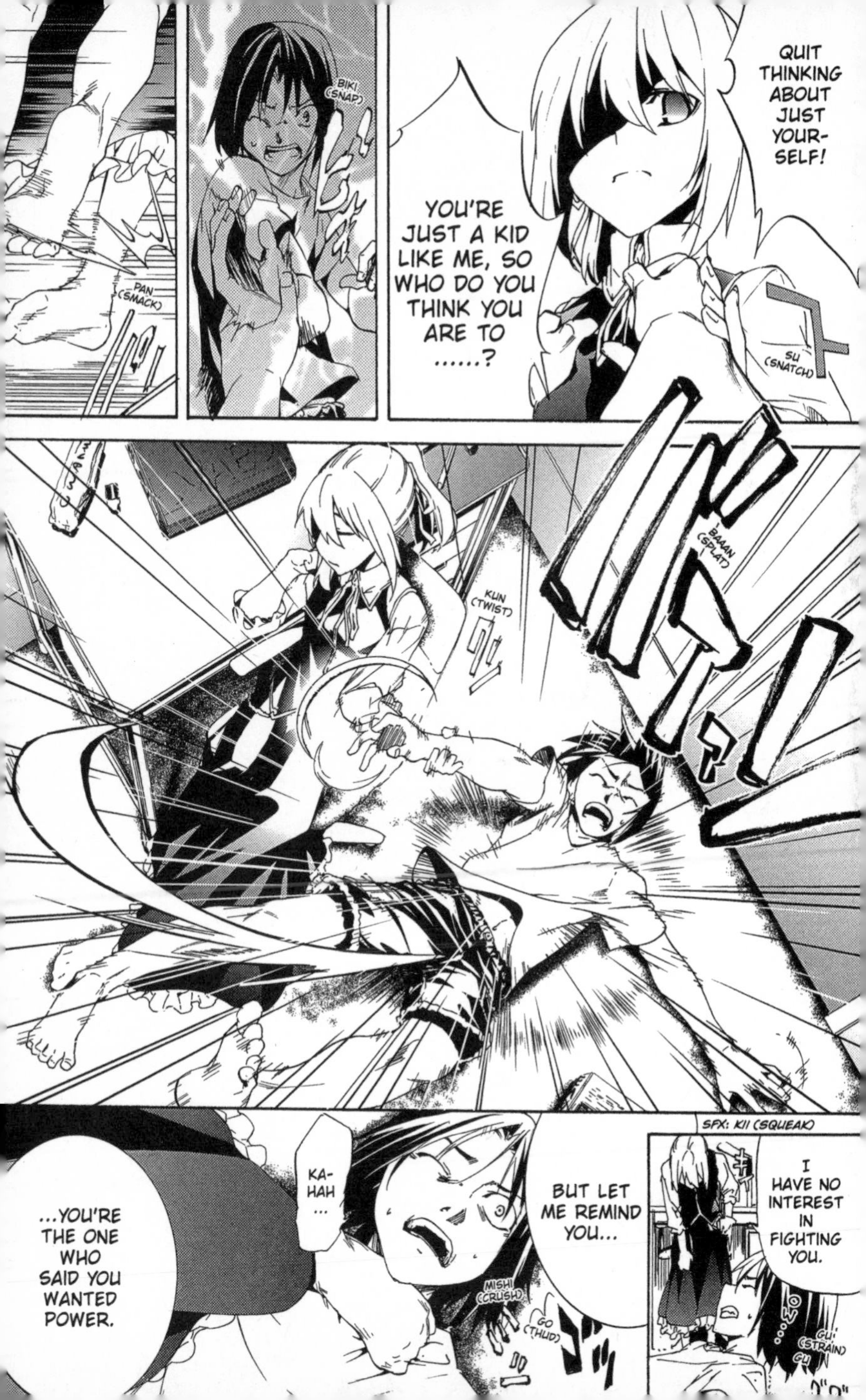
QUIT THINKING ABOUT JUST YOUR-SELF!
YOU'RE JUST A KID LIKE ME, SO WHO DO YOU THINK YOU ARE TO ......?
SU (SNATCH)
BIKI (SNAP)
PAN (SMACK)
BAAAN (SPLAT)
KUN (TWIST)
SFX: KII (SQUEAK)
I HAVE NO INTEREST IN FIGHTING YOU.
GU (STRAIN) GU
BUT LET ME REMIND YOU...
KA-HAH ...
MISHI (CRUSH)
GO (THUD)
...YOU'RE THE ONE WHO SAID YOU WANTED POWER.

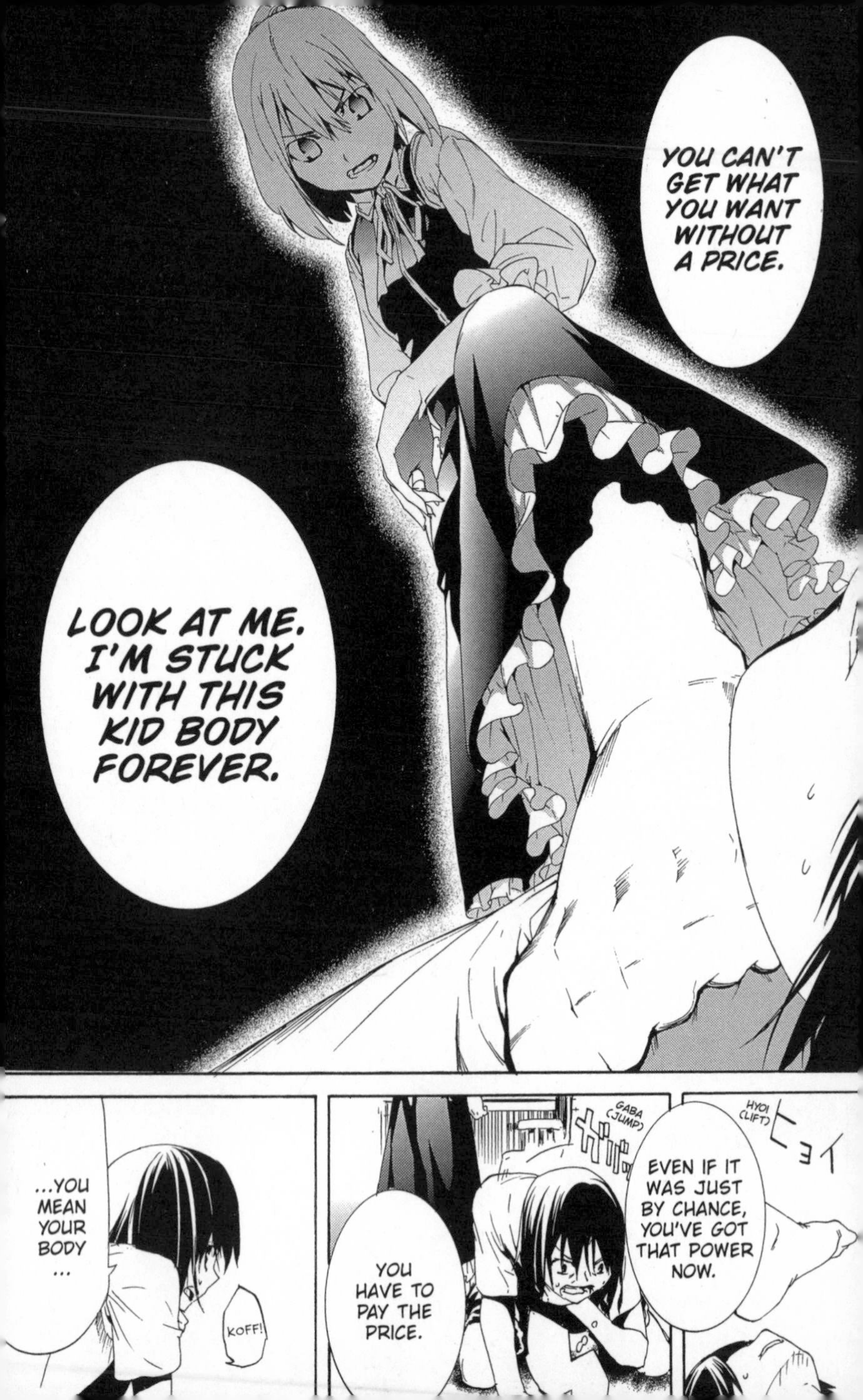
YOU CAN'T GET WHAT YOU WANT WITHOUT A PRICE.
LOOK AT ME. I'M STUCK WITH THIS KID BODY FOREVER.
HYOI (LIFT)
ヒョイ
GABA (JUMP)
ガバッ
EVEN IF IT WAS JUST BY CHANCE, YOU'VE GOT THAT POWER NOW.
YOU HAVE TO PAY THE PRICE.
...YOU MEAN YOUR BODY ...
KOFF!

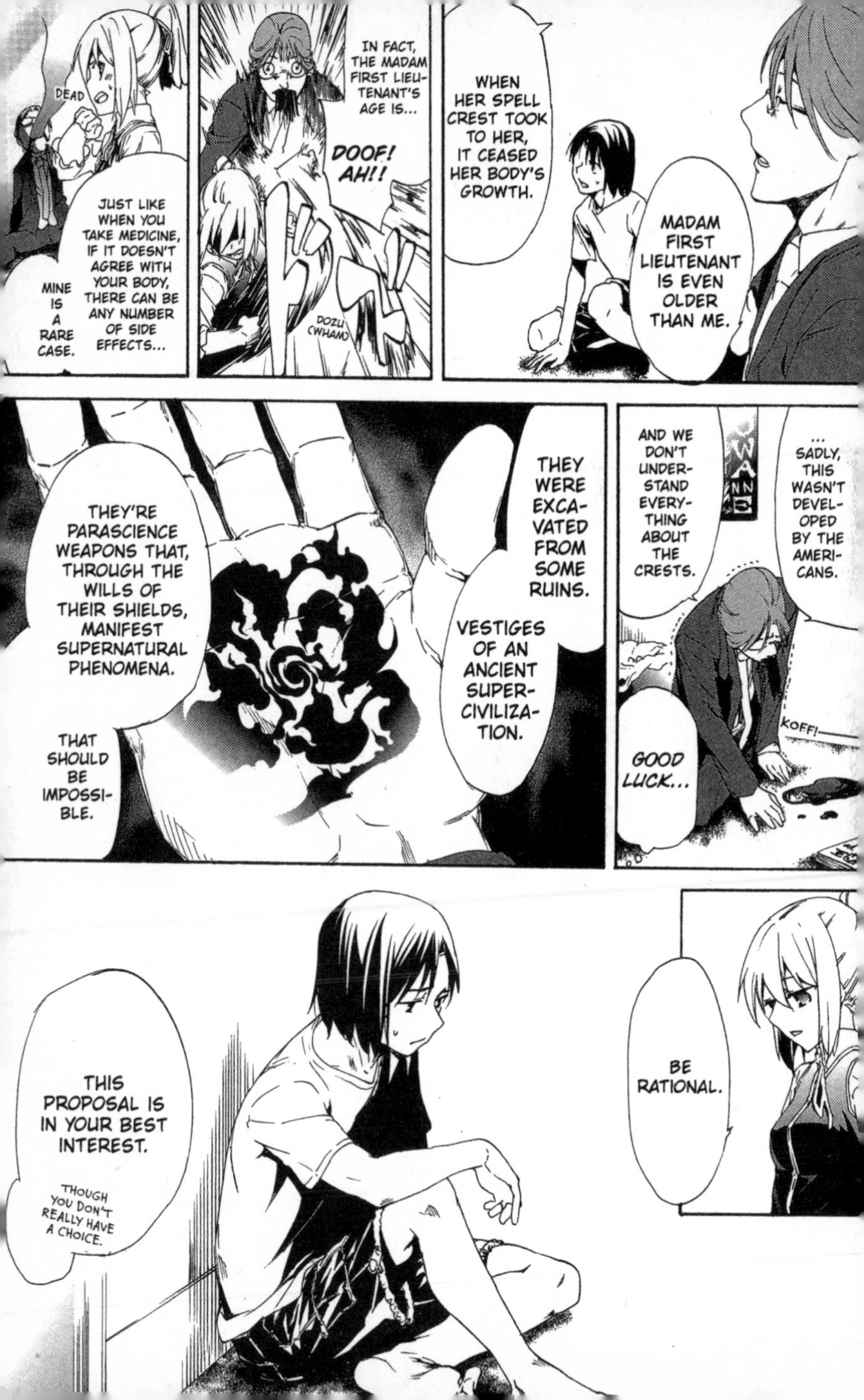
MADAM FIRST LIEUTENANT IS EVEN OLDER THAN ME.
WHEN HER SPELL CREST TOOK TO HER, IT CEASED HER BODY'S GROWTH.
IN FACT, THE MADAM FIRST LIEUTENANT'S AGE IS...
DOOF! AH!!
DOZU (WHAM)
DEAD
JUST LIKE WHEN YOU TAKE MEDICINE, IF IT DOESN'T AGREE WITH YOUR BODY, THERE CAN BE ANY NUMBER OF SIDE EFFECTS...
MINE IS A RARE CASE.
... SADLY, THIS WASN'T DEVELOPED BY THE AMERICANS.
AND WE DON'T UNDERSTAND EVERYTHING ABOUT THE CRESTS.
KOFF!
GOOD LUCK...
THEY WERE EXCAVATED FROM SOME RUINS.
VESTIGES OF AN ANCIENT SUPER-CIVILIZATION.
THEY'RE PARASCIENCE WEAPONS THAT, THROUGH THE WILLS OF THEIR SHIELDS, MANIFEST SUPERNATURAL PHENOMENA.
THAT SHOULD BE IMPOSSIBLE.
BE RATIONAL.
THIS PROPOSAL IS IN YOUR BEST INTEREST.
THOUGH YOU DON'T REALLY HAVE A CHOICE.

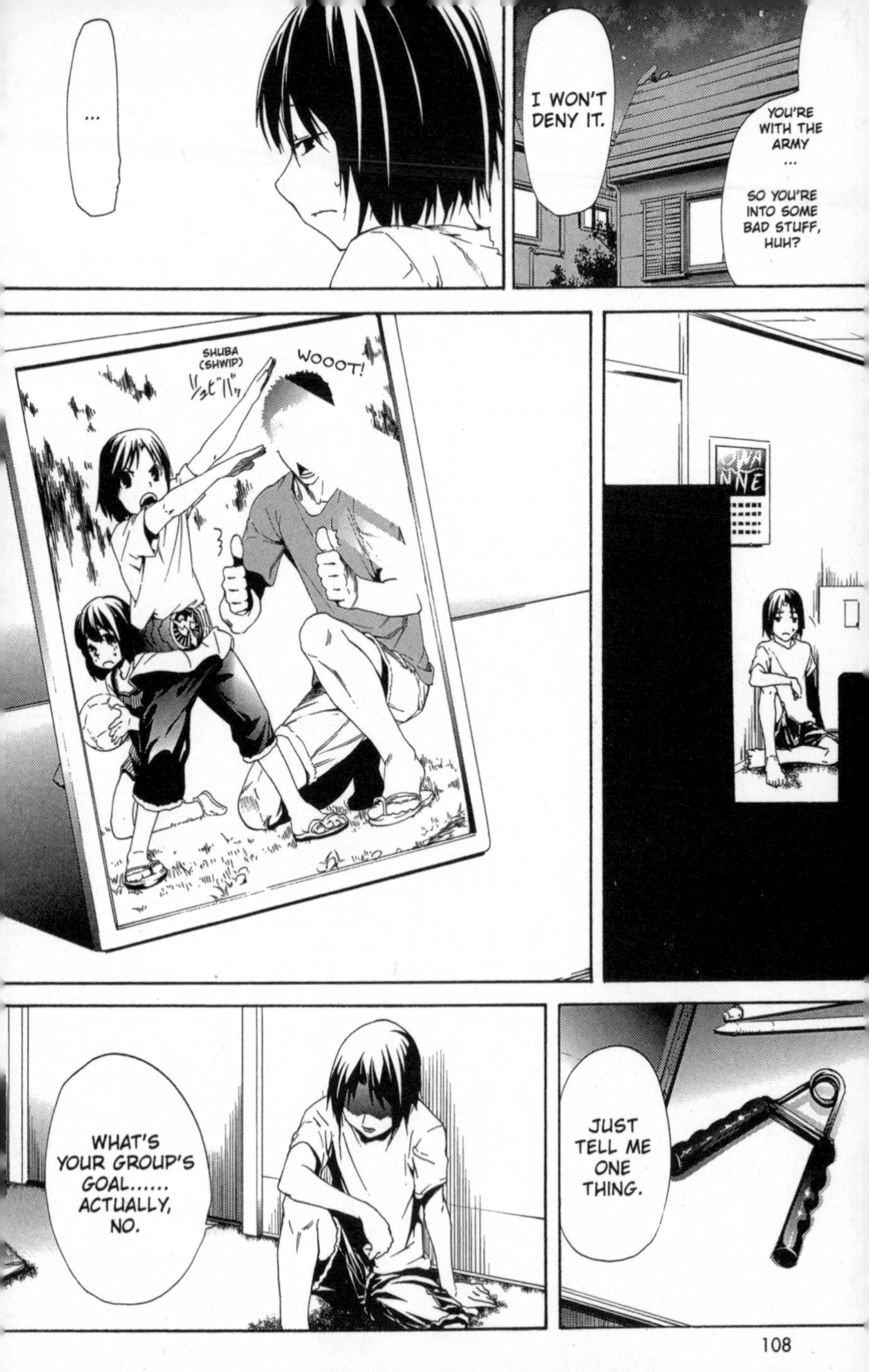
YOU'RE WITH THE ARMY ...
SO YOU'RE INTO SOME BAD STUFF, HUH?
I WON'T DENY IT.
...
WOOOT!
SHUBA (SHWIP)
JUST TELL ME ONE THING.
WHAT'S YOUR GROUP'S GOAL...... ACTUALLY, NO.

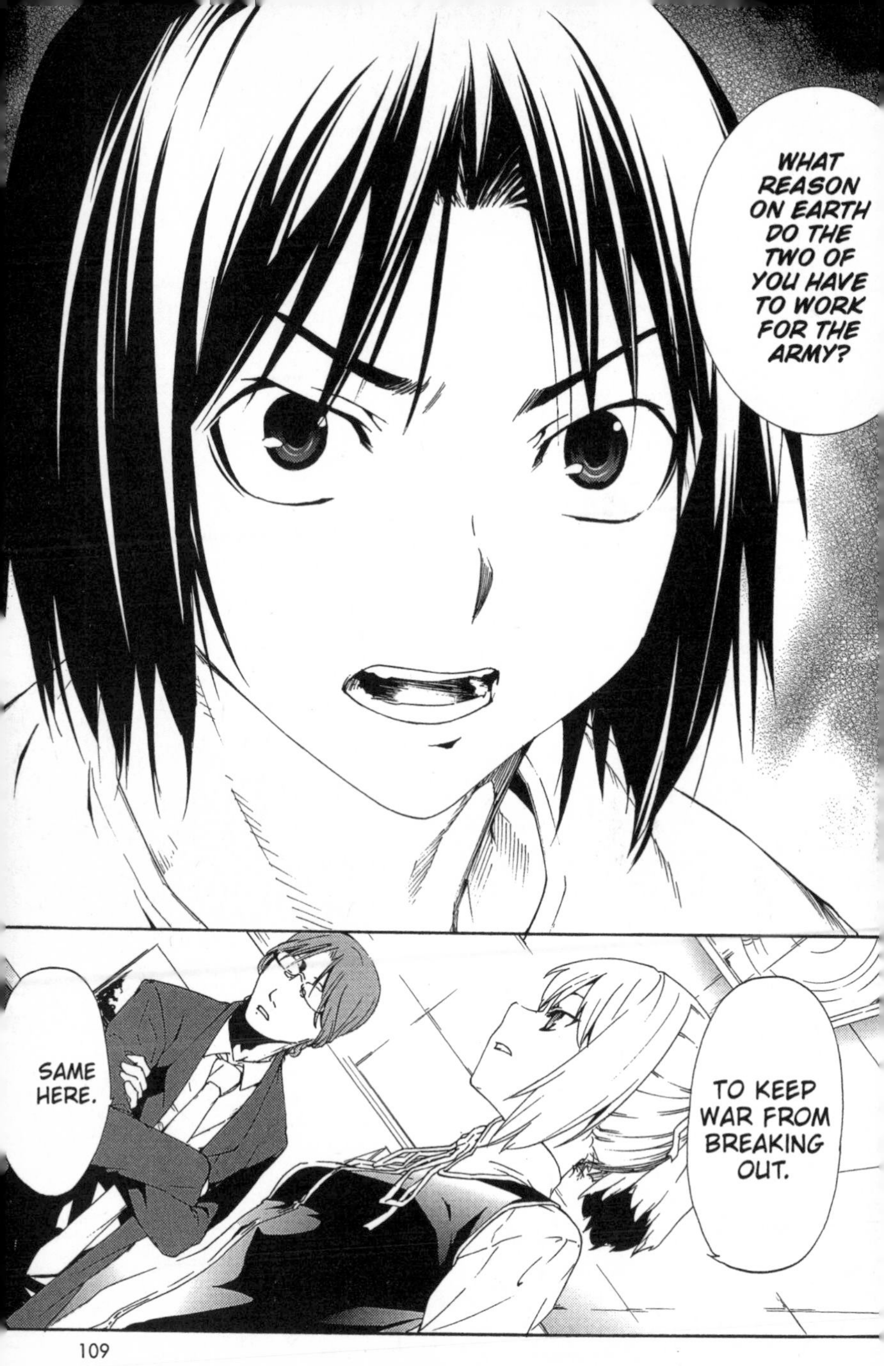
WHAT REASON ON EARTH DO THE TWO OF YOU HAVE TO WORK FOR THE ARMY?
TO KEEP WAR FROM BREAKING OUT.
SAME HERE.

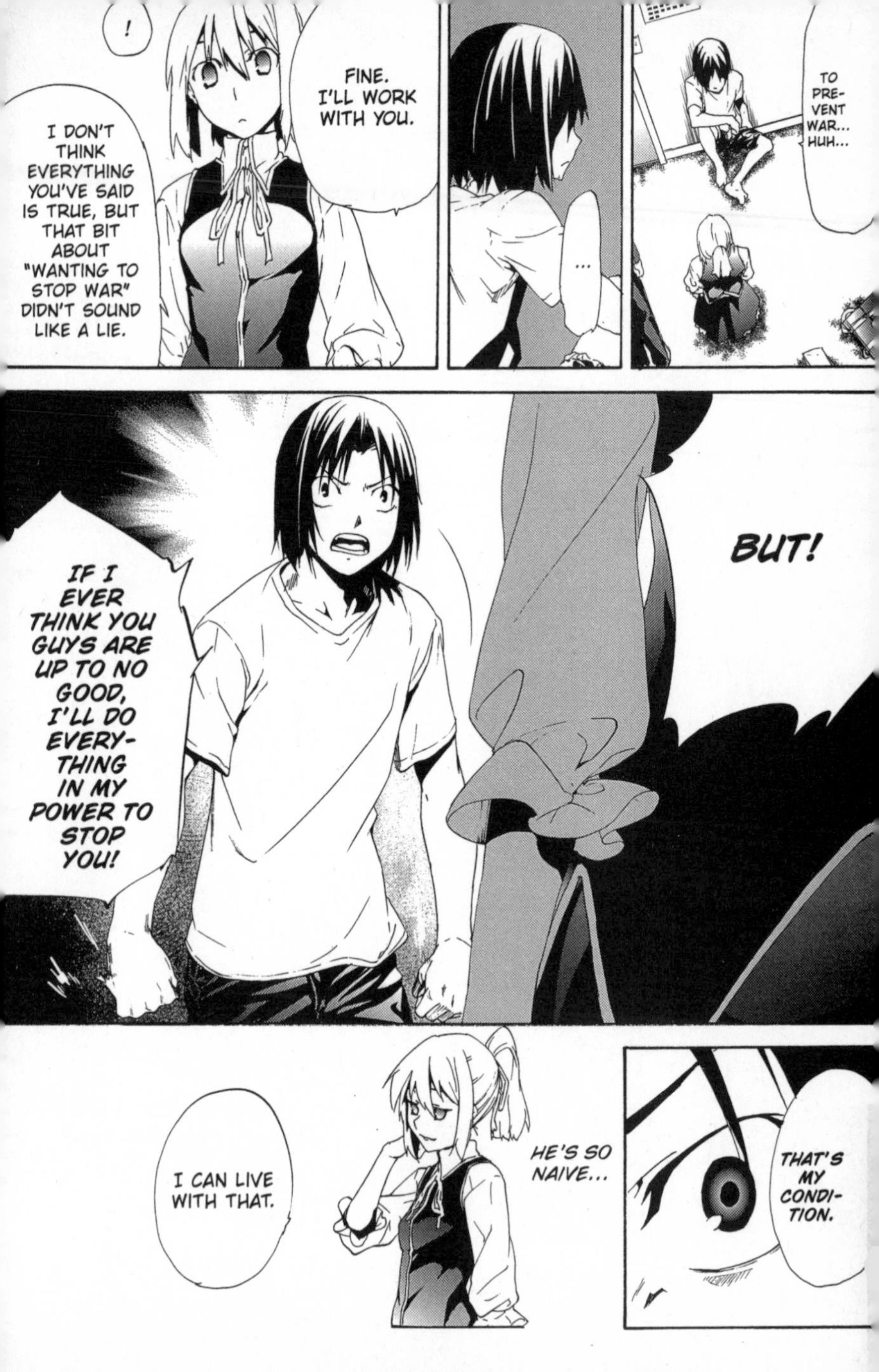
TO PRE-VENT WAR... HUH...
...
FINE. I'LL WORK WITH YOU.
!
I DON'T THINK EVERYTHING YOU'VE SAID IS TRUE, BUT THAT BIT ABOUT "WANTING TO STOP WAR" DIDN'T SOUND LIKE A LIE.
BUT!
IF I EVER THINK YOU GUYS ARE UP TO NO GOOD, I'LL DO EVERY-THING IN MY POWER TO STOP YOU!
THAT'S MY CONDI-TION.
HE'S SO NAIVE...
I CAN LIVE WITH THAT.

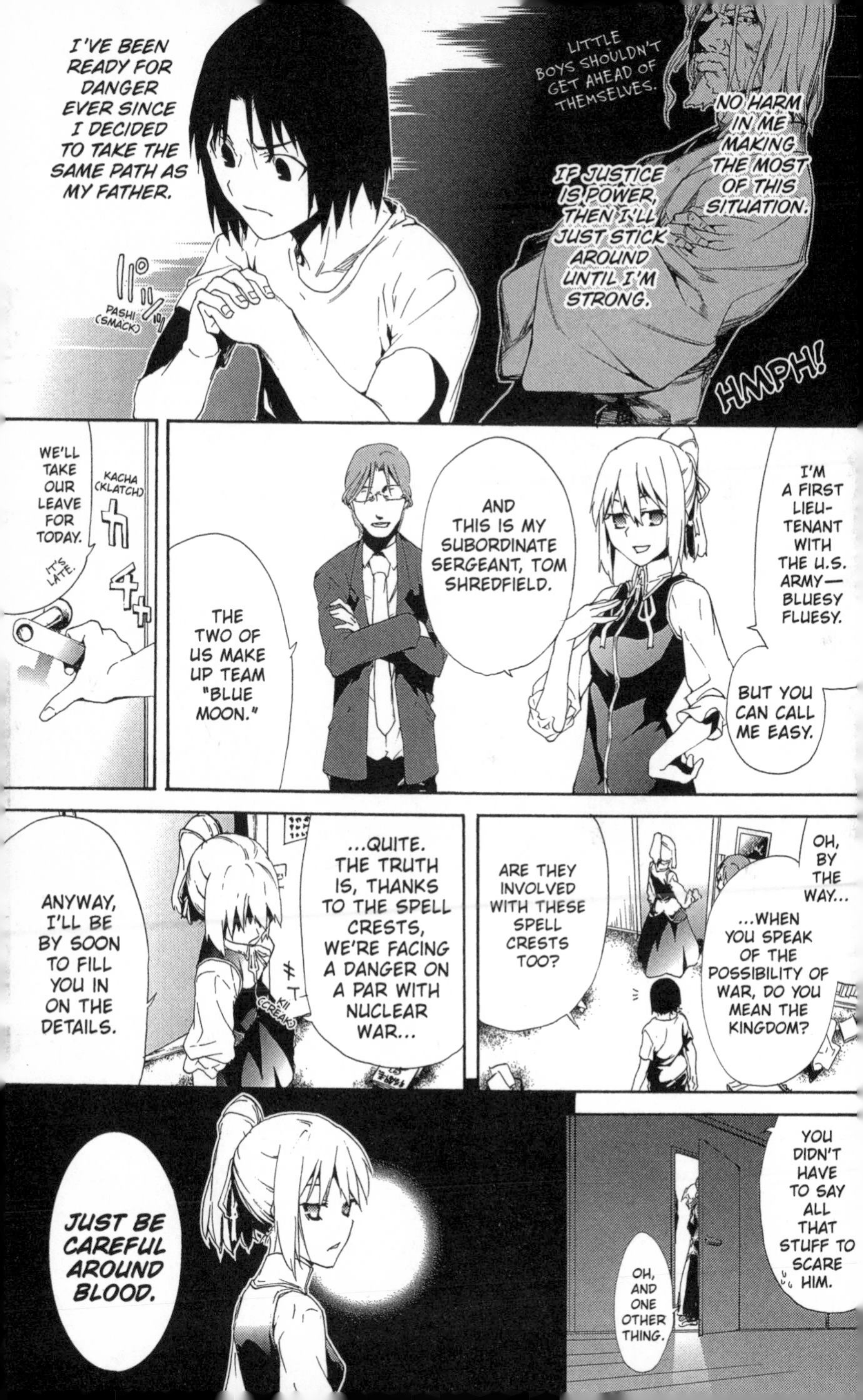
LITTLE BOYS SHOULDN'T GET AHEAD OF THEMSELVES.
NO HARM IN ME MAKING THE MOST OF THIS SITUATION.
IF JUSTICE IS POWER, THEN I'LL JUST STICK AROUND UNTIL I'M STRONG.
HMPH!
I'VE BEEN READY FOR DANGER EVER SINCE I DECIDED TO TAKE THE SAME PATH AS MY FATHER.
PASHI (SMACK)
I'M A FIRST LIEU-TENANT WITH THE U.S. ARMY—BLUESY FLUESY.
BUT YOU CAN CALL ME EASY.
AND THIS IS MY SUBORDINATE SERGEANT, TOM SHREDFIELD.
THE TWO OF US MAKE UP TEAM "BLUE MOON."
WE'LL TAKE OUR LEAVE FOR TODAY.
KACHA (KLATCH)
IT'S LATE.
OH, BY THE WAY...
...WHEN YOU SPEAK OF THE POSSIBILITY OF WAR, DO YOU MEAN THE KINGDOM?
ARE THEY INVOLVED WITH THESE SPELL CRESTS TOO?
...QUITE. THE TRUTH IS, THANKS TO THE SPELL CRESTS, WE'RE FACING A DANGER ON A PAR WITH NUCLEAR WAR...
KII (CREAK)
ANYWAY, I'LL BE BY SOON TO FILL YOU IN ON THE DETAILS.
YOU DIDN'T HAVE TO SAY ALL THAT STUFF TO SCARE HIM.
OH, AND ONE OTHER THING.
JUST BE CAREFUL AROUND BLOOD.

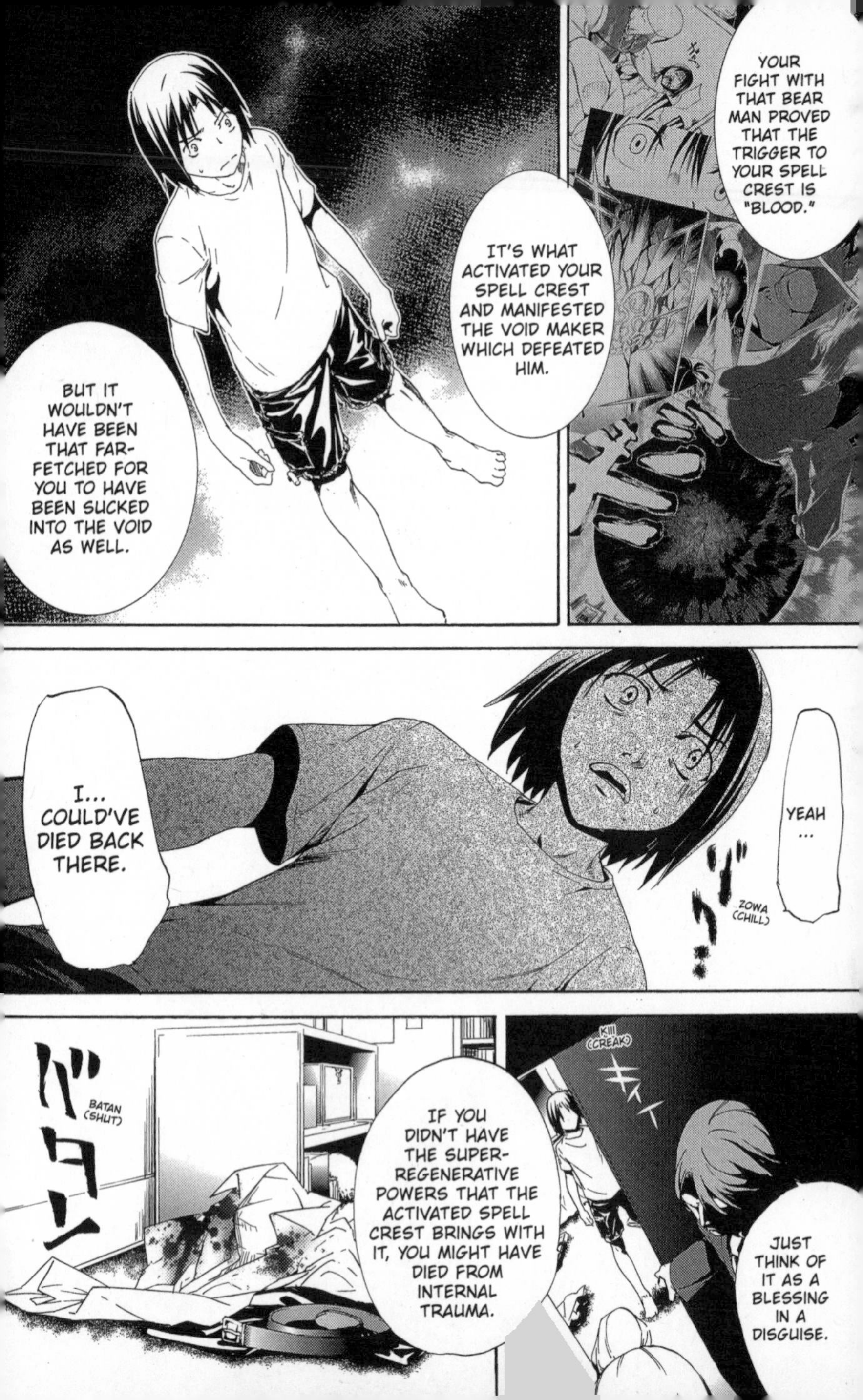
YOUR FIGHT WITH THAT BEAR MAN PROVED THAT THE TRIGGER TO YOUR SPELL CREST IS "BLOOD."
IT'S WHAT ACTIVATED YOUR SPELL CREST AND MANIFESTED THE VOID MAKER WHICH DEFEATED HIM.
BUT IT WOULDN'T HAVE BEEN THAT FAR-FETCHED FOR YOU TO HAVE BEEN SUCKED INTO THE VOID AS WELL.
YEAH ...
ZOWA (CHILL)
I... COULD'VE DIED BACK THERE.
KIII (CREAK)
IF YOU DIDN'T HAVE THE SUPER-REGENERATIVE POWERS THAT THE ACTIVATED SPELL CREST BRINGS WITH IT, YOU MIGHT HAVE DIED FROM INTERNAL TRAUMA.
JUST THINK OF IT AS A BLESSING IN A DISGUISE.
BATAN (SHUT)

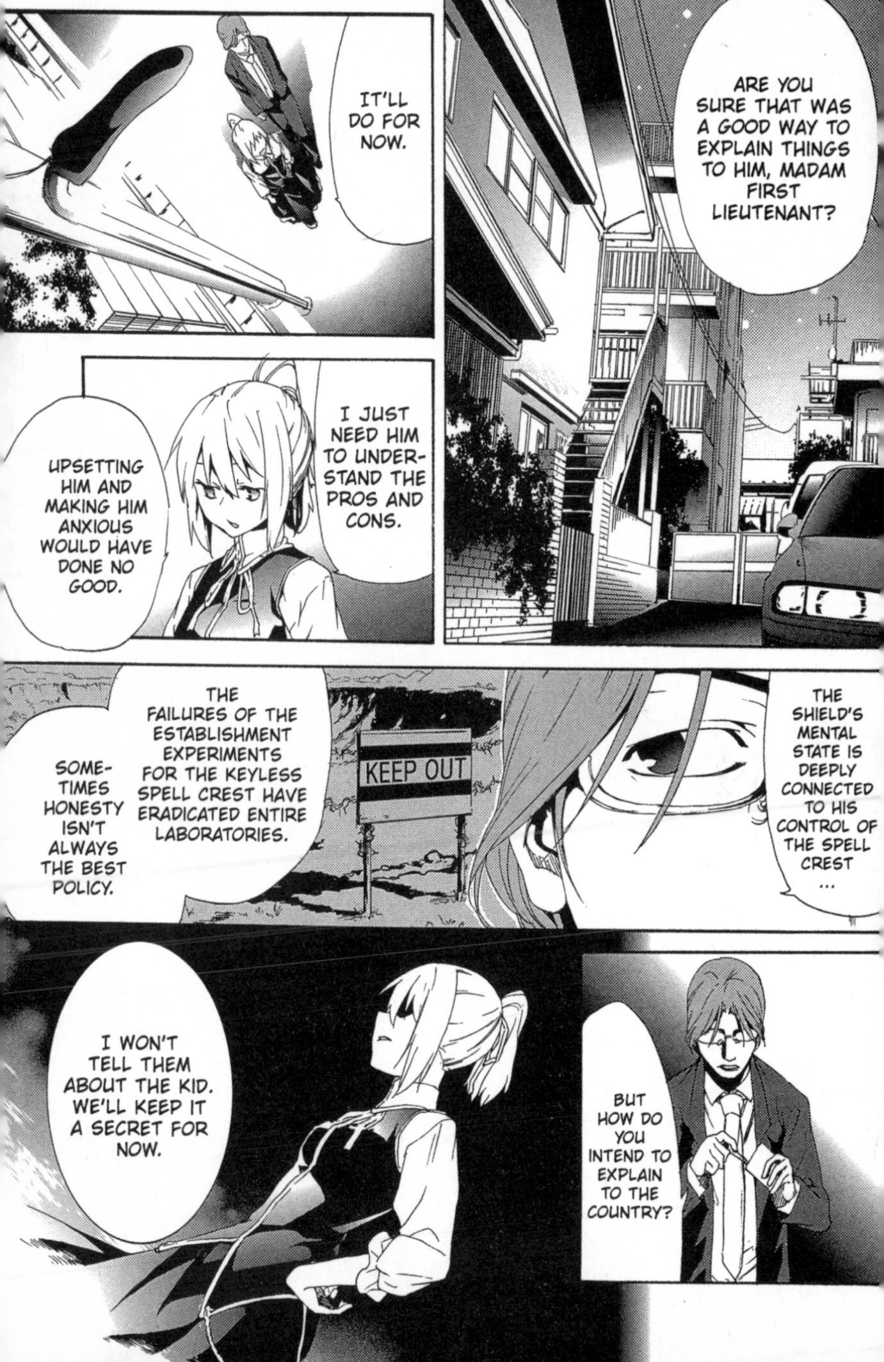
ARE YOU SURE THAT WAS A GOOD WAY TO EXPLAIN THINGS TO HIM, MADAM FIRST LIEUTENANT?
IT'LL DO FOR NOW.
I JUST NEED HIM TO UNDER-STAND THE PROS AND CONS.
UPSETTING HIM AND MAKING HIM ANXIOUS WOULD HAVE DONE NO GOOD.
THE SHIELD'S MENTAL STATE IS DEEPLY CONNECTED TO HIS CONTROL OF THE SPELL CREST ...
KEEP OUT
THE FAILURES OF THE ESTABLISHMENT EXPERIMENTS FOR THE KEYLESS SPELL CREST HAVE ERADICATED ENTIRE LABORATORIES.
SOME-TIMES HONESTY ISN'T ALWAYS THE BEST POLICY.
BUT HOW DO YOU INTEND TO EXPLAIN TO THE COUNTRY?
I WON'T TELL THEM ABOUT THE KID. WE'LL KEEP IT A SECRET FOR NOW.

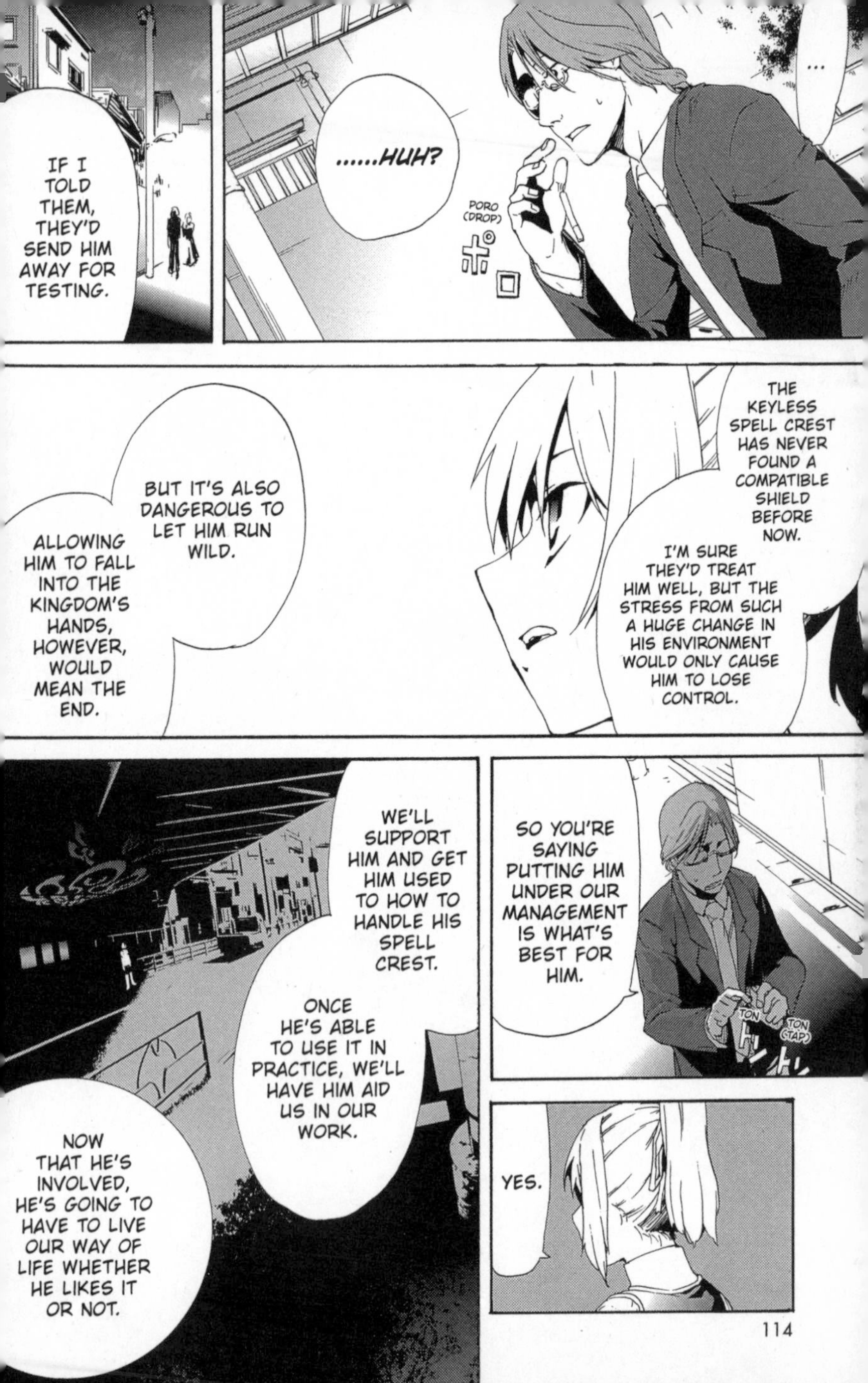
...
......HUH?
PORO (DROP)
IF I TOLD THEM, THEY'D SEND HIM AWAY FOR TESTING.
THE KEYLESS SPELL CREST HAS NEVER FOUND A COMPATIBLE SHIELD BEFORE NOW.
I'M SURE THEY'D TREAT HIM WELL, BUT THE STRESS FROM SUCH A HUGE CHANGE IN HIS ENVIRONMENT WOULD ONLY CAUSE HIM TO LOSE CONTROL.
BUT IT'S ALSO DANGEROUS TO LET HIM RUN WILD.
ALLOWING HIM TO FALL INTO THE KINGDOM'S HANDS, HOWEVER, WOULD MEAN THE END.
SO YOU'RE SAYING PUTTING HIM UNDER OUR MANAGEMENT IS WHAT'S BEST FOR HIM.
TON TON (TAP)
YES.
WE'LL SUPPORT HIM AND GET HIM USED TO HOW TO HANDLE HIS SPELL CREST.
ONCE HE'S ABLE TO USE IT IN PRACTICE, WE'LL HAVE HIM AID US IN OUR WORK.
NOW THAT HE'S INVOLVED, HE'S GOING TO HAVE TO LIVE OUR WAY OF LIFE WHETHER HE LIKES IT OR NOT.

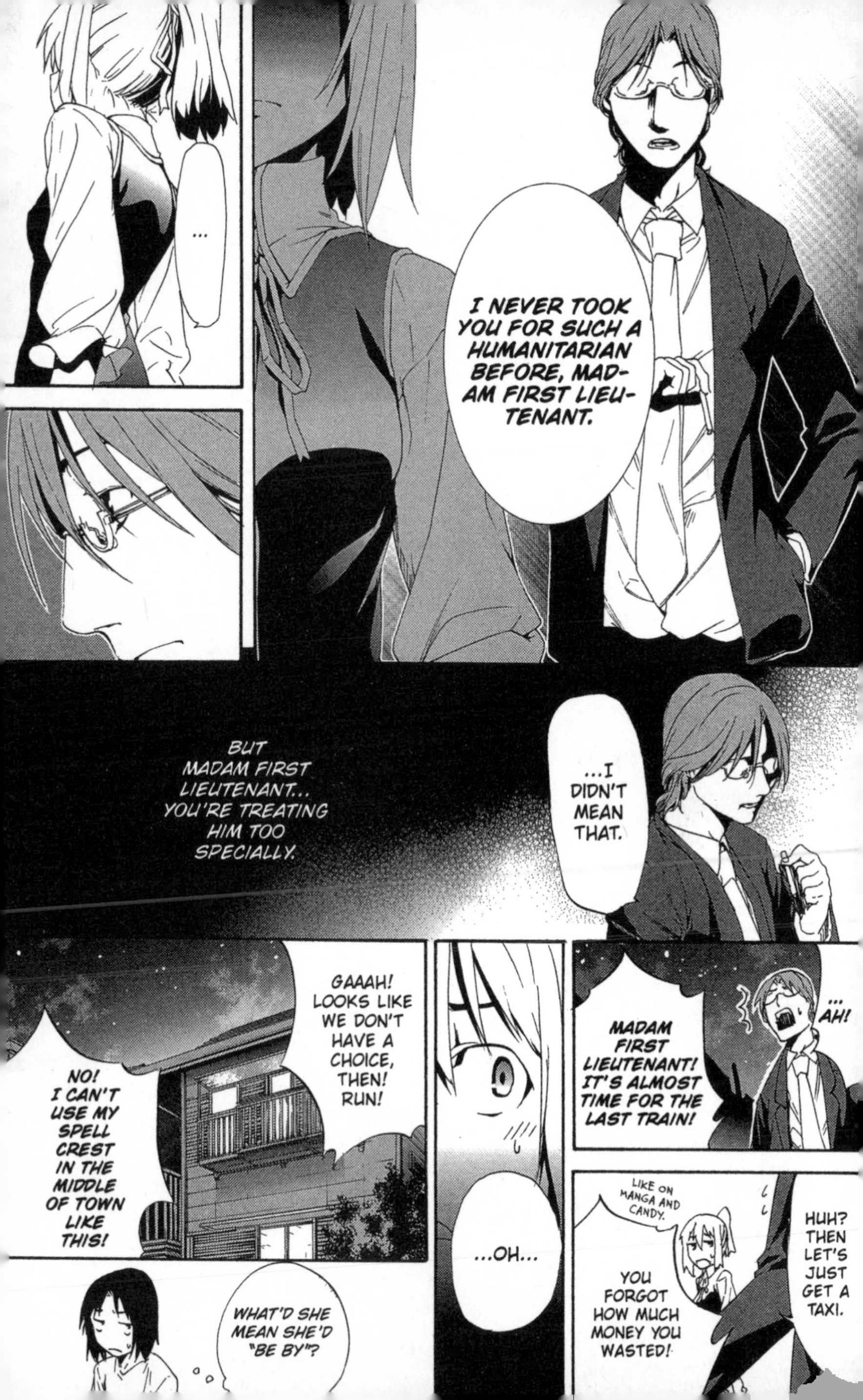
I NEVER TOOK YOU FOR SUCH A HUMANITARIAN BEFORE, MAD-AM FIRST LIEU-TENANT.
...
...I DIDN'T MEAN THAT.
BUT MADAM FIRST LIEUTENANT... YOU'RE TREATING HIM TOO SPECIALLY.
...AH!
MADAM FIRST LIEUTENANT! IT'S ALMOST TIME FOR THE LAST TRAIN!
HUH? THEN LET'S JUST GET A TAXI.
LIKE ON MANGA AND CANDY.
YOU FORGOT HOW MUCH MONEY YOU WASTED!
...OH...
GAAAH! LOOKS LIKE WE DON'T HAVE A CHOICE, THEN! RUN!
NO! I CAN'T USE MY SPELL CREST IN THE MIDDLE OF TOWN LIKE THIS!
WHAT'D SHE MEAN SHE'D "BE BY"?

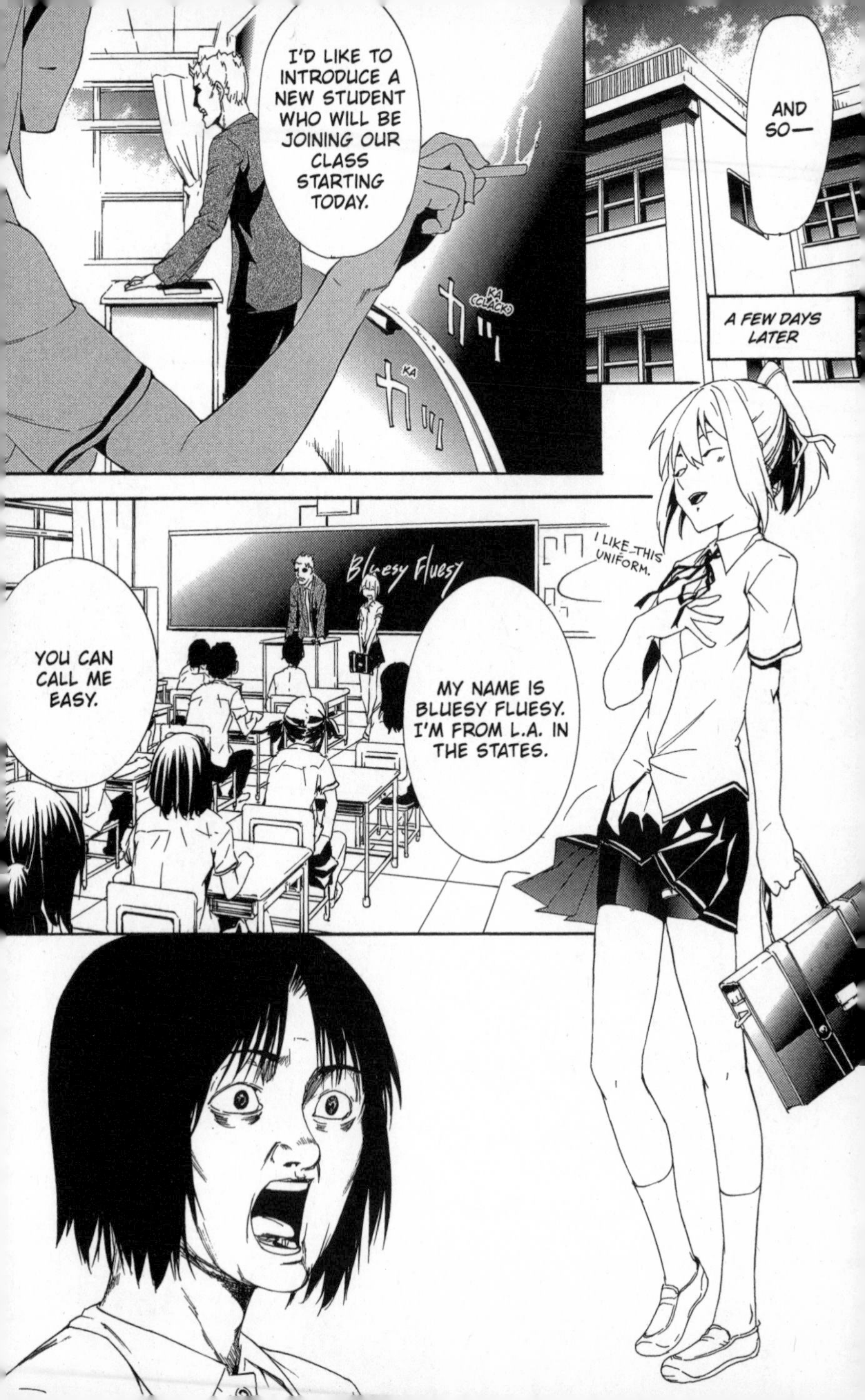
AND SO—
A FEW DAYS LATER
I'D LIKE TO INTRODUCE A NEW STUDENT WHO WILL BE JOINING OUR CLASS STARTING TODAY.
KA (CLACK)
KA
I LIKE THIS UNIFORM.
Bluesy Fluesy
MY NAME IS BLUESY FLUESY. I'M FROM L.A. IN THE STATES.
YOU CAN CALL ME EASY.

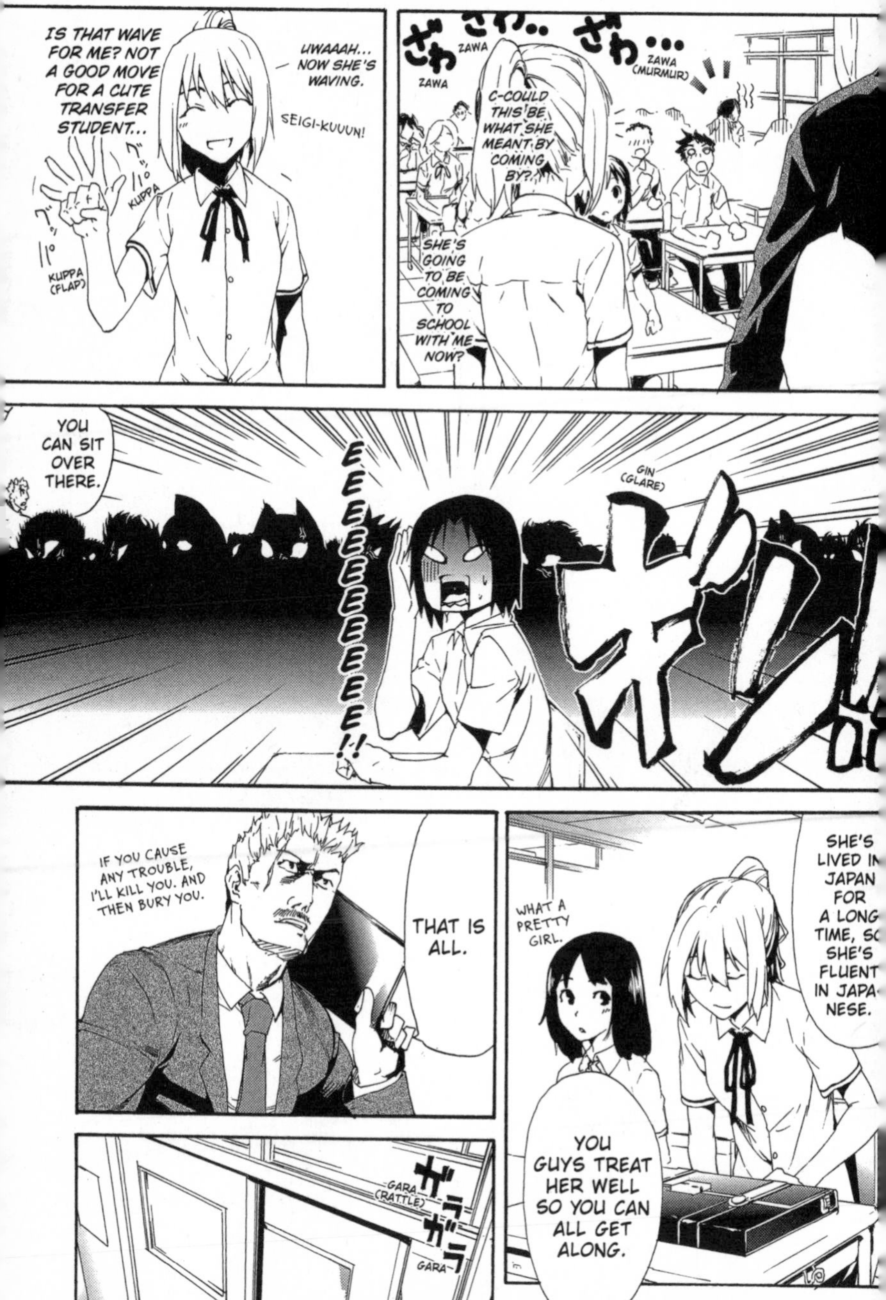

ZAWA
ZAWA
ZAWA (MURMUR)
C-COULD THIS BE WHAT SHE MEANT BY COMING BY?!
SHE'S GOING TO BE COMING TO SCHOOL WITH ME NOW?
UWAAAH... NOW SHE'S WAVING.
SEIGI-KUUUN!
IS THAT WAVE FOR ME? NOT A GOOD MOVE FOR A CUTE TRANSFER STUDENT...
KUPPA
KUPPA (FLAP)
GIN (GLARE)
EEEEEEEEEEEEE!!
YOU CAN SIT OVER THERE.
SHE'S LIVED IN JAPAN FOR A LONG TIME, SO SHE'S FLUENT IN JAPANESE.
WHAT A PRETTY GIRL.
YOU GUYS TREAT HER WELL SO YOU CAN ALL GET ALONG.
THAT IS ALL.
IF YOU CAUSE ANY TROUBLE, I'LL KILL YOU. AND THEN BURY YOU.
GARA (RATTLE)
GARA

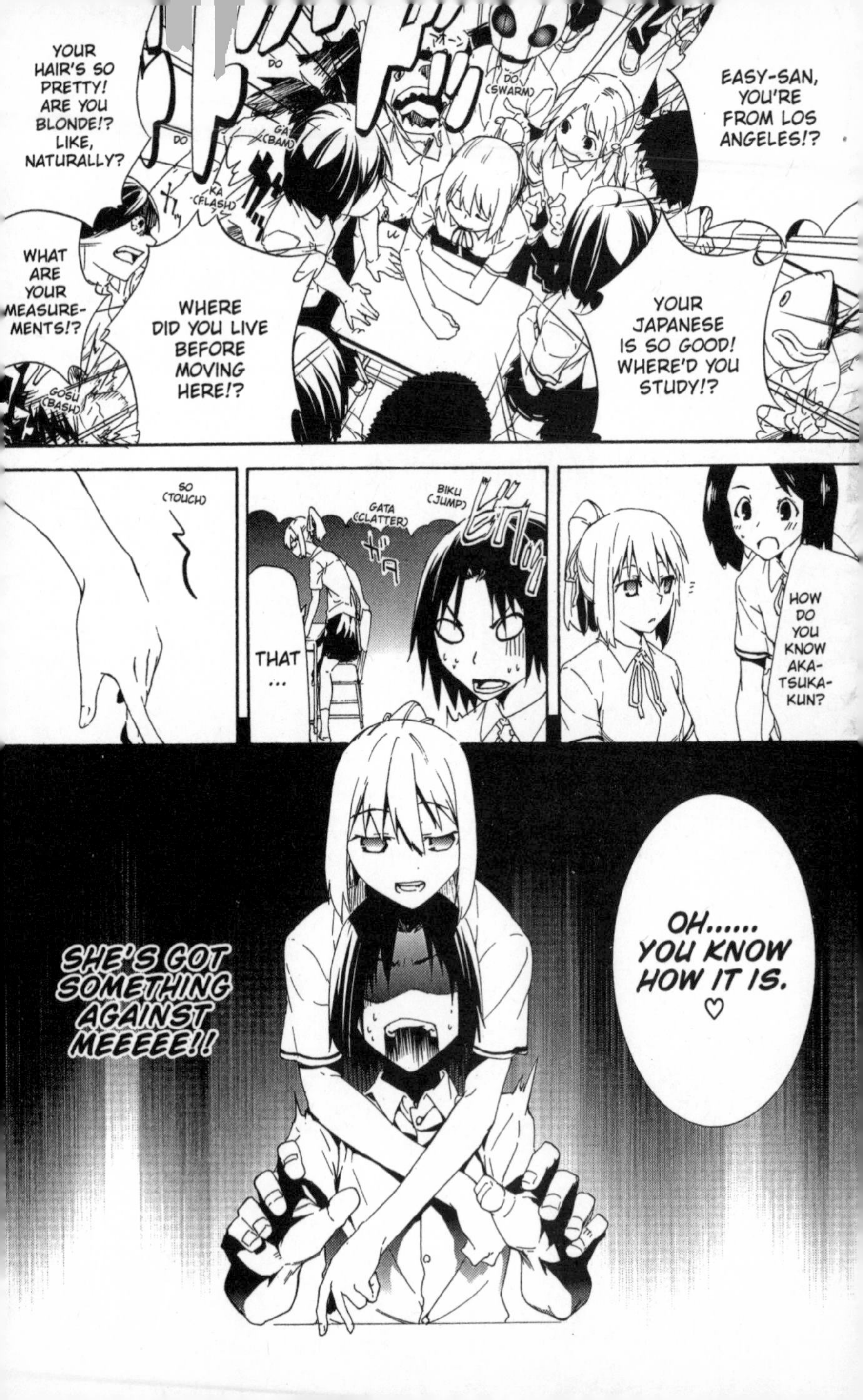
EASY-SAN, YOU'RE FROM LOS ANGELES!?
DO (SWARM)
DO
YOUR HAIR'S SO PRETTY! ARE YOU BLONDE!? LIKE, NATURALLY?
GA (BAM)
DO
KA (FLASH)
YOUR JAPANESE IS SO GOOD! WHERE'D YOU STUDY!?
WHERE DID YOU LIVE BEFORE MOVING HERE!?
WHAT ARE YOUR MEASUREMENTS!?
GOSU (BASH)
HOW DO YOU KNOW AKA-TSUKA-KUN?
BIKU (JUMP)
GATA (CLATTER)
THAT ...
SO (TOUCH)
OH...... YOU KNOW HOW IT IS. ♡
SHE'S GOT SOMETHING AGAINST MEEEEEE!!

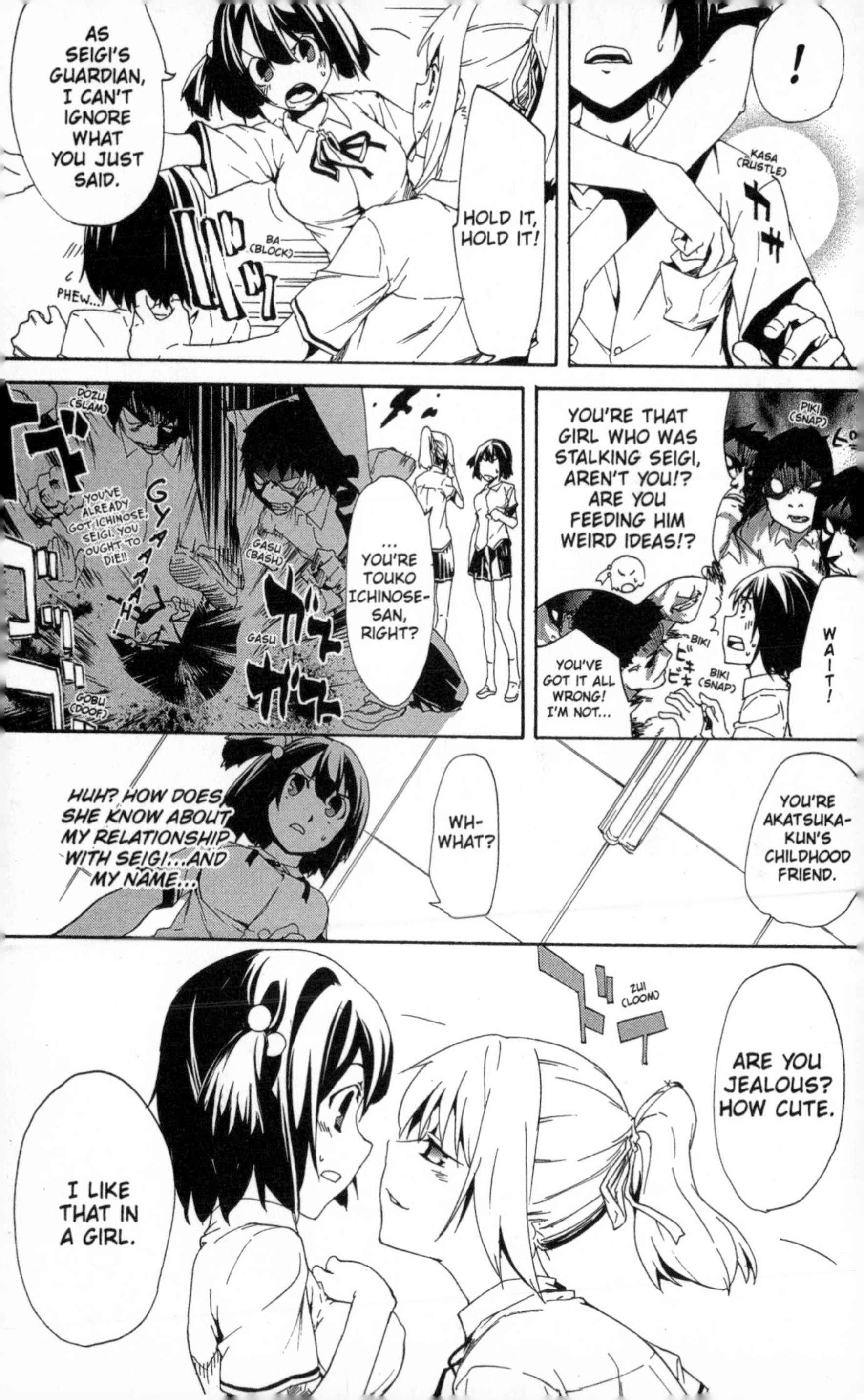
!
KASA (RUSTLE)
AS SEIGI'S GUARDIAN, I CAN'T IGNORE WHAT YOU JUST SAID.
HOLD IT, HOLD IT!
BA (BLOCK)
PHEW...
YOU'RE THAT GIRL WHO WAS STALKING SEIGI, AREN'T YOU!? ARE YOU FEEDING HIM WEIRD IDEAS!?
PIKI (SNAP)
WAIT!
BIKI
BIKI (SNAP)
YOU'VE GOT IT ALL WRONG! I'M NOT...
... YOU'RE TOUKO ICHINOSE-SAN, RIGHT?
DOZU (SLAM)
YOU'VE ALREADY GOT ICHINOSE, SEIGI. YOU OUGHT TO DIE!!
GYAAAAAH!
GASU (BASH)
GASU
GOBU (DOOF)
YOU'RE AKATSUKA-KUN'S CHILDHOOD FRIEND.
WH-WHAT?
HUH? HOW DOES SHE KNOW ABOUT MY RELATIONSHIP WITH SEIGI...AND MY NAME...
ARE YOU JEALOUS? HOW CUTE.
ZUI (LOOM)
I LIKE THAT IN A GIRL.

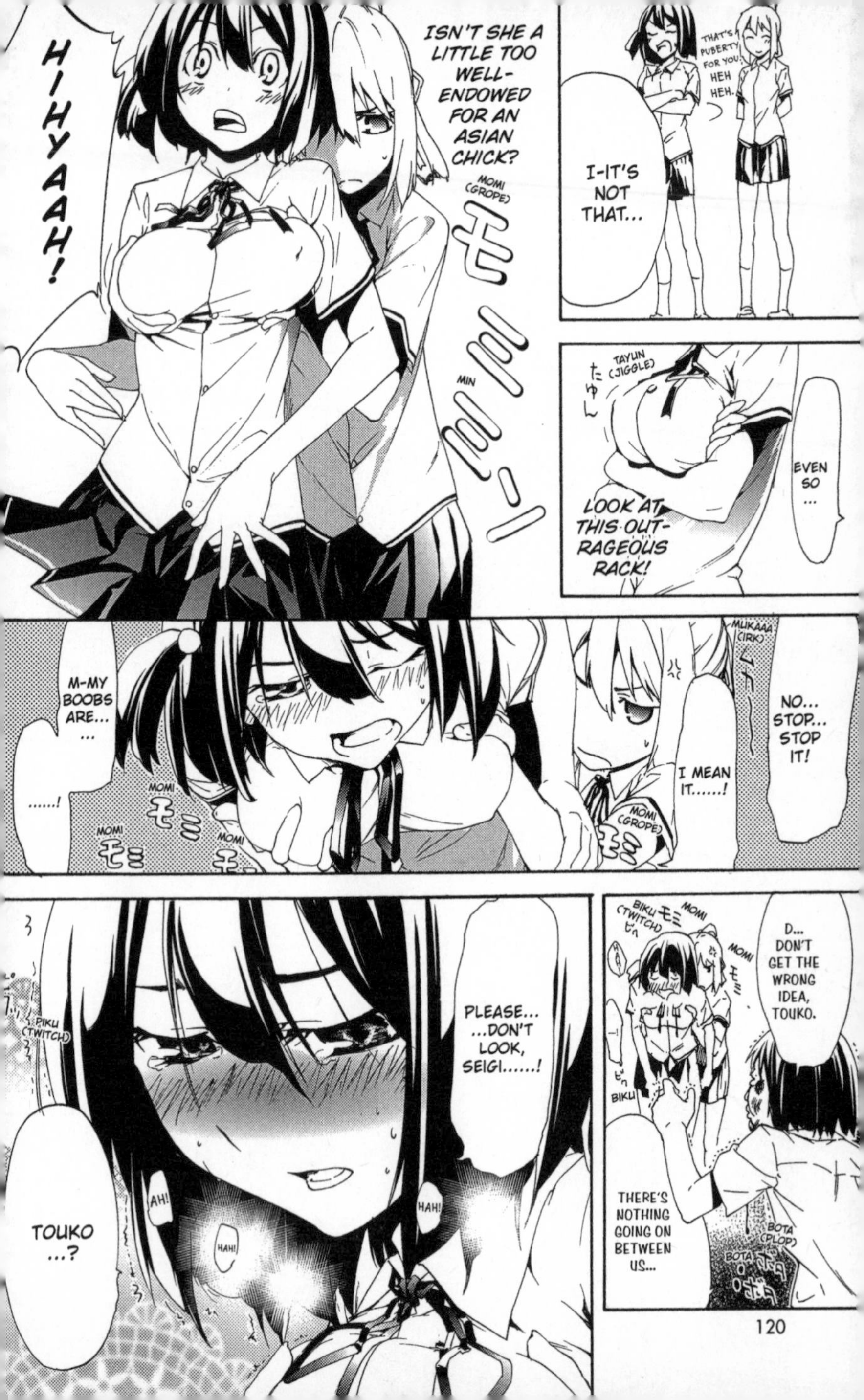
THAT'S PUBERTY FOR YOU. HEH HEH.
I-IT'S NOT THAT...
EVEN SO ...
TAYUN (JIGGLE)
LOOK AT THIS OUT-RAGEOUS RACK!
ISN'T SHE A LITTLE TOO WELL-ENDOWED FOR AN ASIAN CHICK?
MOMI (GROPE)
MIN
HIHYAAAH!
MUKAAA (IRK)
NO... STOP... STOP IT!
I MEAN IT......!
MOMI (GROPE)
M-MY BOOBS ARE... ...
MOMI
MOMI
MOMI
......!
D... DON'T GET THE WRONG IDEA, TOUKO.
MOMI
MOMI
BIKU (TWITCH)
BIKU
THERE'S NOTHING GOING ON BETWEEN US...
BOTA (PLOP)
BOTA
PLEASE... ...DON'T LOOK, SEIGI......!
HAH!
HAH!
AH!
PIKU (TWITCH)
TOUKO ...?

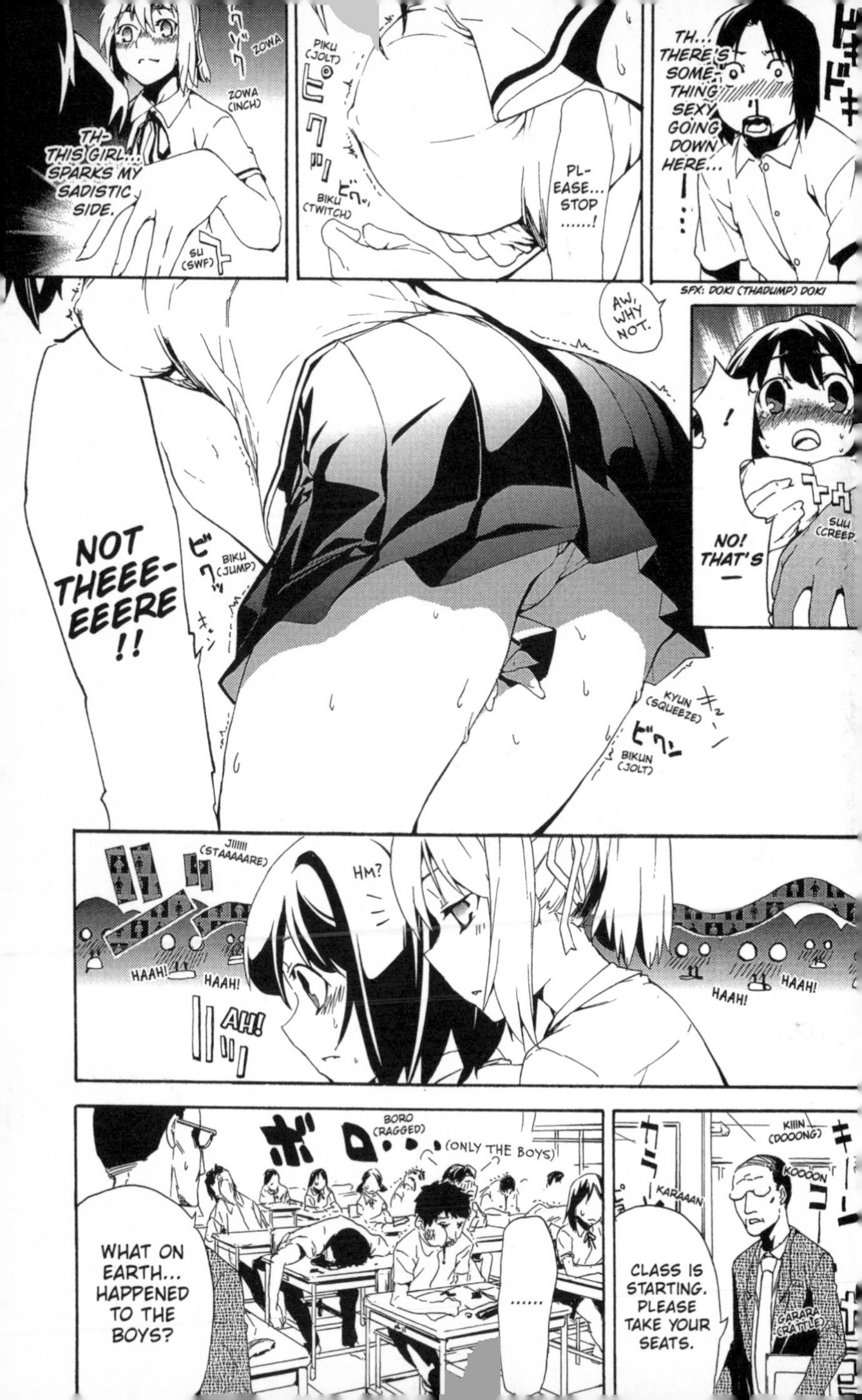
TH... THERE'S SOMETHING SEXY GOING DOWN HERE...
SFX: DOKI (THADUMP) DOKI
PIKU (JOLT)
PL-EASE... STOP ......!
BIKU (TWITCH)
ZOWA
ZOWA (INCH)
TH-THIS GIRL... SPARKS MY SADISTIC SIDE.
SU (SWF)
!
SUU (CREEP)
NO! THAT'S —
AW, WHY NOT.
BIKU (JUMP)
NOT THEEE-EEERE!!
KYUN (SQUEEZE)
BIKUN (JOLT)
JIIIIII (STAAAAARE)
HM?
HAAH!
HAAH!
HAAH!
HAAH!
AH!
KIIIN (DOOONG)
KOOOON
KARAAAN
CLASS IS STARTING. PLEASE TAKE YOUR SEATS.
GARARA (RATTLE)
BORO (RAGGED)
(ONLY THE BOYS)
......
WHAT ON EARTH... HAPPENED TO THE BOYS?

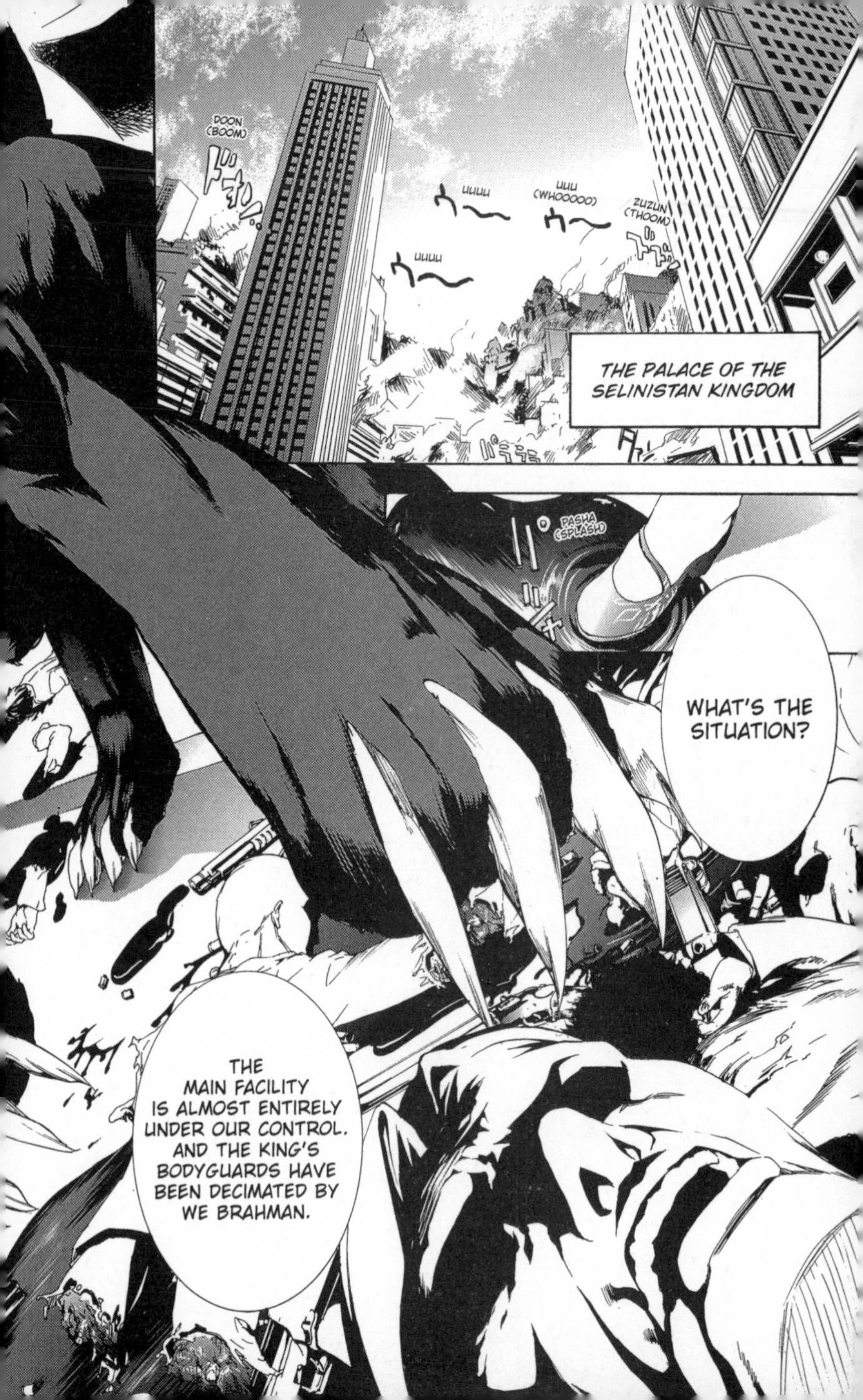
ZUZUN (THOOM)
UUU (WHOOOOO)
UUUU
DOON (BOOM)
UUUU
THE PALACE OF THE SELINISTAN KINGDOM
PASHA (SPLASH)
WHAT'S THE SITUATION?
THE MAIN FACILITY IS ALMOST ENTIRELY UNDER OUR CONTROL. AND THE KING'S BODYGUARDS HAVE BEEN DECIMATED BY WE BRAHMAN.

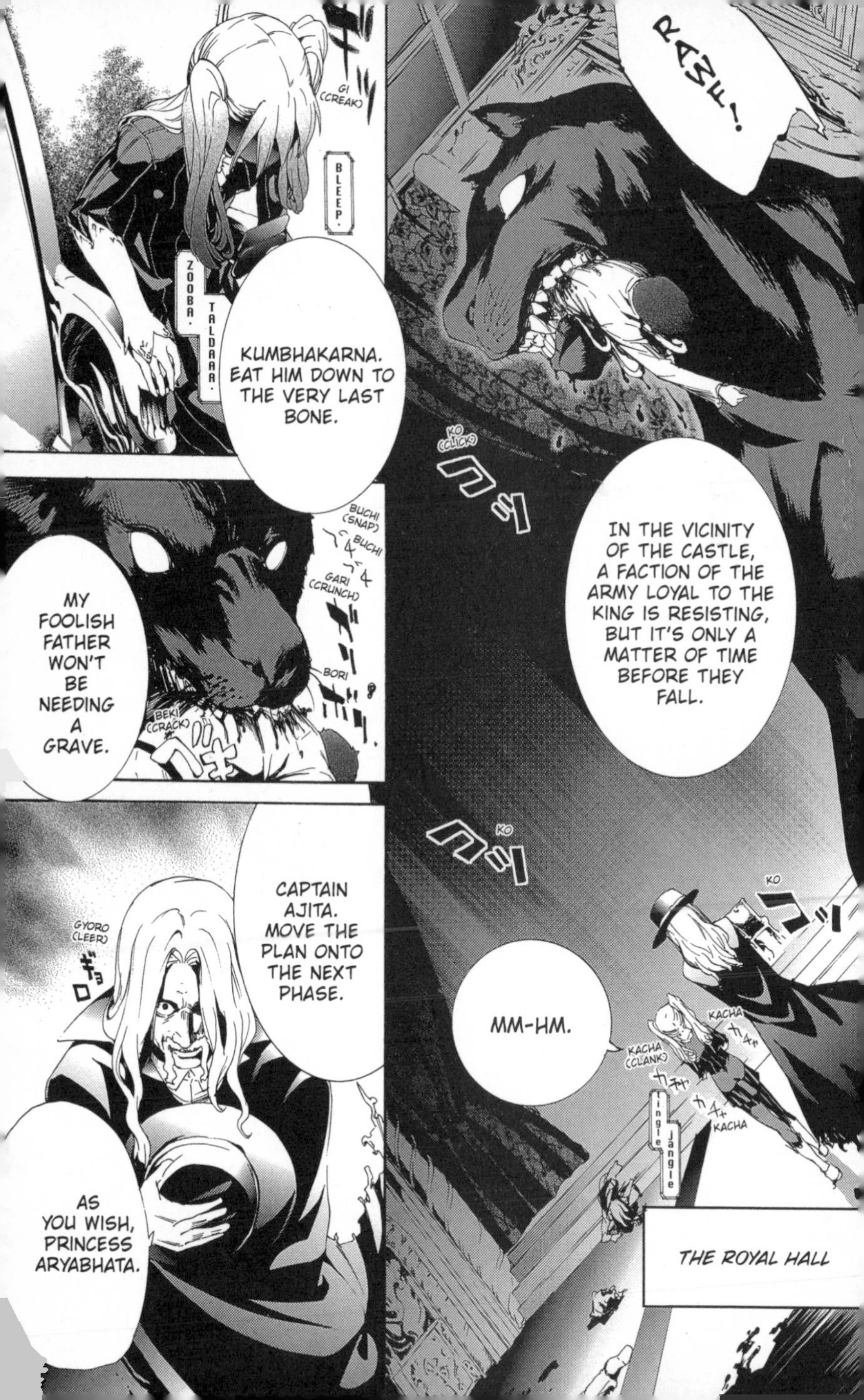
RASH!!
KO (CLICK)
IN THE VICINITY OF THE CASTLE, A FACTION OF THE ARMY LOYAL TO THE KING IS RESISTING, BUT IT'S ONLY A MATTER OF TIME BEFORE THEY FALL.
KO
KO
MM-HM.
KACHA
KACHA (CLANK)
KACHA
jingle jangle
THE ROYAL HALL
GI (CREAK)
BLEEP.
ZOOBA.
TALDAAA.
KUMBHAKARNA. EAT HIM DOWN TO THE VERY LAST BONE.
BUCHI (SNAP)
BUCHI
GARI (CRUNCH)
BORI
BEKI (CRACK)
MY FOOLISH FATHER WON'T BE NEEDING A GRAVE.
CAPTAIN AJITA. MOVE THE PLAN ONTO THE NEXT PHASE.
GYORO (LEER)
AS YOU WISH, PRINCESS ARYABHATA.

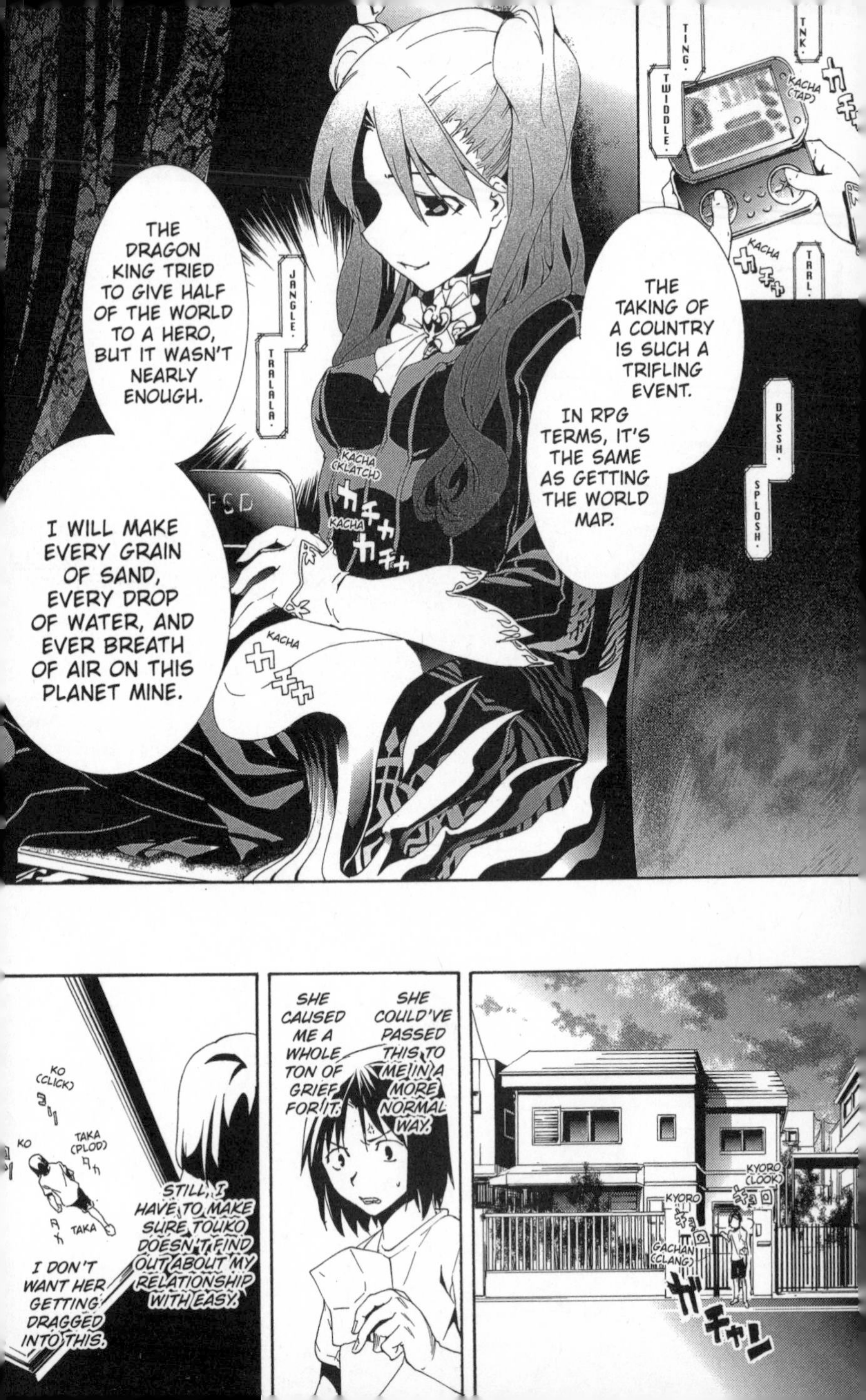
TNK.
TING.
TWIDDLE.
KACHA (TAP)
KACHA
TRRL.
THE TAKING OF A COUNTRY IS SUCH A TRIFLING EVENT.
IN RPG TERMS, IT'S THE SAME AS GETTING THE WORLD MAP.
DKSSH.
SPLOSH.
THE DRAGON KING TRIED TO GIVE HALF OF THE WORLD TO A HERO, BUT IT WASN'T NEARLY ENOUGH.
JANGLE.
TRALALA.
KACHA (KLATCH)
KACHA
I WILL MAKE EVERY GRAIN OF SAND, EVERY DROP OF WATER, AND EVER BREATH OF AIR ON THIS PLANET MINE.
KACHA
KYORO (LOOK)
KYORO
GACHAN (CLANG)
SHE COULD'VE PASSED THIS TO ME IN A MORE NORMAL WAY.
SHE CAUSED ME A WHOLE TON OF GRIEF FOR IT.
STILL, I HAVE TO MAKE SURE TOUKO DOESN'T FIND OUT ABOUT MY RELATIONSHIP WITH EASY.
KO (CLICK)
KO
TAKA (PLOD)
TAKA
I DON'T WANT HER GETTING DRAGGED INTO THIS.

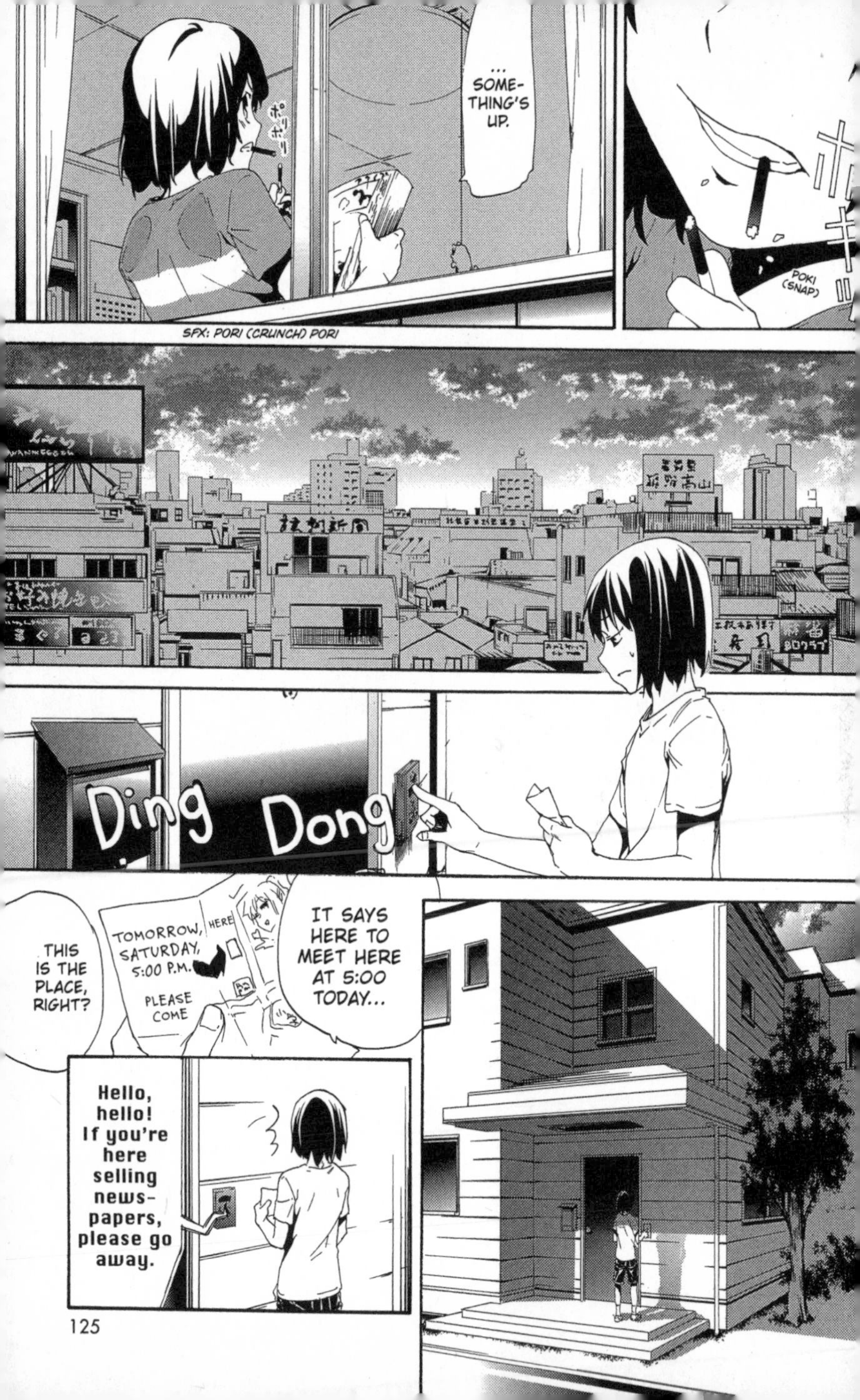
POKI (SNAP)
... SOME-THING'S UP.
SFX: PORI (CRUNCH) PORI
Ding Dong
IT SAYS HERE TO MEET HERE AT 5:00 TODAY...
TOMORROW, SATURDAY, 5:00 P.M.
HERE
PLEASE COME
THIS IS THE PLACE, RIGHT?
Hello, hello! If you're here selling news-papers, please go away.

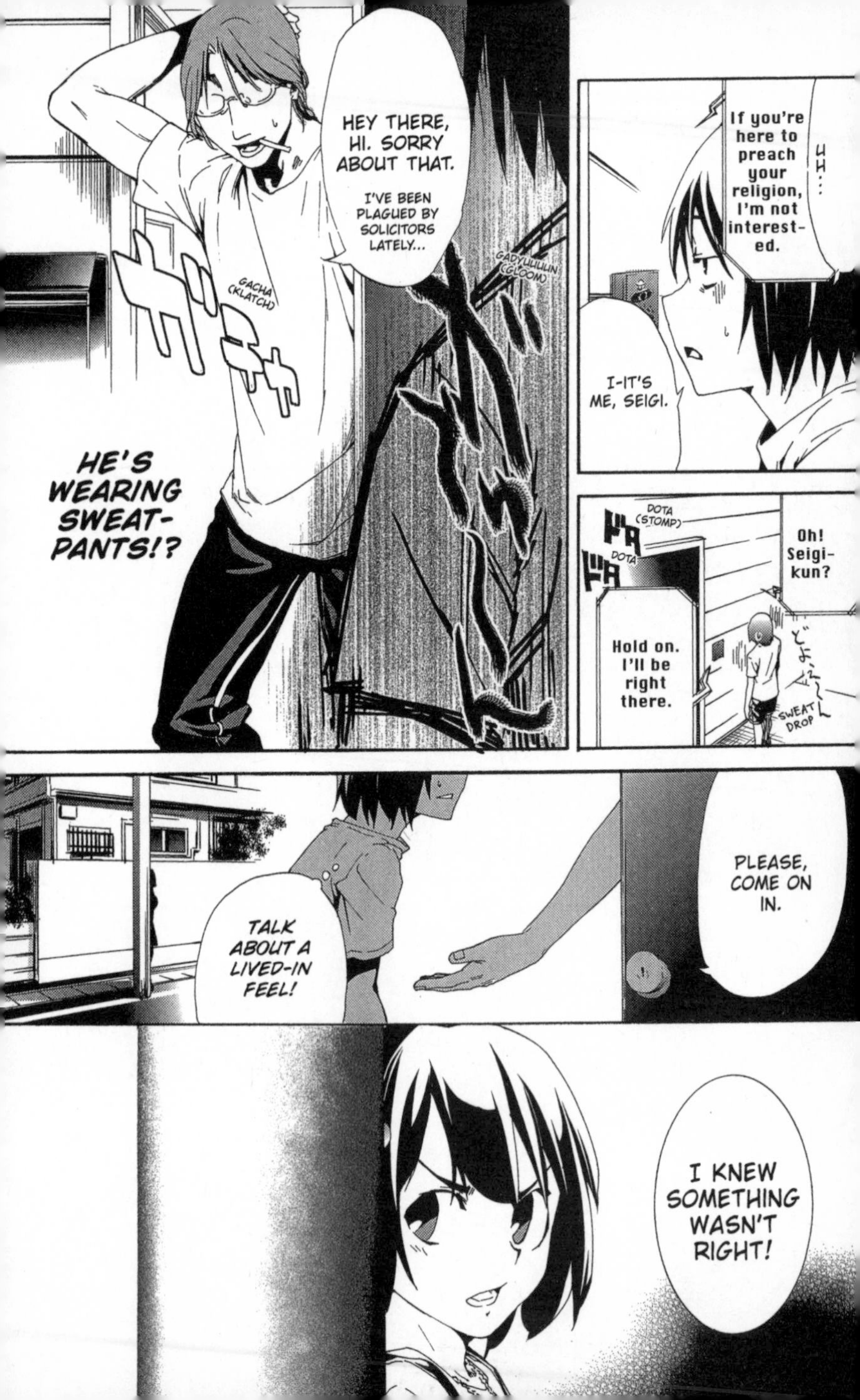
UH...
If you're here to preach your religion, I'm not interested.
I-IT'S ME, SEIGI.
DOTA (STOMP)
DOTA
Oh! Seigi-kun?
Hold on. I'll be right there.
SWEAT DROP
GADYUUUUN (GLOOM)
HEY THERE, HI. SORRY ABOUT THAT.
I'VE BEEN PLAGUED BY SOLICITORS LATELY...
GACHA (KLATCH)
HE'S WEARING SWEAT-PANTS!?
PLEASE, COME ON IN.
TALK ABOUT A LIVED-IN FEEL!
I KNEW SOMETHING WASN'T RIGHT!

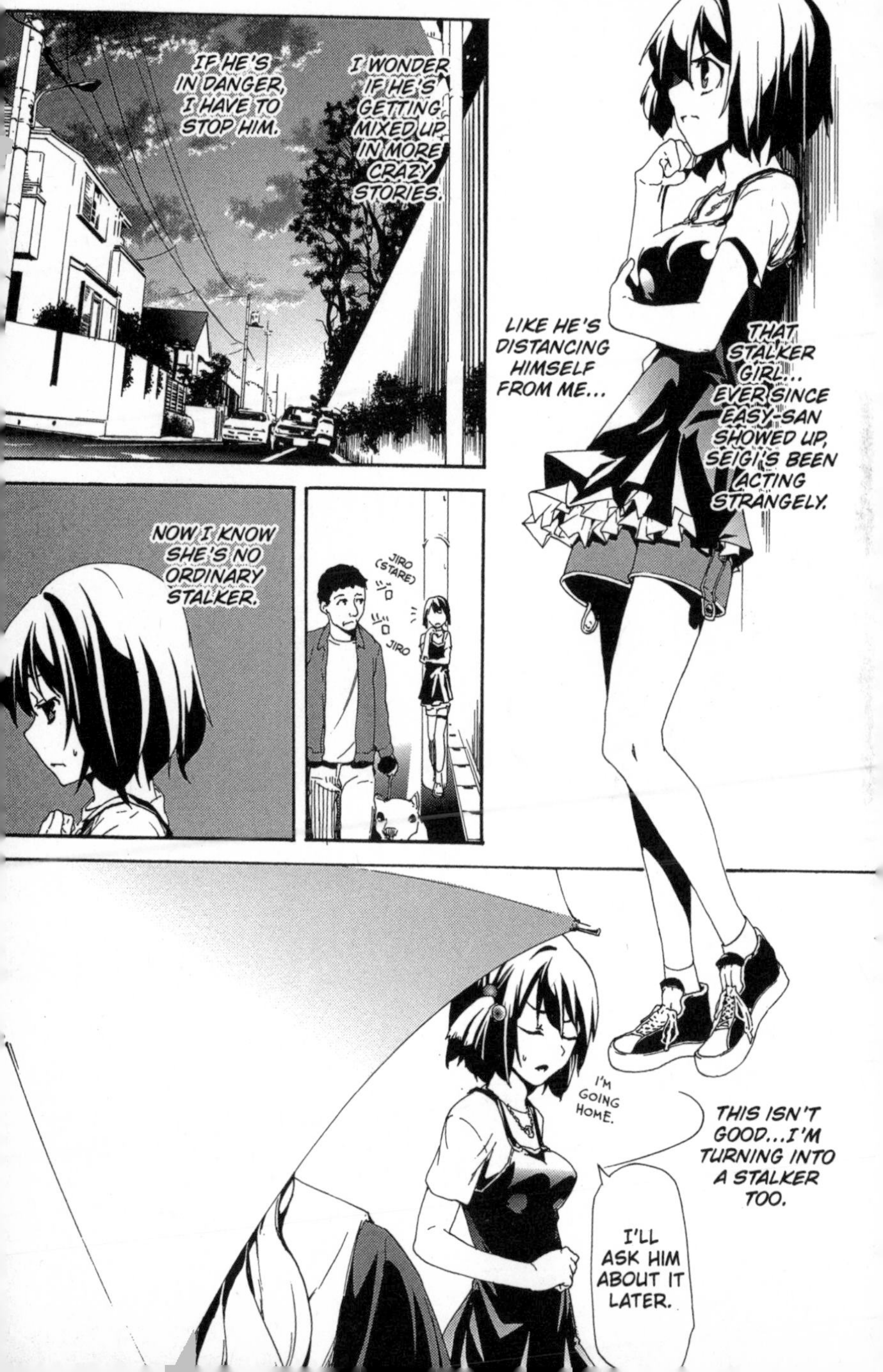
THAT STALKER GIRL... EVER SINCE EASY-SAN SHOWED UP, SEIGI'S BEEN ACTING STRANGELY.
LIKE HE'S DISTANCING HIMSELF FROM ME...
I WONDER IF HE'S GETTING MIXED UP IN MORE CRAZY STORIES.
IF HE'S IN DANGER, I HAVE TO STOP HIM.
JIRO (STARE)
JIRO
NOW I KNOW SHE'S NO ORDINARY STALKER.
THIS ISN'T GOOD...I'M TURNING INTO A STALKER TOO.
I'M GOING HOME.
I'LL ASK HIM ABOUT IT LATER.

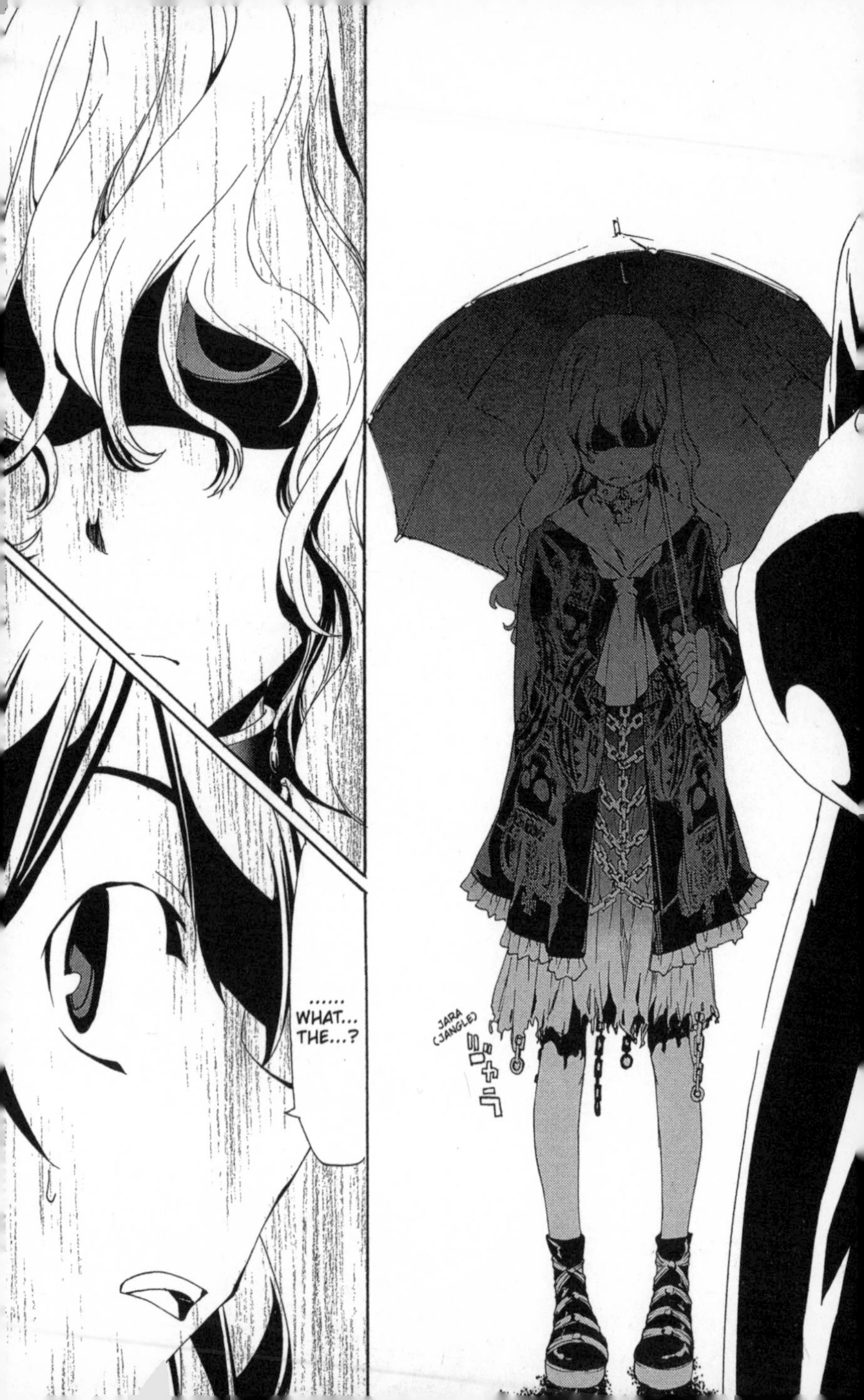
JARA (JANGLE)
ジャラ
......WHAT... THE...?

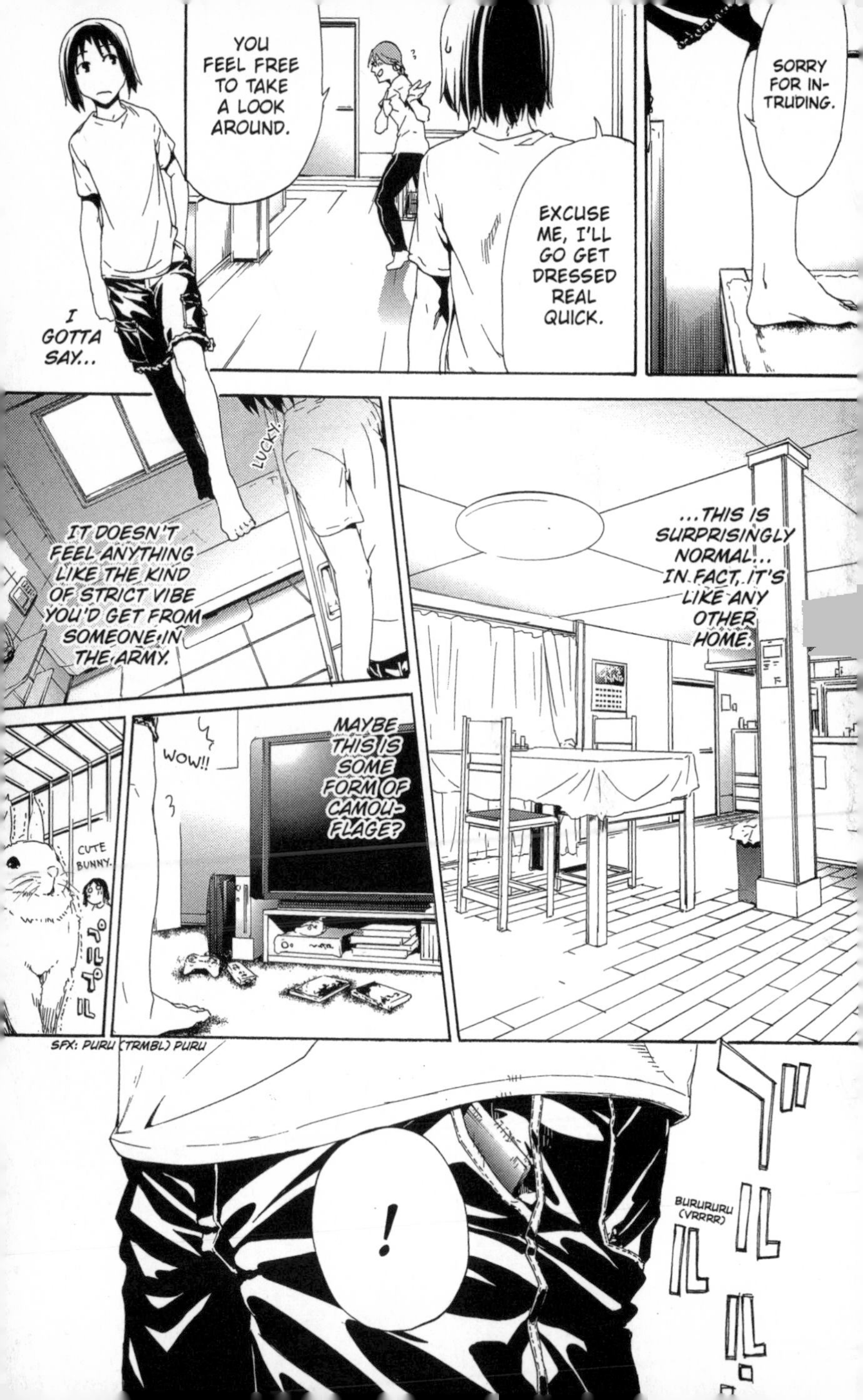
SORRY FOR IN-TRUDING.
YOU FEEL FREE TO TAKE A LOOK AROUND.
EXCUSE ME, I'LL GO GET DRESSED REAL QUICK.
I GOTTA SAY...
...THIS IS SURPRISINGLY NORMAL... IN FACT, IT'S LIKE ANY OTHER HOME.
LUCKY.
IT DOESN'T FEEL ANYTHING LIKE THE KIND OF STRICT VIBE YOU'D GET FROM SOMEONE IN THE ARMY.
MAYBE THIS IS SOME FORM OF CAMOU-FLAGE?
WOW!!
CUTE BUNNY.
SFX: PURU (TRMBL) PURU
!
BURURURU (VRRRR)

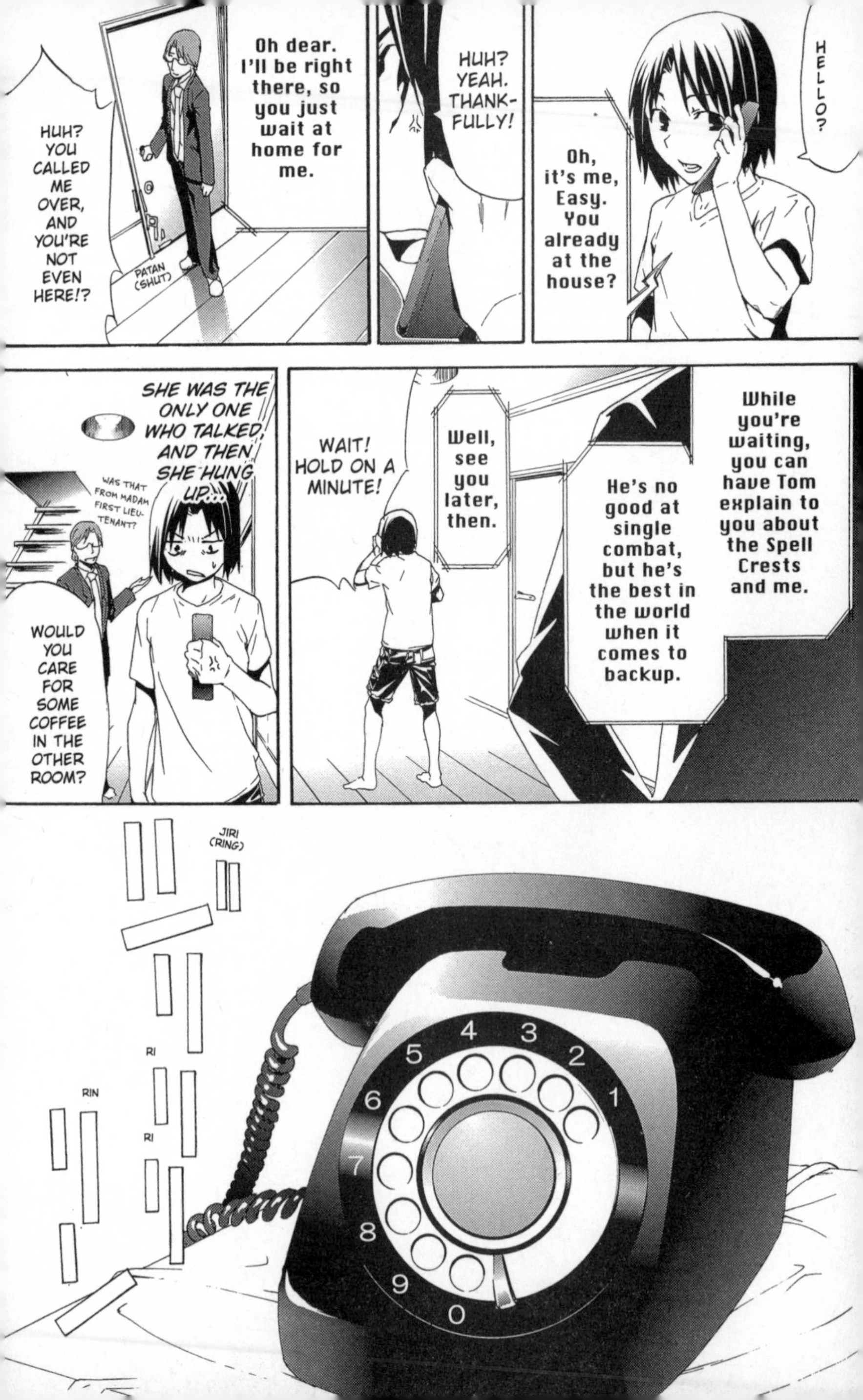
HELLO?
Oh, it's me, Easy. You already at the house?
HUH? YEAH. THANKFULLY!
Oh dear. I'll be right there, so you just wait at home for me.
HUH? YOU CALLED ME OVER, AND YOU'RE NOT EVEN HERE!?
PATAN (SHUT)
While you're waiting, you can have Tom explain to you about the Spell Crests and me.
He's no good at single combat, but he's the best in the world when it comes to backup.
Well, see you later, then.
WAIT! HOLD ON A MINUTE!
SHE WAS THE ONLY ONE WHO TALKED, AND THEN SHE HUNG UP...
WAS THAT FROM MADAM FIRST LIEUTENANT?
WOULD YOU CARE FOR SOME COFFEE IN THE OTHER ROOM?
JIRI (RING)
RI
RIN
RI

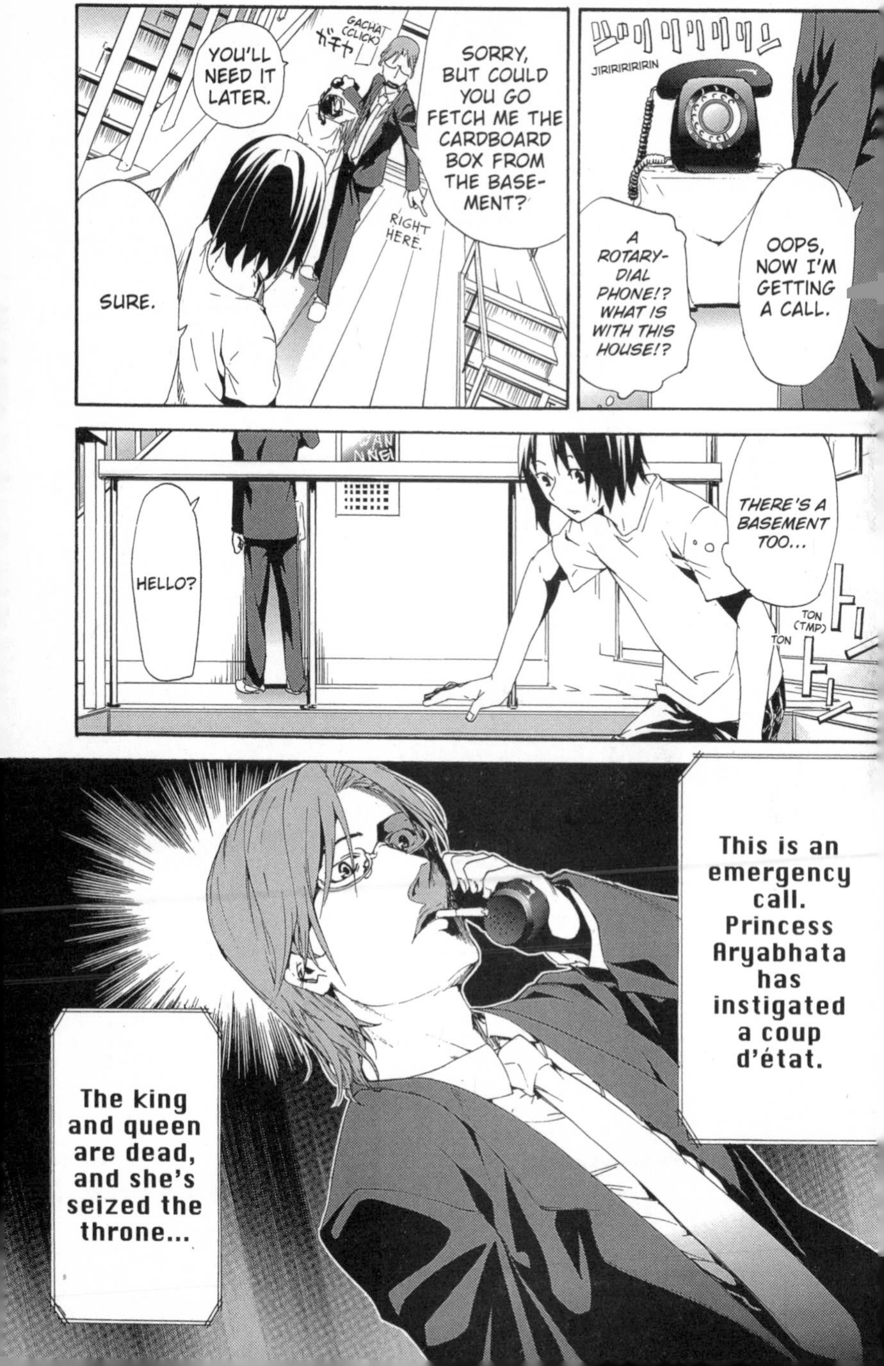
JIRIRIRIRIRIN
OOPS, NOW I'M GETTING A CALL.
A ROTARY-DIAL PHONE!? WHAT IS WITH THIS HOUSE!?
SORRY, BUT COULD YOU GO FETCH ME THE CARDBOARD BOX FROM THE BASEMENT?
ガチャ
GACHA (CLICK)
RIGHT HERE.
YOU'LL NEED IT LATER.
SURE.
THERE'S A BASEMENT TOO...
TON (TMP)
TON
HELLO?
This is an emergency call. Princess Aryabhata has instigated a coup d'état.
The king and queen are dead, and she's seized the throne...

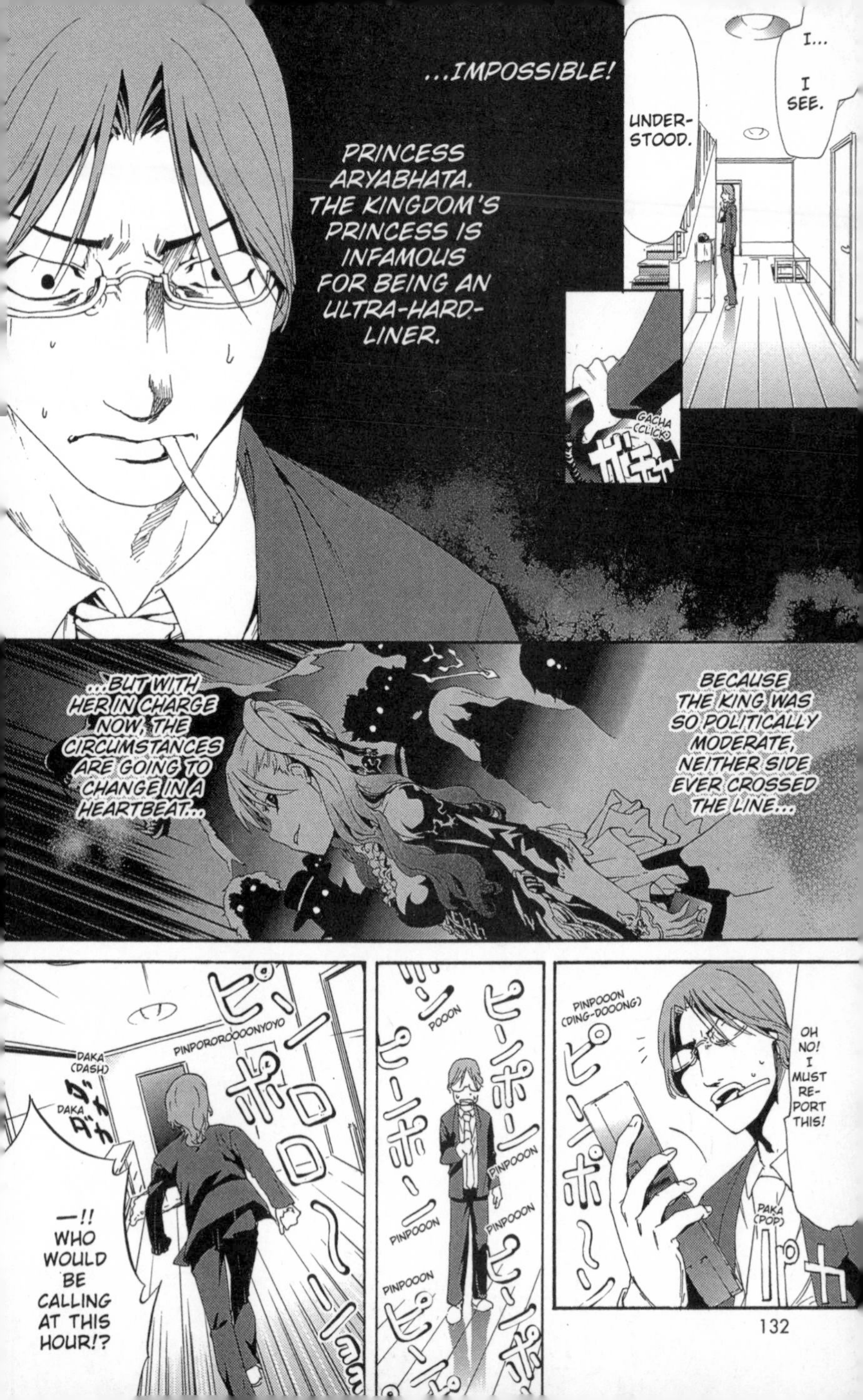

I... I SEE.
UNDER-STOOD.
GACHA (CLICK)
...IMPOSSIBLE!
PRINCESS ARYABHATA. THE KINGDOM'S PRINCESS IS INFAMOUS FOR BEING AN ULTRA-HARD-LINER.
BECAUSE THE KING WAS SO POLITICALLY MODERATE, NEITHER SIDE EVER CROSSED THE LINE...
...BUT WITH HER IN CHARGE NOW, THE CIRCUMSTANCES ARE GOING TO CHANGE IN A HEARTBEAT...
PINPOOON (DING-DOOONG)
OH NO! I MUST RE-PORT THIS!
PAKA (POP)
POOON
PINPOOON
PINPOOON
PINPOOON
PINPOOON
PINPORORОOOONYOYO
DAKA (DASH)
DAKA
—!! WHO WOULD BE CALLING AT THIS HOUR!?

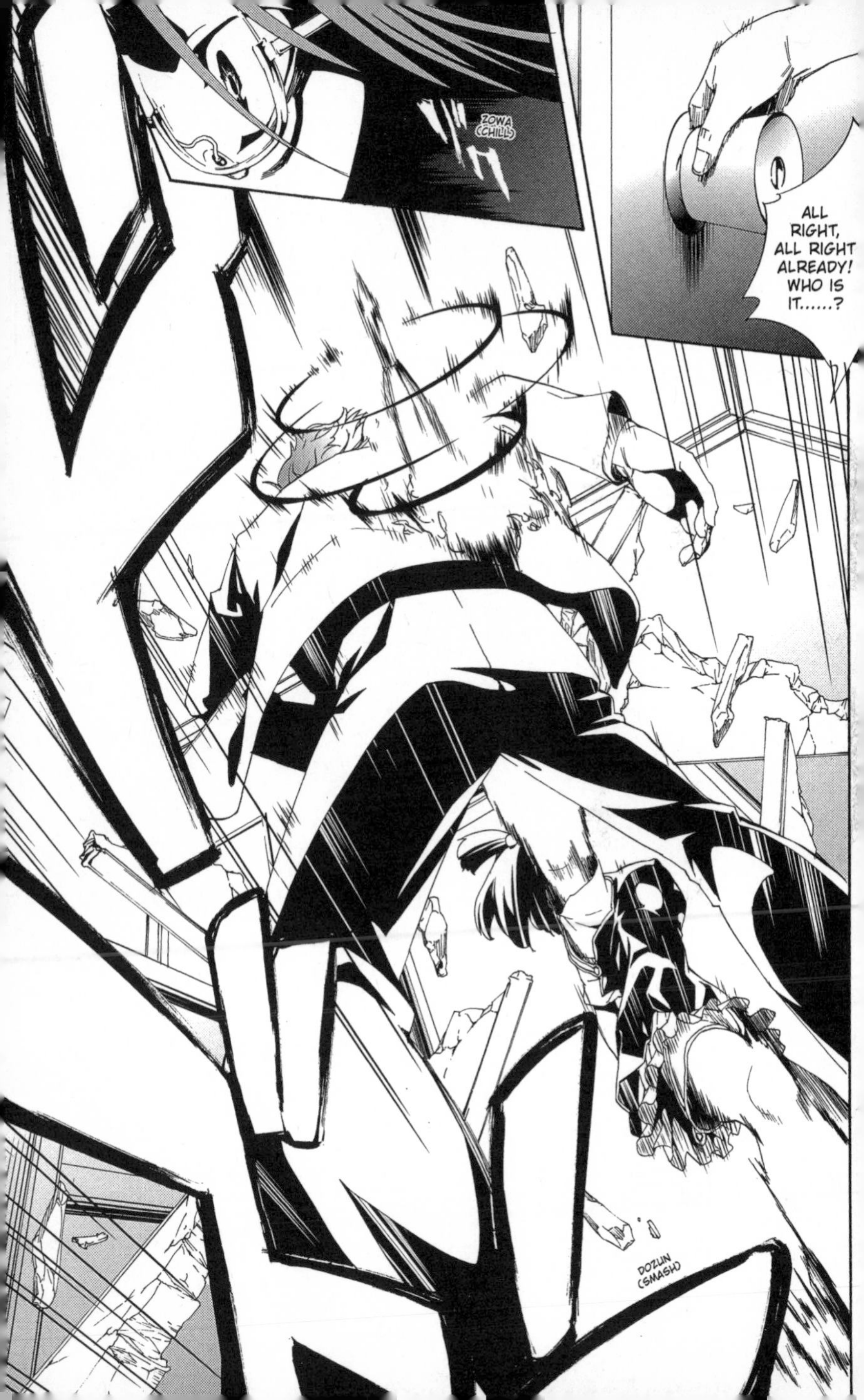
ALL RIGHT, ALL RIGHT ALREADY! WHO IS IT......?
ZOWA (CHILL)
DOZUN (SMASH)

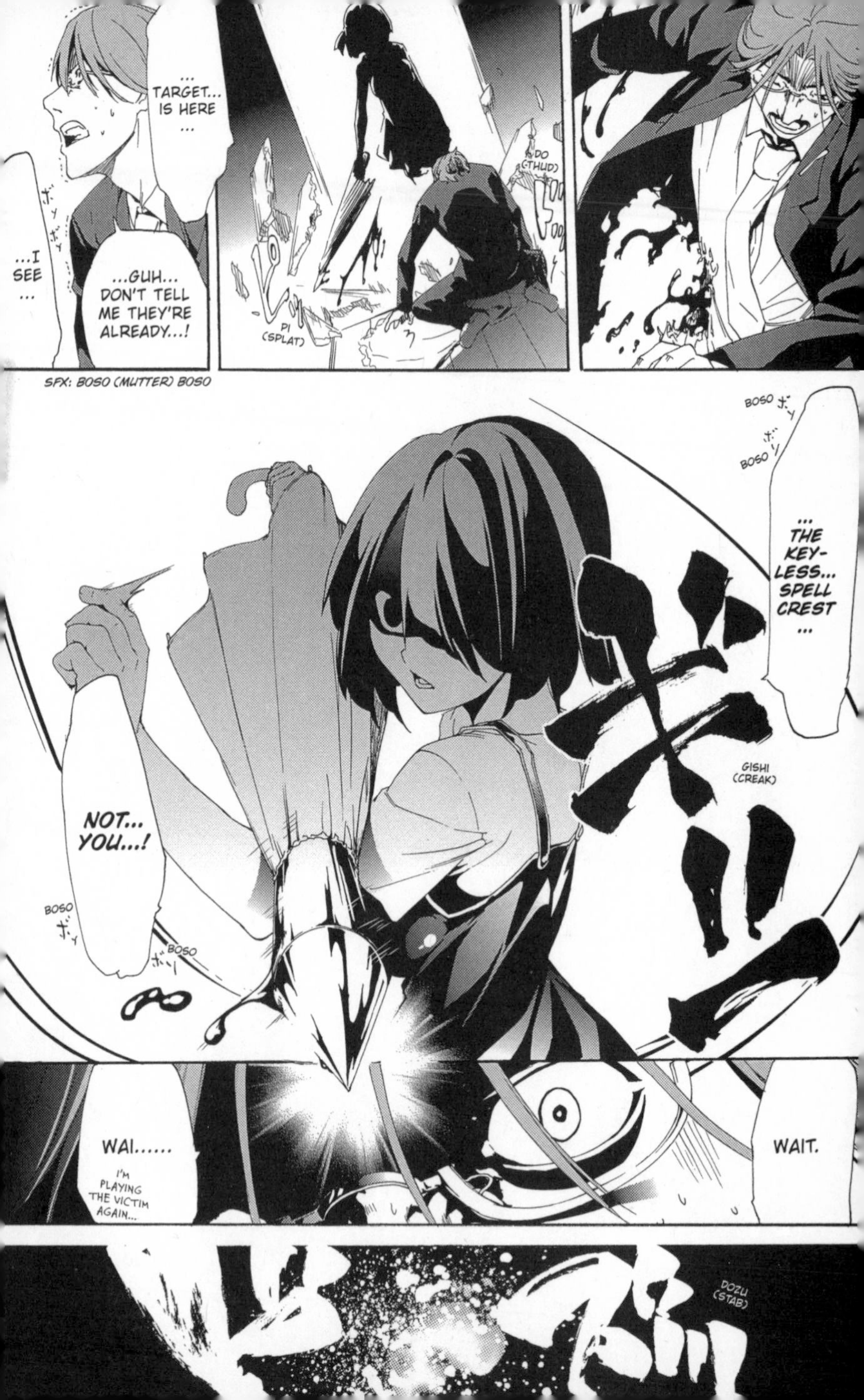
DO
(THUD)
PI
(SPLAT)
... TARGET... IS HERE ...
...GUH... DON'T TELL ME THEY'RE ALREADY...!
...I SEE ...
SFX: BOSO (MUTTER) BOSO
BOSO
BOSO
... THE KEY-LESS... SPELL CREST ...
GISHI
(CREAK)
NOT... YOU...!
BOSO
BOSO
WAIT.
WAI......
I'M PLAYING THE VICTIM AGAIN...
DOZU
(STAB)

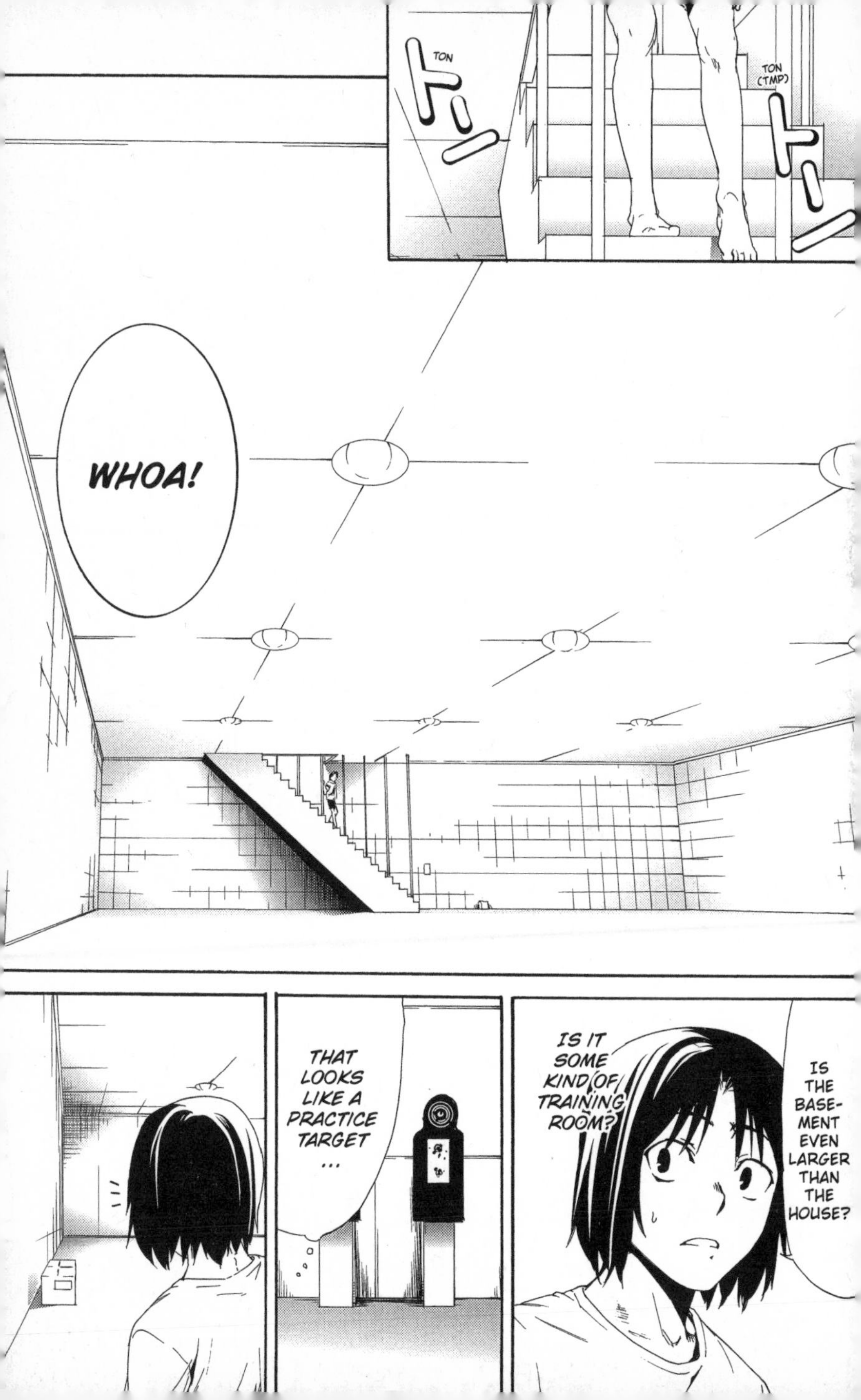
TON (TMP)
TON
WHOA!
IS THE BASE-MENT EVEN LARGER THAN THE HOUSE?
IS IT SOME KIND OF TRAINING ROOM?
THAT LOOKS LIKE A PRACTICE TARGET ...

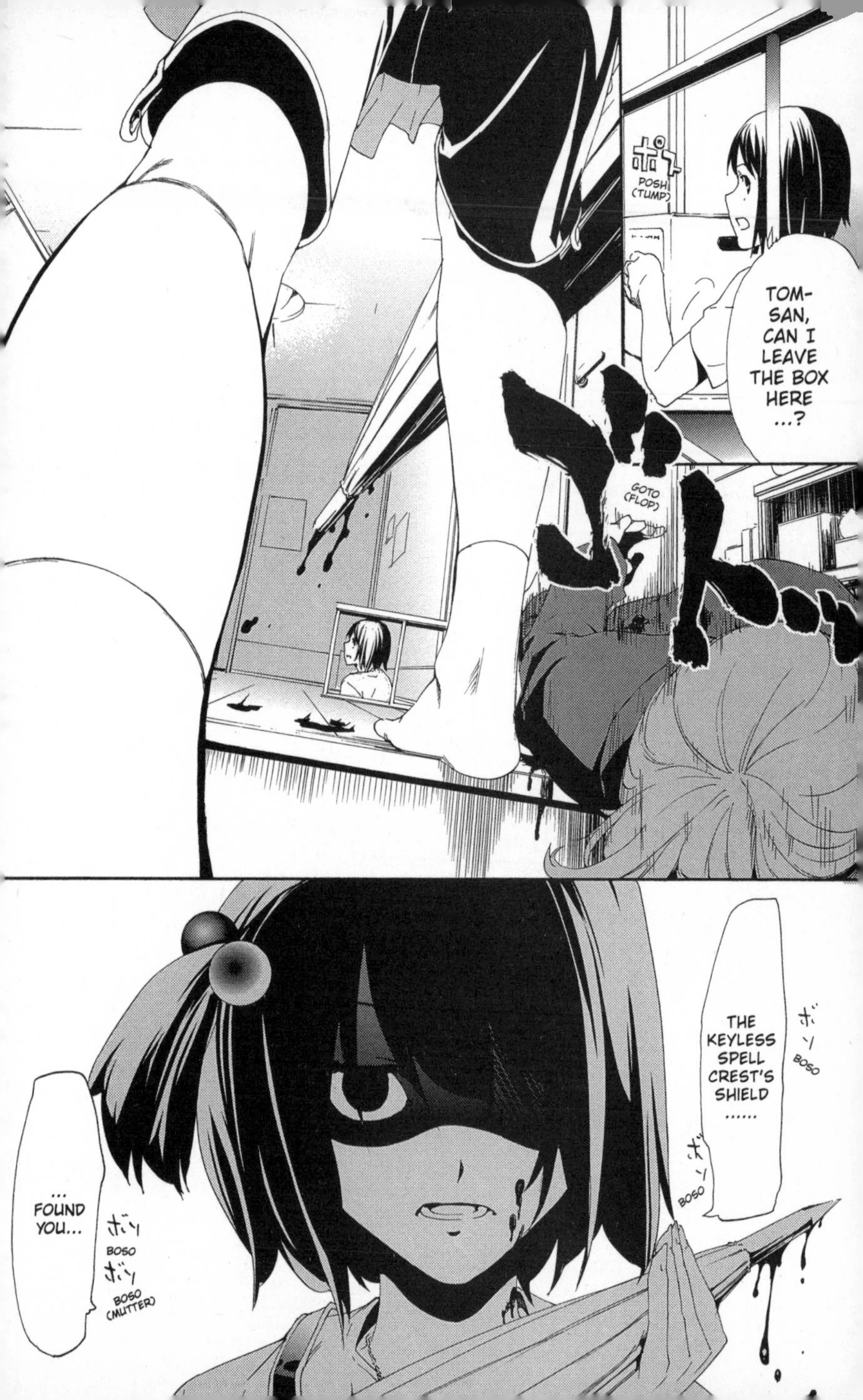
POSHI (TUMP)
TOM-SAN, CAN I LEAVE THE BOX HERE ...?
GOTO (FLOP)
THE KEYLESS SPELL CREST'S SHIELD ......
ボソ BOSO
ボソ BOSO
... FOUND YOU...
ボソ BOSO
ボソ BOSO (MUTTER)

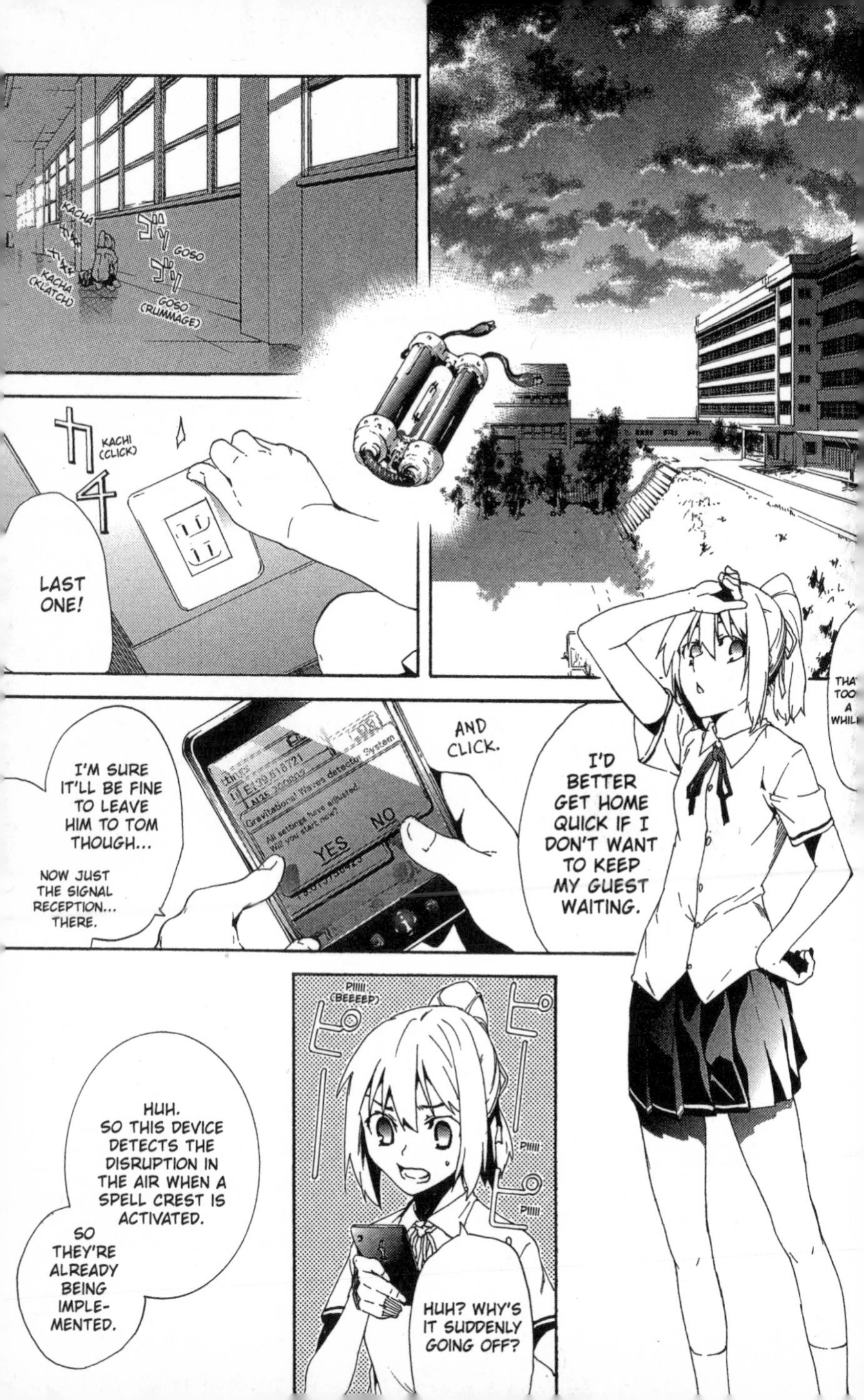
THA TOO A WHIL
KACHA
GOSO
KACHA (KLATCH)
GOSO (RUMMAGE)
KACHI (CLICK)
LAST ONE!
I'D BETTER GET HOME QUICK IF I DON'T WANT TO KEEP MY GUEST WAITING.
AND CLICK.
I'M SURE IT'LL BE FINE TO LEAVE HIM TO TOM THOUGH...
NOW JUST THE SIGNAL RECEPTION... THERE.
PIIIII (BEEEEP)
PIIIII
PIIIII
HUH? WHY'S IT SUDDENLY GOING OFF?
HUH. SO THIS DEVICE DETECTS THE DISRUPTION IN THE AIR WHEN A SPELL CREST IS ACTIVATED.
SO THEY'RE ALREADY BEING IMPLE-MENTED.

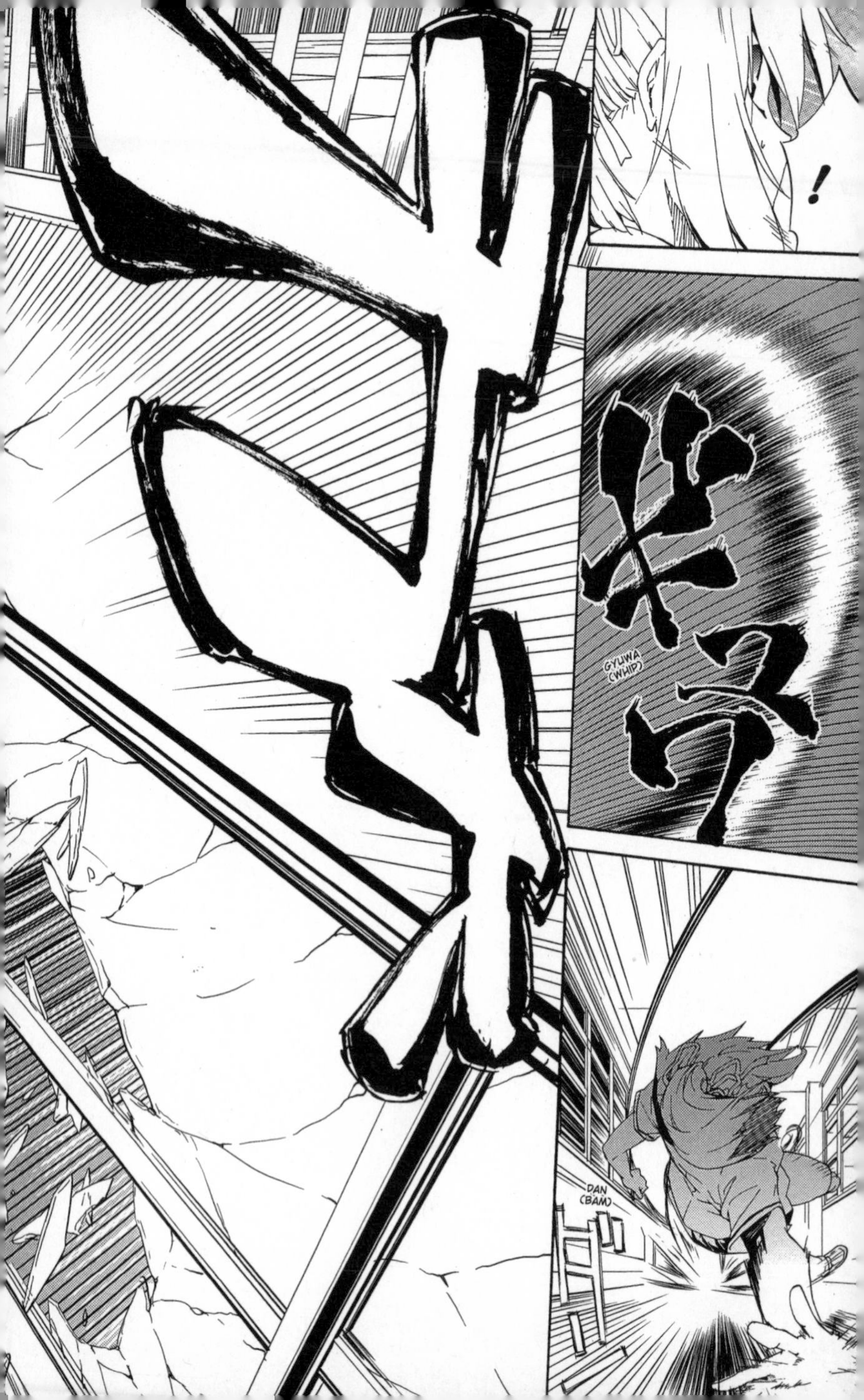
!
GYUWA (WHIP)
DAN (BAM)

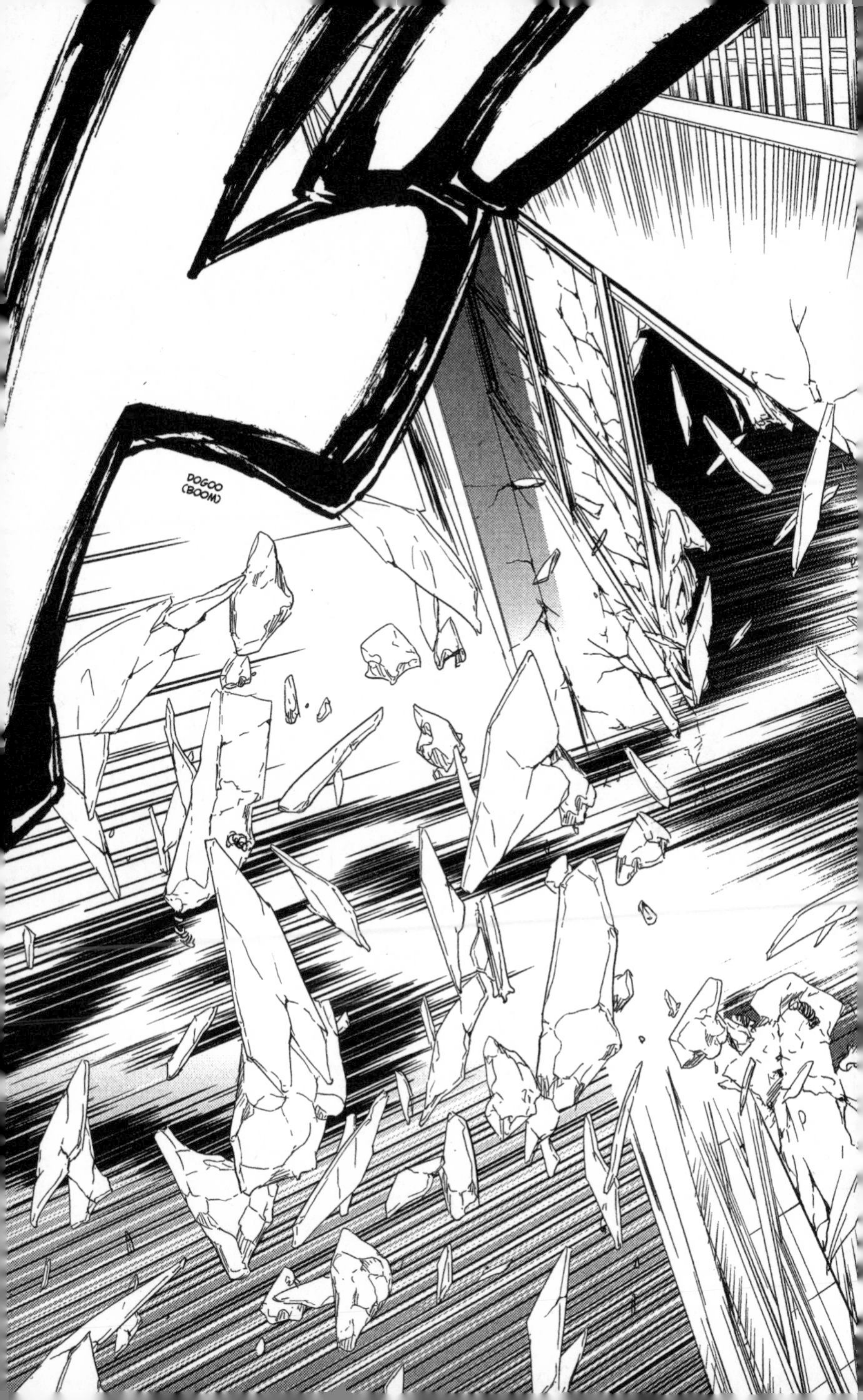
DOGOO (BOOM)

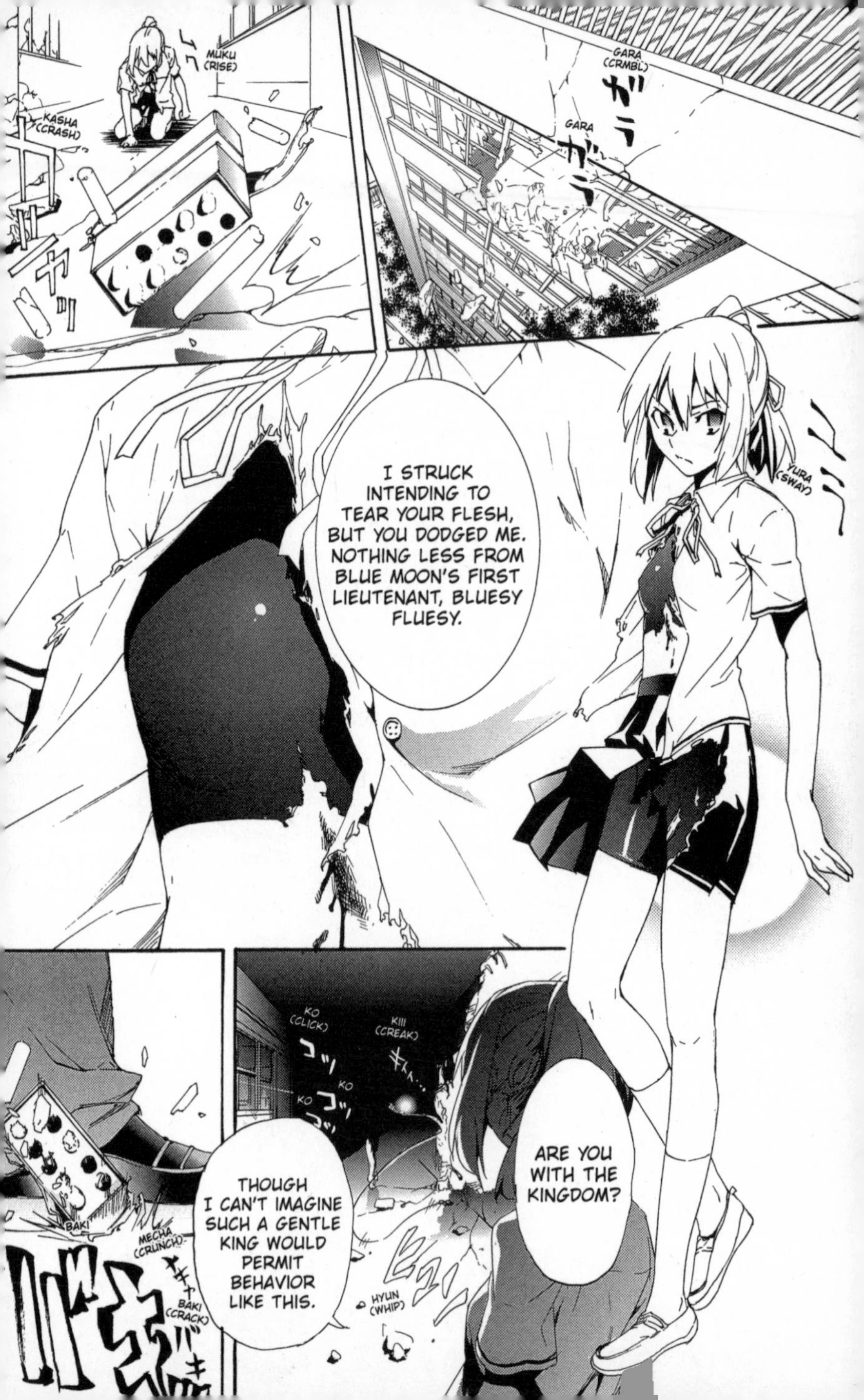

GARA (CRMBL)
GARA
MUKU (RISE)
KASHA (CRASH)
YURA (SWAY)
I STRUCK INTENDING TO TEAR YOUR FLESH, BUT YOU DODGED ME. NOTHING LESS FROM BLUE MOON'S FIRST LIEUTENANT, BLUESY FLUESY.
KIII (CREAK)
KO (CLICK)
KO
KO
ARE YOU WITH THE KINGDOM?
HYUN (WHIP)
THOUGH I CAN'T IMAGINE SUCH A GENTLE KING WOULD PERMIT BEHAVIOR LIKE THIS.
BAKI
MECHA (CRUNCH)
BAKI (CRACK)

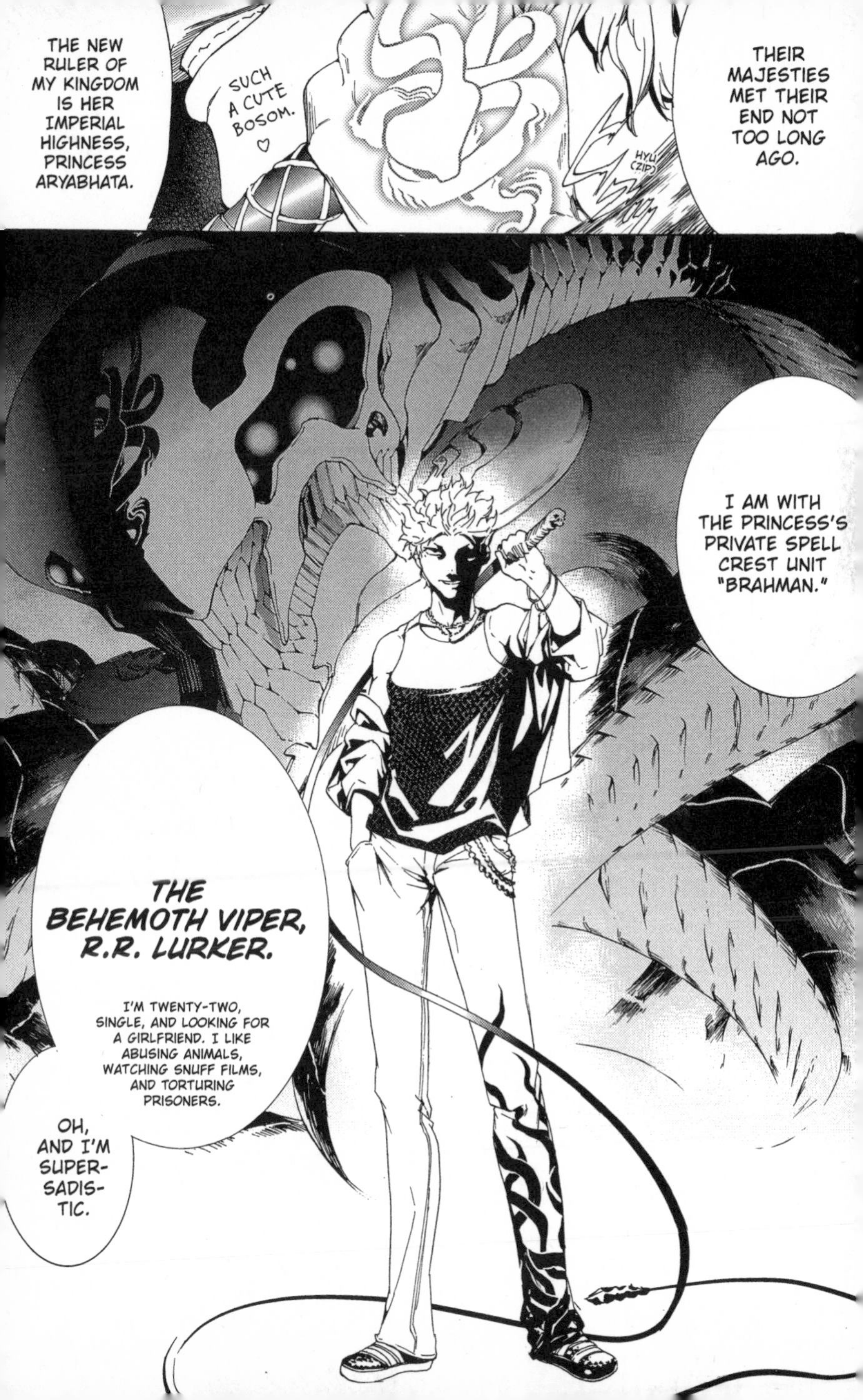
THEIR MAJESTIES MET THEIR END NOT TOO LONG AGO.
HYU (ZIP)
SUCH A CUTE BOSOM. ♡
THE NEW RULER OF MY KINGDOM IS HER IMPERIAL HIGHNESS, PRINCESS ARYABHATA.
I AM WITH THE PRINCESS'S PRIVATE SPELL CREST UNIT "BRAHMAN."
THE BEHEMOTH VIPER, R.R. LURKER.
I'M TWENTY-TWO, SINGLE, AND LOOKING FOR A GIRLFRIEND. I LIKE ABUSING ANIMALS, WATCHING SNUFF FILMS, AND TORTURING PRISONERS.
OH, AND I'M SUPER-SADIS-TIC.

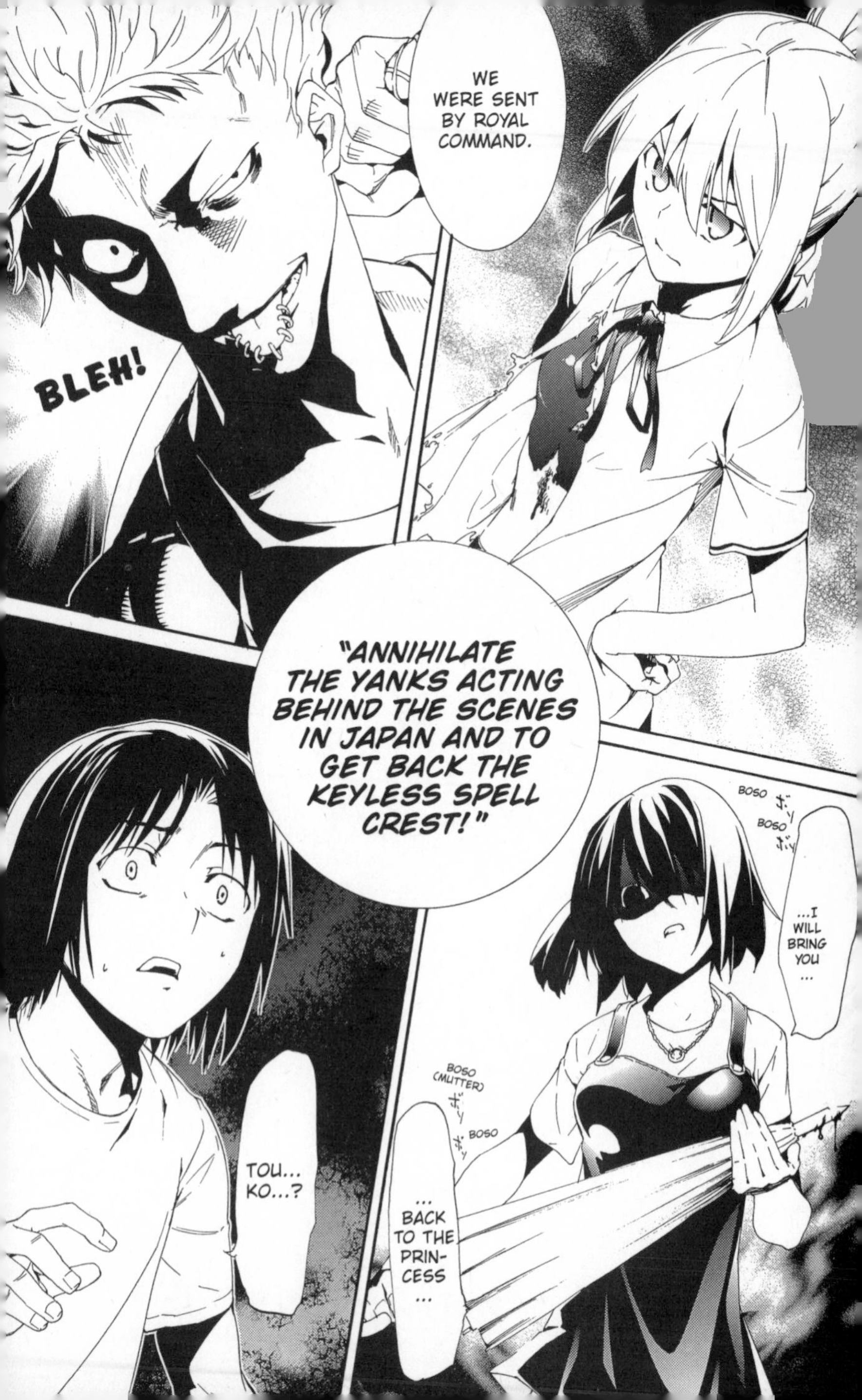
WE WERE SENT BY ROYAL COMMAND.
BLEH!
"ANNIHILATE THE YANKS ACTING BEHIND THE SCENES IN JAPAN AND TO GET BACK THE KEYLESS SPELL CREST!"
BOSO BOSO
...I WILL BRING YOU ...
BOSO (MUTTER) BOSO
... BACK TO THE PRIN- CESS ...
TOU... KO...?

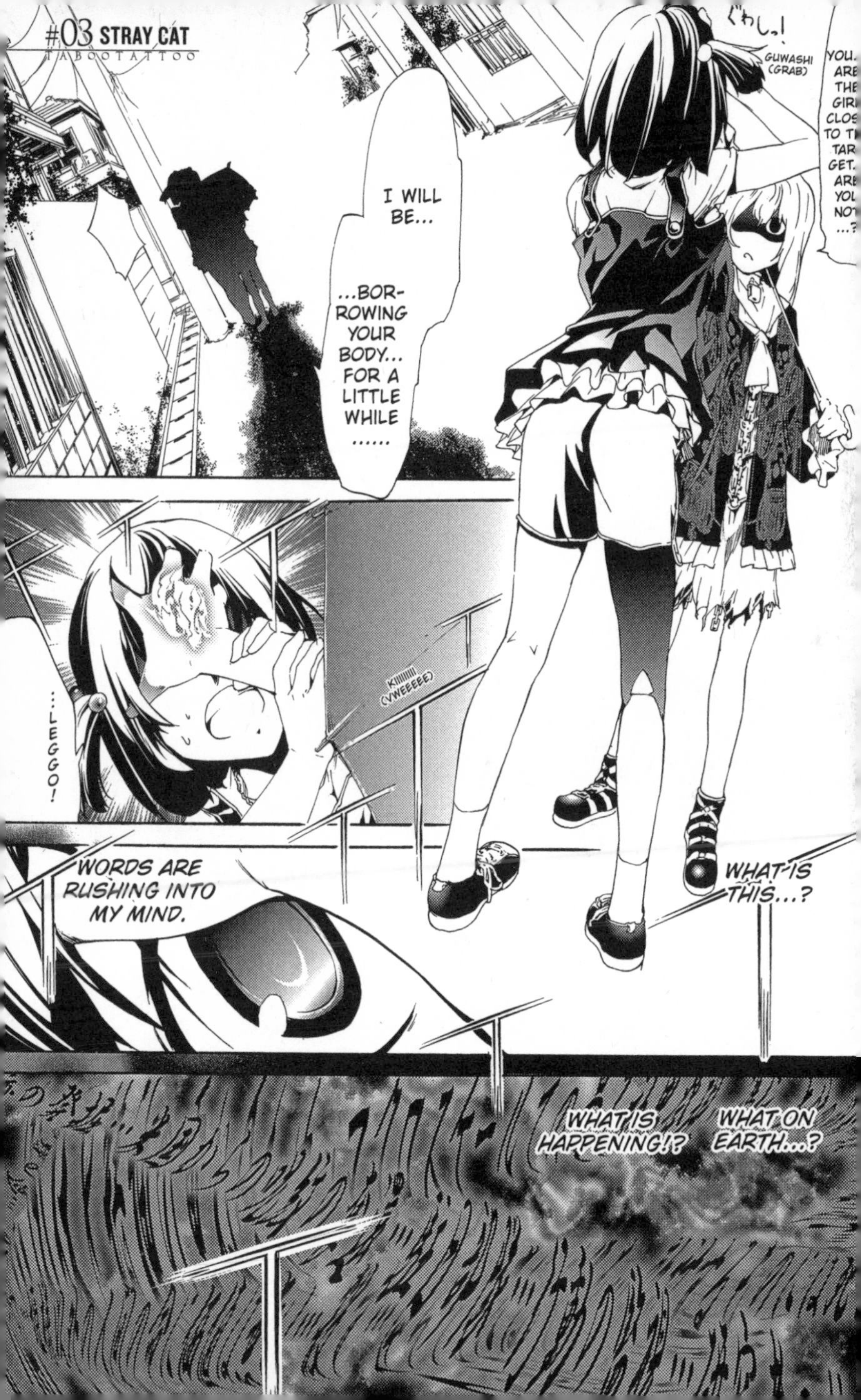
ぐわしっ!
GUWASHI (GRAB)
YOU... ARE THE GIR CLOS TO T TAR GET. ARE YOU NOT ...?
I WILL BE...
...BOR-ROWING YOUR BODY... FOR A LITTLE WHILE ......
KIIIIIII (VWEEEEE)
...LEGGO!
WHAT IS THIS...?
WORDS ARE RUSHING INTO MY MIND.
WHAT ON EARTH...?
WHAT IS HAPPENING!?

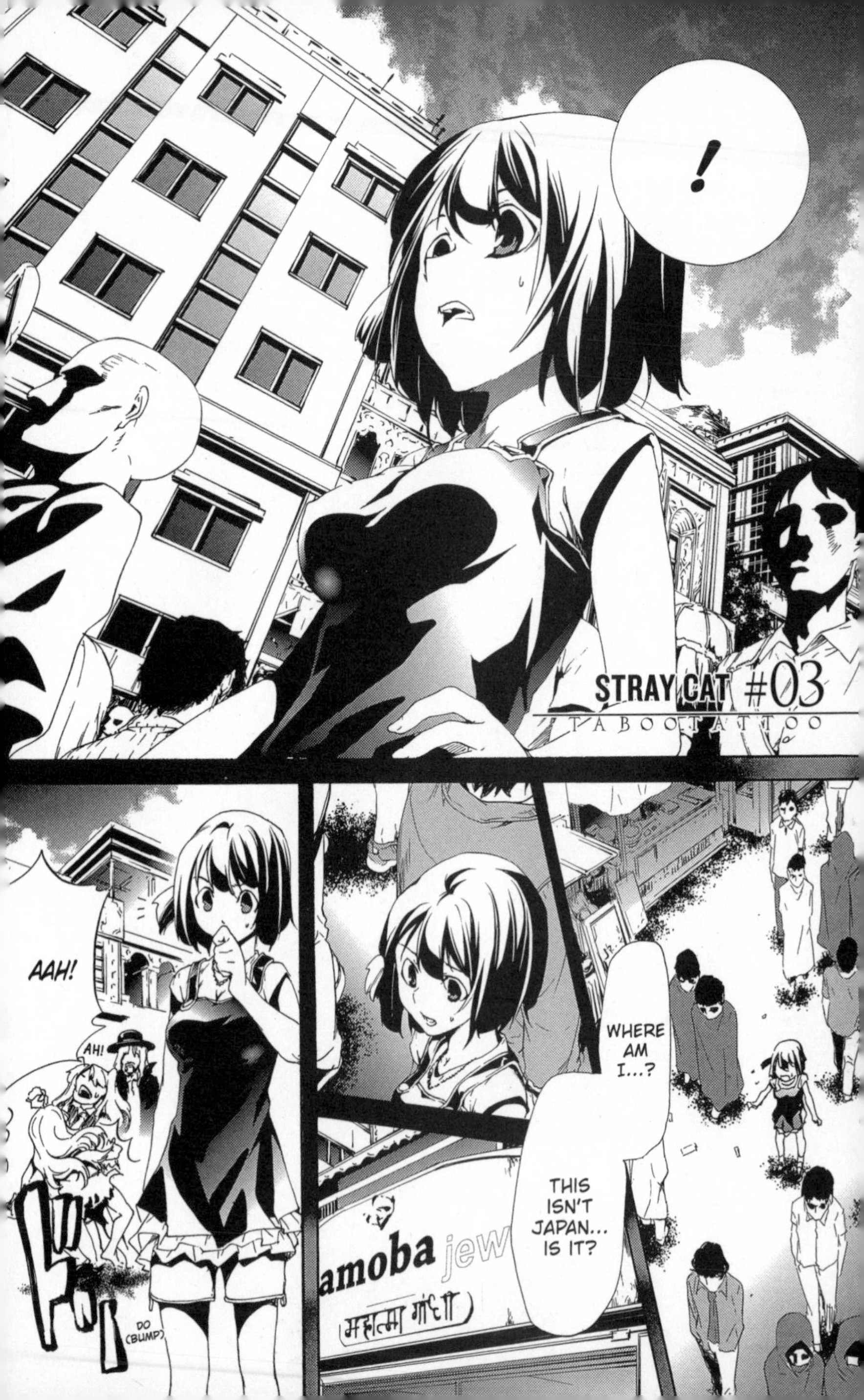
!
STRAY CAT #03
TABOO TATTOO
WHERE AM I...?
THIS ISN'T JAPAN... IS IT?
AAH!
AH!
DO (BUMP)

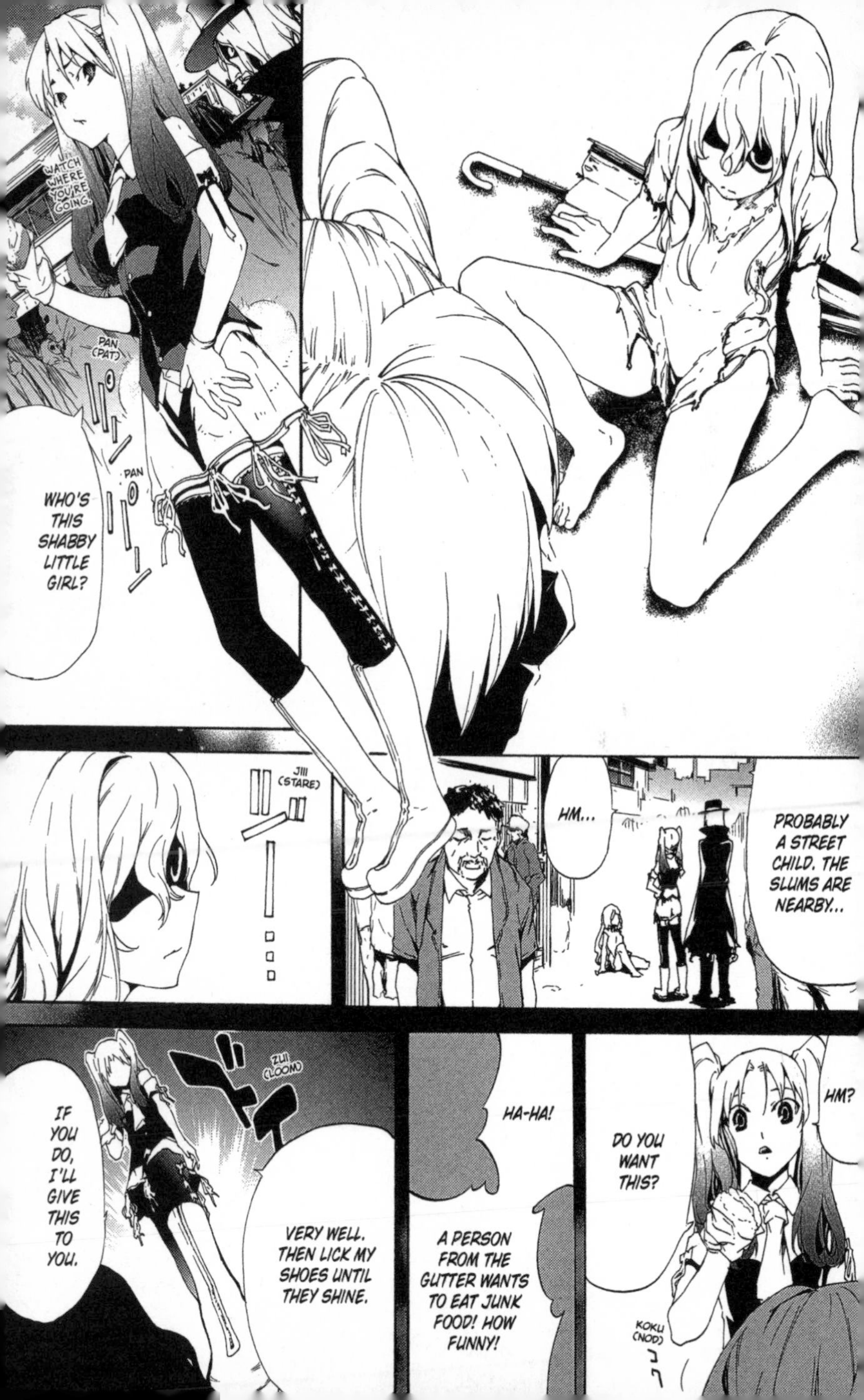
WATCH WHERE YOU'RE GOING.
PAN (PAT)
PAN
WHO'S THIS SHABBY LITTLE GIRL?
PROBABLY A STREET CHILD. THE SLUMS ARE NEARBY...
HM...
JIII (STARE)
...
HM?
DO YOU WANT THIS?
KOKU (NOD)
HA-HA!
A PERSON FROM THE GUTTER WANTS TO EAT JUNK FOOD! HOW FUNNY!
ZUI (LOOM)
VERY WELL. THEN LICK MY SHOES UNTIL THEY SHINE.
IF YOU DO, I'LL GIVE THIS TO YOU.

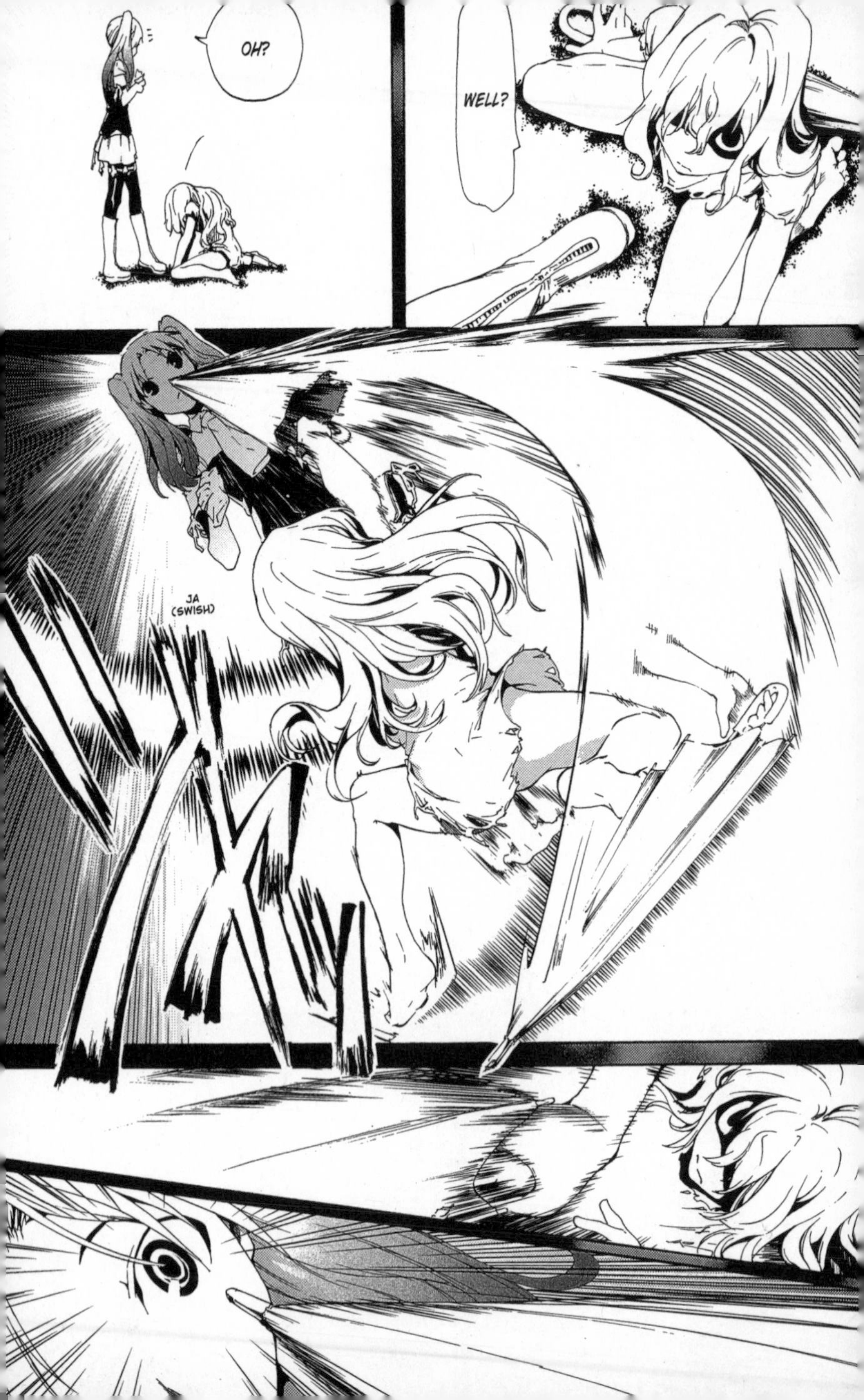
WELL?
OH?
JA
(SWISH)

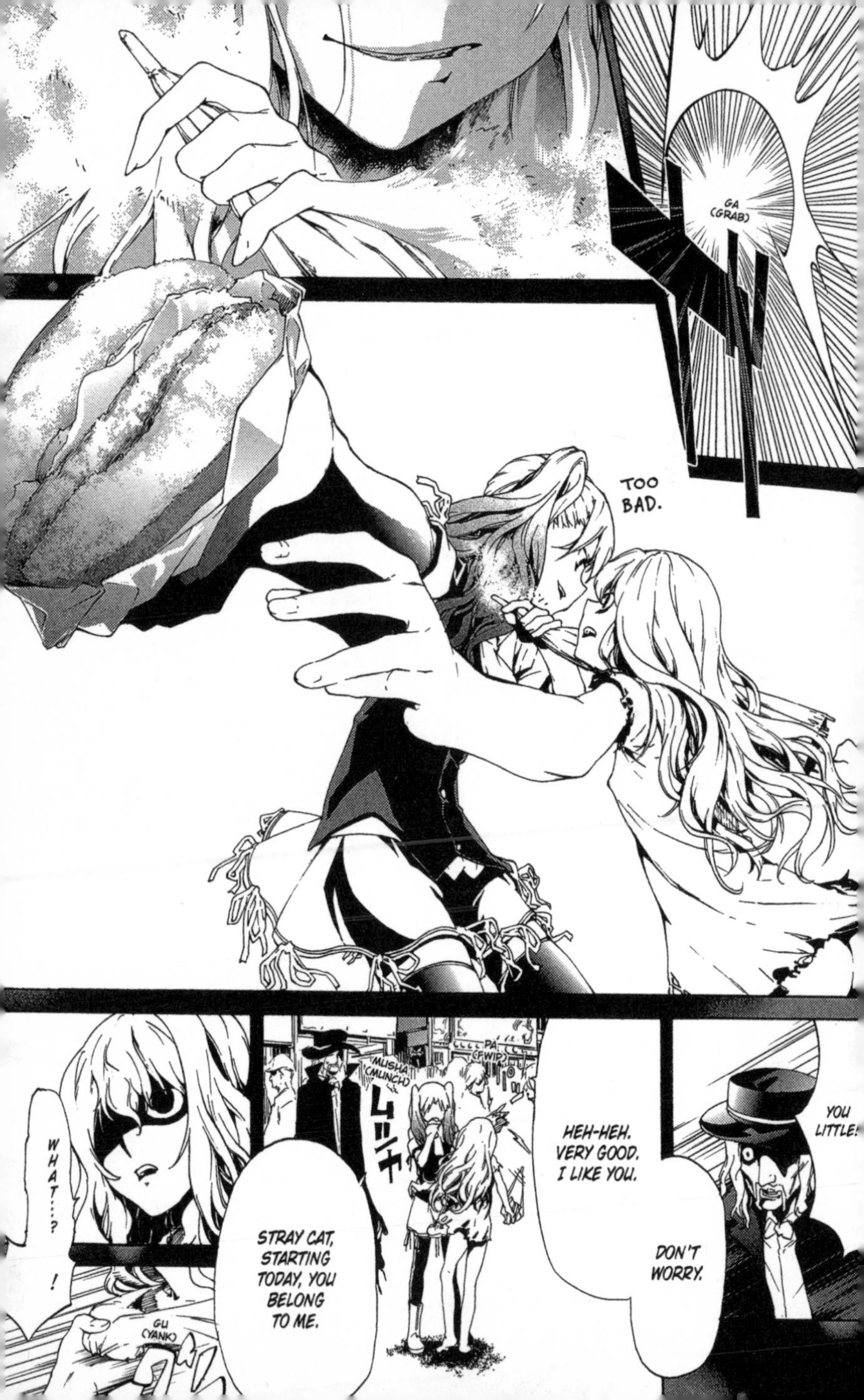
GA (GRAB)
TOO BAD.
YOU LITTLE!
HEH-HEH. VERY GOOD. I LIKE YOU.
DON'T WORRY.
STRAY CAT, STARTING TODAY, YOU BELONG TO ME.
PA (FWIP)
MUSHA (MUNCH)
WHAT...?
!
GU (YANK)

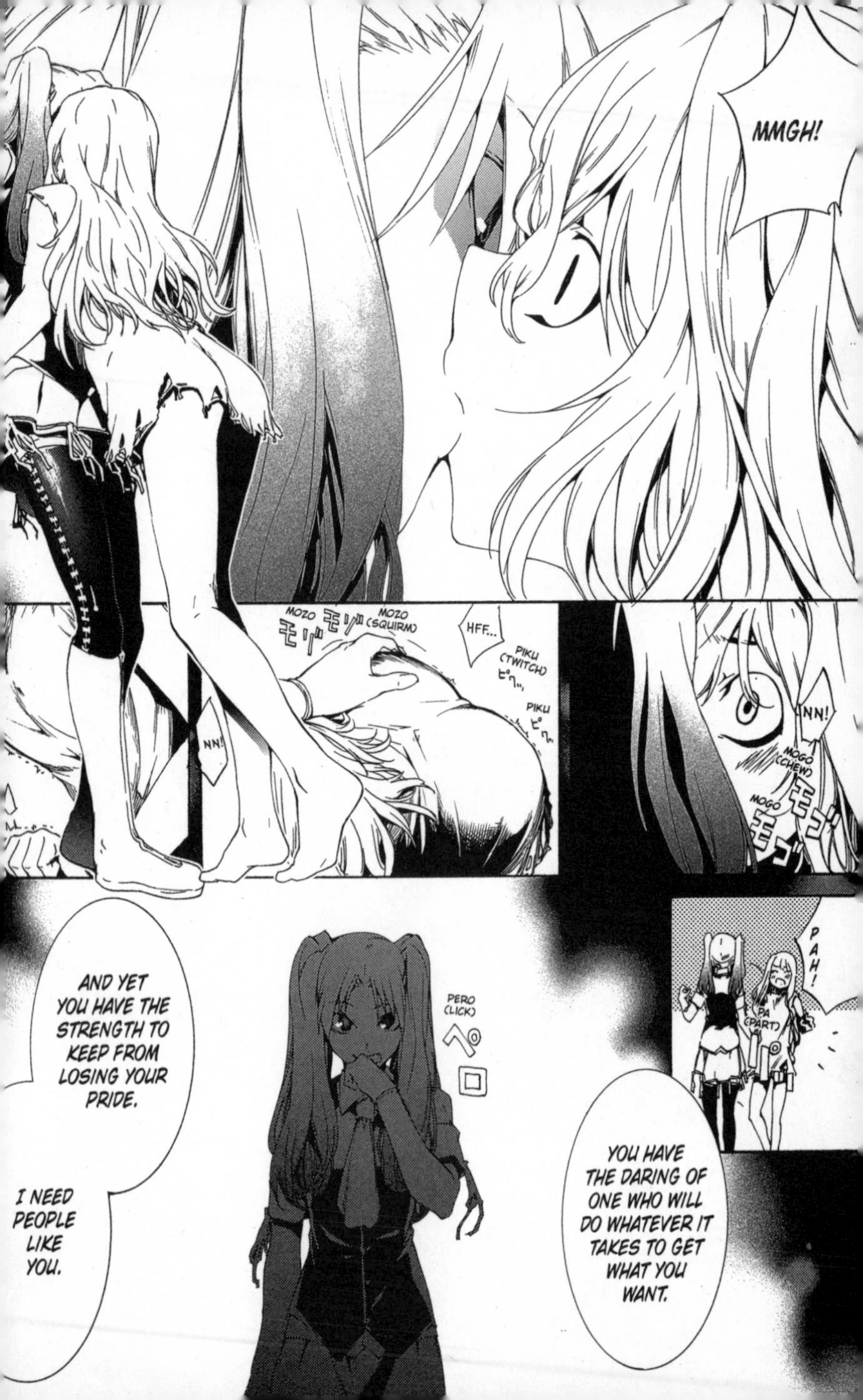
MMGH!
NN!
MOGO (CHEW)
MOGO
MOZO MOZO (SQUIRM)
HFF...
PIKU (TWITCH)
PIKU
NN!
PAH!
PA (PART)
YOU HAVE THE DARING OF ONE WHO WILL DO WHATEVER IT TAKES TO GET WHAT YOU WANT.
PERO (LICK)
AND YET YOU HAVE THE STRENGTH TO KEEP FROM LOSING YOUR PRIDE.
I NEED PEOPLE LIKE YOU.

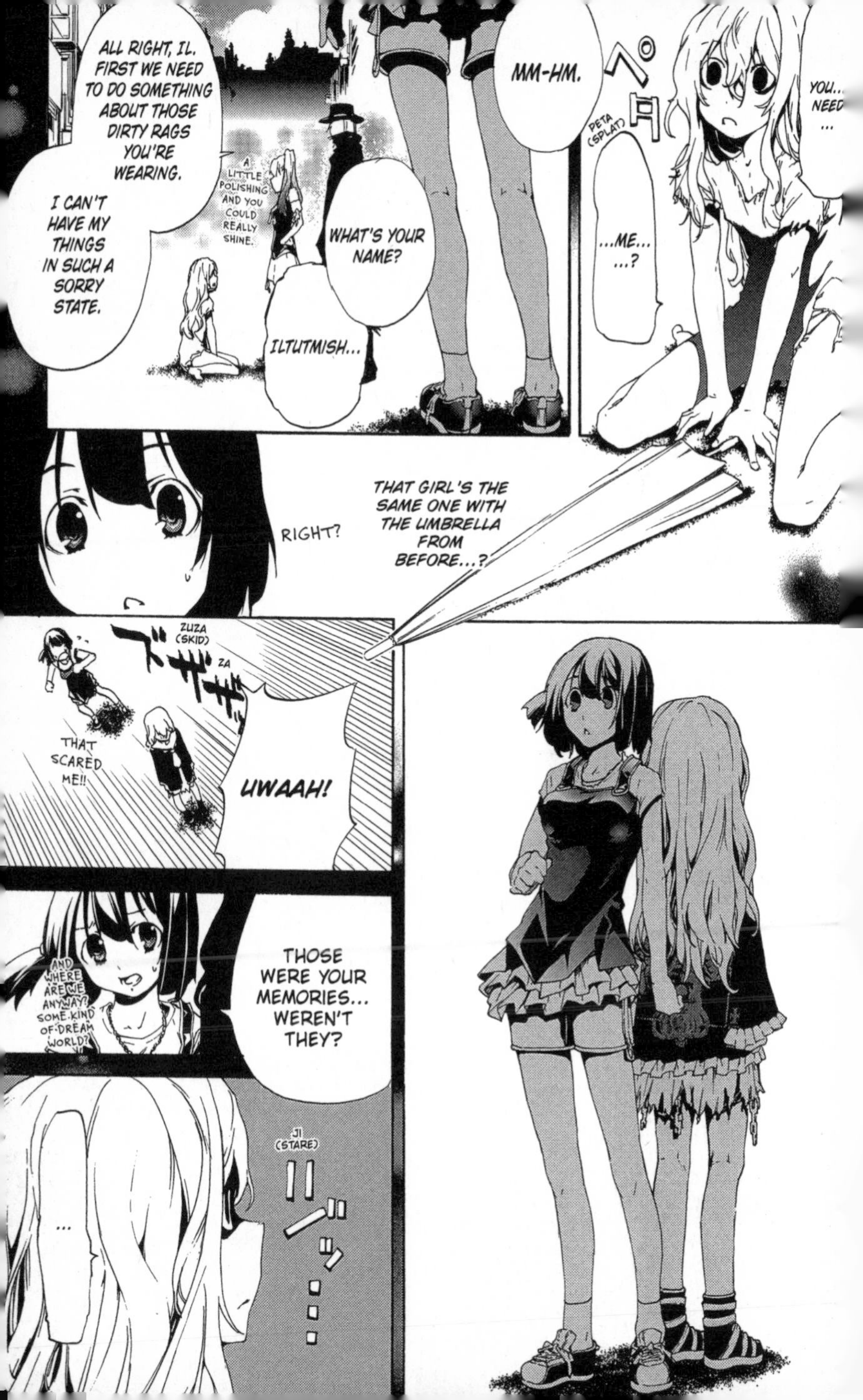
YOU... NEED ...
PETA (SPLAT)
...ME... ...?
MM-HM.
WHAT'S YOUR NAME?
ILTUTMISH...
ALL RIGHT, IL. FIRST WE NEED TO DO SOMETHING ABOUT THOSE DIRTY RAGS YOU'RE WEARING.
A LITTLE POLISHING AND YOU COULD REALLY SHINE.
I CAN'T HAVE MY THINGS IN SUCH A SORRY STATE.
THAT GIRL'S THE SAME ONE WITH THE UMBRELLA FROM BEFORE...?
RIGHT?
ZUZA (SKID)
ZA
UWAAH!
THAT SCARED ME!!
THOSE WERE YOUR MEMORIES... WEREN'T THEY?
AND WHERE ARE WE ANYWAY? SOME KIND OF DREAM WORLD?
JI (STARE)
...

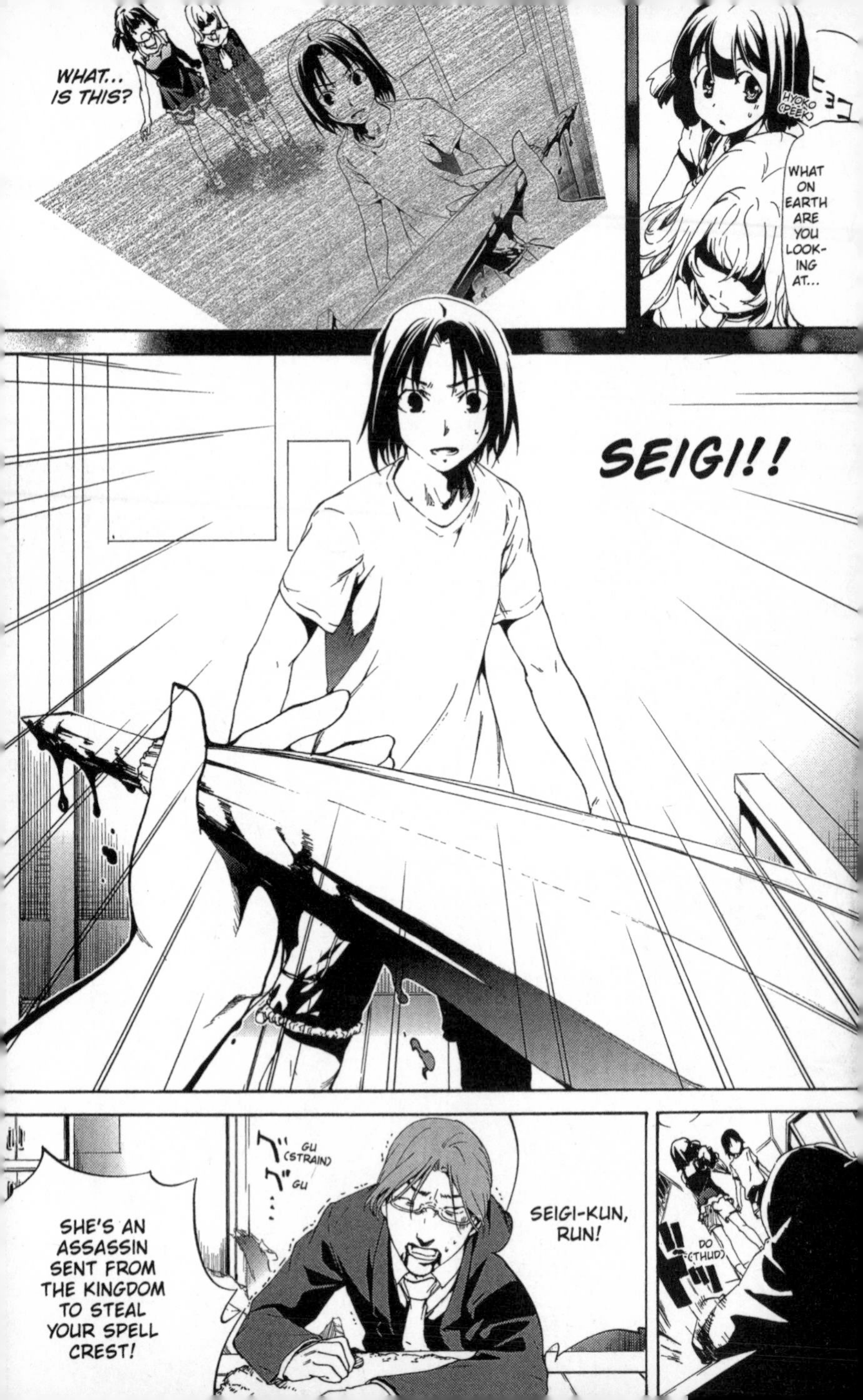

HYOKO (PEEK)
WHAT ON EARTH ARE YOU LOOKING AT...
WHAT... IS THIS?
SEIGI!!
DO (THUD)
SEIGI-KUN, RUN!
GU (STRAIN)
GU
SHE'S AN ASSASSIN SENT FROM THE KINGDOM TO STEAL YOUR SPELL CREST!

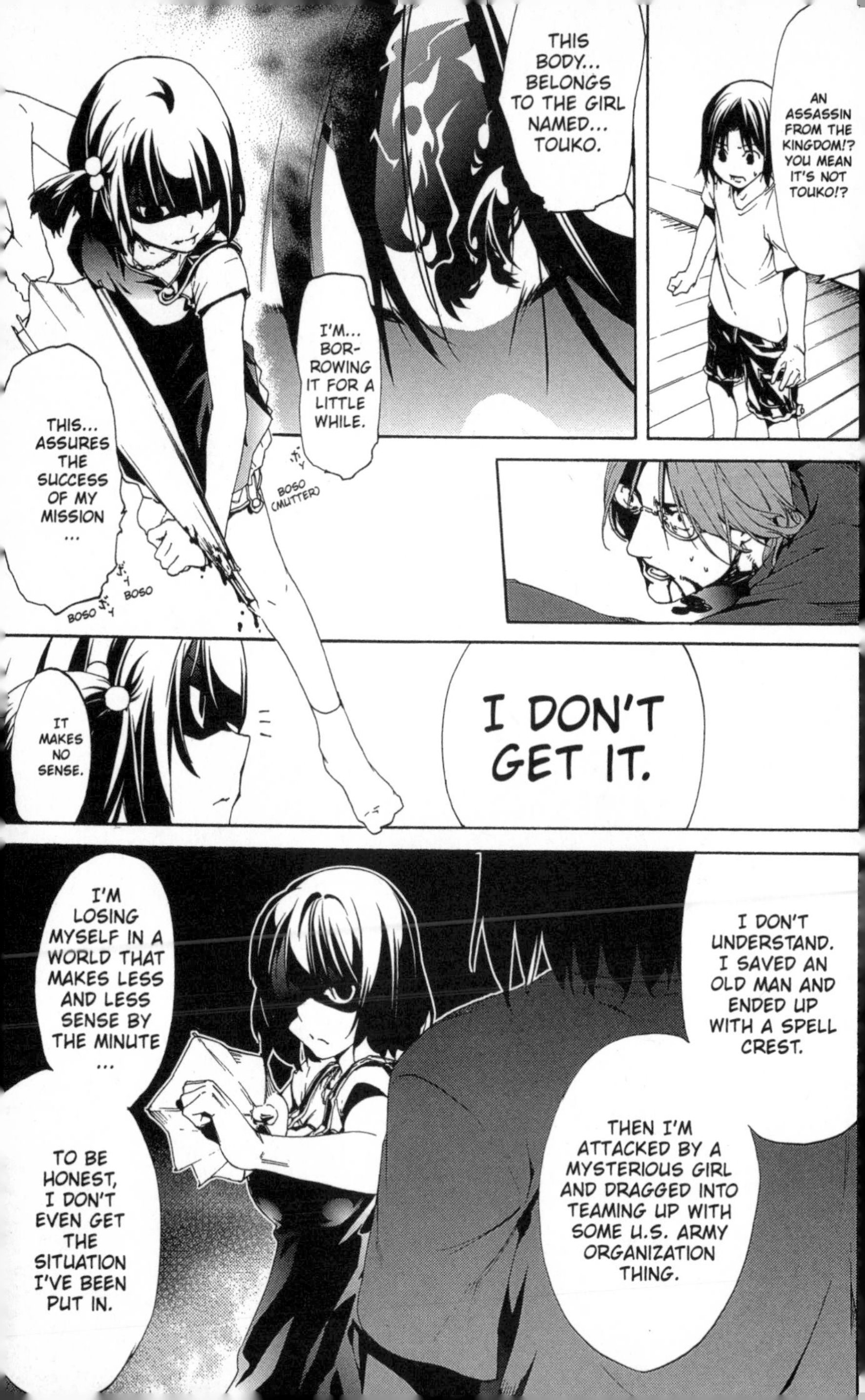
AN ASSASSIN FROM THE KINGDOM!? YOU MEAN IT'S NOT TOUKO!?
THIS BODY... BELONGS TO THE GIRL NAMED... TOUKO.
I'M... BOR-ROWING IT FOR A LITTLE WHILE.
BOSO (MUTTER)
THIS... ASSURES THE SUCCESS OF MY MISSION ...
BOSO
BOSO
I DON'T GET IT.
IT MAKES NO SENSE.
I DON'T UNDERSTAND. I SAVED AN OLD MAN AND ENDED UP WITH A SPELL CREST.
THEN I'M ATTACKED BY A MYSTERIOUS GIRL AND DRAGGED INTO TEAMING UP WITH SOME U.S. ARMY ORGANIZATION THING.
I'M LOSING MYSELF IN A WORLD THAT MAKES LESS AND LESS SENSE BY THE MINUTE ...
TO BE HONEST, I DON'T EVEN GET THE SITUATION I'VE BEEN PUT IN.

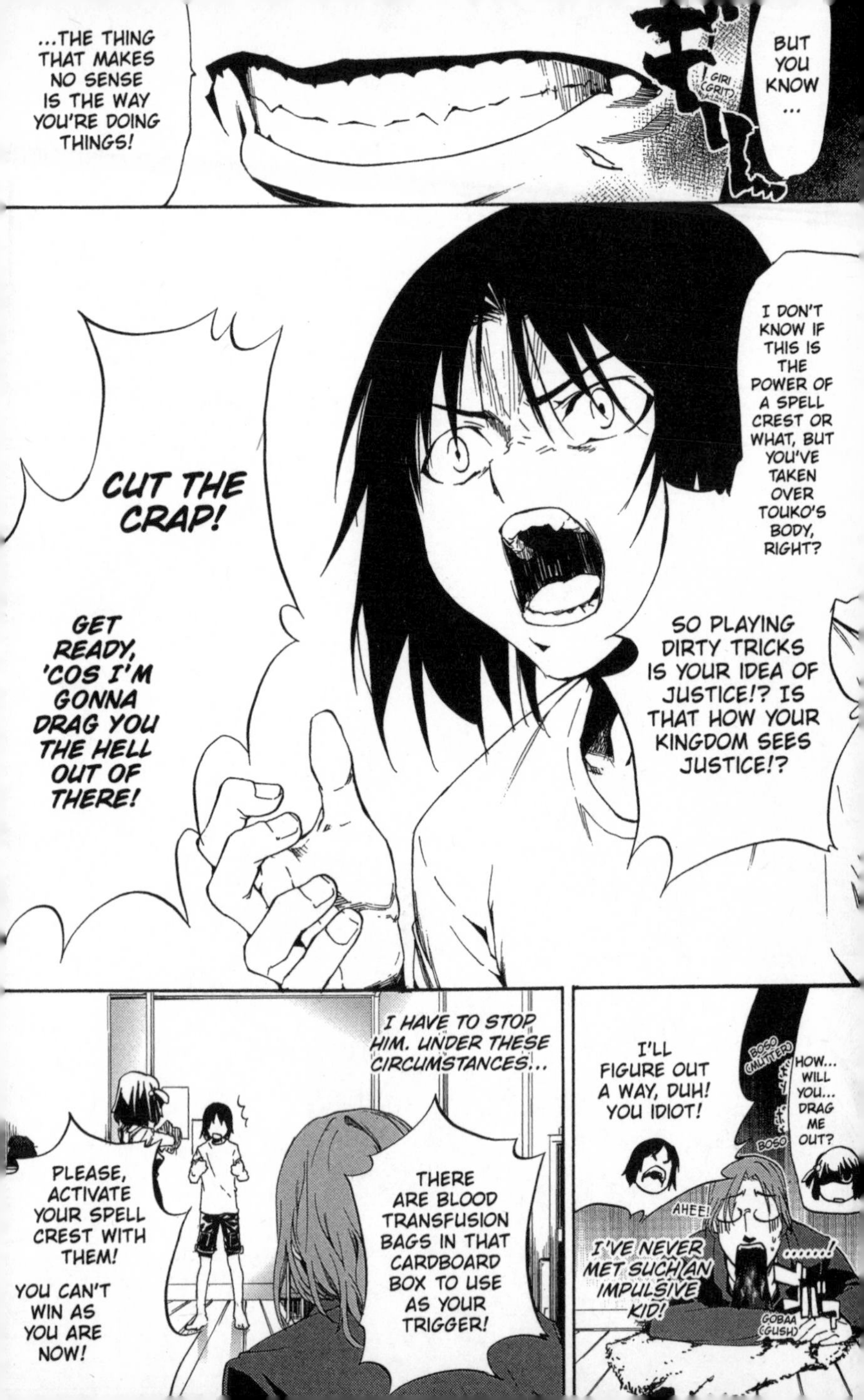

BUT YOU KNOW ...
GIRI (GRIT)
...THE THING THAT MAKES NO SENSE IS THE WAY YOU'RE DOING THINGS!
I DON'T KNOW IF THIS IS THE POWER OF A SPELL CREST OR WHAT, BUT YOU'VE TAKEN OVER TOUKO'S BODY, RIGHT?
SO PLAYING DIRTY TRICKS IS YOUR IDEA OF JUSTICE!? IS THAT HOW YOUR KINGDOM SEES JUSTICE!?
CUT THE CRAP!
GET READY, 'COS I'M GONNA DRAG YOU THE HELL OUT OF THERE!
HOW... WILL YOU... DRAG ME OUT?
BOSO (MUTTER)
BOSO
I'LL FIGURE OUT A WAY, DUH! YOU IDIOT!
AHEE!
......!
I'VE NEVER MET SUCH AN IMPULSIVE KID!
GOBAA (GUSH)
I HAVE TO STOP HIM. UNDER THESE CIRCUMSTANCES...
THERE ARE BLOOD TRANSFUSION BAGS IN THAT CARDBOARD BOX TO USE AS YOUR TRIGGER!
PLEASE, ACTIVATE YOUR SPELL CREST WITH THEM!
YOU CAN'T WIN AS YOU ARE NOW!

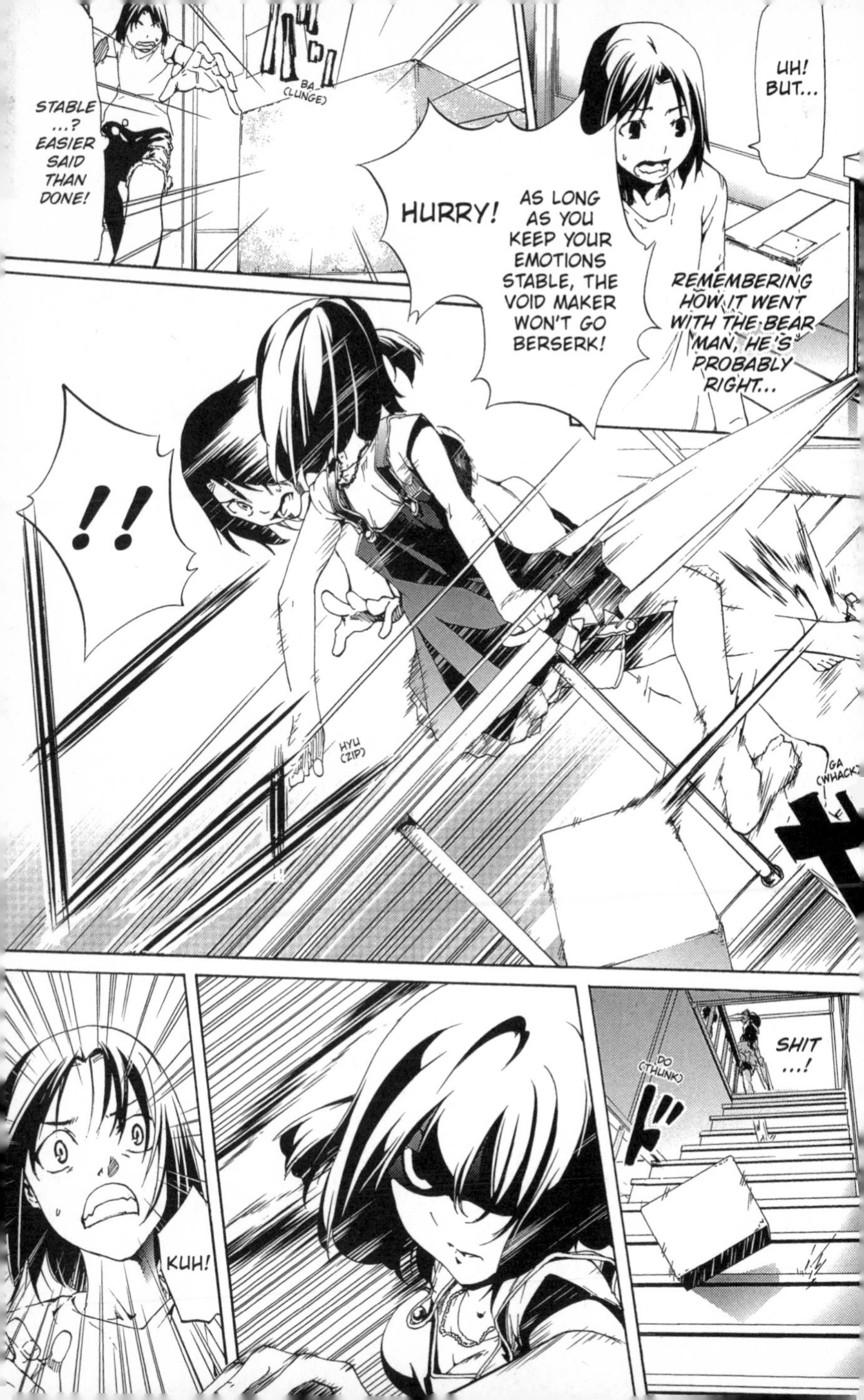

UH! BUT...
HURRY!
AS LONG AS YOU KEEP YOUR EMOTIONS STABLE, THE VOID MAKER WON'T GO BERSERK!
REMEMBERING HOW IT WENT WITH THE BEAR MAN, HE'S PROBABLY RIGHT...
BA (LUNGE)
STABLE ...? EASIER SAID THAN DONE!
GA (WHACK)
HYU (ZIP)
!!
SHIT ...!
DO (THUNK)
KUH!

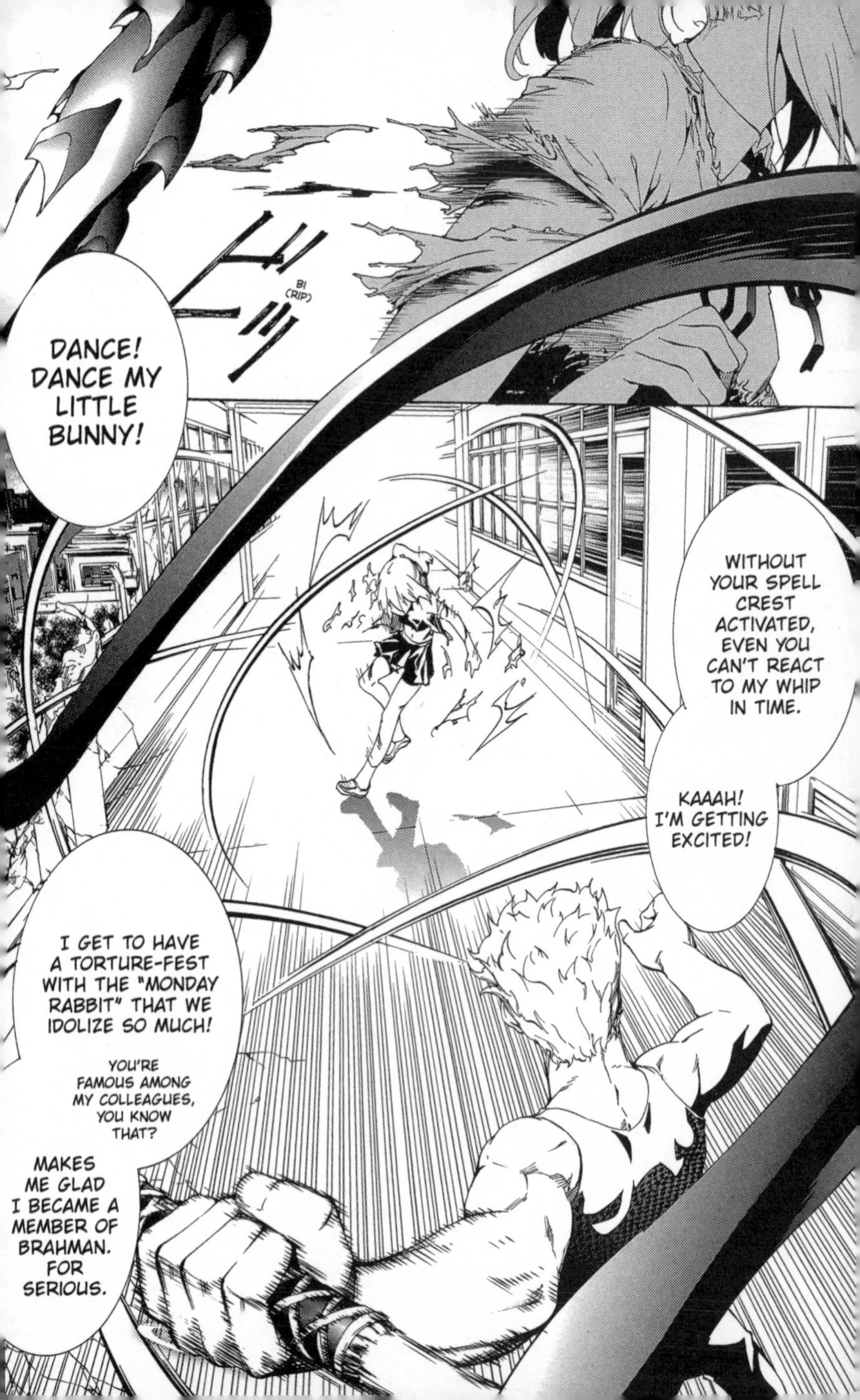
BI (RIP)
DANCE! DANCE MY LITTLE BUNNY!
WITHOUT YOUR SPELL CREST ACTIVATED, EVEN YOU CAN'T REACT TO MY WHIP IN TIME.
KAAAH! I'M GETTING EXCITED!
I GET TO HAVE A TORTURE-FEST WITH THE "MONDAY RABBIT" THAT WE IDOLIZE SO MUCH!
YOU'RE FAMOUS AMONG MY COLLEAGUES, YOU KNOW THAT?
MAKES ME GLAD I BECAME A MEMBER OF BRAHMAN. FOR SERIOUS.

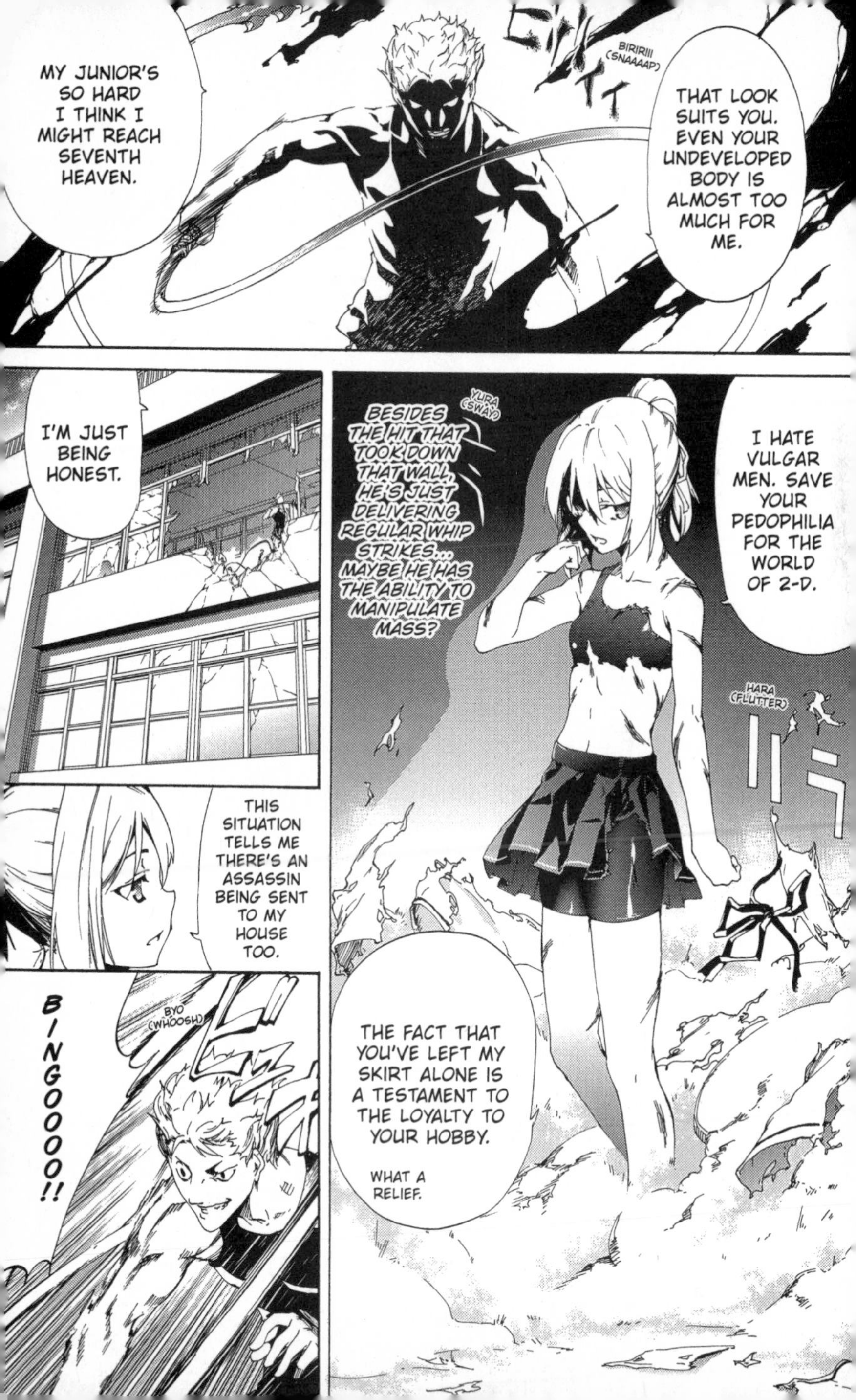
BIRIRIII (SNAAAAP)
THAT LOOK SUITS YOU. EVEN YOUR UNDEVELOPED BODY IS ALMOST TOO MUCH FOR ME.
MY JUNIOR'S SO HARD I THINK I MIGHT REACH SEVENTH HEAVEN.
I HATE VULGAR MEN. SAVE YOUR PEDOPHILIA FOR THE WORLD OF 2-D.
YURA (SWAY)
BESIDES THE HIT THAT TOOK DOWN THAT WALL, HE'S JUST DELIVERING REGULAR WHIP STRIKES... MAYBE HE HAS THE ABILITY TO MANIPULATE MASS?
HARA (FLUTTER)
THE FACT THAT YOU'VE LEFT MY SKIRT ALONE IS A TESTAMENT TO THE LOYALTY TO YOUR HOBBY.
WHAT A RELIEF.
I'M JUST BEING HONEST.
THIS SITUATION TELLS ME THERE'S AN ASSASSIN BEING SENT TO MY HOUSE TOO.
BYO (WHOOSH)
BINGOOOOO!!

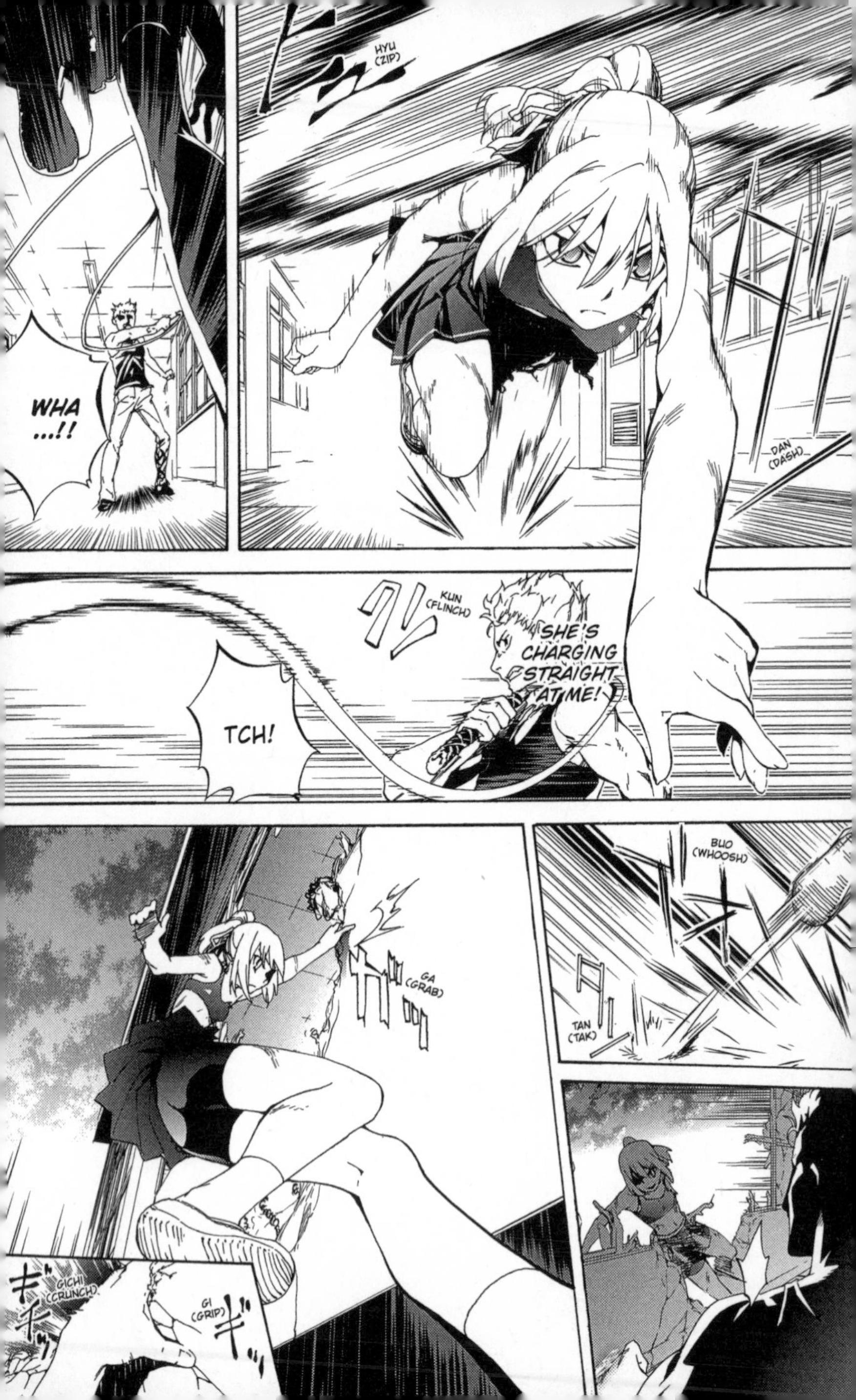

HYU (ZIP)
DAN (DASH)
WHA ...!!
KUN (FLINCH)
SHE'S CHARGING STRAIGHT AT ME!
TCH!
BUO (WHOOSH)
TAN (TAK)
GA (GRAB)
GI (GRIP)
GICHI (CRUNCH)

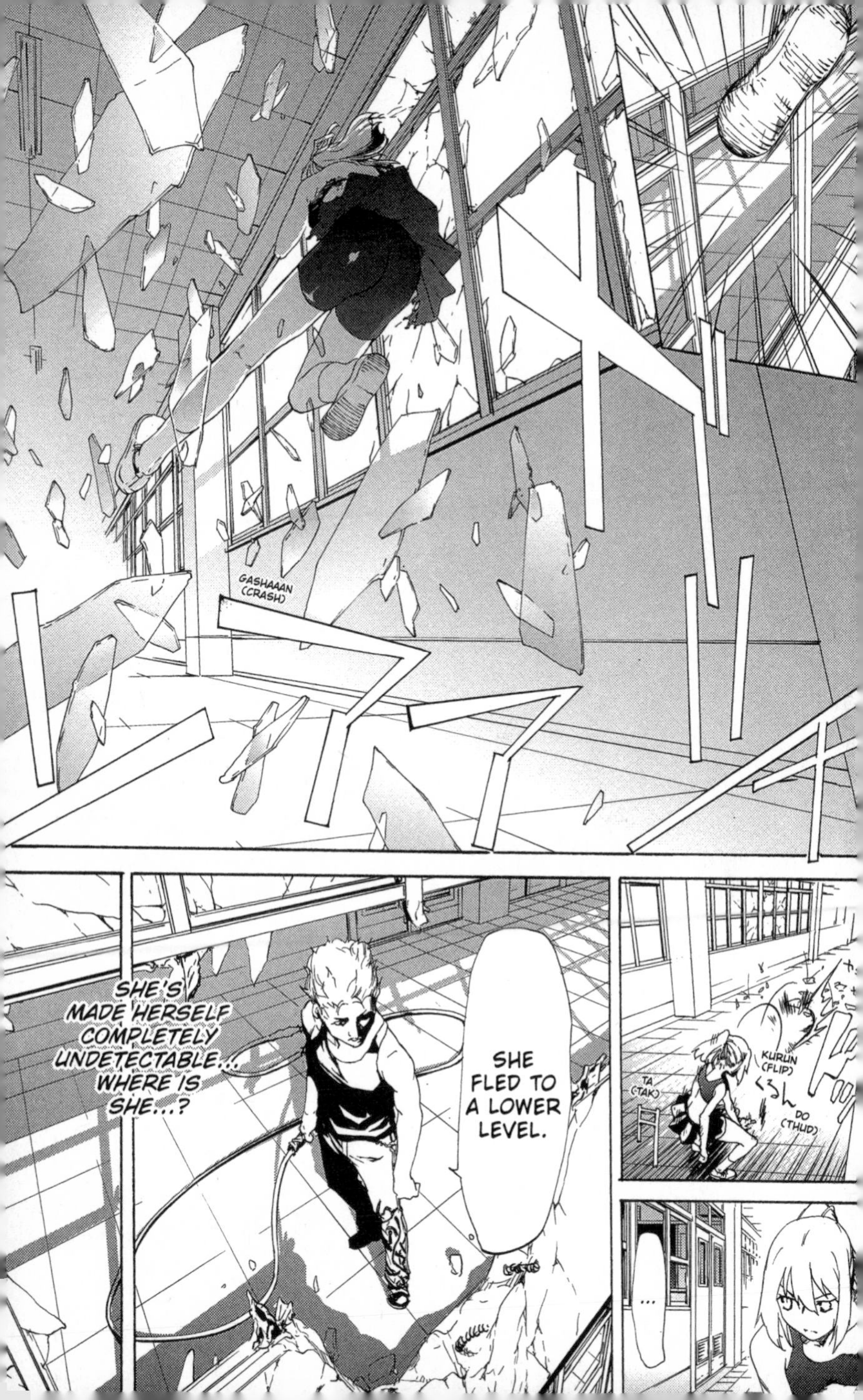
GASHAAAN (CRASH)
KURUN (FLIP)
くるん
TA (TAK)
DO (THUD)
...
SHE'S MADE HERSELF COMPLETELY UNDETECTABLE... WHERE IS SHE...?
SHE FLED TO A LOWER LEVEL.

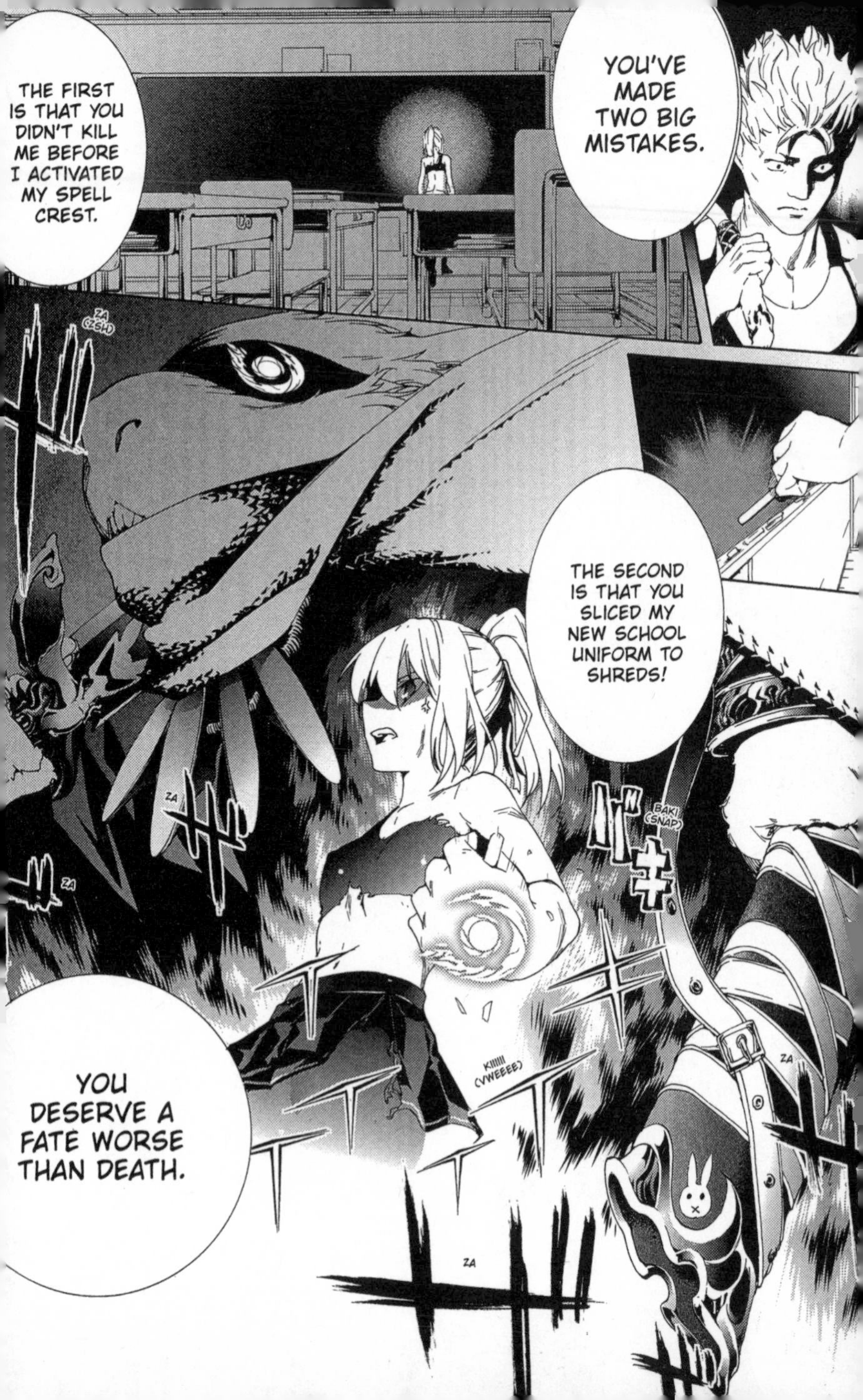
YOU'VE MADE TWO BIG MISTAKES.
THE FIRST IS THAT YOU DIDN'T KILL ME BEFORE I ACTIVATED MY SPELL CREST.
ZA (ZSHD)
THE SECOND IS THAT YOU SLICED MY NEW SCHOOL UNIFORM TO SHREDS!
BAKI (SNAP)
ZA
ZA
ZA
KIIIII (VWEEEE)
YOU DESERVE A FATE WORSE THAN DEATH.
ZA

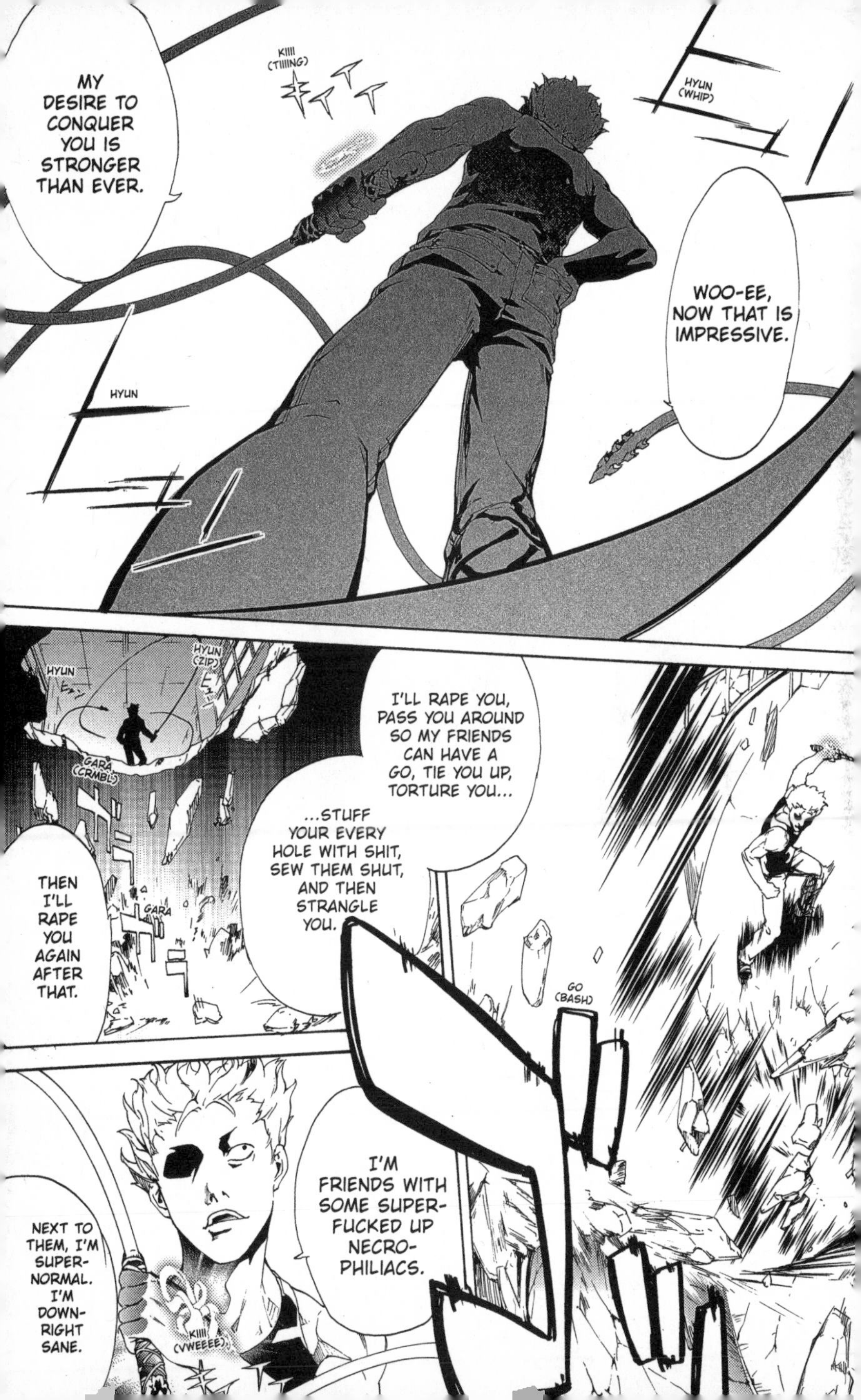
HYUN (WHIP)
WOO-EE, NOW THAT IS IMPRESSIVE.
KIIII (TIIIING)
MY DESIRE TO CONQUER YOU IS STRONGER THAN EVER.
HYUN
GO (BASH)
I'LL RAPE YOU, PASS YOU AROUND SO MY FRIENDS CAN HAVE A GO, TIE YOU UP, TORTURE YOU...
...STUFF YOUR EVERY HOLE WITH SHIT, SEW THEM SHUT, AND THEN STRANGLE YOU.
HYUN (ZIP)
HYUN
GARA (CRMBL)
GARA
THEN I'LL RAPE YOU AGAIN AFTER THAT.
I'M FRIENDS WITH SOME SUPER-FUCKED UP NECRO-PHILIACS.
NEXT TO THEM, I'M SUPER-NORMAL. I'M DOWN-RIGHT SANE.
KIIII (VWEEEE)

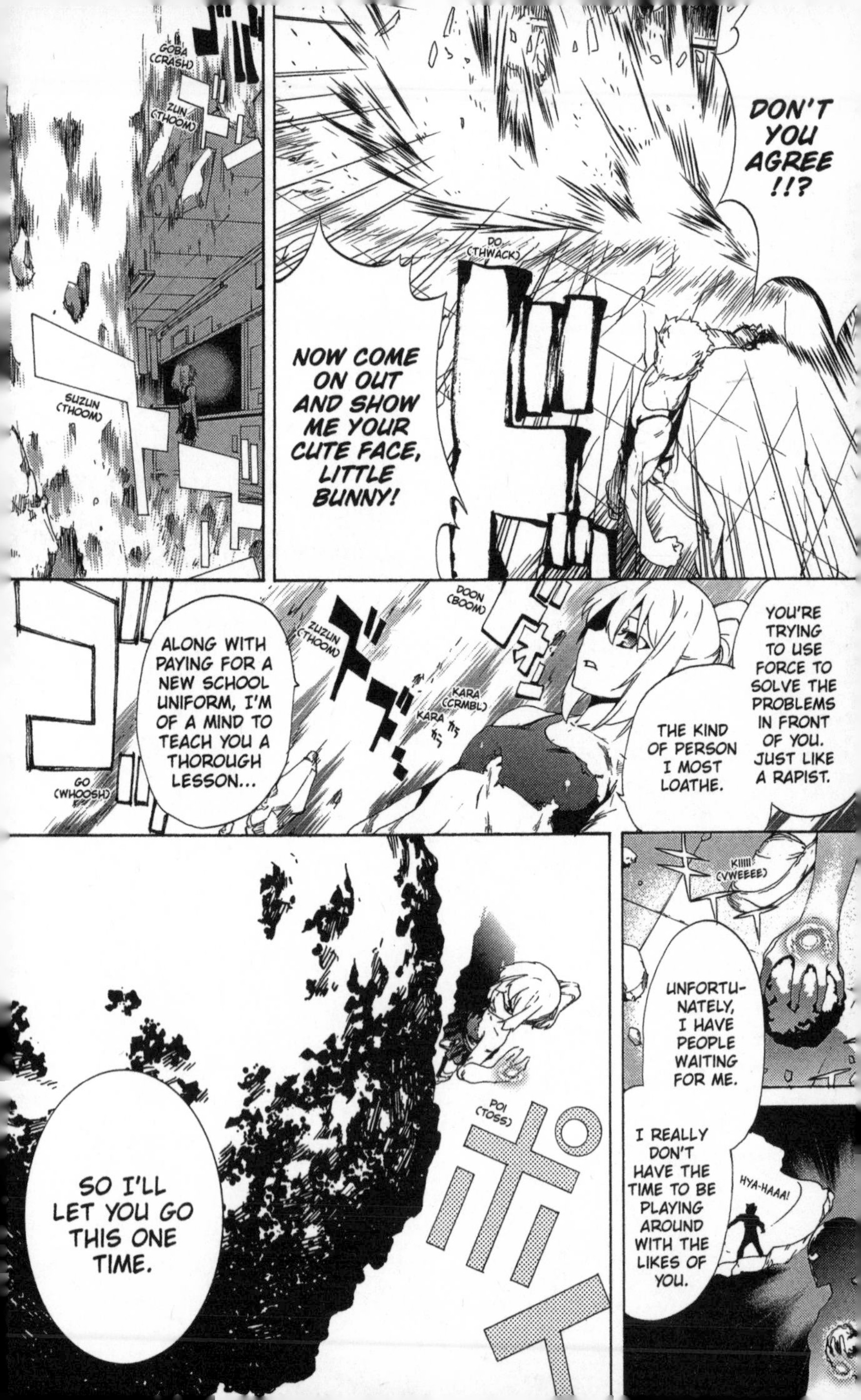
DON'T YOU AGREE!!?
DO (THWACK)
NOW COME ON OUT AND SHOW ME YOUR CUTE FACE, LITTLE BUNNY!
GOBA (CRASH)
ZUN (THOOM)
SUZUN (THOOM)
YOU'RE TRYING TO USE FORCE TO SOLVE THE PROBLEMS IN FRONT OF YOU. JUST LIKE A RAPIST.
THE KIND OF PERSON I MOST LOATHE.
DOON (BOOM)
KARA (CRMBL) KARA
ZUZUN (THOOM)
ALONG WITH PAYING FOR A NEW SCHOOL UNIFORM, I'M OF A MIND TO TEACH YOU A THOROUGH LESSON...
GO (WHOOSH)
KIIII (VWEEEE)
UNFORTU-NATELY, I HAVE PEOPLE WAITING FOR ME.
I REALLY DON'T HAVE THE TIME TO BE PLAYING AROUND WITH THE LIKES OF YOU.
HYA-HAAA!
POI (TOSS)
SO I'LL LET YOU GO THIS ONE TIME.

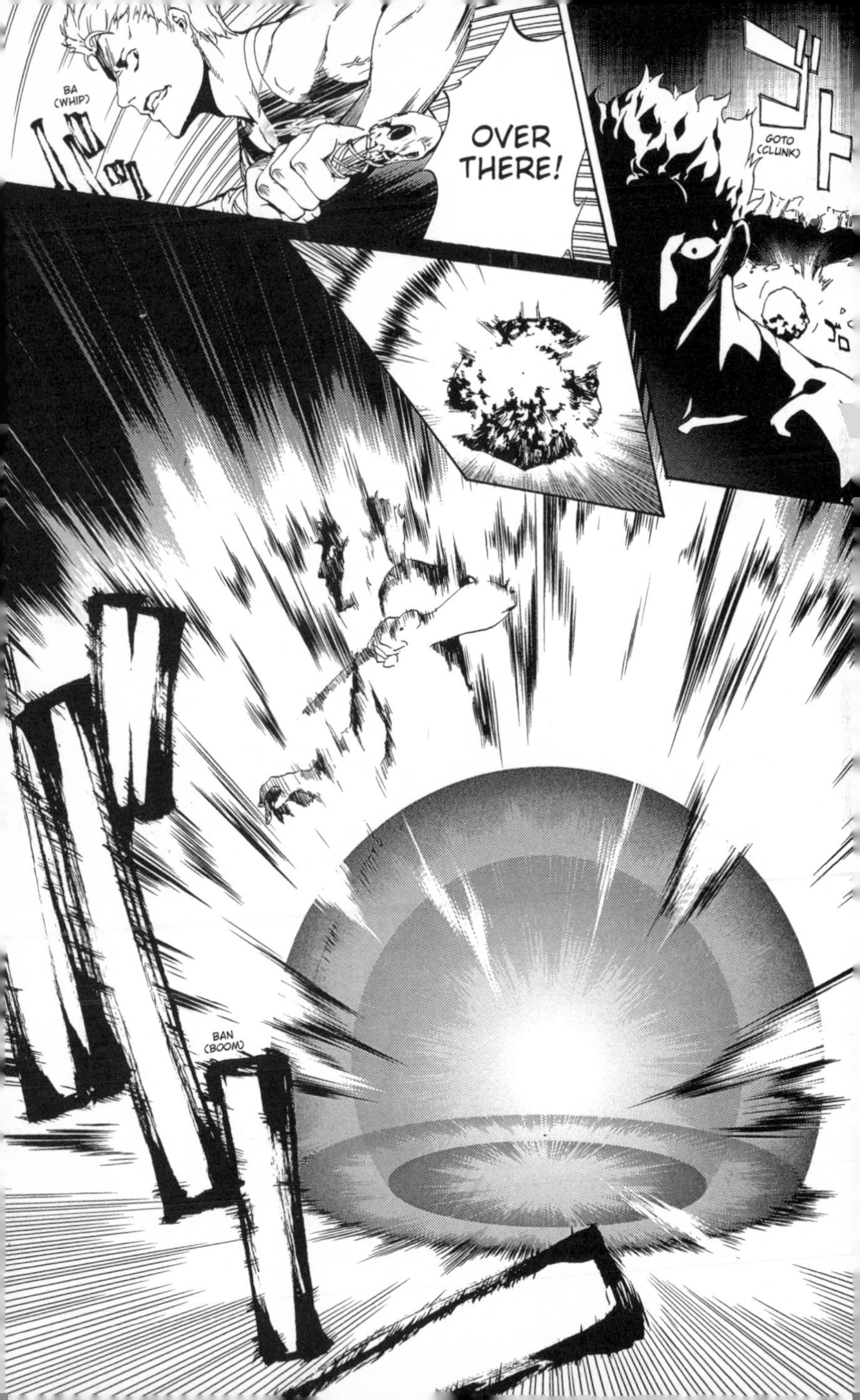
ゴト
GOTO (CLUNK)
BA (WHIP)
OVER THERE!
BAN (BOOM)

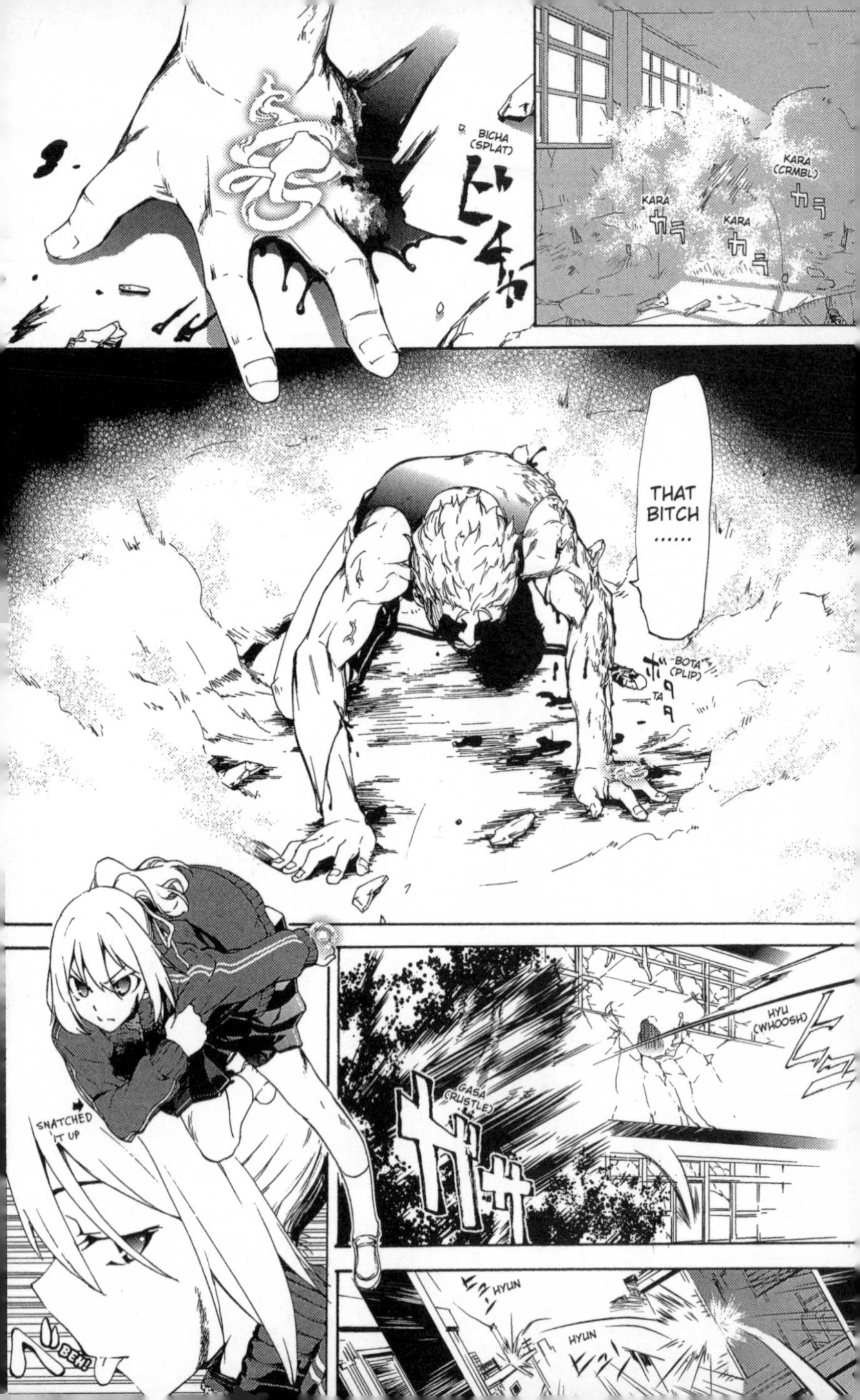
KARA (CRMBL)
KARA
KARA
BICHA (SPLAT)
THAT BITCH ......
BOTA (PLIP)
TA
HYU (WHOOSH)
GASA (RUSTLE)
HYUN
HYUN
SNATCHED IT UP
BEH!

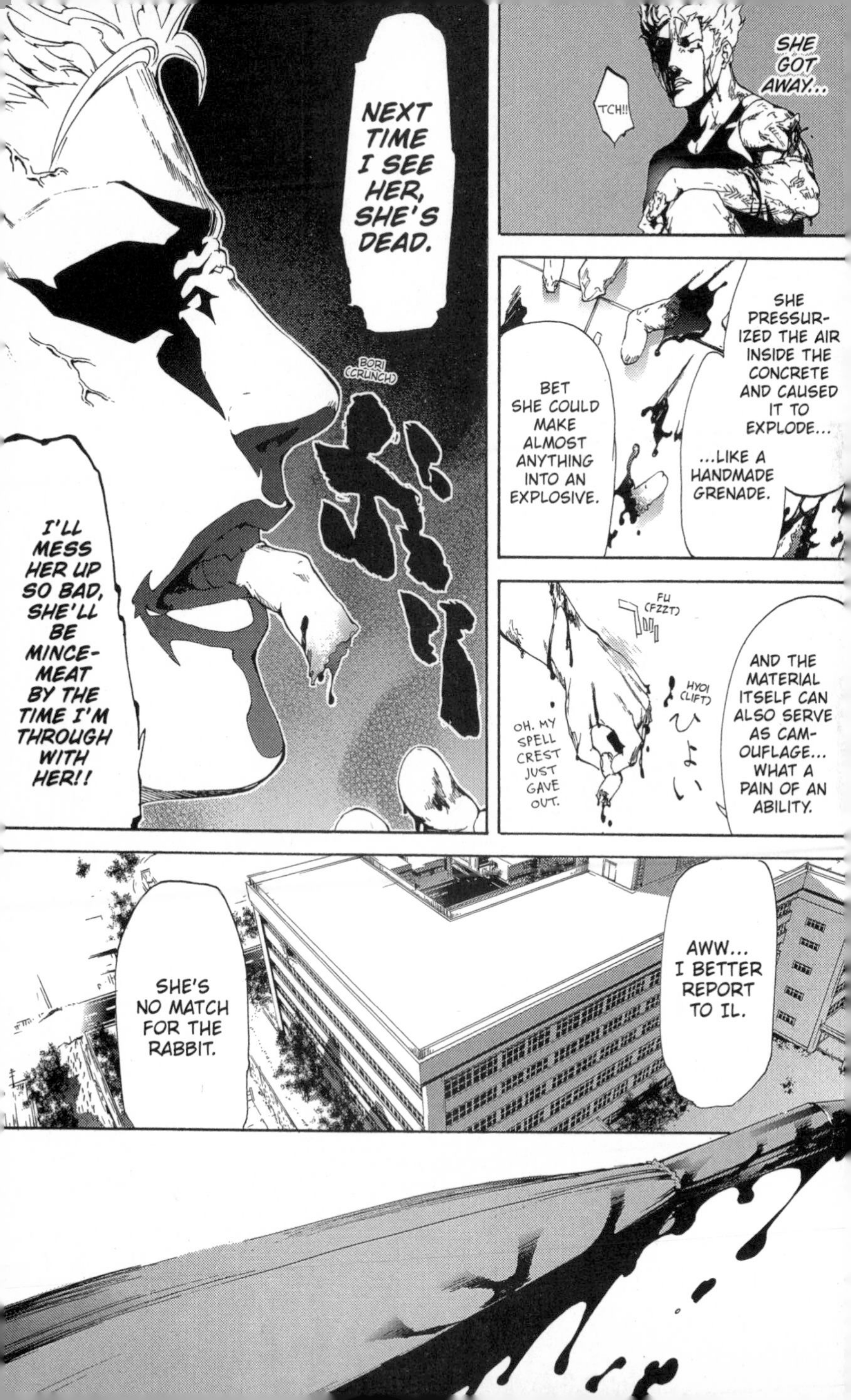
SHE GOT AWAY...
TCH!!
SHE PRESSURIZED THE AIR INSIDE THE CONCRETE AND CAUSED IT TO EXPLODE...
...LIKE A HANDMADE GRENADE.
BET SHE COULD MAKE ALMOST ANYTHING INTO AN EXPLOSIVE.
FU (FZZT)
AND THE MATERIAL ITSELF CAN ALSO SERVE AS CAMOUFLAGE... WHAT A PAIN OF AN ABILITY.
HYOI (LIFT)
OH. MY SPELL CREST JUST GAVE OUT.
NEXT TIME I SEE HER, SHE'S DEAD.
BORI (CRUNCH)
I'LL MESS HER UP SO BAD, SHE'LL BE MINCEMEAT BY THE TIME I'M THROUGH WITH HER!!
AWW... I BETTER REPORT TO IL.
SHE'S NO MATCH FOR THE RABBIT.

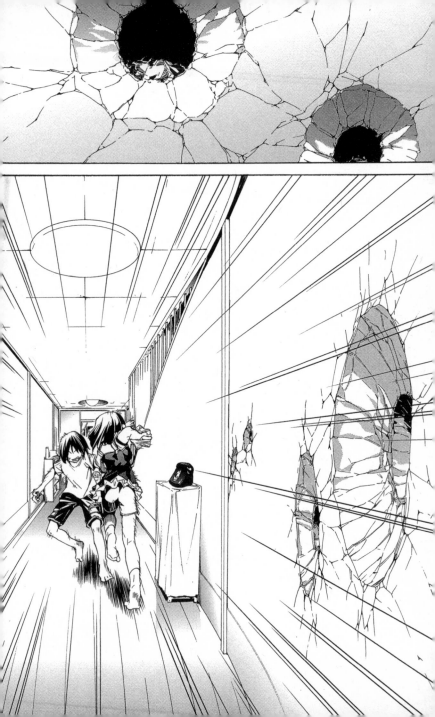

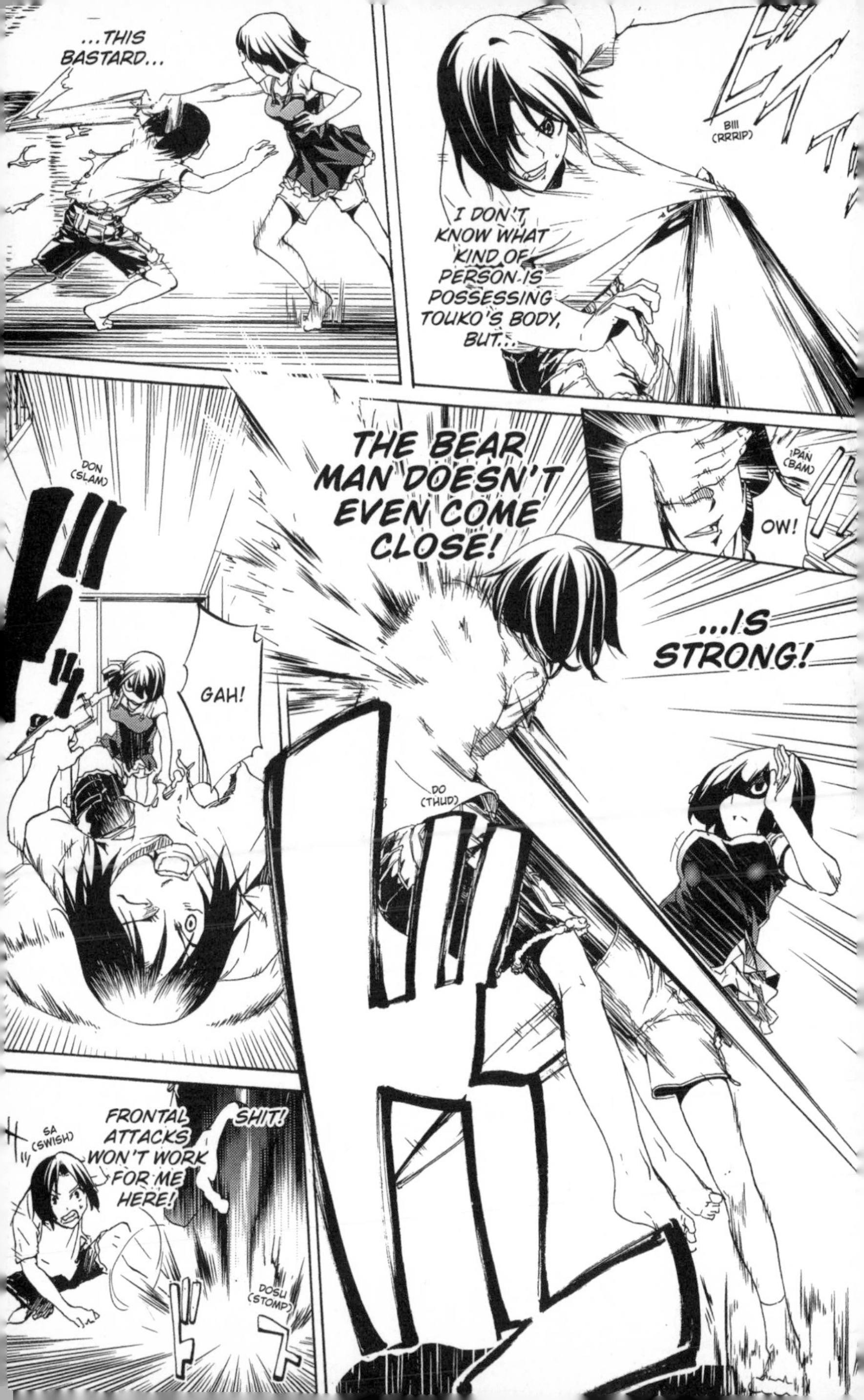
BIII (RRRIP)
I DON'T KNOW WHAT KIND OF PERSON IS POSSESSING TOUKO'S BODY, BUT...
...THIS BASTARD...
PAN (BAM)
OW!
THE BEAR MAN DOESN'T EVEN COME CLOSE!
...IS STRONG!
DO (THUD)
DON (SLAM)
GAH!
SHIT!
FRONTAL ATTACKS WON'T WORK FOR ME HERE!
SA (SWISH)
DOSU (STOMP)

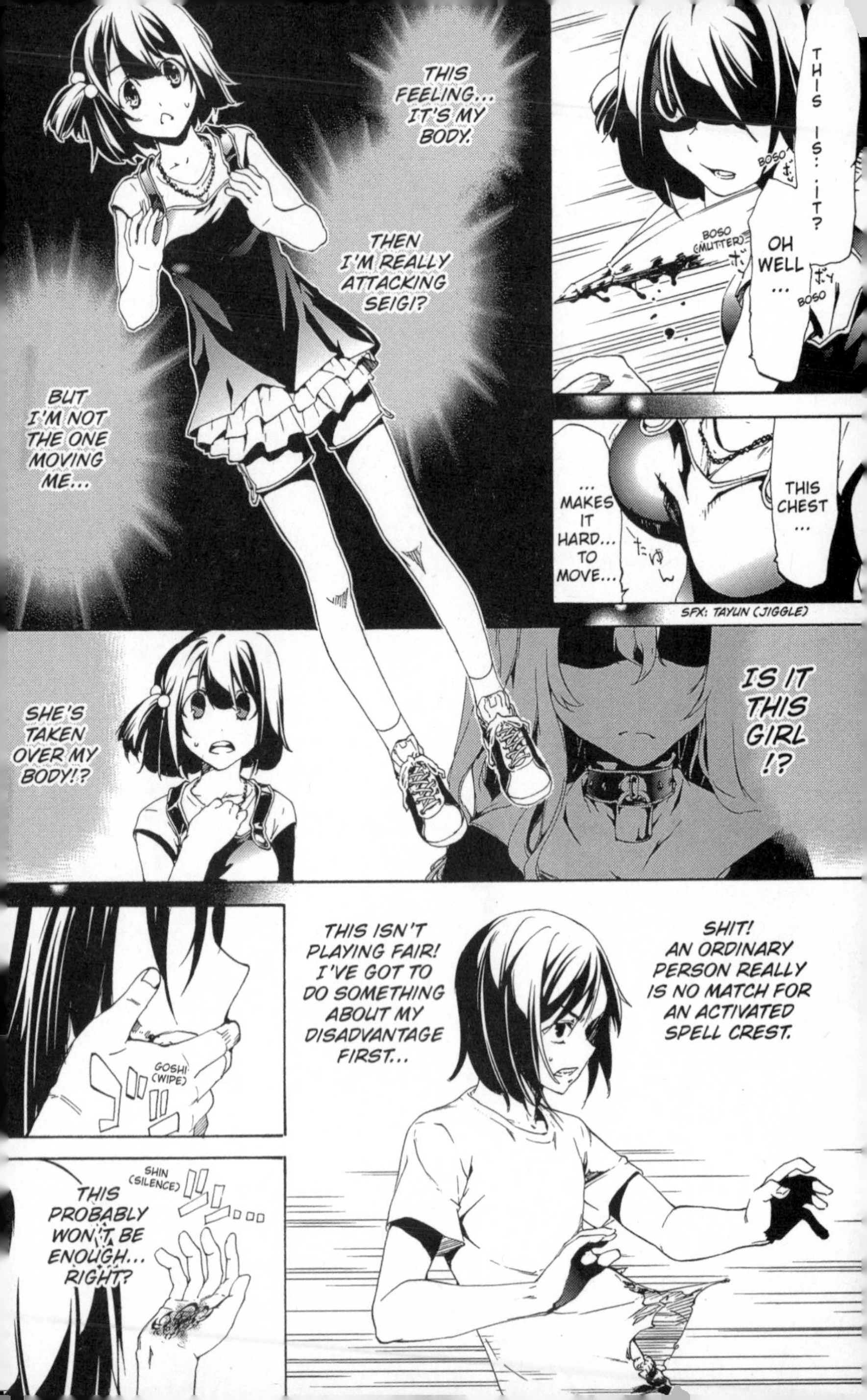
THIS IS... IT?
BOSO
BOSO (MUTTER)
OH WELL...
BOSO
THIS CHEST...
...MAKES IT HARD... TO MOVE...
SFX: TAYUN (JIGGLE)
THIS FEELING... IT'S MY BODY.
THEN I'M REALLY ATTACKING SEIGI?
BUT I'M NOT THE ONE MOVING ME...
IS IT THIS GIRL!?
SHE'S TAKEN OVER MY BODY!?
SHIT! AN ORDINARY PERSON REALLY IS NO MATCH FOR AN ACTIVATED SPELL CREST.
THIS ISN'T PLAYING FAIR! I'VE GOT TO DO SOMETHING ABOUT MY DISADVANTAGE FIRST...
GOSHI (WIPE)
SHIN (SILENCE)
THIS PROBABLY WON'T BE ENOUGH... RIGHT?

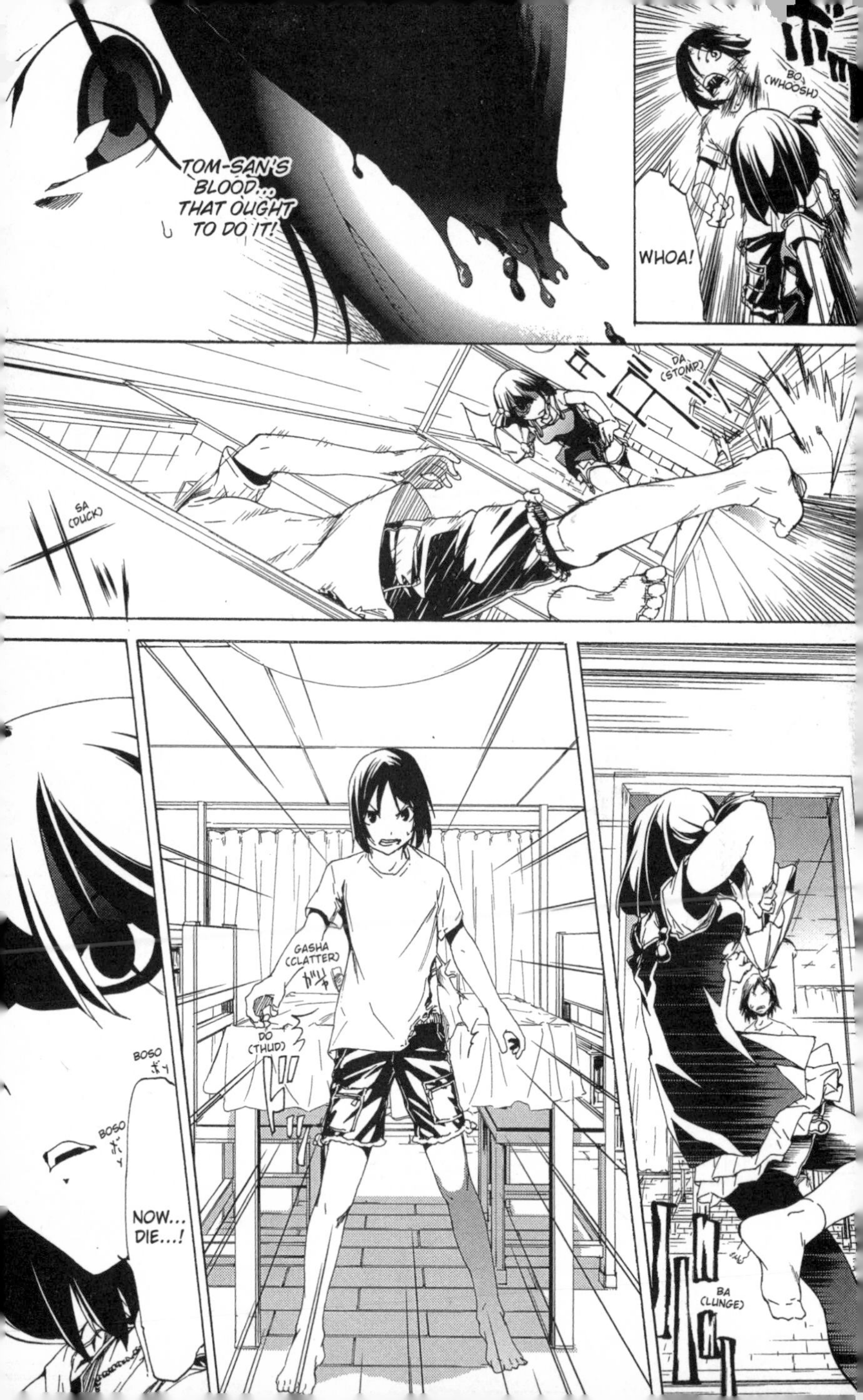
BO (WHOOSH)
WHOA!
TOM-SAN'S BLOOD... THAT OUGHT TO DO IT!
DA (STOMP)
SA (DUCK)
BA (LUNGE)
GASHA (CLATTER)
DO (THUD)
BOSO
BOSO
NOW... DIE...!

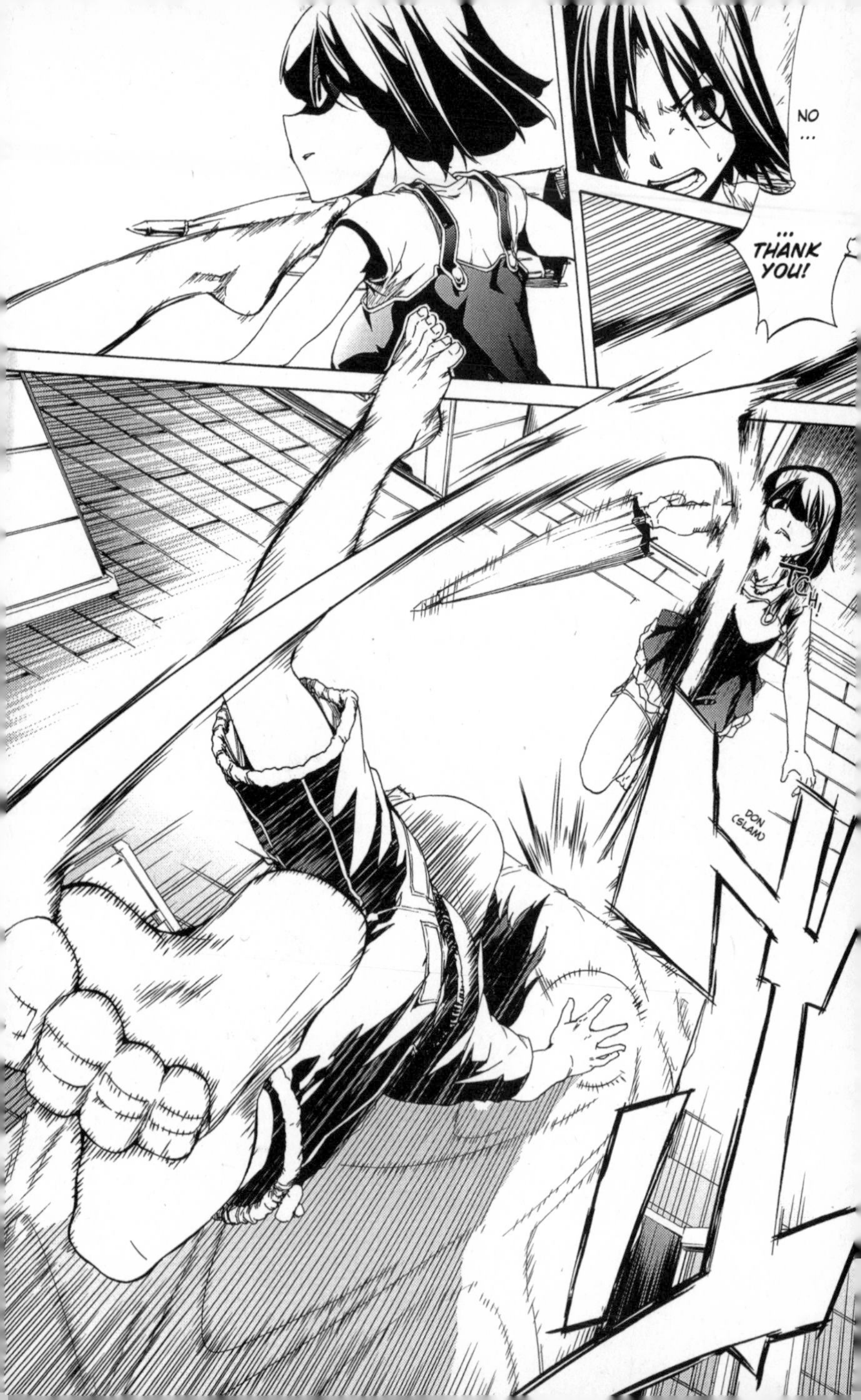
NO ...
... THANK YOU!
TCH!
DON (SLAM)

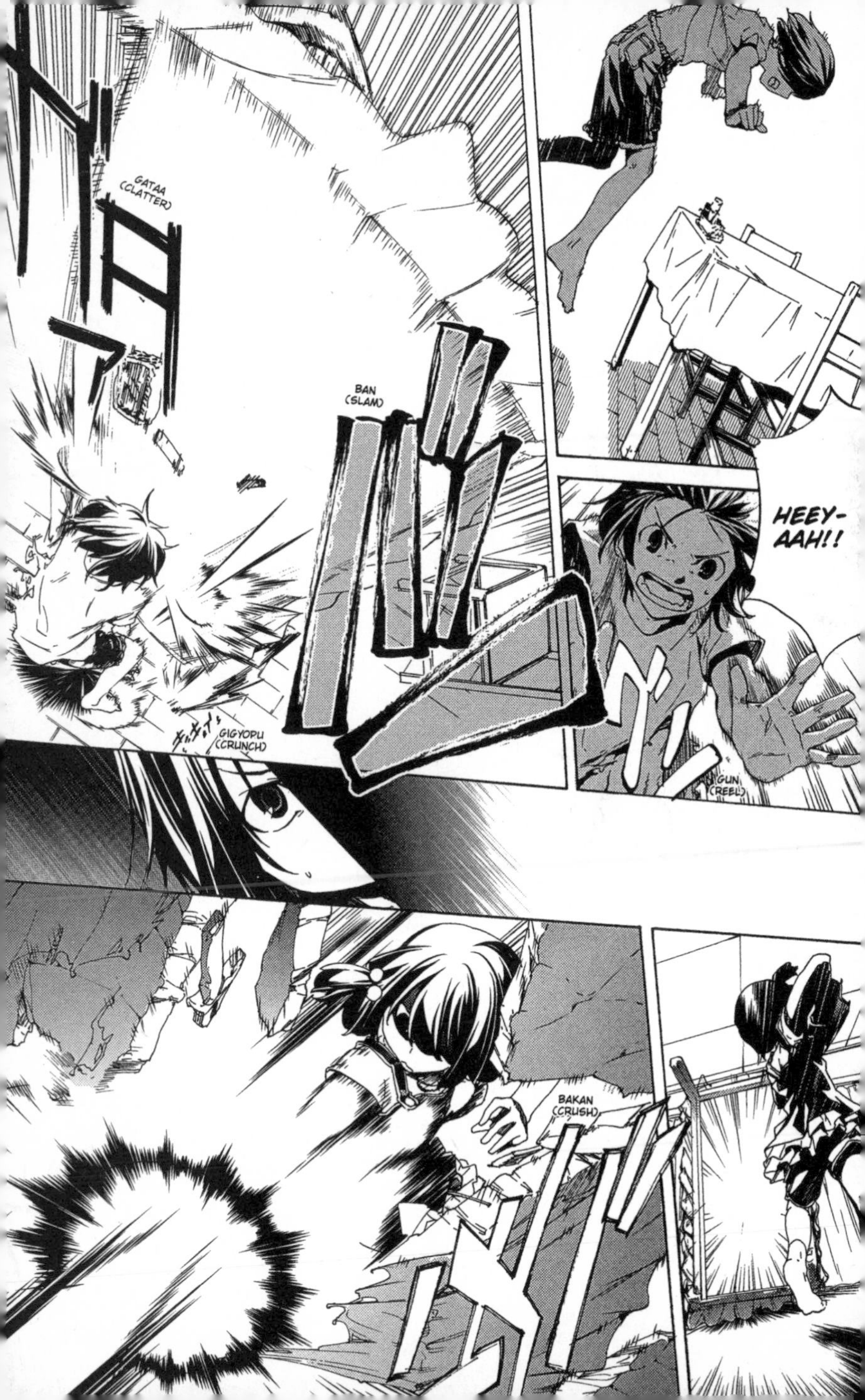
HEEY-AAH!!
GUN (REEL)
GATAA (CLATTER)
BAN (SLAM)
GIGYOPU (CRUNCH)
BAKAN (CRUSH)

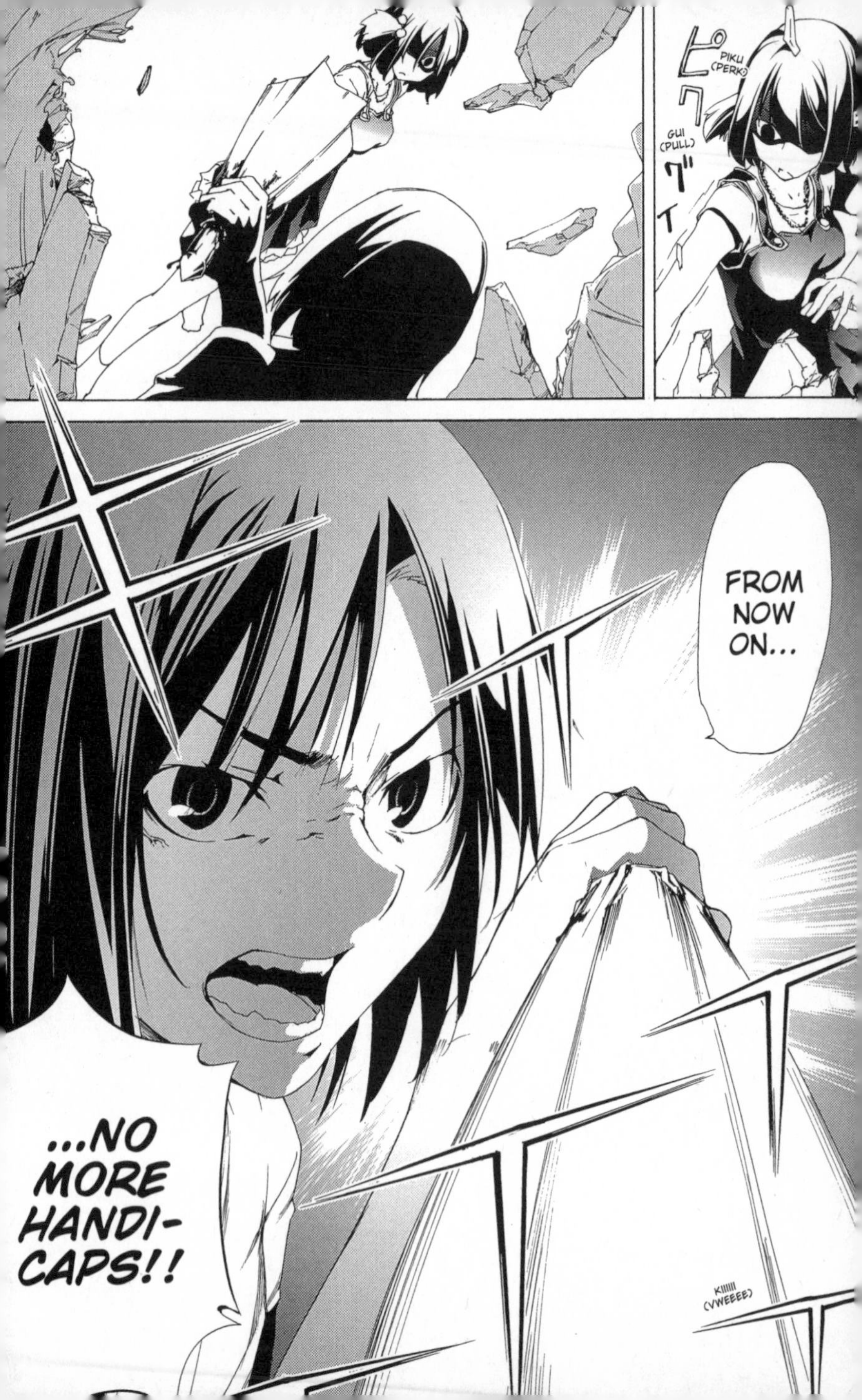
ピク
PIKU (PERK)
グイ
GUI (PULL)
FROM NOW ON...
...NO MORE HANDI-CAPS!!
KIIIII (VWEEEE)

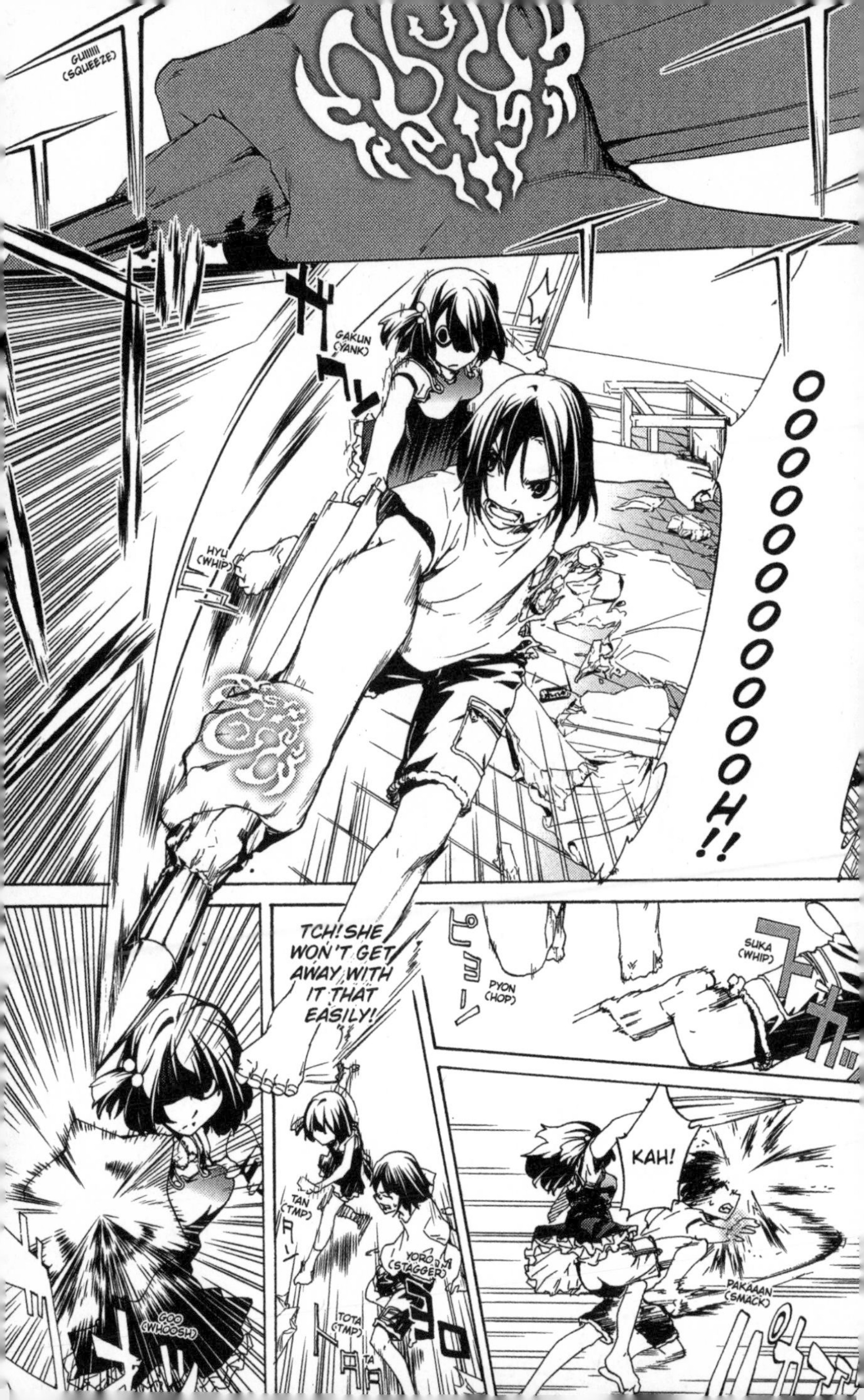
OOOOOOOOOOOH!!
GAKUN (YANK)
GUIIIII (SQUEEZE)
HYU (WHIP)
SUKA (WHIP)
PYON (HOP)
TCH! SHE WON'T GET AWAY WITH IT THAT EASILY!
KAH!
PAKAAAN (SMACK)
YORO (STAGGER)
TAN (TMP)
TOTA (TMP)
TA
GOO (WHOOSH)

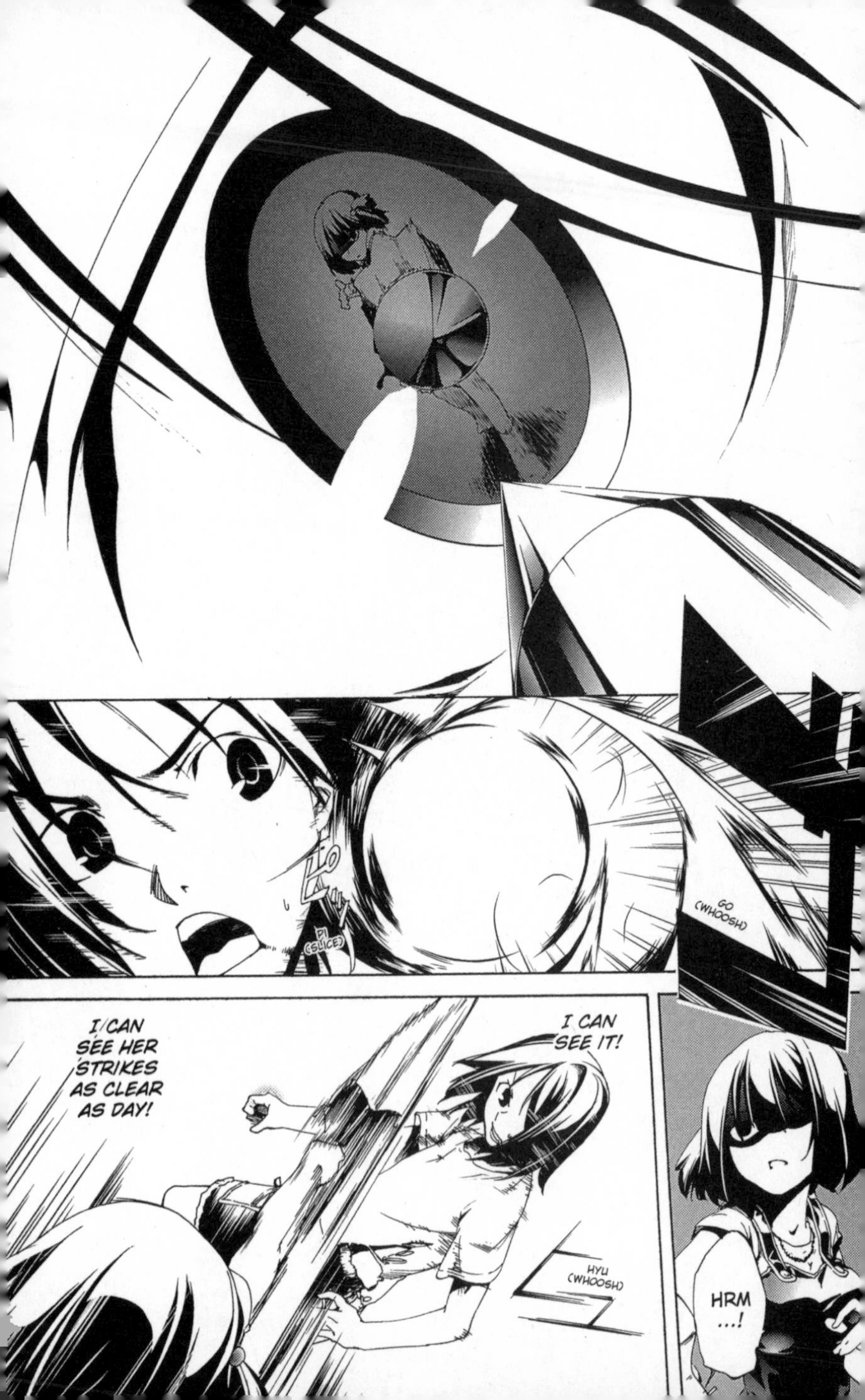
GO (WHOOSH)
PI (SLICE)
HRM ...!
I CAN SEE IT!
I CAN SEE HER STRIKES AS CLEAR AS DAY!
HYU (WHOOSH)

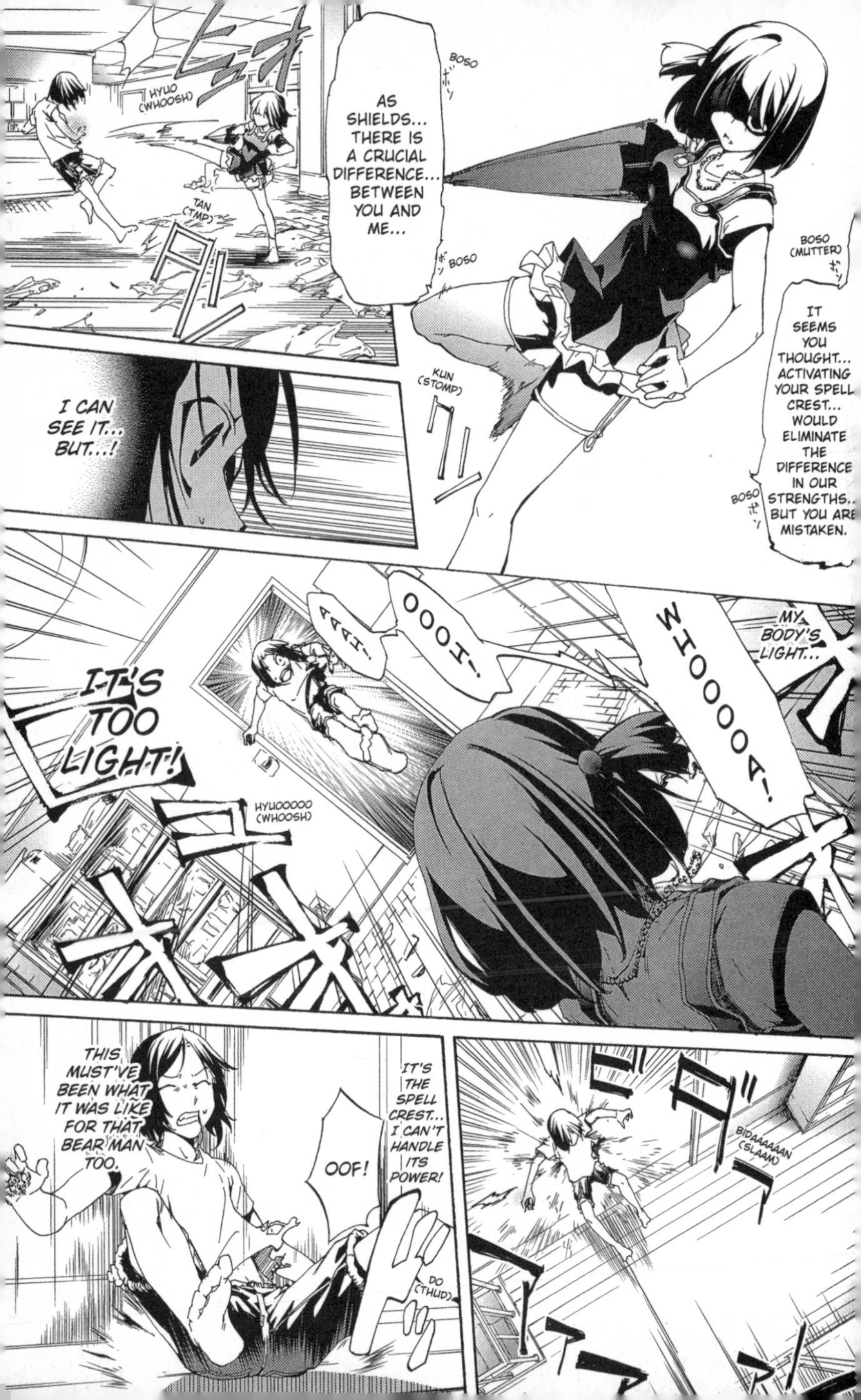
BOSO
AS SHIELDS... THERE IS A CRUCIAL DIFFERENCE... BETWEEN YOU AND ME...
BOSO
BOSO (MUTTER)
IT SEEMS YOU THOUGHT... ACTIVATING YOUR SPELL CREST... WOULD ELIMINATE THE DIFFERENCE IN OUR STRENGTHS... BUT YOU ARE MISTAKEN.
KUN (STOMP)
BOSO
HYUO (WHOOSH)
TAN (TMP)
I CAN SEE IT... BUT...!
MY BODY'S LIGHT...
WHOOOOOA!
OOOI!
IAAA!
IT'S TOO LIGHT!
HYUOOOOO (WHOOSH)
BIDAAAAAAN (SLAAM)
IT'S THE SPELL CREST... I CAN'T HANDLE ITS POWER!
THIS MUST'VE BEEN WHAT IT WAS LIKE FOR THAT BEAR MAN TOO.
OOF!
DO (THUD)

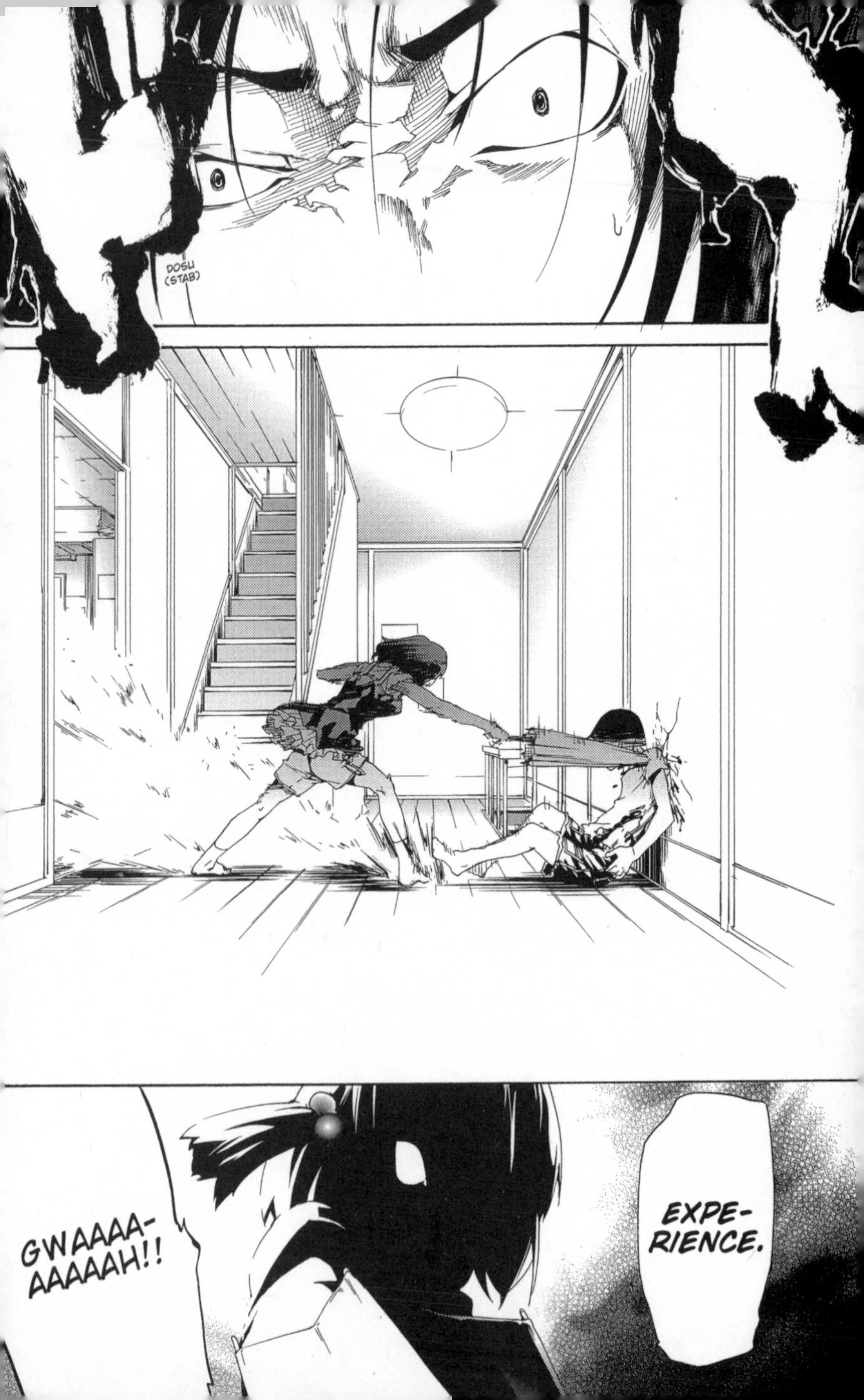
DOSU (STAB)
EXPE-RIENCE.
GWAAAA-AAAAAH!!

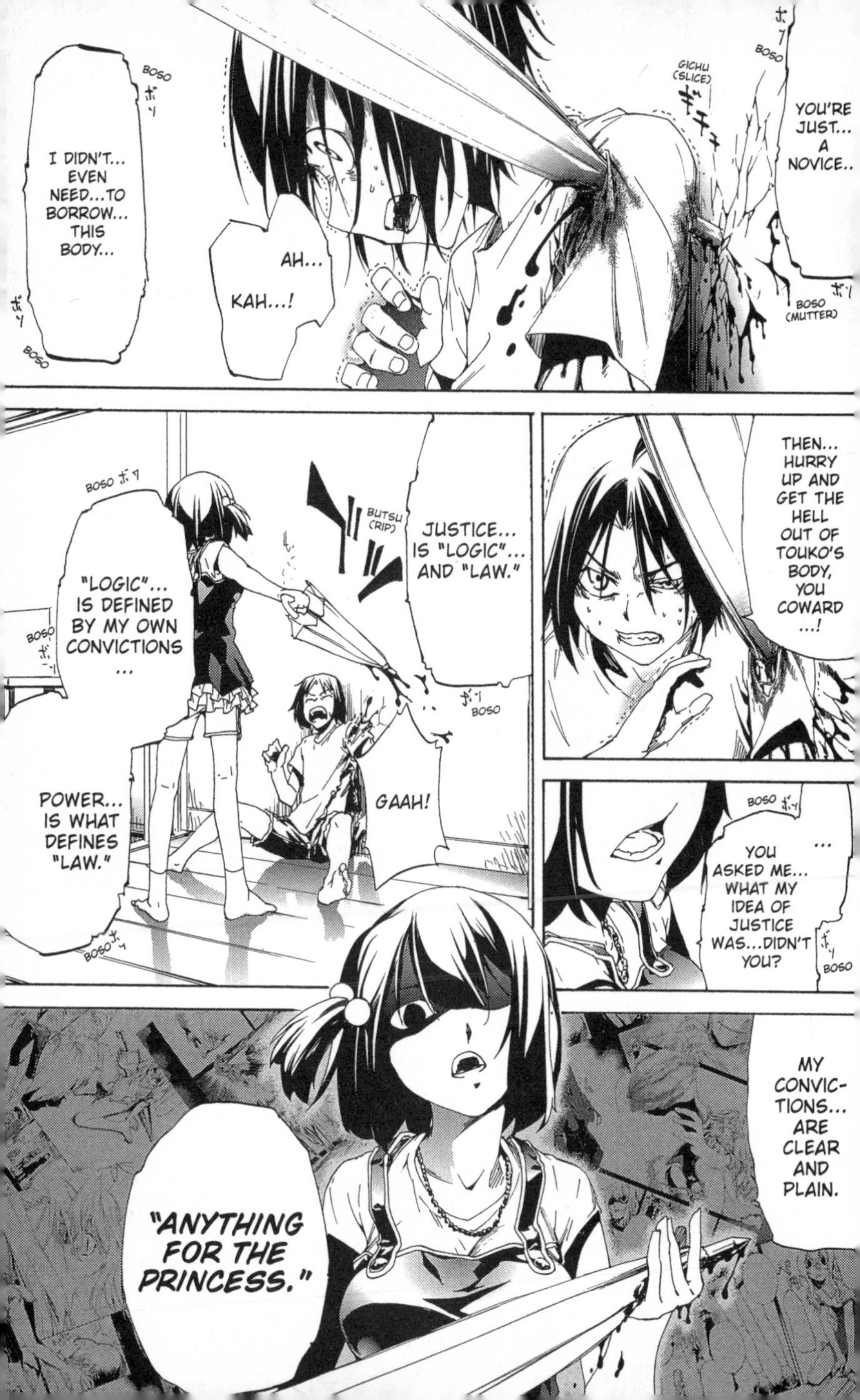
BOSO
GICHU (SLICE)
YOU'RE JUST... A NOVICE..
BOSO (MUTTER)
AH... KAH...!
I DIDN'T... EVEN NEED...TO BORROW... THIS BODY...
BOSO
THEN... HURRY UP AND GET THE HELL OUT OF TOUKO'S BODY, YOU COWARD ...!
BOSO
...
YOU ASKED ME... WHAT MY IDEA OF JUSTICE WAS...DIDN'T YOU?
BOSO
JUSTICE... IS "LOGIC"... AND "LAW."
BUTSU (RIP)
BOSO
GAAH!
BOSO
"LOGIC"... IS DEFINED BY MY OWN CONVICTIONS ...
BOSO
POWER... IS WHAT DEFINES "LAW."
BOSO
MY CONVIC-TIONS... ARE CLEAR AND PLAIN.
"ANYTHING FOR THE PRINCESS."

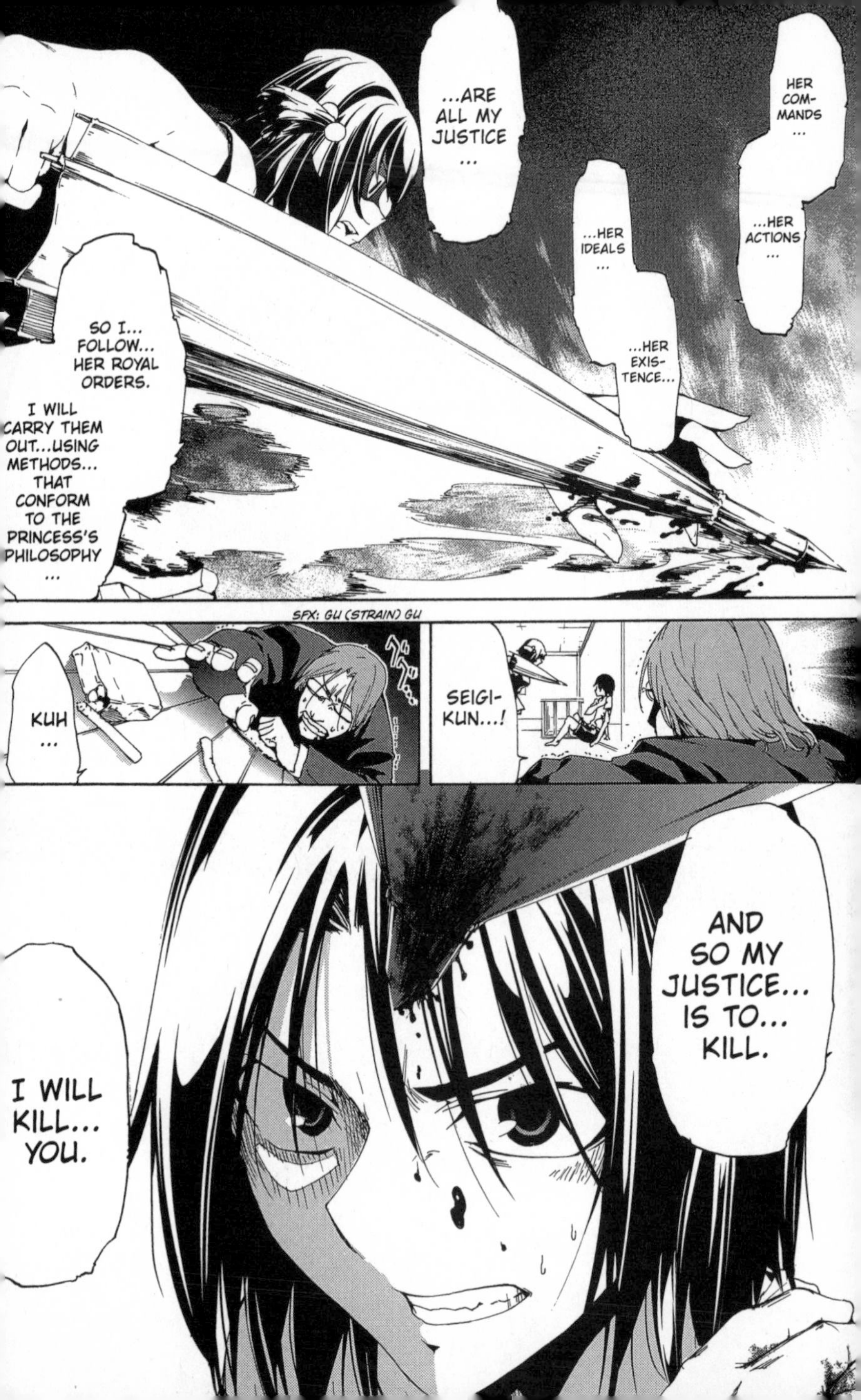
HER COMMANDS...
...HER ACTIONS...
...HER IDEALS...
...HER EXISTENCE...
...ARE ALL MY JUSTICE...
SO I... FOLLOW... HER ROYAL ORDERS.
I WILL CARRY THEM OUT...USING METHODS... THAT CONFORM TO THE PRINCESS'S PHILOSOPHY...
SFX: GU (STRAIN) GU
SEIGI-KUN...!
KUH...
AND SO MY JUSTICE... IS TO... KILL.
I WILL KILL... YOU.

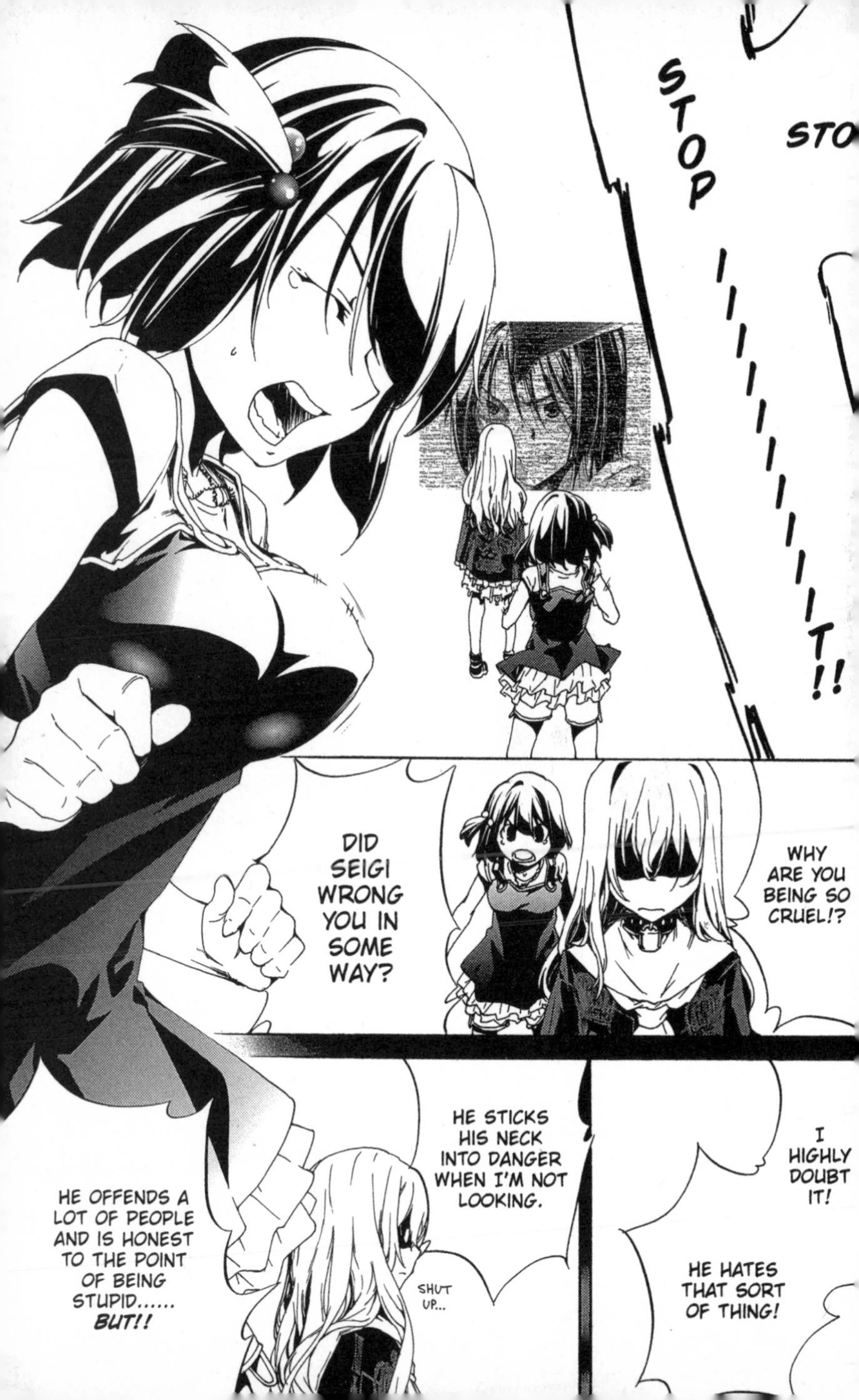

STO
STOP IIIIIIIT!!
WHY ARE YOU BEING SO CRUEL!?
DID SEIGI WRONG YOU IN SOME WAY?
I HIGHLY DOUBT IT!
HE HATES THAT SORT OF THING!
HE STICKS HIS NECK INTO DANGER WHEN I'M NOT LOOKING.
SHUT UP...
HE OFFENDS A LOT OF PEOPLE AND IS HONEST TO THE POINT OF BEING STUPID...... *BUT!!*

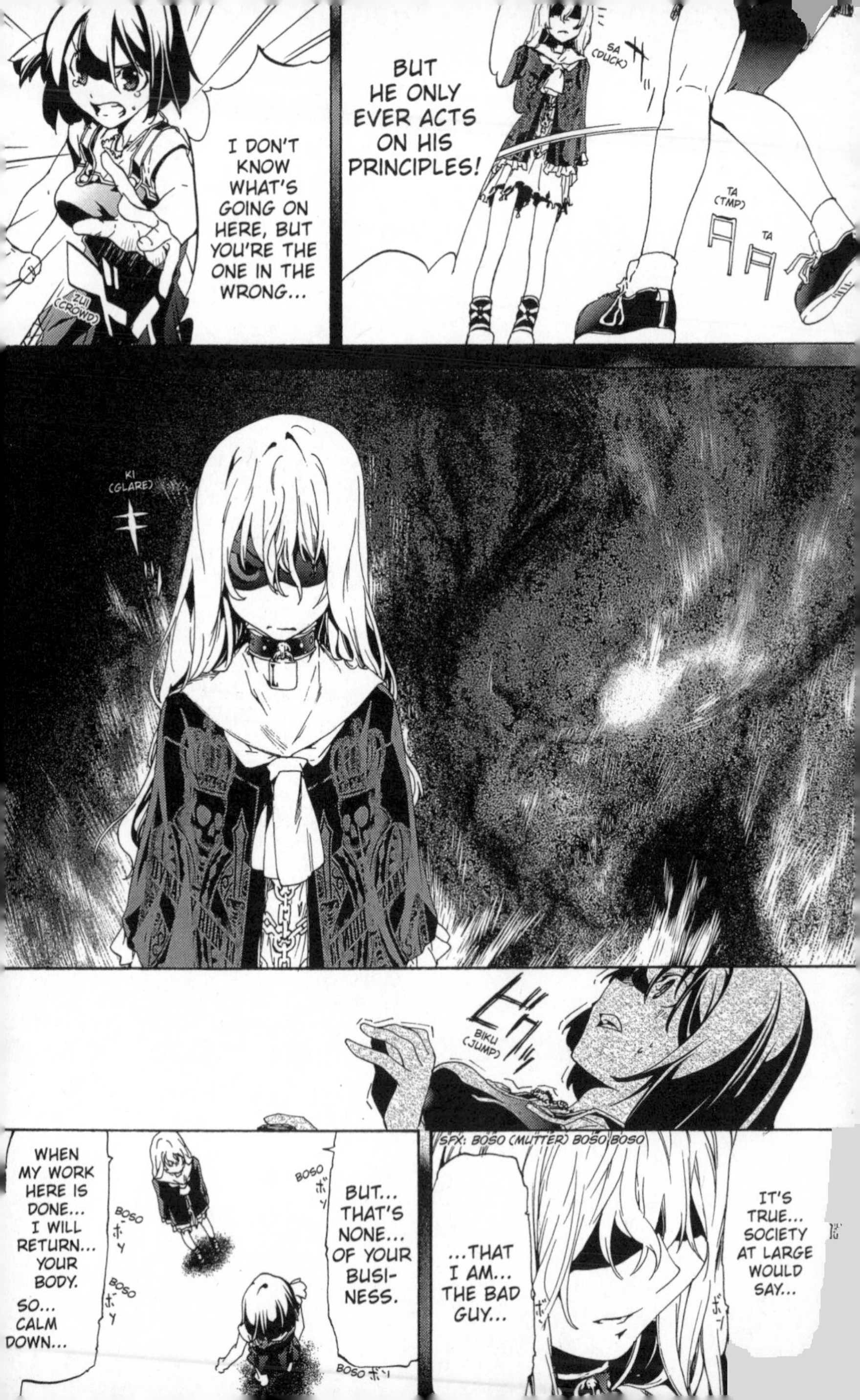
BUT HE ONLY EVER ACTS ON HIS PRINCIPLES!
SA (DUCK)
TA (TMP)
TA
I DON'T KNOW WHAT'S GOING ON HERE, BUT YOU'RE THE ONE IN THE WRONG...
ZUI (CROWD)
KI (GLARE)
BIKU (JUMP)
SFX: BOSO (MUTTER) BOSO BOSO
IT'S TRUE... SOCIETY AT LARGE WOULD SAY...
...THAT I AM... THE BAD GUY...
BUT... THAT'S NONE... OF YOUR BUSINESS.
BOSO
WHEN MY WORK HERE IS DONE... I WILL RETURN... YOUR BODY.
SO... CALM DOWN...
BOSO
BOSO
BOSO

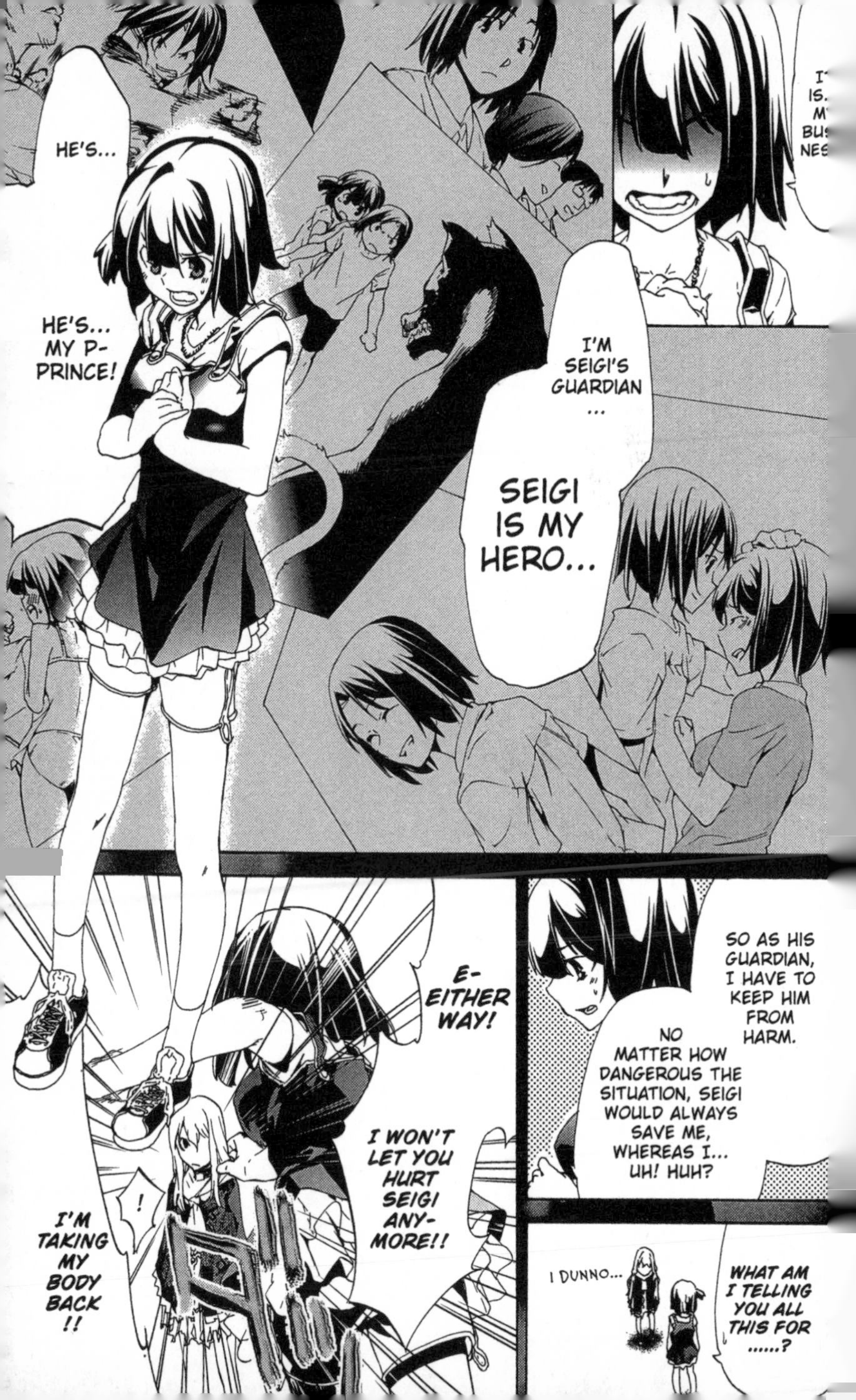

I' IS.. M' BUS NES
I'M SEIGI'S GUARDIAN ...
SEIGI IS MY HERO...
HE'S...
HE'S... MY P-PRINCE!
SO AS HIS GUARDIAN, I HAVE TO KEEP HIM FROM HARM.
NO MATTER HOW DANGEROUS THE SITUATION, SEIGI WOULD ALWAYS SAVE ME, WHEREAS I... UH! HUH?
WHAT AM I TELLING YOU ALL THIS FOR ......?
I DUNNO...
E-EITHER WAY!
I WON'T LET YOU HURT SEIGI ANY-MORE!!
!
I'M TAKING MY BODY BACK!!

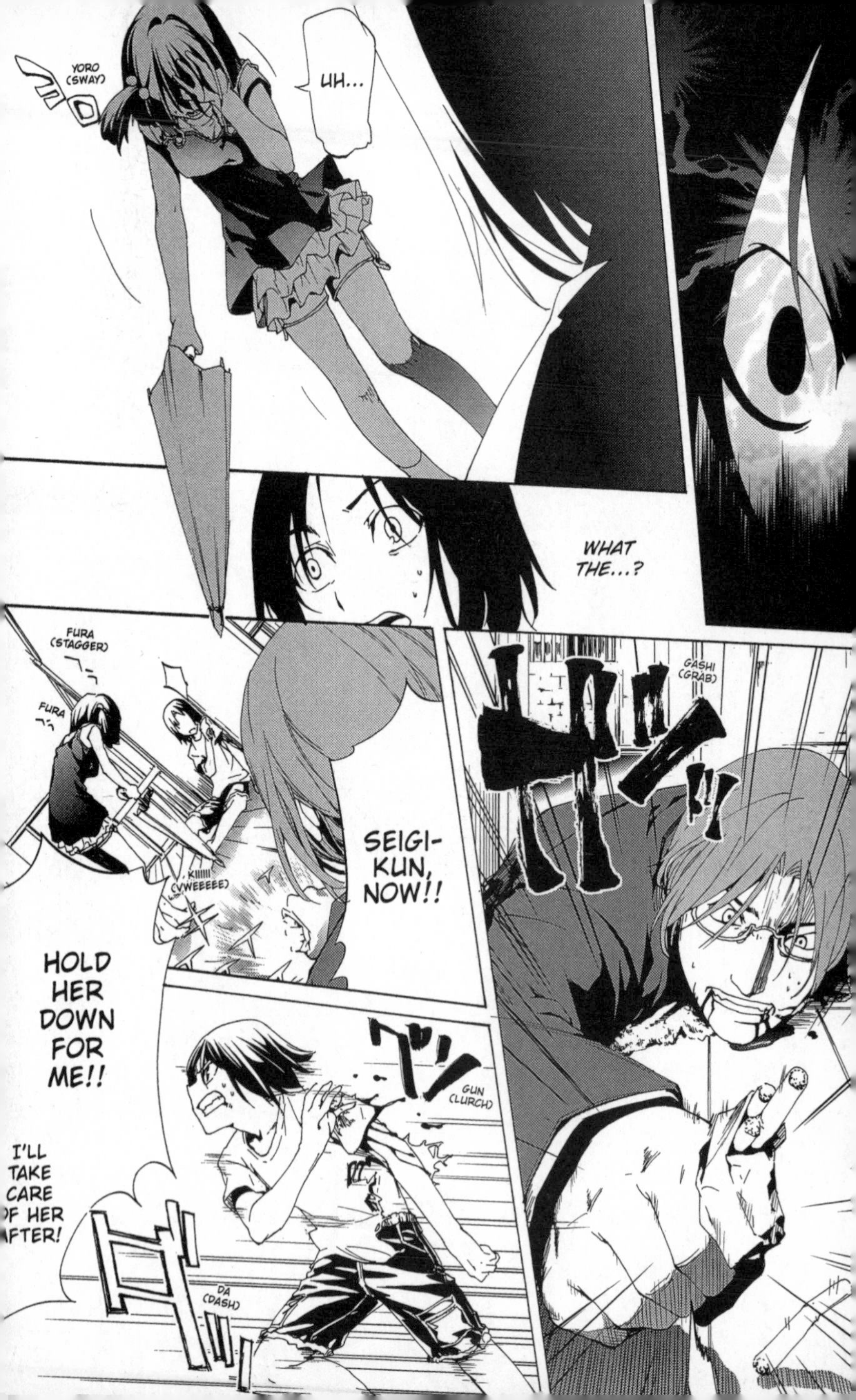

UH...
YORO (SWAY)
WHAT THE...?
GASHI (GRAB)
SEIGI-KUN, NOW!!
KIIIII (VWEEEEE)
FURA (STAGGER)
FURA
HOLD HER DOWN FOR ME!!
I'LL TAKE CARE OF HER AFTER!
GUN (LURCH)
DA (DASH)

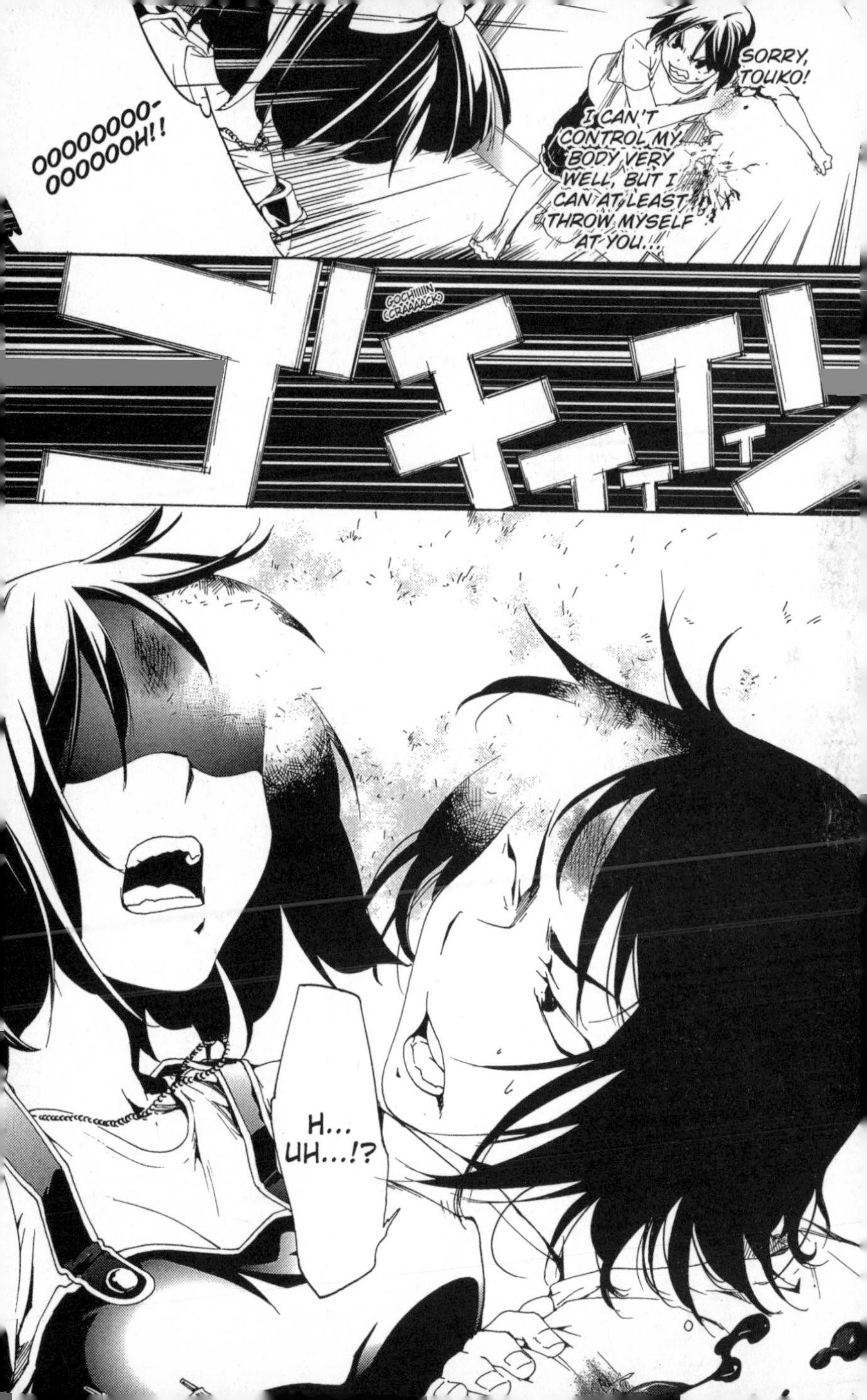
SORRY, TOUKO!
I CAN'T CONTROL MY BODY VERY WELL, BUT I CAN AT LEAST THROW MYSELF AT YOU...!
OOOOOOOO-OOOOOOOH!!
ゴキィィィン
GOCHIIIIIIN (CRAAAACK)
H... UH...!?

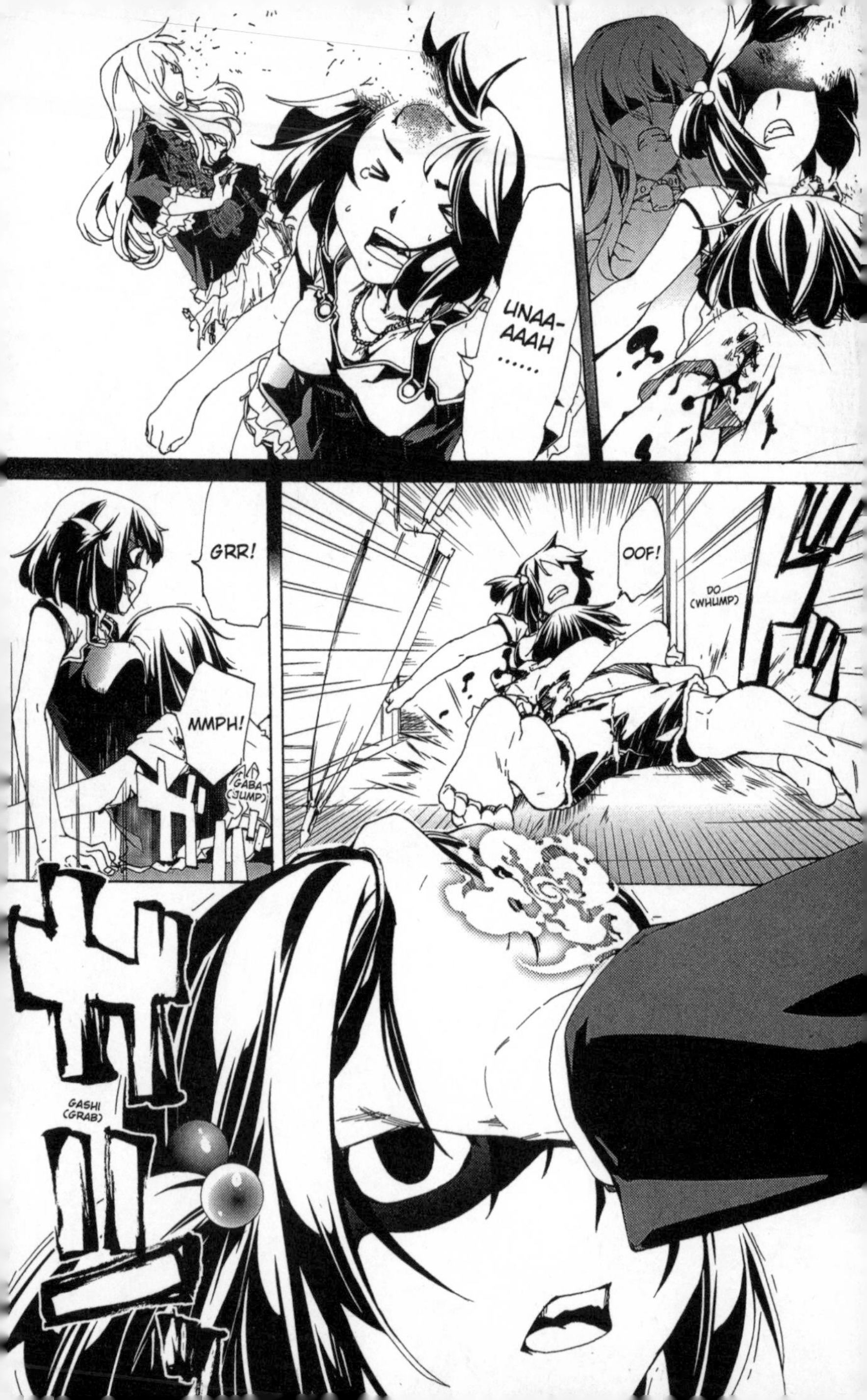
UNAA-AAAH ......
OOF!
DO (WHUMP)
GRR!
MMPH!
GABA (JUMP)
GASHI (GRAB)

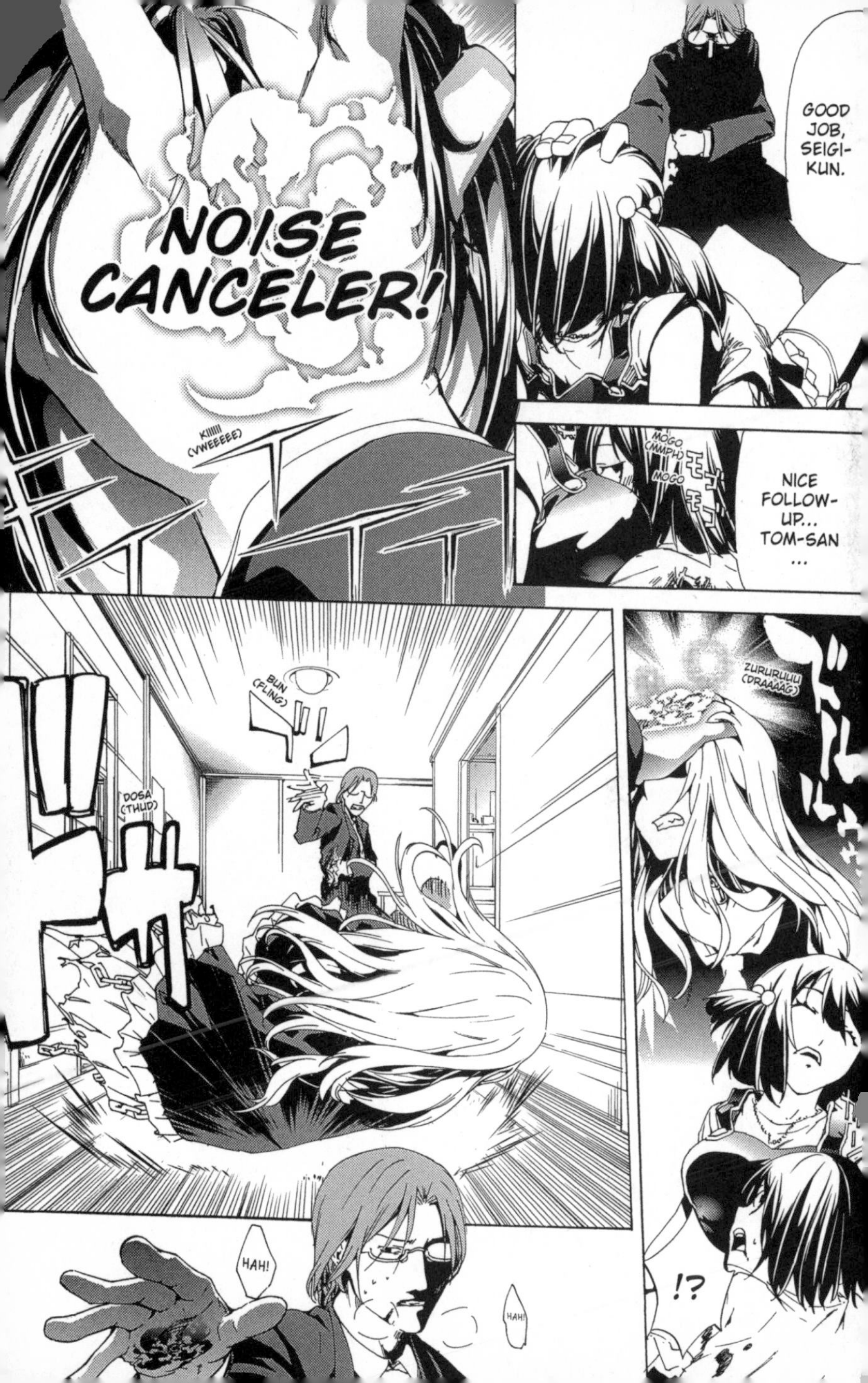

GOOD JOB, SEIGI-KUN.
MOGO (MMPH) MOGO
NICE FOLLOW-UP... TOM-SAN ...
NOISE CANCELER!
KIIIII (VWEEEEE)
ZURURUUU (DRAAAAG)
!?
BUN (FLING)
DOSA (THUD)
HAH!
HAH!

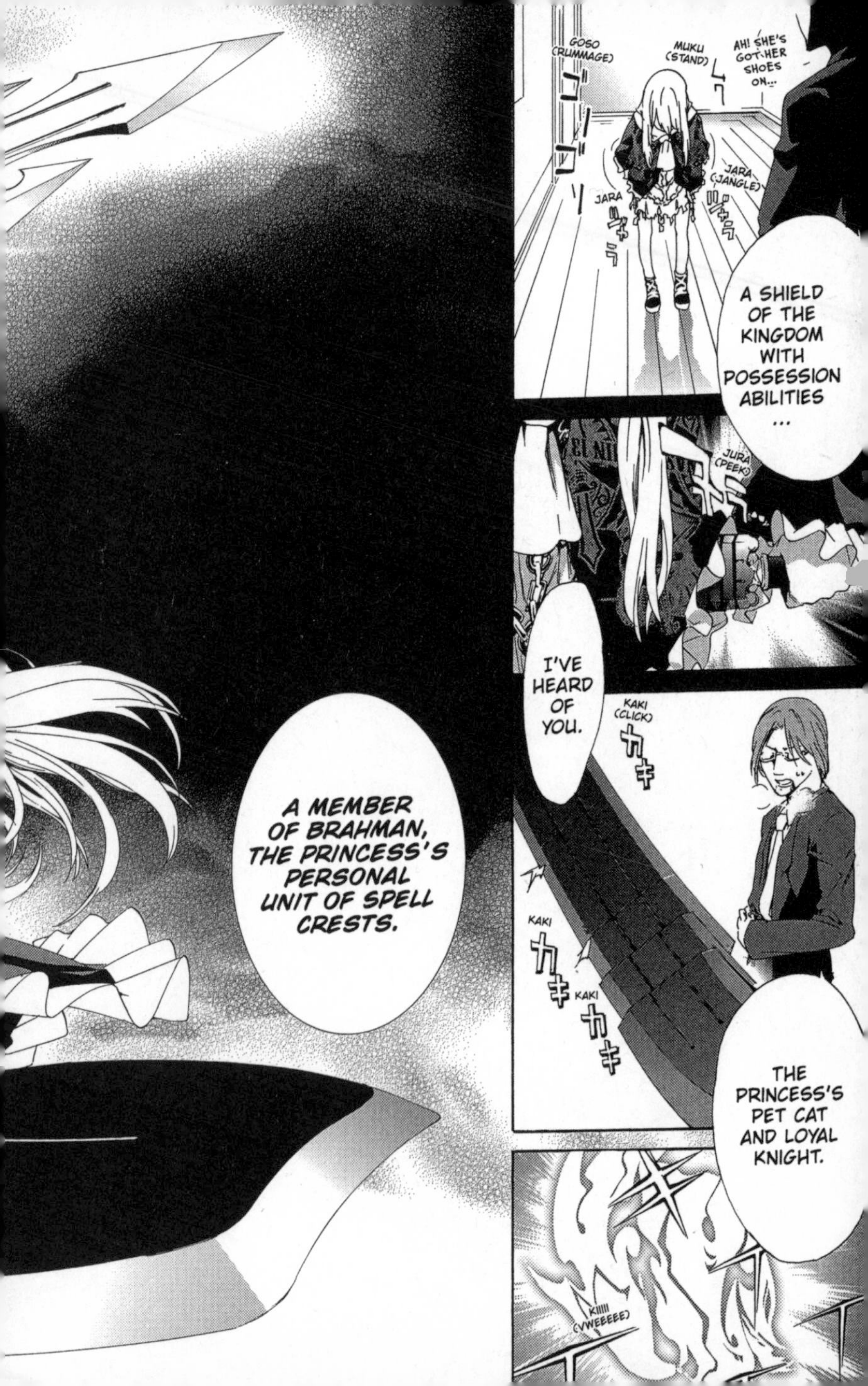
AH! SHE'S GOT HER SHOES ON...
MUKU (STAND)
GOSO (RUMMAGE)
JARA (JANGLE)
JARA
A SHIELD OF THE KINGDOM WITH POSSESSION ABILITIES ...
JURA (PEEK)
I'VE HEARD OF YOU.
KAKI (CLICK)
KAKI
KAKI
THE PRINCESS'S PET CAT AND LOYAL KNIGHT.
KIIIII (VWEEEEE)
A MEMBER OF BRAHMAN, THE PRINCESS'S PERSONAL UNIT OF SPELL CRESTS.

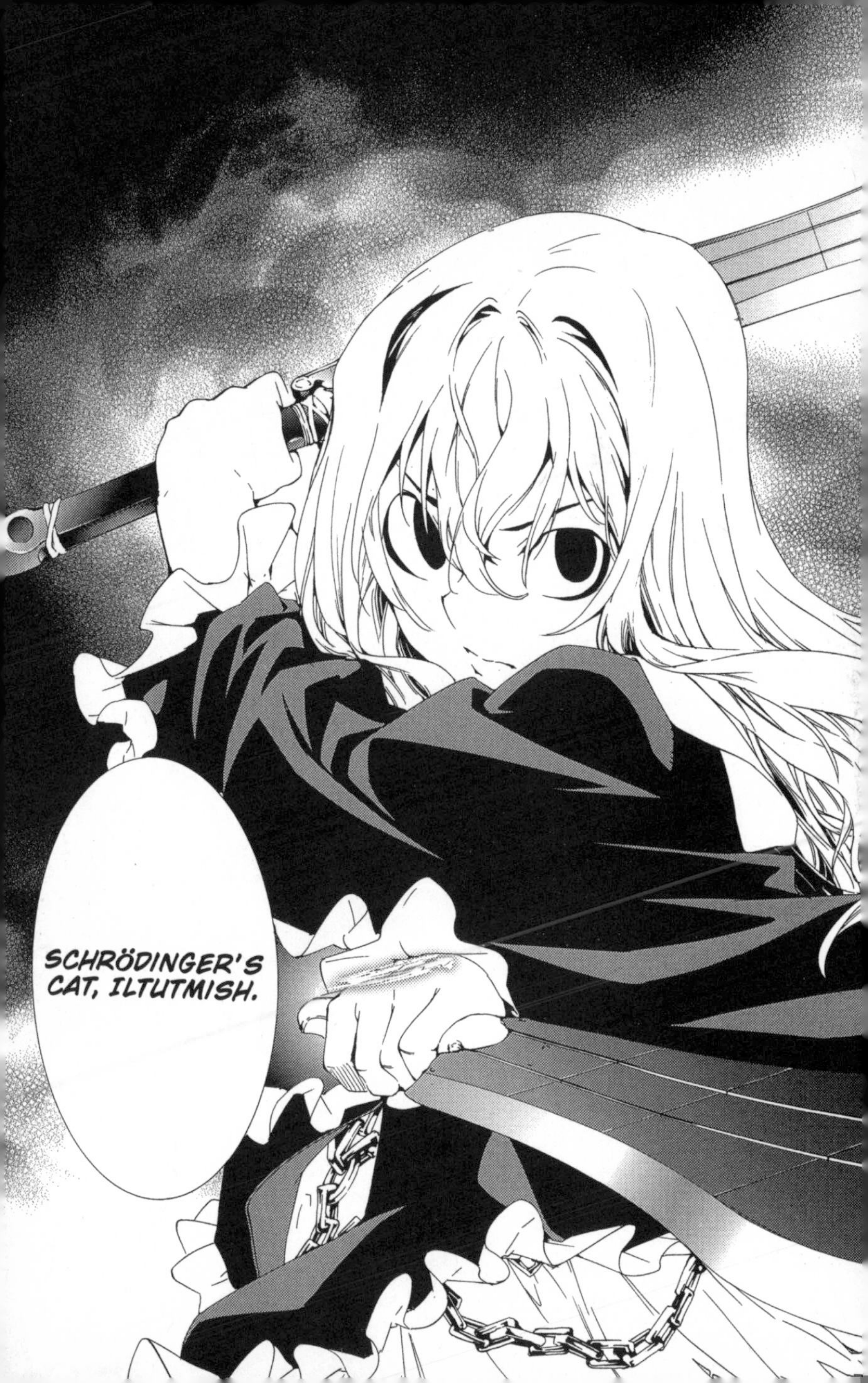
SCHRÖDINGER'S CAT, ILTUTMISH.

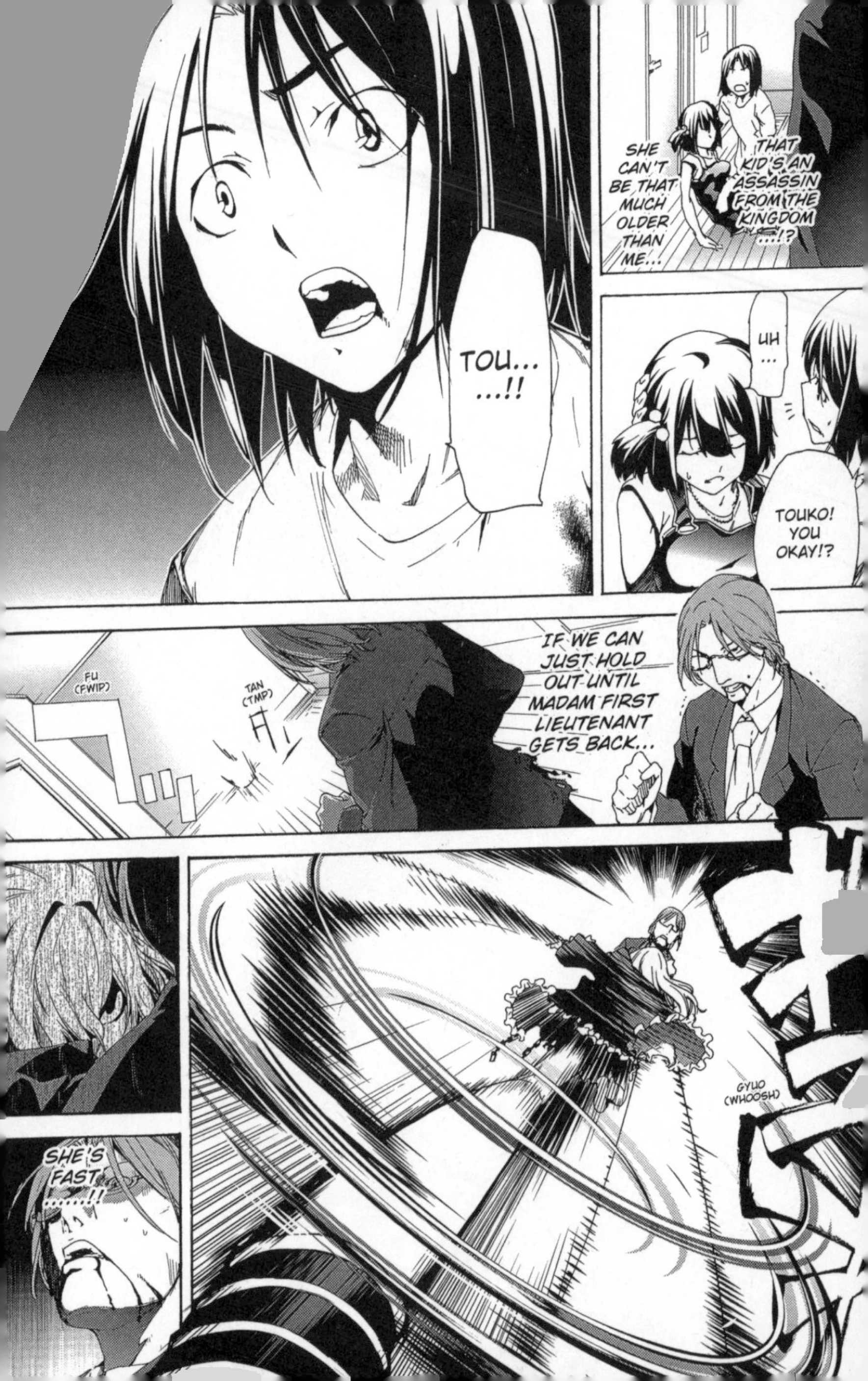
THAT KID'S AN ASSASSIN FROM THE KINGDOM ......!?
SHE CAN'T BE THAT MUCH OLDER THAN ME...
UH ...
TOUKO! YOU OKAY!?
TOU... ...!!
IF WE CAN JUST HOLD OUT UNTIL MADAM FIRST LIEUTENANT GETS BACK...
TAN (TMP)
FU (FWIP)
GYUO (WHOOSH)
SHE'S FAST ......!!

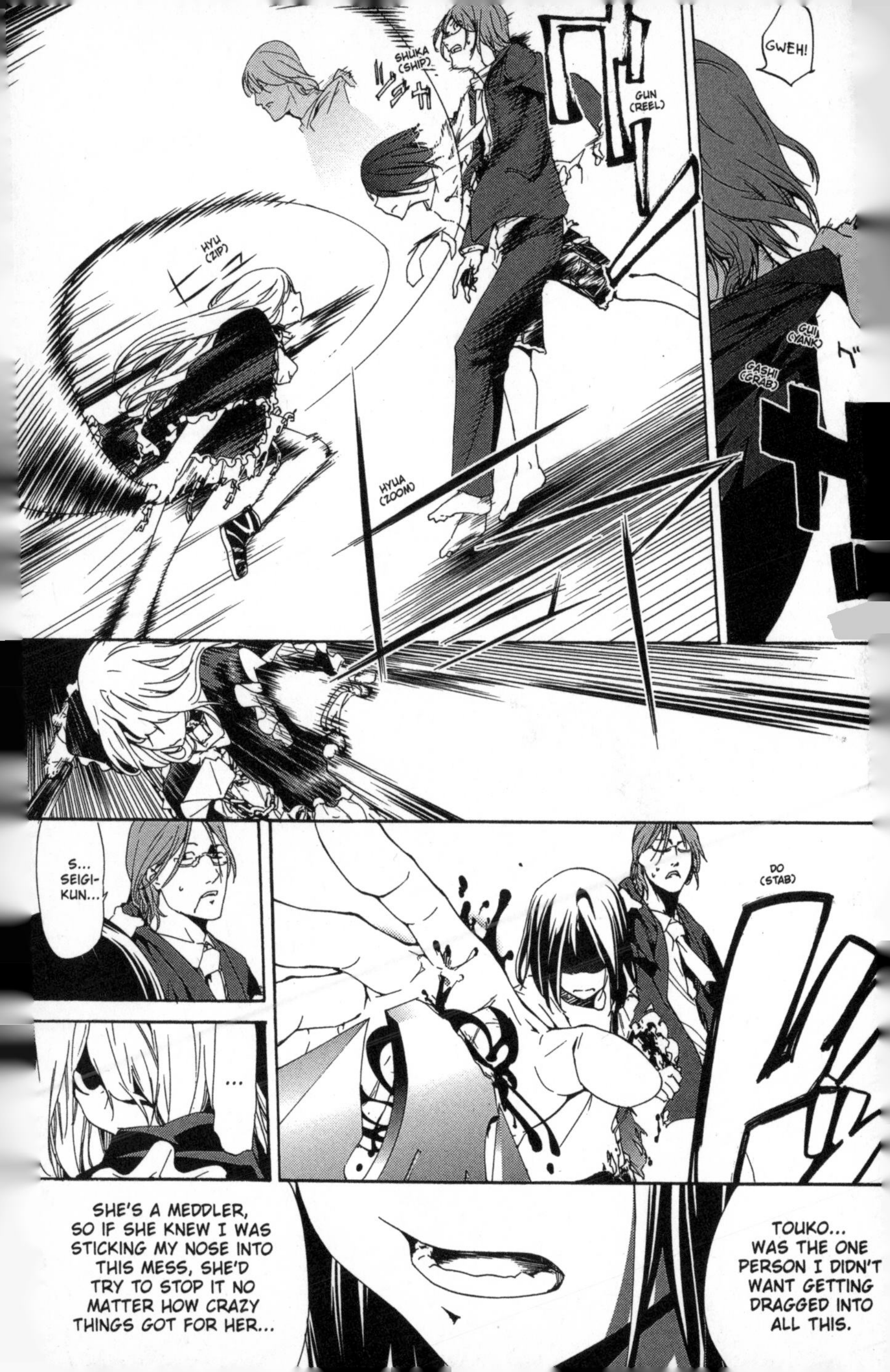
GWEH!
GUN (REEL)
SHUKA (SHIP)
GUI (YANK)
GASHI (GRAB)
HYU (ZIP)
HYUA (ZOOM)
DO (STAB)
S... SEIGI-KUN...
...
TOUKO... WAS THE ONE PERSON I DIDN'T WANT GETTING DRAGGED INTO ALL THIS.
SHE'S A MEDDLER, SO IF SHE KNEW I WAS STICKING MY NOSE INTO THIS MESS, SHE'D TRY TO STOP IT NO MATTER HOW CRAZY THINGS GOT FOR HER...

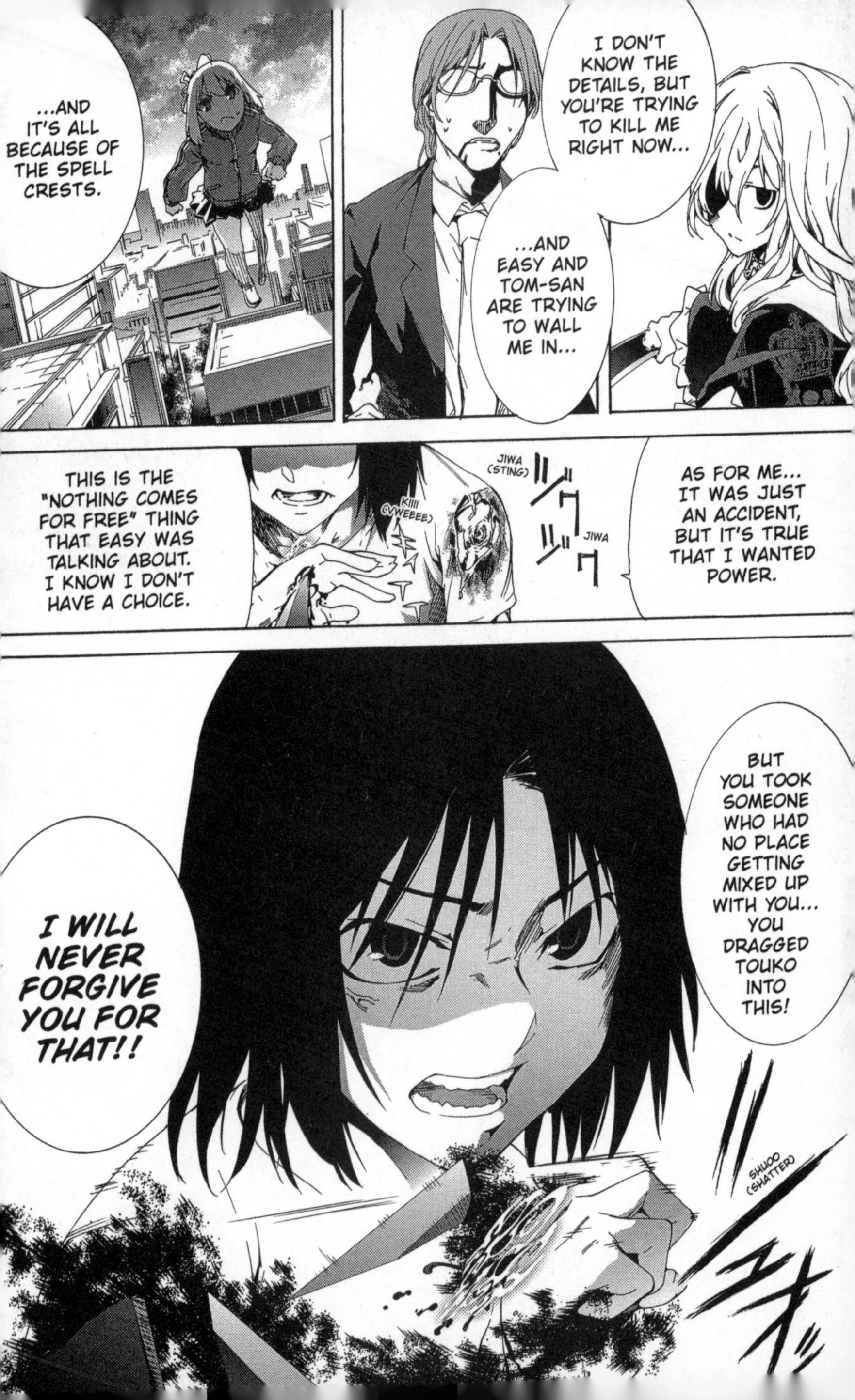
I DON'T KNOW THE DETAILS, BUT YOU'RE TRYING TO KILL ME RIGHT NOW...
...AND EASY AND TOM-SAN ARE TRYING TO WALL ME IN...
...AND IT'S ALL BECAUSE OF THE SPELL CRESTS.
AS FOR ME... IT WAS JUST AN ACCIDENT, BUT IT'S TRUE THAT I WANTED POWER.
JIWA (STING)
JIWA
KIIII (VWEEEE)
THIS IS THE "NOTHING COMES FOR FREE" THING THAT EASY WAS TALKING ABOUT. I KNOW I DON'T HAVE A CHOICE.
BUT YOU TOOK SOMEONE WHO HAD NO PLACE GETTING MIXED UP WITH YOU... YOU DRAGGED TOUKO INTO THIS!
I WILL NEVER FORGIVE YOU FOR THAT!!
SHUOO (SHATTER)

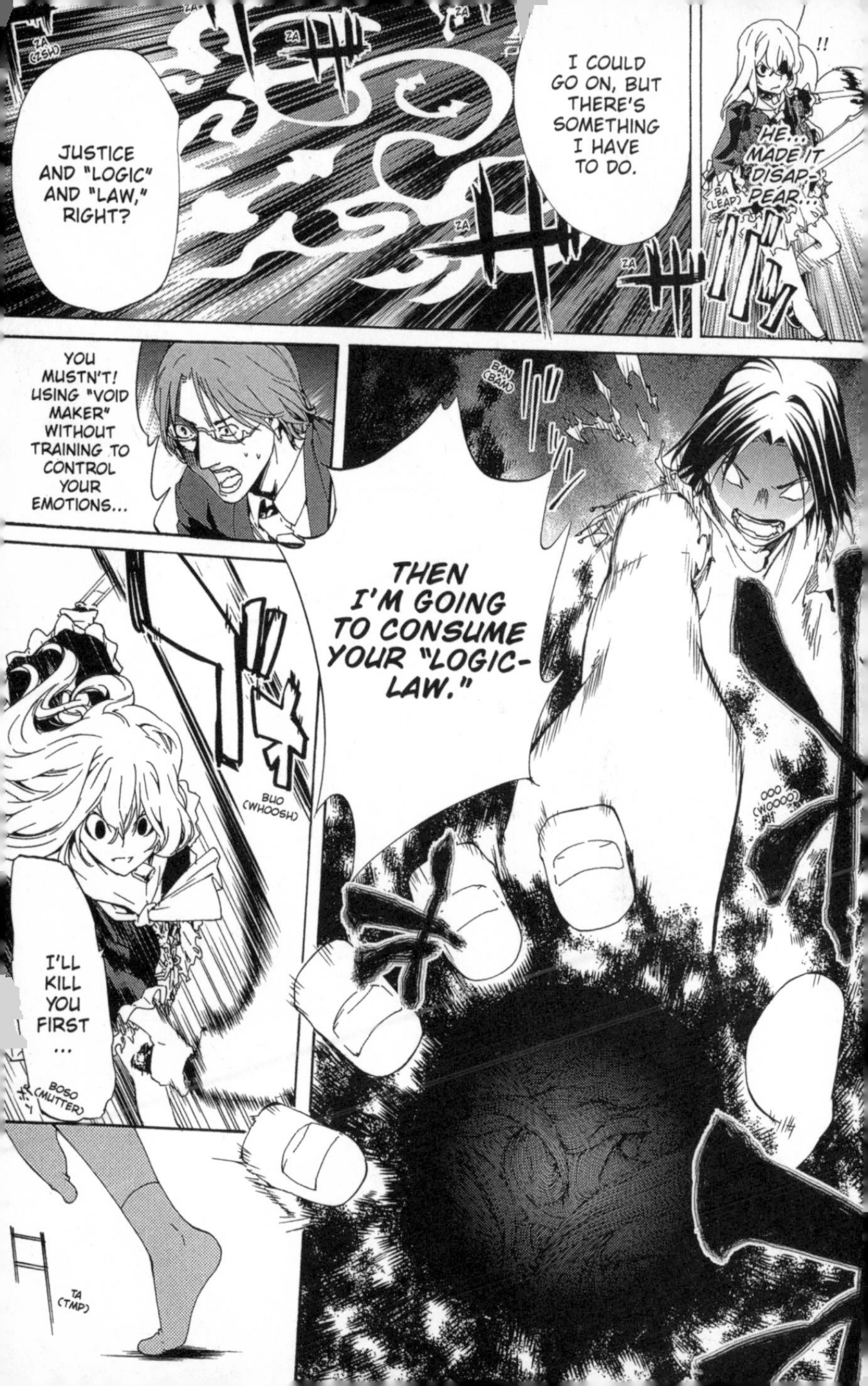
!!
HE... MADE IT DISAPPEAR...
BA (LEAP)
I COULD GO ON, BUT THERE'S SOMETHING I HAVE TO DO.
ZA
ZA
ZA
ZA
ZA (ZSH)
JUSTICE AND "LOGIC" AND "LAW," RIGHT?
BAN (BAM)
THEN I'M GOING TO CONSUME YOUR "LOGIC-LAW."
OOO (WOOOO)
YOU MUSTN'T! USING "VOID MAKER" WITHOUT TRAINING TO CONTROL YOUR EMOTIONS...
BUO (WHOOSH)
I'LL KILL YOU FIRST ...
BOSO (MUTTER)
TA (TMP)

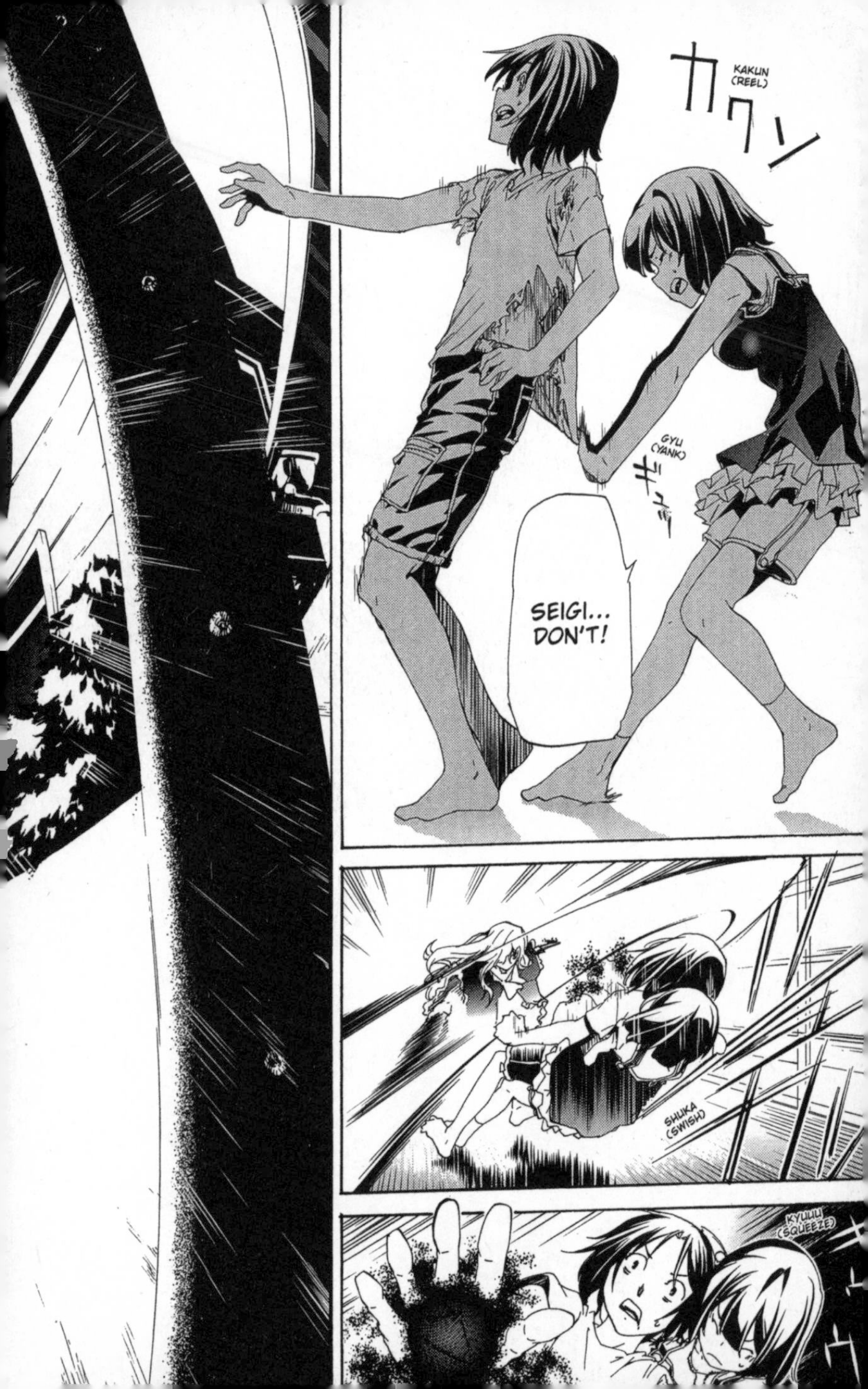
カクン
KAKUN (REEL)
GYU (YANK)
SEIGI... DON'T!
SHUKA (SWISH)
KYUUU (SQUEEZE)

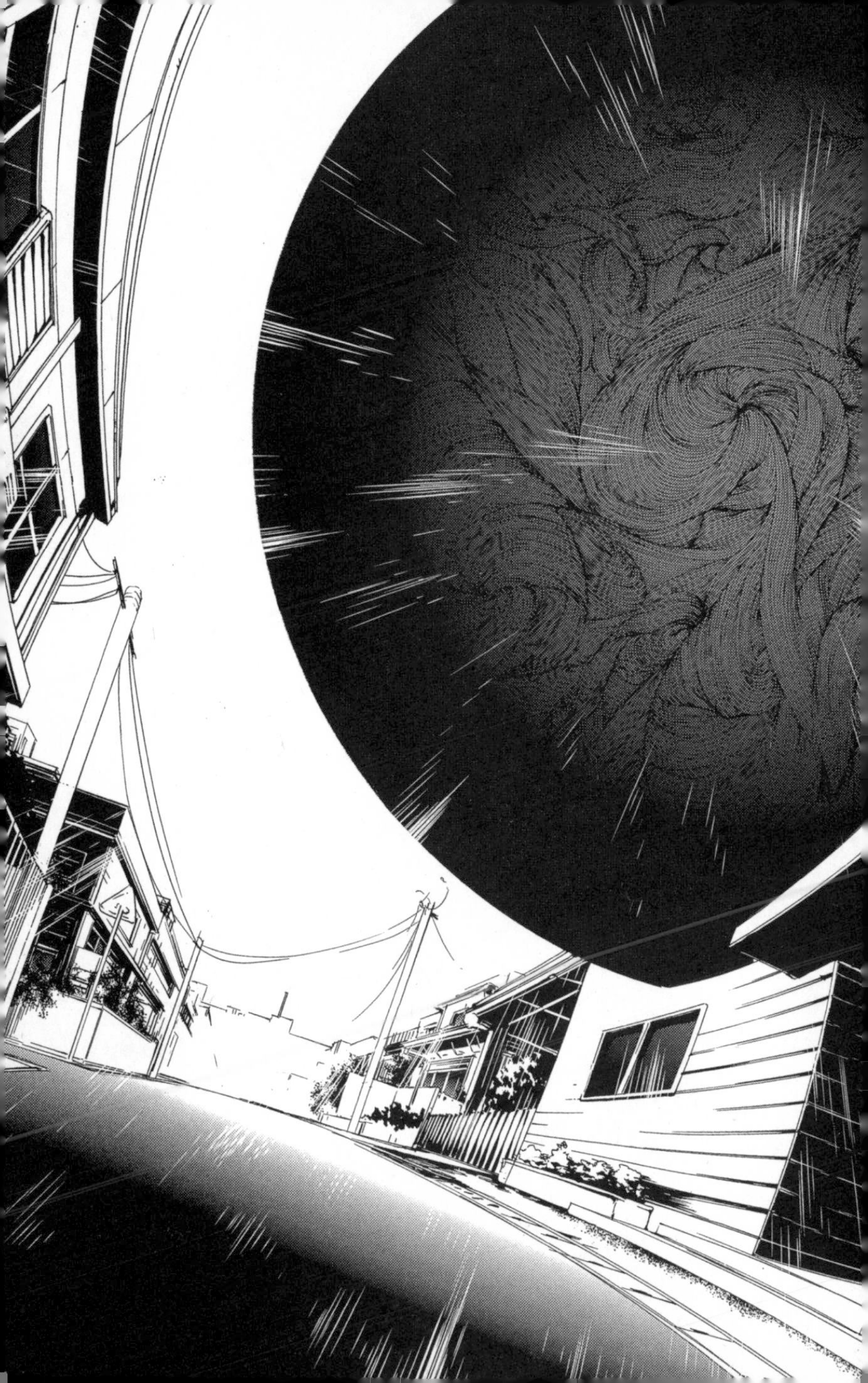

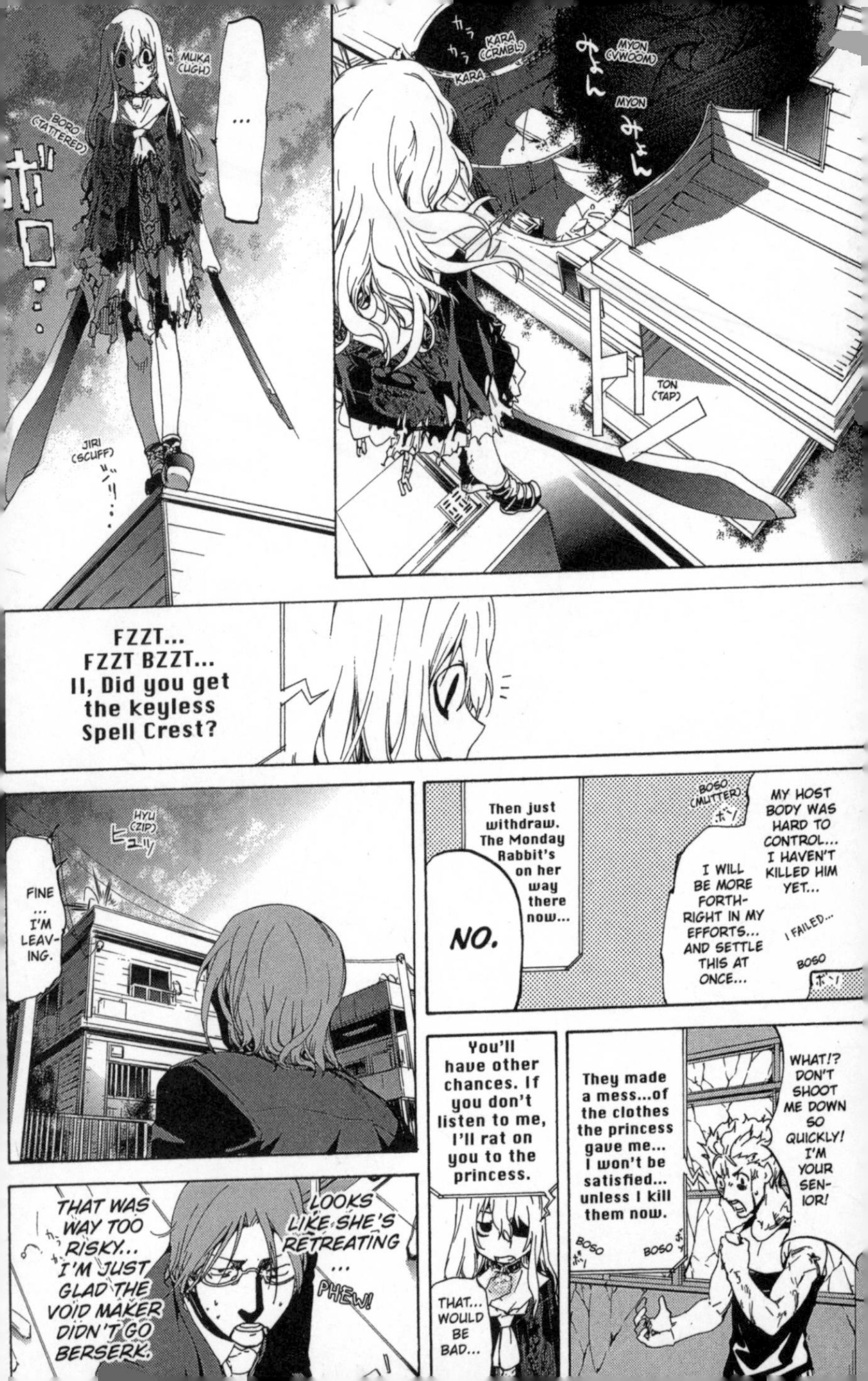
KARA (CRMBL)
KARA
カラ カラ
MYON (VWOOM)
MYON
みょん みょん
TON (TAP)
MUKA (UGH)
...
BORO (TATTERED)
ボロ...
JIRI (SCUFF)
ジリ...
FZZT... FZZT BZZT... II, Did you get the keyless Spell Crest?
BOSO (MUTTER)
MY HOST BODY WAS HARD TO CONTROL... I HAVEN'T KILLED HIM YET...
I FAILED...
BOSO
I WILL BE MORE FORTH-RIGHT IN MY EFFORTS... AND SETTLE THIS AT ONCE...
Then just withdraw. The Monday Rabbit's on her way there now...
NO.
WHAT!? DON'T SHOOT ME DOWN SO QUICKLY! I'M YOUR SEN-IOR!
They made a mess...of the clothes the princess gave me... I won't be satisfied... unless I kill them now.
BOSO
BOSO
You'll have other chances. If you don't listen to me, I'll rat on you to the princess.
THAT... WOULD BE BAD...
HYU (ZIP)
ヒュッ
FINE ... I'M LEAV-ING.
LOOKS LIKE SHE'S RETREATING ...
PHEW!
THAT WAS WAY TOO RISKY... I'M JUST GLAD THE VOID MAKER DIDN'T GO BERSERK.

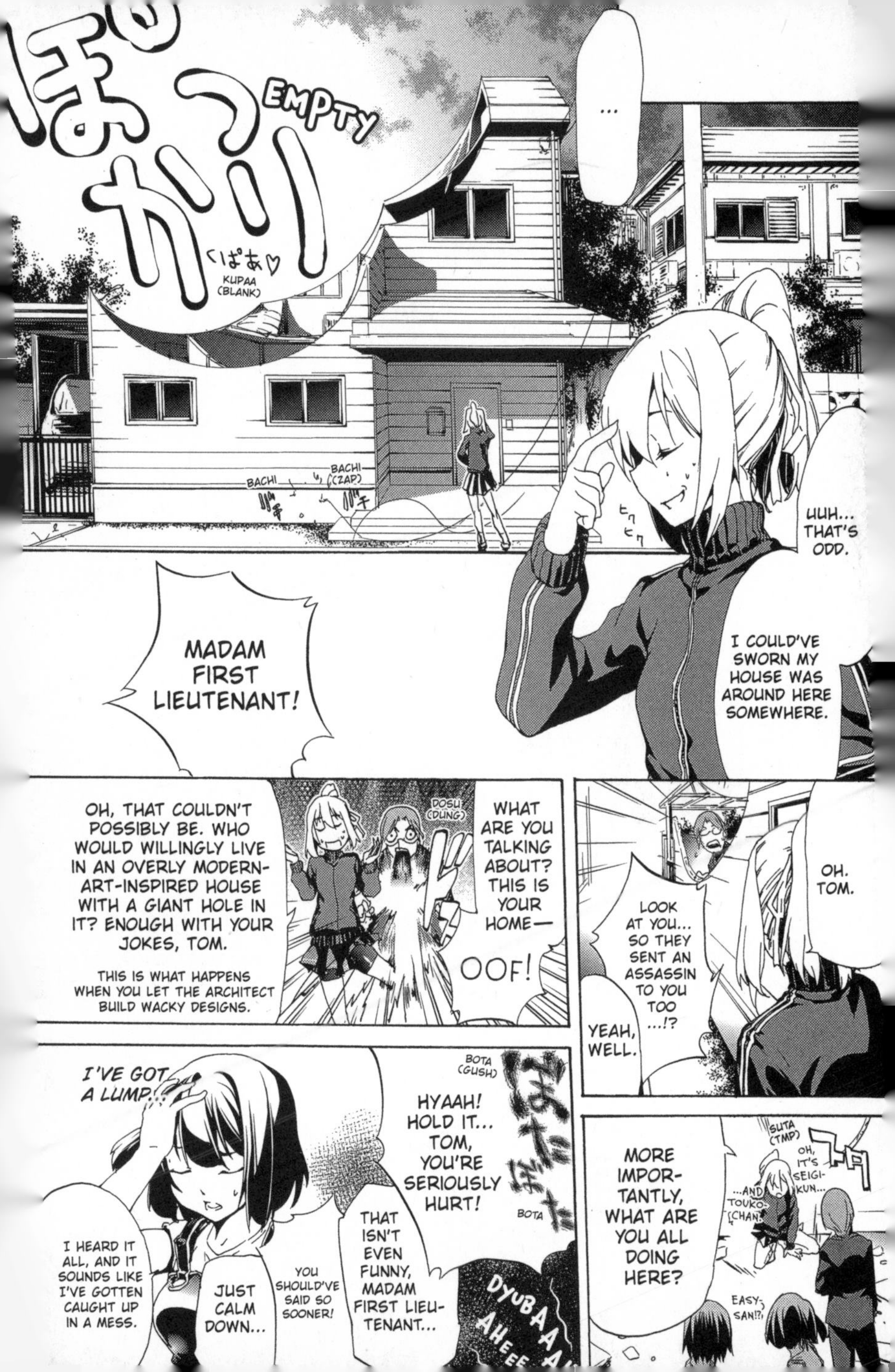
...
ぽっかり
EMPTY
くぱあ♡
KUPAA (BLANK)
UUH... THAT'S ODD.
I COULD'VE SWORN MY HOUSE WAS AROUND HERE SOMEWHERE.
BACHI (ZAP)
BACHI
MADAM FIRST LIEUTENANT!
OH. TOM.
LOOK AT YOU... SO THEY SENT AN ASSASSIN TO YOU TOO ...!?
YEAH, WELL.
WHAT ARE YOU TALKING ABOUT? THIS IS YOUR HOME—
DOSU (DUNG)
OOF!
OH, THAT COULDN'T POSSIBLY BE. WHO WOULD WILLINGLY LIVE IN AN OVERLY MODERN-ART-INSPIRED HOUSE WITH A GIANT HOLE IN IT? ENOUGH WITH YOUR JOKES, TOM.
THIS IS WHAT HAPPENS WHEN YOU LET THE ARCHITECT BUILD WACKY DESIGNS.
SUTA (TMP)
OH, IT'S SEIGI-KUN...
...AND TOUKO-CHAN.
MORE IMPORTANTLY, WHAT ARE YOU ALL DOING HERE?
EASY-SAN!?
BOTA (GUSH)
HYAAH! HOLD IT... TOM, YOU'RE SERIOUSLY HURT!
BOTA
THAT ISN'T EVEN FUNNY, MADAM FIRST LIEUTENANT...
DYUBAAA AHEEE
YOU SHOULD'VE SAID SO SOONER!
I'VE GOT A LUMP...
JUST CALM DOWN...
I HEARD IT ALL, AND IT SOUNDS LIKE I'VE GOTTEN CAUGHT UP IN A MESS.

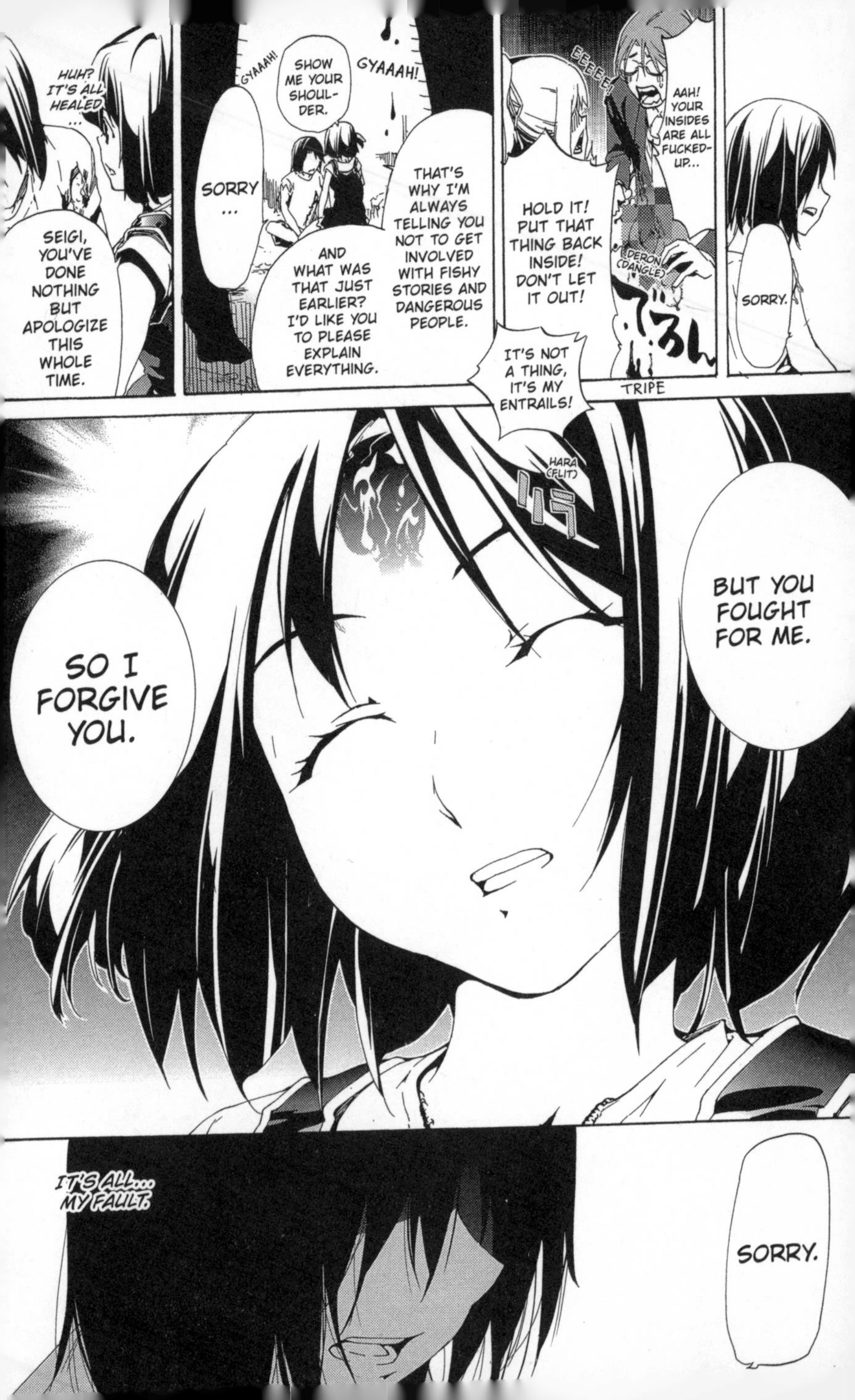
SORRY.
AAH! YOUR INSIDES ARE ALL FUCKED-UP...
BEEEEE!
HOLD IT! PUT THAT THING BACK INSIDE! DON'T LET IT OUT!
DERON (DANGLE)
IT'S NOT A THING, IT'S MY ENTRAILS!
TRIPE
GYAAAH!
SHOW ME YOUR SHOULDER.
GYAAAH!
THAT'S WHY I'M ALWAYS TELLING YOU NOT TO GET INVOLVED WITH FISHY STORIES AND DANGEROUS PEOPLE.
AND WHAT WAS THAT JUST EARLIER? I'D LIKE YOU TO PLEASE EXPLAIN EVERYTHING.
SORRY...
HUH? IT'S ALL HEALED...
SEIGI, YOU'VE DONE NOTHING BUT APOLOGIZE THIS WHOLE TIME.
HARA (FLIT)
BUT YOU FOUGHT FOR ME.
SO I FORGIVE YOU.
SORRY.
IT'S ALL... MY FAULT.

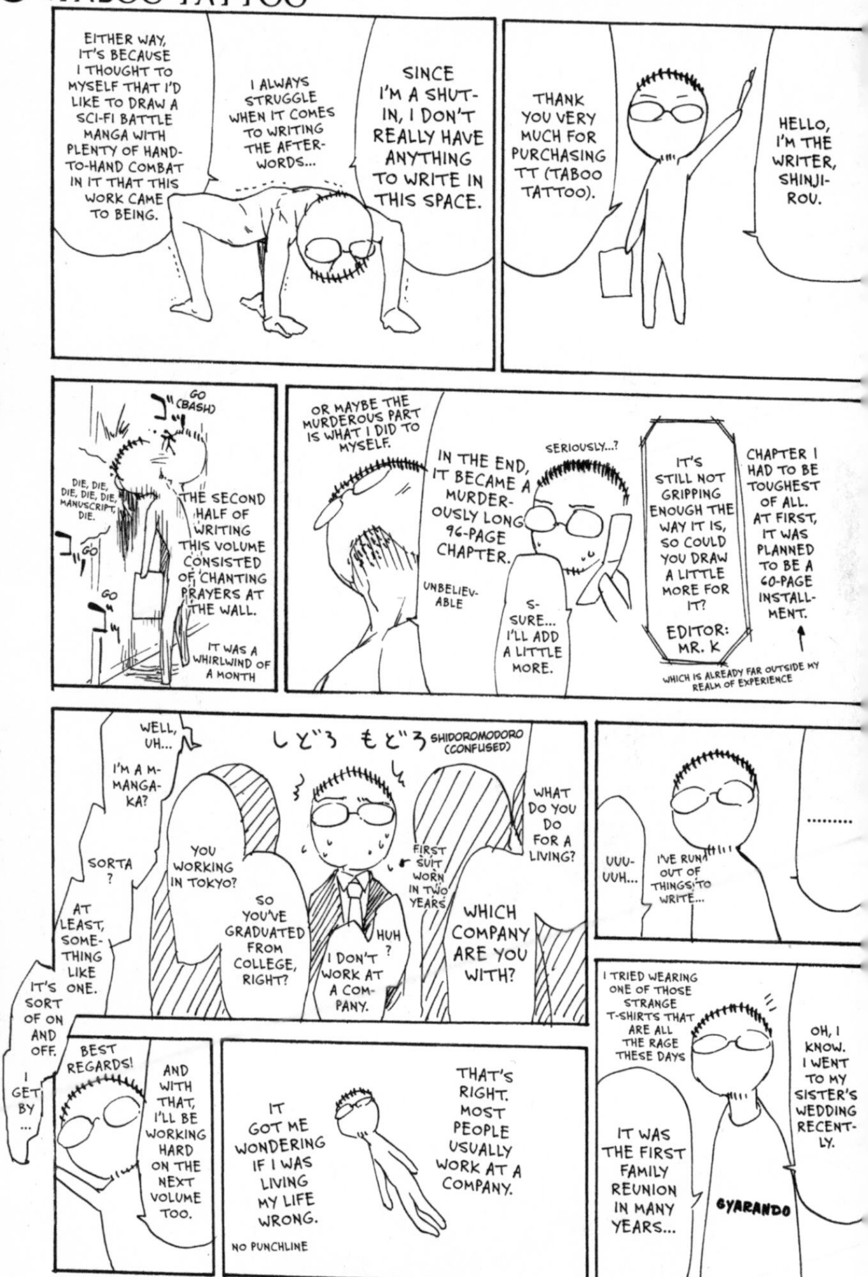
HELLO, I'M THE WRITER, SHINJI-ROU.
THANK YOU VERY MUCH FOR PURCHASING TT (TABOO TATTOO).
SINCE I'M A SHUT-IN, I DON'T REALLY HAVE ANYTHING TO WRITE IN THIS SPACE.
I ALWAYS STRUGGLE WHEN IT COMES TO WRITING THE AFTER-WORDS...
EITHER WAY, IT'S BECAUSE I THOUGHT TO MYSELF THAT I'D LIKE TO DRAW A SCI-FI BATTLE MANGA WITH PLENTY OF HAND-TO-HAND COMBAT IN IT THAT THIS WORK CAME TO BEING.
CHAPTER 1 HAD TO BE TOUGHEST OF ALL. AT FIRST, IT WAS PLANNED TO BE A 60-PAGE INSTALL-MENT.
WHICH IS ALREADY FAR OUTSIDE MY REALM OF EXPERIENCE
IT'S STILL NOT GRIPPING ENOUGH THE WAY IT IS, SO COULD YOU DRAW A LITTLE MORE FOR IT?
EDITOR: MR. K
SERIOUSLY...?
S-SURE... I'LL ADD A LITTLE MORE.
IN THE END, IT BECAME A MURDER-OUSLY LONG 96-PAGE CHAPTER.
UNBELIEV-ABLE
OR MAYBE THE MURDEROUS PART IS WHAT I DID TO MYSELF.
GO (BASH)
THE SECOND HALF OF WRITING THIS VOLUME CONSISTED OF CHANTING PRAYERS AT THE WALL.
DIE, DIE, DIE, DIE, DIE, MANUSCRIPT, DIE.
GO
GO
IT WAS A WHIRLWIND OF A MONTH
....
I'VE RUN OUT OF THINGS TO WRITE...
UUU-UUH...
OH, I KNOW. I WENT TO MY SISTER'S WEDDING RECENT-LY.
I TRIED WEARING ONE OF THOSE STRANGE T-SHIRTS THAT ARE ALL THE RAGE THESE DAYS
GYARANDO
IT WAS THE FIRST FAMILY REUNION IN MANY YEARS...
WHAT DO YOU DO FOR A LIVING?
しどろ もどろ SHIDOROMODORO (CONFUSED)
WELL, UH...
I'M A M-MANGA-KA?
SORTA?
AT LEAST, SOME-THING LIKE ONE.
YOU WORKING IN TOKYO?
FIRST SUIT WORN IN TWO YEARS
WHICH COMPANY ARE YOU WITH?
HUH?
I DON'T WORK AT A COM-PANY.
SO YOU'VE GRADUATED FROM COLLEGE, RIGHT?
IT'S SORT OF ON AND OFF.
I GET BY...
THAT'S RIGHT. MOST PEOPLE USUALLY WORK AT A COMPANY.
IT GOT ME WONDERING IF I WAS LIVING MY LIFE WRONG.
NO PUNCHLINE
AND WITH THAT, I'LL BE WORKING HARD ON THE NEXT VOLUME TOO.
BEST REGARDS!

THOUGH IT IS EASY.

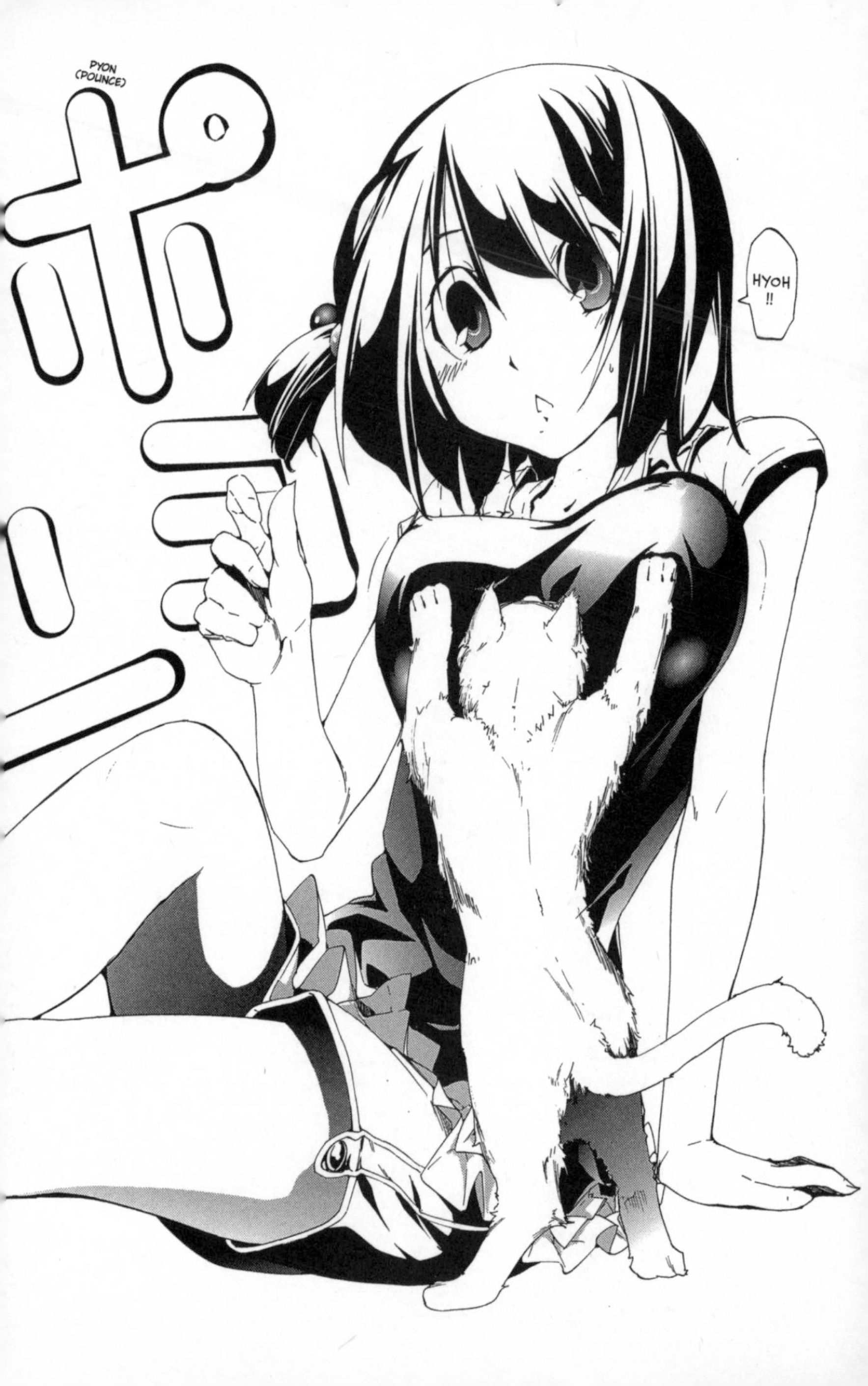
HYOH !!
PYON (POUNCE)

LANGUAGE BARRIER

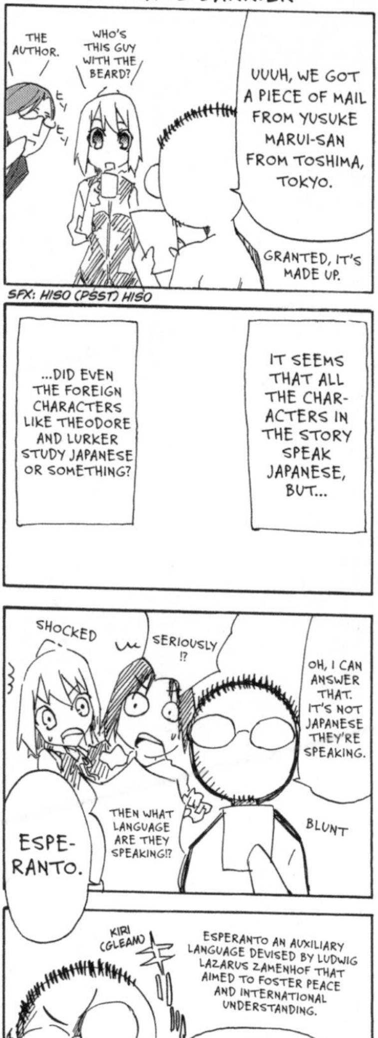
UUUH, WE GOT A PIECE OF MAIL FROM YUSUKE MARUI-SAN FROM TOSHIMA, TOKYO.
WHO'S THIS GUY WITH THE BEARD?
THE AUTHOR.
GRANTED, IT'S MADE UP.
SFX: HISO (PSST) HISO
IT SEEMS THAT ALL THE CHARACTERS IN THE STORY SPEAK JAPANESE, BUT...
...DID EVEN THE FOREIGN CHARACTERS LIKE THEODORE AND LURKER STUDY JAPANESE OR SOMETHING?
OH, I CAN ANSWER THAT. IT'S NOT JAPANESE THEY'RE SPEAKING.
SERIOUSLY!?
SHOCKED
BLUNT
THEN WHAT LANGUAGE ARE THEY SPEAKING!?
ESPERANTO.
ESPERANTO AN AUXILIARY LANGUAGE DEVISED BY LUDWIG LAZARUS ZAMENHOF THAT AIMED TO FOSTER PEACE AND INTERNATIONAL UNDERSTANDING.
KIRI (GLEAM)
IN THE WORLD OF TT, ESPERANTO IS WIDELY USED, SO THAT THERE ARE NO LANGUAGE BARRIERS.
AND DON'T ARGUE WITH ME ABOUT IT!
SFX: CHA (CHK)

A PEACEFUL DAY

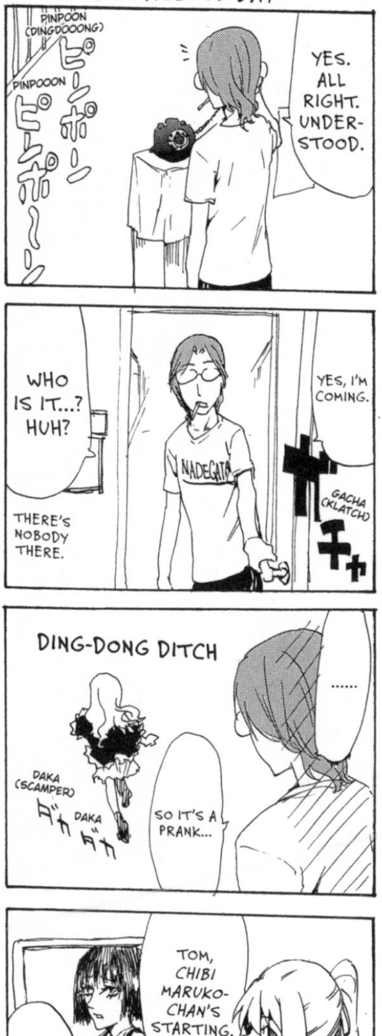
YES. ALL RIGHT. UNDERSTOOD.
PINPOON (DINGDOOONG)
PINPOOON
YES, I'M COMING.
GACHA (KLATCH)
WHO IS IT...? HUH?
NADEGATA
THERE'S NOBODY THERE.
......
DING-DONG DITCH
SO IT'S A PRANK...
DAKA (SCAMPER)
DAKA
TOM, CHIBI MARUKO-CHAN'S STARTING.
COMING!

TRANSLATION NOTES

COMMON HONORIFICS

no honorific: Indicates familiarity or closeness; if used without permission or reason, addressing someone in this manner would constitute an insult.

-san: The Japanese equivalent of Mr./Mrs./Miss. If a situation calls for politeness, this is the fail-safe honorific.

-kun: Used most often when referring to boys, this indicates affection or familiarity. Occasionally used by older men among their peers, but it may also be used by anyone referring to a person of lower standing.

-chan: An affectionate honorific indicating familiarity used mostly in reference to girls; also used in reference to cute persons or animals of either gender.

Page 14
The sign is an inside joke on the author's part because he had to write such a tormentingly long first chapter for this story. (96 pages!!) He gripes about it later in the book during his Afterword as well.

Page 20
The chalkboard houses further commentary by the author about how much work he has to do.

Page 33
DQN name
A fad of Japanese parents who give their children very unique names by assigning peculiar interpretations and readings to the kanji in their names. So a child with the name "泡姫" which literally means "bubble princess" might have it pronounced "ari-e-ru" (Ariel, like from *The Little Mermaid*). The word "DQN" comes from the SFX *dokyun*, like when you get a sudden surprise and your heart jumps.

Page 56
The chalkboard again has more references to the author's suffering from this insanely long chapter.

Page 57
The sign in front of the café has another glib reference to the length of the first chapter.

Page 61
Cat-tongued
In Japanese, the condition of being sensitive to hot foods or beverages is described as "cat-tongued" since cats notoriously only lap up their drinks a little at a time. This is further illustrating the catlike nature of Easy.

Page 101
"Meat" on the forehead
Referring to the classic Japanese manga *Kinnikuman*, where the main character has the symbol for meat on his forehead.

Page 184
Shoes on inside
In Japanese homes, it is unheard of to wear your outside shoes inside the home, hence why Tom would point it out.

Page 195
"Gyarando"
The name of a single by Hideki Saijo from 1983.

Chibi Maruko-chan
A cute children's TV program based on a manga by the same name.

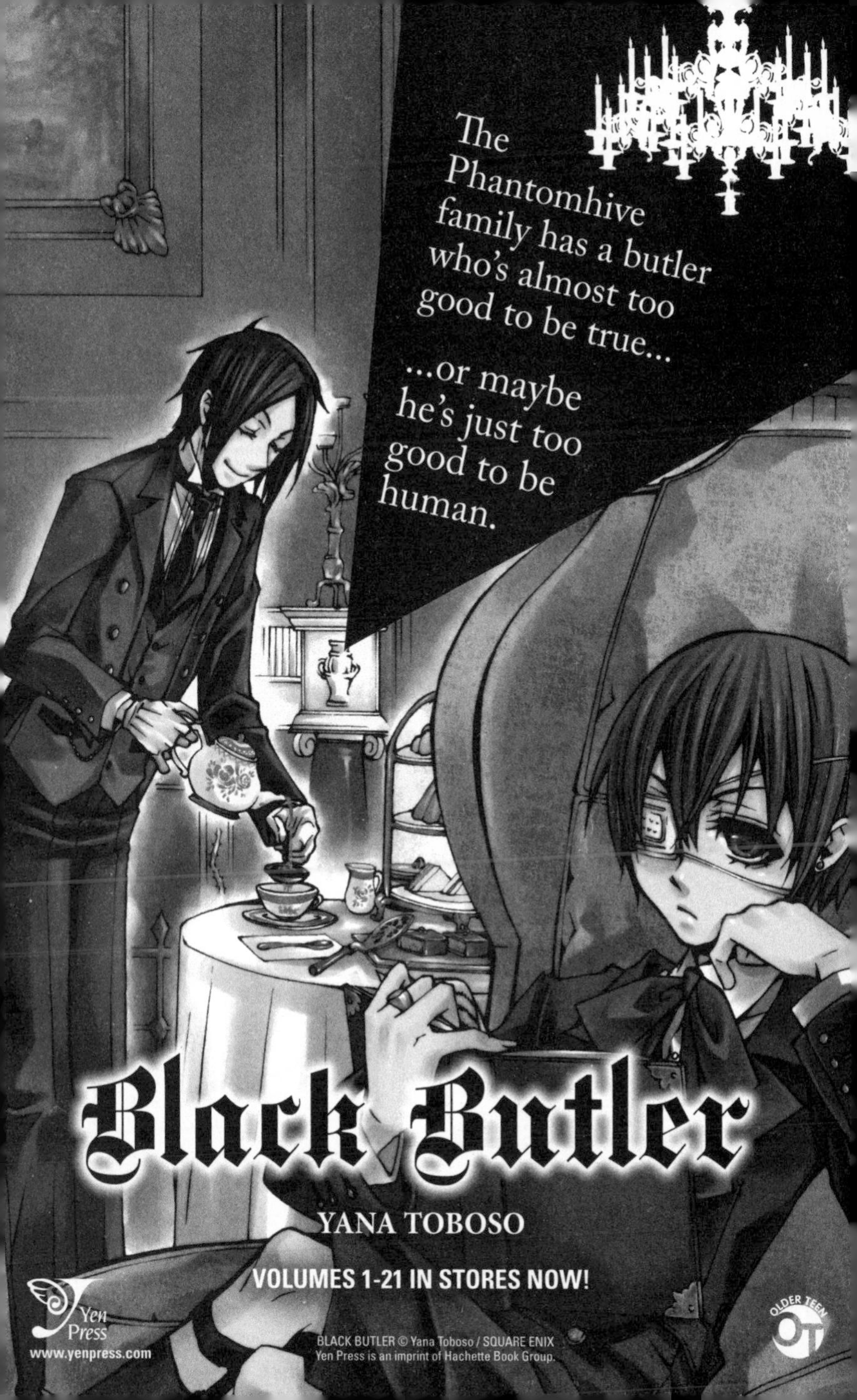

The Phantomhive family has a butler who's almost too good to be true...
...or maybe he's just too good to be human.
Black Butler
YANA TOBOSO
VOLUMES 1-21 IN STORES NOW!
Yen Press
www.yenpress.com
BLACK BUTLER © Yana Toboso / SQUARE ENIX
Yen Press is an imprint of Hachette Book Group.
OLDER TEEN
OT

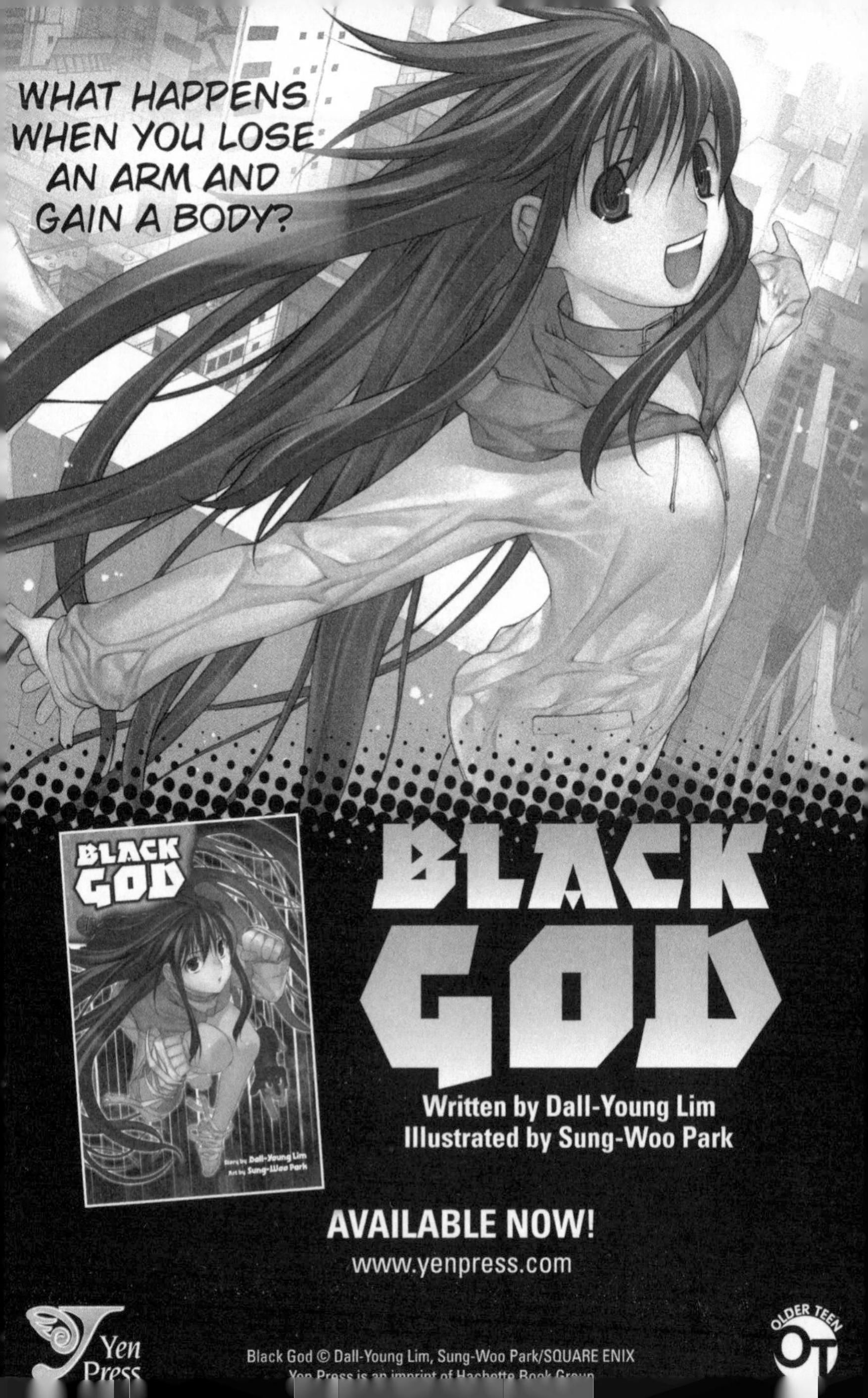
WHAT HAPPENS WHEN YOU LOSE AN ARM AND GAIN A BODY?
BLACK GOD
BLACK GOD
Story by Dall-Young Lim
Art by Sung-Woo Park
Written by Dall-Young Lim
Illustrated by Sung-Woo Park
AVAILABLE NOW!
www.yenpress.com
Yen Press
Black God © Dall-Young Lim, Sung-Woo Park/SQUARE ENIX
OLDER TEEN
OT

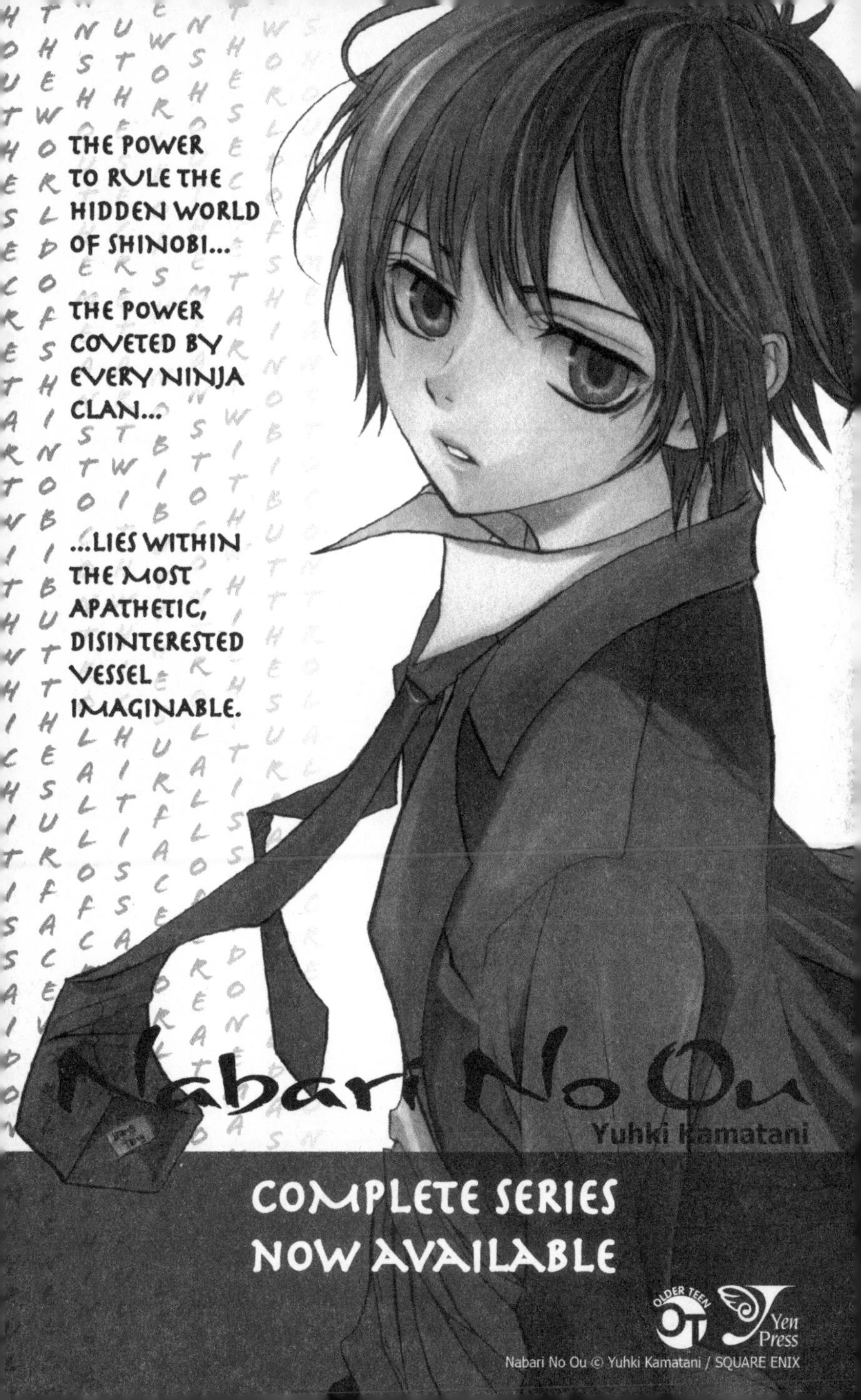
THE POWER TO RULE THE HIDDEN WORLD OF SHINOBI...
THE POWER COVETED BY EVERY NINJA CLAN...
...LIES WITHIN THE MOST APATHETIC, DISINTERESTED VESSEL IMAGINABLE.
Nabari No Ou
Yuhki Kamatani
COMPLETE SERIES NOW AVAILABLE
OLDER TEEN OT
Yen Press
Nabari No Ou © Yuhki Kamatani / SQUARE ENIX

WELCOME TO IKEBUKURO, WHERE TOKYO'S WILDEST CHARACTERS GATHER!!

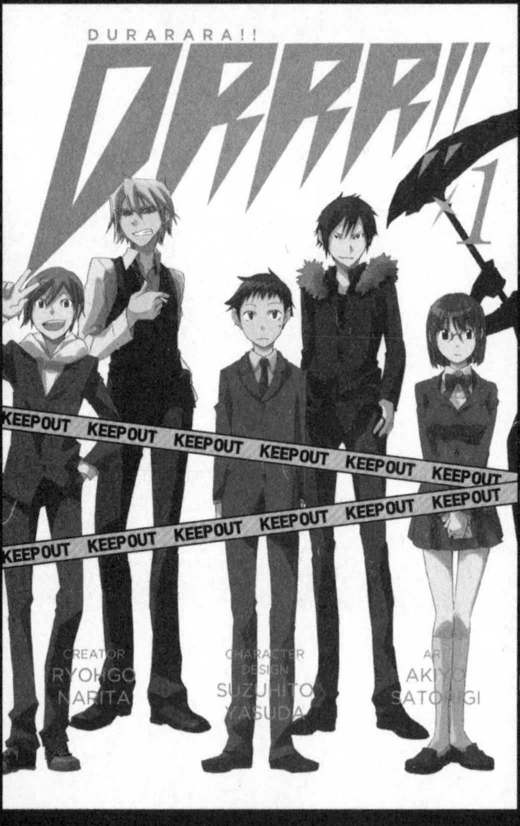
DURARARA!!
DRRR!!
1
KEEPOUT KEEPOUT KEEPOUT KEEPOUT KEEPOUT KEEPOUT
CREATOR
RYOHGO NARITA
CHARACTER DESIGN
SUZUHITO YASUDA
ART
AKIYO SATORIGI

AS THEIR PATHS CROSS, THIS ECCENTRIC CAST WEAVES A TWISTED, CRACKED LOVE STORY...

AVAILABLE NOW!!

COMPLETE SERIES
NOW AVAILABLE!

DING-DONG!
DEAD-DONG!

DON'T BE LATE FOR THE "NOT" CLASS AT DEATH WEAPON MEISTER ACADEMY!

OLDER TEEN
OT

Yen Press

SOUL EATER NOT!

ATSUSHI OHKUBO

TABOO TATTOO

by SHINJIRO

Translation: Christine Dashiell • Lettering: Phil Christie

TABOO TATTOO
© Shinjiro 2010
Edited by MEDIA FACTORY
First published in Japan in 2010 by KADOKAWA CORPORATION. English translation rights reserved by HACHETTE BOOK GROUP, INC. under the license from KADOKAWA CORPORATION, Tokyo through TUTTLE-MORI AGENCY, Inc., Tokyo.

Translation © 2016 by Hachette Book Group, Inc.

Yen Press
Hachette Book Group
1290 Avenue of the Americas
New York, NY 10104

www.HachetteBookGroup.com • www.YenPress.com

Yen Press is an imprint of Hachette Book Group, Inc.
The Yen Press name and logo are trademarks of Hachette Book Group, Inc.

The publisher is not responsible for websites (or their content) that are not owned by the publisher.

First Yen Press Edition: January 2016

Library of Congress Control Number: 2015952591

ISBN: 978-0-316-26890-5

10 9 8 7 6 5 4 3 2 1

BVG

Printed in the United States of America